VOCABULARY INSTRUCTION

vocabulary
INSTRUCTION

Research to Practice

Second Edition

TOURO COLLEGE LIBRARY
Kings Hwy

Edited by
Edward J. Kame'enui
James F. Baumann

THE GUILFORD PRESS
New York   London

KH

© 2012 The Guilford Press
A Division of Guilford Publications, Inc.
72 Spring Street, New York, NY 10012
www.guilford.com

Printed in the United States of America

This book is printed on acid-free paper.

Last digit is print number: 9   8   7   6   5   4   3   2   1

Library of Congress Cataloging-in-Publication Data
Vocabulary instruction : research to practice / edited by Edward J. Kame'enui,
James F. Baumann. — 2nd ed.
      p. cm.
   Includes bibliographical references and index.
   ISBN 978-1-4625-0397-1 (pbk.) — ISBN 978-1-4625-0398-8 (hardcover)
   1. Vocabulary—Study and teaching. 2. Reading. I. Kame'enui, Edward J.
II. Baumann, James F.
   LB1574.5.V63 2012
   372.44—dc23

                                                                    2012005662

9/19/12

To Metztli Kai Kame'enui Ramirez (4½)
and Kiele Atlan Kame'enui Ramirez (1½),
who already appreciate the "truthiness" of words
—E. J. K.

and

To Nancy, Kate, and Tim,
who always have been there to support Dad
—J. F. B.

About the Editors

Edward J. Kame'enui, PhD, is Dean–Knight Professor of Education, Associate Dean for Research and Outreach, and Director of the Center on Teaching and Learning and the Institute for the Development of Educational Achievement in the College of Education, University of Oregon. He was founding Commissioner of the National Center for Special Education Research in the Institute of Education Sciences. His research interests include instructional design, vocabulary development and instruction, and learning disabilities.

James F. Baumann, PhD, holds the Chancellor's Chair for Excellence in Literacy Education at the University of Missouri–Columbia, where he teaches courses in reading and advises graduate students. His research interests include elementary reading instruction, vocabulary teaching and learning, and teacher inquiry.

Contributors

James F. Baumann, PhD, Department of Learning, Teaching, and Curriculum, University of Missouri–Columbia, Columbia, Missouri

Isabel L. Beck, PhD, Learning Research and Development Center, University of Pittsburgh, Pittsburgh, Pennsylvania

Andrew Biemiller, PhD, Institute of Child Study, Department of Human Development and Applied Psychology, University of Toronto, Toronto, Ontario, Canada

Camille L. Z. Blachowicz, PhD, National College of Education, National Louis University, Evanston, Illinois

Eileen Boland, MEd, Roosevelt High School and California State University, Fresno, Fresno, California

Ashley Capozzoli-Oldham, MA, Department of Educational Psychology, Neag School of Education, University of Connecticut, Storrs, Connecticut

Jill Castek, PhD, Graduate School of Education, University of California, Berkeley, Berkeley, California

Gina N. Cervetti, PhD, School of Education, University of Michigan, Ann Arbor, Michigan

Michael D. Coyne, PhD, Department of Educational Psychology, Neag School of Education, University of Connecticut, Storrs, Connecticut

Anne E. Cunningham, PhD, Graduate School of Education, University of California, Berkeley, Berkeley, California

Bridget Dalton, EdD, Department of Teaching and Learning, Vanderbilt University, Nashville, Tennessee

Elizabeth Carr Edwards, PhD, Department of Curriculum Foundations and Reading, Georgia Southern University, Statesboro, Georgia

Peter Fisher, PhD, National College of Education, National Louis University, Evanston, Illinois

Susan Leigh Flinspach, PhD, Department of Education, University of California, Santa Cruz, Santa Cruz, California

George Font, PhD, Department of Early, Elementary, and Reading Education, James Madison University, Harrisonburg, Virginia

Michael F. Graves, PhD (Emeritus), Department of Literacy Education, University of Minnesota, Minneapolis, Minnesota

Dana L. Grisham, PhD, School of Education, National University, La Jolla, California

Elfrieda H. Hiebert, PhD, TextProject, University of California, Santa Cruz, Santa Cruz, California

Bonnie Johnson, PhD, Human Development and Learning, School of Education, Dowling College, Oakdale, New York

Dale D. Johnson, PhD, Literacy Education, School of Education, Dowling College, Oakdale, New York

Edward J. Kame'enui, PhD, College of Education, University of Oregon, Eugene, Oregon

Michael L. Kamil, PhD (Emeritus), School of Education, Stanford University, Stanford, California

Patrick C. Manyak, PhD, Department of Elementary and Early Childhood Education, University of Wyoming, Laramie, Wyoming

Margaret G. McKeown, PhD, Learning Research and Development Center, University of Pittsburgh, Pittsburgh, Pennsylvania

Tatiana F. Miller, PhD candidate, Department of Education, University of California, Santa Cruz, Santa Cruz, California

Colleen Ryan O'Donnell, PhD, Institute for Human Development, University of California, Berkeley, Berkeley, California

P. David Pearson, PhD, Graduate School of Education, University of California, Berkeley, Berkeley, California

Melanie Ruda, MA, Seward Inc., Minneapolis, Minnesota

Gregory C. Sales, PhD, Seward Inc., Minneapolis, Minnesota

Cheryl Sandora, PhD, Learning Research and Development Center, University of Pittsburgh, Pittsburgh, Pennsylvania

Kathleen Schlichting, PhD, Watson School of Education, University of North Carolina Wilmington, Wilmington, North Carolina

Judith A. Scott, PhD, Department of Education, University of California, Santa Cruz, Santa Cruz, California

Deborah C. Simmons, PhD, Department of Educational Psychology, Texas A&M University, College Station, Texas

Katherine A. Dougherty Stahl, EdD, Steinhardt School of Education, New York University, New York, New York

Steven A. Stahl, EdD (deceased), Curriculum and Instruction, College of Education, University of Illinois at Urbana–Champaign, Urbana–Champaign, Illinois

Shane Templeton, PhD (Emeritus), Department of Educational Specialties, College of Education, University of Nevada, Reno, Reno, Nevada

Acknowledgments

The preparation of this book was supported in part by two sources: the Center on Teaching and Learning, College of Education, University of Oregon; and the Institute of Education Sciences, U.S. Department of Education, through Grant No. R305A090163 to the University of Missouri–Columbia, University of Wyoming, and National Louis University. The opinions expressed are those of the authors and do not represent views of their universities or the U.S. Department of Education.

Contents

Introduction

Chapter 1

Context for Vocabulary Instruction

Edward J. Kame'enui
James F. Baumann

In his book *Bryson's Dictionary of Troublesome Words: A Writer's Guide to Getting it Right*, Bill Bryson (2002) observes:

> One of the abiding glories of English is that it has no governing authority; no group of august worthies empowered to decree how words may be spelled and deployed. We are a messy democracy, and all the more delightful for it. . . . When we tire of a meaning or usage or spelling—when we decide, for example, that *masque* would be niftier as *mask*—we change it, not by fiat but by consensus. The result is a language that is wonderfully fluid and accommodating, but also complex, undirected, and often puzzling—in a word, troublesome. (p. xi)

In contrived but mindful disagreement with Bryson's declaration about English lacking a "governing authority," as editors of this second edition of *Vocabulary Instruction: Research to Practice*, we have convened and empowered a "group of august worthies" in this "messy democracy" to earnestly "decree how words may be spelled and deployed." In doing so, we have taken particular care, of course, for the strategic employment of words and their intended and unintended meanings. Naturally, the scholars that were invited to pen these chapters are also in wild agreement with Bryson's celebration of language as wonderfully fluid, accommodating, complex, undirected, puzzling, and perhaps a tad troublesome.

As with the first edition, the primary and unambiguous focus of the second edition of *Vocabulary Instruction: Research to Practice* is the application of research-based findings and principles to the teaching and instruction of vocabulary. But as an active and informed reader in this "messy democracy," you could ask, "What does this *really mean* for me as a teacher, the curriculum directors I work with, and the school administrators who, like me, are intimately engaged in the pulse of practice on a daily basis?" Well, as editors who have had the privilege of working with the authors of these chapters, we are confident it means that readers will gain clear and immediate access to elaborate and in some cases new ideas, instructional strategies, and concrete and extended examples, often in unforgiving detail, about how to teach the meanings of words, and how to expand children's knowledge of and disposition toward words—all kinds of words. Of course, in doing so, the authors knowingly and vigorously celebrate what Bryson notes as the "abiding glories of English" that has "no governing authority" but operates on "consensus." And, as in the first edition, the authors convey tacitly their appreciation for what Pinker (1999) characterizes as the "first trick" to appreciating the "boundless expressive power" of our language (pp. 1–2); that is, understanding the important associations between word pronunciations and word meanings—that is, the "trick" of acquiring a reading vocabulary.

In this edition, we again replicate the three-part organization of the first edition, which knowingly aligns with three of Graves's (2000) four components of a comprehensive vocabulary approach: Part I—Teaching Specific Vocabulary; Part II—Teaching Vocabulary-Learning Strategies; and Part III—Teaching Vocabulary through Word Consciousness and Language Play. For this edition, we introduce a new and timely section as Part IV—Special Topics in Vocabulary Instruction—which includes five new chapters on a range of ripe and pressing issues. In this section, we have recruited notable research scholars in the field of reading and vocabulary development to provide their insights on vocabulary assessment (P. David Pearson, Elfrieda H. Hiebert, and Michael L. Kamil), independent reading and vocabulary growth (Anne E. Cunningham and Colleen Ryan O'Donnell), vocabulary instruction for English learners (Patrick C. Manyak), the use of multimedia to support vocabulary learning (Jill Castek, Bridget Dalton, and Dana L. Grisham), and a framework for selecting words to teach in informational and narrative texts (Elfrieda H. Hiebert and Gina N. Cervetti).

PART I: TEACHING SPECIFIC VOCABULARY

As in the first edition, we open Part I with a chapter titled "Direct and Rich Vocabulary Instruction Needs to Start Early," by Margaret G. McKeown and Isabel L. Beck, who are joined in this edition by Cheryl Sandora. In their chapter, the authors report on their research-based program of "rich instruction" designed to produce "deep and facile word knowledge . . . needed to affect comprehension" (p. 20). The aim of rich instruction, which as the authors note, should include "even the very youngest learners" (p. 17), is to have students engage "in active thinking about word meanings, about how they might use the words in different situations, and about the relationships among words" (p. 20). They, like other authors in this edition, invoke Perfetti and Hart's (2002) "lexical quality hypothesis" in calling for a deeper processing of word meanings in which students are not only given "ample opportunities . . . to think and talk about words" but are "challenged to examine and articulate their thinking" (p. 25). As in the first edition, McKeown, Beck, and Sandora again deliver the details on "which words to teach," "how to build generalizable and flexible representations of words," "how to build 'high-quality practice' in order to build rich, nuanced, flexible representations of word meaning," and "how to keep vocabulary going."

In Chapter 3, Andrew Biemiller reminds readers, as he did in the first edition, "From grade 3 on, the main limiting factor for the majority of children is vocabulary, not reading mechanics (decoding print into words)" (p. 34). In his chapter, titled "Teaching Vocabulary in the Primary Grades: Vocabulary Instruction Needed," Biemiller observes that "Our chances of successfully addressing vocabulary differences in school are greatest in the preschool and early primary years" (p. 36). These "vocabulary differences" are decidedly and vividly nontrivial; as Biemiller notes: "By the end of grade 2, children in the lowest vocabulary quartile had acquired slightly more than 1.5 root words a day over 7 years, for a total of about 4,000 root word meanings. In contrast, children in the highest quartile had acquired more than 3 root words a day, for a total of about 8,000 root word meanings" (p. 34). Moreover, a major barrier to such an effort, according to Biemiller, is the "difficulty of assessing vocabulary under classroom conditions" (p. 36). Again, like McKeown, Beck, and Sandora, Biemiller believes that instruction and what teachers do matter, especially for children with limited vocabularies. In this chapter, he offers guidelines on the words worth teaching, including choosing books to read to children, selecting words for explanation, and keeping track of words taught.

In Chapter 4, Coyne, Capozzoli-Oldham, and Simmons offer an update of their empirically tested shared storybook reading strategy to develop the vocabulary knowledge of children who enter the primary grades knowing fewer word meanings than their peers. These researchers assert what McKeown et al. and Biemiller also argue: "Early intervention matters, and it matters more for children who enter with less" (p. 52). In translating their program of research for practitioners, Coyne and his colleagues developed an 18-week program of direct and extended instruction designed to increase children's vocabulary knowledge. The critical features of this program to accelerate vocabulary growth within the context of storybook reading activities is anchored in the following research principles indicating the need for (1) carefully selected target words, (2) simple definitions within the context of the story, (3) conspicuous instruction, (4) extended instruction, (5) multiple exposures to target words, and (6) carefully scheduled review and practice.

In the last chapter of Part I, Katherine A. Dougherty Stahl and Steven A. Stahl provide readers with specific ways to expand prekindergarten to grade 2 children's experiences with words, including talking to children "around words," reading storybooks because that's "where the words are," using Text Talk in read-alouds, picture walks for vocabulary development, Venn diagrams, semantic maps, words walls, and "Word Wizard" activities. As the authors observe, "Good vocabulary teaching in the primary grades involves talking about words when you find them in books, on trips, or in the classroom and bringing them in and sending children out to find more" (p. 90). As in the first edition, and like other authors of Part I, Dougherty Stahl and Stahl recognize the "diversity of vocabulary knowledge among children entering formal educational settings" and that the "variations are evident in the preschool years and persist through the elementary school years, and probably beyond" (p. 74). Like other Part I authors, they too call for teaching word meanings directly, including " 'Goldilocks' words—words that are not too difficult, not too easy, but just right" (p. 76).

PART II: TEACHING VOCABULARY-LEARNING STRATEGIES

In contrast to teaching specific vocabulary words, in Part II we focus on the teaching of vocabulary-learning strategies for unfamiliar words that are not taught directly, word by word, but that can be acquired through the application of a general strategy. As in the first edition, what we gain from the three chapters in this section is a keen respect for the intricate requirements of teaching selected instances of particular words or word parts (e.g., roots, prefixes, suffixes) that permit readers to know or infer more about novel or unknown instances of similar words or classes of words through the application of a vocabulary-learning strategy. To open Part II, Michael F. Graves and his coauthors for this edition, Melanie Ruda, Gregory C. Sales, and James F. Baumann, offer a "broader general approach" to teaching prefixes, and in doing so, they put greater emphasis on motivation, include more "constructivist" activities, and embed prefix instruction into a broader program of word-learning strategies. In the first edition, Graves asked whether our knowledge of teaching prefixes is "as good as it gets" and readily answered, "No." In this edition, he and his colleagues make it obvious why "No" is the right answer. In their "General Approach to Instruction 2011," Graves and colleagues report their work on the development of a "comprehensive supplementary program to teach word-learning strategies" (p. 96). Interestingly, the researchers take care to note that this research was funded by an SBIR grant (Small Business Innovation Research) from the Institute of Education Sciences, which serves as *the* research, evaluation, and statistical arm of the U.S. Department of Education. The program, which is still under development, employs both explicit instruction and "constructivist elements" (pp. 103, 106), and the results, as the authors note, appear "promising."

In Chapter 7, "The Vocabulary–Spelling Connection and Generative Instruction," Shane Templeton offers a clear and worthy decree about "how words may be spelled and deployed" (Bryson, 2002, p. xi). Templeton observes, "Morphological awareness—identifying prefixes, suffixes, bases, and Greek and Latin roots and understanding *how* they combine to form words—is facilitated by attention to the *spelling* of words" (p. 117). As he asserted more than two decades ago, "Words that are related in meaning are often related in spelling as well, despite changes in sound" (Templeton, 1991, p. 194). Students' knowledge of word forms, according to Templeton, is the "*generative* engine that can drive students' independent word learning from the intermediate grades and beyond" (p. 117). In the final section of his chapter, titled "Instruction," Templeton offers readers concrete examples of activities and strategies for learning words, including teacher "walk-throughs" that involve teacher modeling (e.g., "You know what's neat about all of this? More and more often, you're going to notice words when you read that you don't know but which remind you of words you *do* know because of their similarity in spelling," p. 128), scaffolding, and a "mix of teacher-guided and student-exploratory aspects" (p. 126) of sound instruction.

In Chapter 8, the final chapter of Part II, Elizabeth Carr Edwards, James F. Baumann, Eileen Boland, and George Font offer readers another empirically tested set of generalized strategies and guidelines for "unlocking word meanings" through teaching morphemic and contextual analysis. After acknowledging the elements of Graves's (2000) comprehensive vocabulary development program and providing a concise review of research on teaching morphemic and contextual analyses, these researchers provide readers with an instructive analysis for why morphemic and contextual analyses deserve attention. In addition, they offer a set of guidelines for teaching morphemic and contextual analysis, including teaching these strategies in tandem.

PART III: TEACHING VOCABULARY THROUGH WORD CONSCIOUSNESS AND LANGUAGE PLAY

The three chapters that make up Part III are of a very different ilk and character from the previous chapters in Part I on teaching specific words and in Part II on word-learning strategies. In fact, these chapters are arguably not about "words" per se, but about the "awareness," "intuition," or "sense" about words. As the title of each chapter makes boldly conspicuous, these chapters, in short, are about *word consciousness*. As in the first edition, the chapters address an important and "fun" aspect of vocabulary development that might even please Mr. Bryson, an author himself of humorous books on the English language (e.g., *A Short History about Everything*; Bryson, 2002), who no doubt appreciates both the troublesome and mischievous nature of words.

In the first chapter to Part III, Chapter 9, "Developing Word Consciousness: Lessons from Highly Diverse Fourth-Grade Classrooms," Judith A. Scott, Tatiana F. Miller, and Susan Leigh Flinspach report the results of their research project titled VINE (Vocabulary Innovations in Education, funded by the Institute of Education Sciences), an intervention designed to help teachers develop "word-conscious instruction" (p. 170). The authors report that "VINE was based on the premise that teachers who are more word conscious teach in ways that help students become more word conscious, which accelerates vocabulary development" (p. 171). Scott and her colleagues identify three domains of word-conscious teaching that include (1) metacognitive knowledge and awareness (e.g., how people learn new words, why words are important, how words make people feel), (2) metalinguistic knowledge and awareness (e.g., recognizing Spanish–English cognates, word play and games such as Root Relay and Word Wizzle), and (3) the affective aspects of word learning. VINE, the authors note, was based in part on the "Gift of Words" project that Scott and Nagy (2004) described in their chapter of the first edition of this text.

In the second chapter of this section on word consciousness, Chapter 10, Camille L. Z. Blachowicz and Peter Fisher insist, as they did in the first edition, on keeping the "fun" in fundamental, because as a teacher in a staff development session on word play once conveyed to the authors, "Vocabulary instruction can be pretty grim sometimes" (p. 189). To deter this grimness, Blachowicz and Fisher vigorously employ research-based principles to support "four goals for classroom word play: (1) create a word-rich environment; (2) call on students to reflect metacognitively on words, word parts, and context; (3) encourage active engagement with discussion; and (4) emphasize relatedness in rehearsal and practice" (p. 206). As in the first edition, Blachowicz and Fisher have been around words and classrooms enough to appreciate that research-based statements are simply inadequate, if not potentially irrelevant, if not applied to classroom practice. In a section titled, "Practice: Making It Happen," they provide readers with the instructional details; engaging activities and games; specific recommendations for materials, vocabulary websites, media resources, drama and art activities; and the creative categories of words that are essential to creating a "word-rich classroom."

It seems only appropriate to conclude Part III with a chapter by Dale D. Johnson, Bonnie Johnson, and Kathleen Schlichting, who open their treatise by taking readers on a ride of a #2 New York City subway to Penn Station and offering a provocative description of the prominence of "figurative expressions" (e.g., an ad sponsored by the New York State Lottery that says "Get Fat") as a ubiquitous part of "modern Americans' vocabulary" (p. 210). These authors provide readers with a brief description of seven categories of *language play* or *word play*, which they define as "the adaptation or use of words to achieve an effect, and it is accomplished through the manipulation of meanings, arrangements, sounds, spellings, and various other dimensions of words, phrases, and sentences" (p. 211). However, for this edition, they provide particular focus on two categories: figurative language (e.g., idioms, proverbs, in-betweens, catchphrases, slogans, similes and metaphors, euphemisms) and onomastics (i.e., the study of names, including eponyms, toponyms, demonyms, odonyms, and anemonyms). After all, names are everywhere, and as in the first edition, "these authors are especially clever in communicating the playful wit underlying so many words, names, and expressions in the English language" (Baumann & Kame'enui, 2004, p. 8).

PART IV: SPECIAL TOPICS IN VOCABULARY INSTRUCTION

As we noted previously, Part IV is brand-spanking new to this edition of *Vocabulary Instruction: Research to Practice*. In fact, the chapters in this final section of the book are designed to explicitly address some very important and pressing issues in vocabulary development and instruction, beginning with the assessment of vocabulary development, and continuing with reading and vocabulary growth, vocabulary instruction for English Learners, the use of multimedia to support vocabulary learning, and concluding with a chapter on selecting words to teach in stories.

The assessment of vocabulary learning is perhaps the most elusive and troublesome technical, theoretical, and conceptual issue that researchers continue to face in vocabulary research and development. As we noted at least two decades ago (Baumann & Kame'enui, 1991), echoing the earlier insights of others (Anderson & Freebody, 1979; Beck & McKeown, 1980; Kame'enui, Carnine, & Freschi, 1982), it is difficult to plan for vocabulary instruction if the technical adequacy of our vocabulary assessment tools and our explicit purpose for assessing vocabulary learning are undetermined or underdetermined. What should we assess—words only that are stripped of any linguistic environmental support, or target words fully embedded in other familiar words but lodged in unfamiliar content? Or should we merely assess isolated words with selected meanings represented in pictures? Additionally, how do we decide when a child truly "knows" the full meanings of a word and can use said word flexibly and imaginatively?

Of course, the questions we could ask about the assessment of vocabulary learning—epistemological, empirical, conceptual, technical, pedagogical, and practical—are large in number, varied in complexity, and all in urgent need of clear, research-based, and thoughtful responses. Thus, to address these questions while posing and answering other equally important and poignant questions, we sought the insights and experience of three researchers who truly know vocabulary research and the assessment of vocabulary learning—P. David Pearson, Elfrieda H. Hiebert, and Michael L. Kamil. In their chapter titled "Vocabulary Assessment: Making Do with What We Have While We Create the Tools We Need," these authors assert that "vocabulary assessment is grossly underdeveloped, both in its theoretical and practical aspects" (p. 231), then pose and answer three questions:

1. What do vocabulary assessments (both past and current) measure?
2. What could vocabulary assessments measure, as illustrated by conceptual frameworks, and what development and validation efforts are needed to make such assessments a reality?
3. What assessments should teachers use, create, or modify while we wait for the research that is needed for wide-scale change? (p. 232).

These questions are important and the answers that Pearson, Hiebert, and Kamil offer readers are timely, provocative, and thoughtful and will "do" while "we create the tools we need."

In Chapter 13, the second chapter of Part IV, Anne E. Cunningham and Colleen Ryan O'Donnell grapple directly and insightfully with yet another issue that has long troubled researchers interested in advancing or accelerating language and vocabulary development—that of *intentional* vocabulary development and instruction (as represented in the chapters found in Part I on teaching specific vocabulary) versus *incidental* vocabulary development, which the authors define as "the derivation and learning of new word meanings encountered through exposure to language" (p. 257). Cunningham and O'Donnell are quick to note that "there is strong evidence of the value of providing children with direct and explicit vocabulary instruction as a means of building word knowledge" (p. 261). However, they further argue that "there are also compelling reasons to believe that a sizable amount of vocabulary development occurs through authentic experiences with language," especially exposure to "written language (i.e., reading)" and the "differences in sophistication of the words found in print as compared to oral language" (p. 261). These authors offer readers guidance on understanding the "variables associated with the development of positive reading habits," (p. 268) including, for example, "reading ability, social support, and access to print" (p. 268).

As editors of this edition on vocabulary instruction, we would unwittingly declare our benign indifference (and irrelevance) to the currency of educational research in general, and vocabulary research in particular, if we did not include a chapter on the vocabulary development of English learners (ELs). It is now well established that ELs are unequivocally the fastest growing student population in U.S. schools, and all indications suggest that this trend is likely to continue (August & Shanahan, 2006). According to the National Center for Education Statistics in the Institute of Education Sciences, there appear to be approximately 440 different home languages spoken by children in U.S. schools. However, Spanish speakers comprise approximately 80% of ELs and are by far the largest EL group in the country (Hubler, 2005, as cited in Burns, 2011). Moreover, as the author of Chapter 14, Patrick C. Manyak states, "Today, a growing body of research confirms what my teaching colleagues and I observed in our classrooms two decades ago: many English learners (ELs) face a large deficit in English vocabulary knowledge, and this deficit represents a major obstacle to achievement in critical areas such as reading comprehension" (p. 280).

In his chapter titled, "Powerful Vocabulary Instruction for English Learners," Manyak readily recognizes that "*English learner*, like many categorical terms, can gloss over the diversity among students from families that speak languages other than English" (p. 281). As such, as an opening, he describes "six ways in which ELs may differ from one another" (p. 281) that makes obvious the limitation of a "one-size-fits-all" approach to vocabulary instruction. In reporting the established and emerging research on vocabulary instruction for ELs, Manyak navigates an expansive and complex empirical problem space, including, for example, the effectiveness of a read-aloud strategy for teaching individual words, multimedia-enhanced instruction, "intensive, multiyear vocabulary instruction" involving "Dutch vocabulary to limited-Dutch-speaking immigrants in The Netherlands" (p. 289); vocabulary instruction in mixed native-English-speaking–EL classrooms, multifaceted vocabulary instruction, diverse pedagogical strategies, an unwieldy topic to be sure, and a range of other topics that are equally intricate. Manyak concludes his chapter with "six key practical guidelines for planning and implementing instruction" that he anticipates "will have a powerful positive effect on ELs' vocabulary development and long-term academic achievement" (p. 294).

While addressing the needs of ELs may arguably serve as a litmus test on the "ripeness" of the content of this second edition on vocabulary instruction, certainly including a chapter on digital media and Web 2.0 tools that "offer unique opportunities for students to explore vocabulary, create multimodal products, and collaborate in online communities" (p. 303) is a "no brainer," especially in the current and unforgiving preoccupation with "all things" involving the digital, technological, fiber-optic cable, work flow software, and other innovative and subtle "forces that flattened the world" (Friedman, 2005, p. 50). To deliver on this important and potentially unwieldy task, Jill Castek, Bridget Dalton, and Dana L. Grisham offer a compelling case for "integrating multimodal expression into vocabulary instruction," and in doing so, they offer "several strategies and digital tools to promote students' active word learning" (p. 303).

In Chapter 15 on "Using Multimedia to Support Generative Vocabulary Learning," Castek, Dalton, and Grisham describe "digital literacy events" in vocabulary learning that they consider "generative"; that is, the events involve "instruction that actively engages students in using language and media to express themselves and to create products that represent their new knowledge" (p. 304). Following a brief review of the research on word learning, these authors examine multimodal learning and vocabulary and argue that there is "both indirect and direct research evidence for multimodal word learning" that can be extended to "digital environments" (i.e., digital media and the Internet) that "offer multiple means of access to new words and concepts, including auditory, visual, and animated supports" (p. 307). Appropriately and importantly, Castek and her colleagues offer readers a range of strategies for "learning words through multimodal expression" (p. 307). These strategies include, for example: (1) student-created vocabulary videos (or "vocab vids") in which students "act out the word's meaning, situating it in a specific context"; (2) the use of "VoiceThread" that allows students to create a multimedia slide show using multimodal responses in the form of "text, recorded audio, or webcam-created video files" (p. 309); (3) student-created "hypertext versions of the text that include links to other media" in which the "original text represents the first layer, and students' personal connections and interpretations represent the second, hyperlinked layer" (p. 310); and (4) the use of *Visual Thesaurus* and the *Oxford Dictionary of English* as Internet resources for learning about words and language. These authors conclude their chapter with a note that "giving students experience with the digital technologies required in the 21st century will be motivationally, as well as academically beneficial" (p. 319).

We conclude Part IV with a focus on a topic that has pestered vocabulary researchers and practitioners alike for some time, and continues to do so. In Chapter 16, titled "What Differences in Narrative and Informational Texts Mean for the Learning and Instruction of Vocabulary," Elfrieda H.

Hiebert (known to her colleagues as well as some readers as "Freddy") and Gina N. Cervetti offer an argument that is rather obvious to most of us; that is, narrative and informational texts are indeed different, because they are comprised of words that are substantially different. As Hiebert and Cervetti report, words in science texts are conceptually complex and unfamiliar, often "dense with rare words" (p. 339), which is in contrast to narrative texts that generally "represent concepts with which most students are familiar" (p. 341). However, what is not obvious is their analysis of the differences in the vocabularies of narrative and informational texts, including their frequency, morphological families, conceptual complexity and semantic relatedness, as well as their selective and appropriate analysis of the word features of a sample of fourth-grade "exemplar texts." The new counsel that Hiebert and Cervetti offer readers about these differences are worthy of our attention and consideration.

CONCLUSION

As we noted in the first edition, more than 15 years ago, Hart and Risley (1995) documented that children came to school with considerable variation in their vocabulary knowledge. The second edition of *Vocabulary Instruction: Research to Practice* again bears witness to the importance of ensuring that all children, regardless of their place in the vocabulary development continuum, are taught, encouraged, and inspired to gain access to the meanings of words. As in the first edition, as editors, we are privileged to receive the contributions of these authors—these "worthy scholars" who represent many of the field's most knowledgeable scholars of vocabulary teaching and learning. As with the first edition, the message of this second edition is again unremarkable: Learning the meanings of unfamiliar words is essential to fully understand the story—the plot, if you will. Central to understanding the "plot" of the vocabulary development, learning, and instruction story, therefore, is that the manner in which teachers create instructional environments, craft lessons, and engage students in activities that promote students' vocabulary learning really matters. As Bloom (2001) reminds us, reading and understanding the meanings of the words read is indeed the most "healing of pleasures" (p. 19).

REFERENCES

Anderson, R. C., & Freebody, P. (1979). *Vocabulary knowledge* (Technical Report No. 136). Champaign–Urbana: Center for the Study of Reading, University of Illinois.

August, D., & Shanahan, T. (2006). *Developing literacy in second-language learners: Report of the National Literacy Panel on language-minority children and youth.* Mahwah, NJ: Erlbaum.

Baumann, J. F., & Kame'enui, E. J. (1991). Vocabulary instruction: Ode to Voltaire. In J. Flood, J. Jensen, D. Lapp, & J. R. Squire (Eds.), *Handbook of research on teaching the English language arts* (pp. 604–632). New York: Macmillan.

Baumann, J. F., & Kame'enui, E. J. (2004). *Reading vocabulary instruction: Research to practice.* New York: Guilford Press.

Beck, I. L., McCaslin, E. S., & McKeown, M. G. (1980). *The rationale and design of a program to teach vocabulary to fourth-grade students* (LRDC Publication No. 1980/25). Pittsburgh: Learning Research and Development Center, University of Pittsburgh.

Bloom, H. (2001). *How to read and why.* New York: Simon & Schuster.

Bryson, B. (2002). *Bryson's dictionary of troublesome words: A writer's guide to getting it right.* New York: Broadway Books.

Burns, D. A. (2011). *Examining the effect of an overt transition intervention on the reading development of at-risk English-language learners in first grade.* Doctoral dissertation, University of Oregon, Eugene, OR.

Friedman, T. L. (2005). *The world is flat: A brief history of the twenty-first century.* New York: Farrar, Straus & Giroux.

Graves, M. F. (2000). A vocabulary program to complement and bolster a middle-grade comprehension program. In B. M. Taylor, M. F. Graves, & P. van den Broek (Eds.), *Reading for meaning: Fostering comprehension in the middle grades* (pp. 116–135). Newark, DE: International Reading Association.

Hart, B., & Risley, T. R. (1995). *Meaningful differences in the everyday experiences of young American children.* Baltimore: Brookes.

Kame'enui, E. J., Carnine, D. W., & Freschi, R. (1982). Effects of text construction and instructional procedures for teaching word meanings on comprehension of contrived passages. *Reading Research Quarterly, 17*(3), 367–388.

Perfetti, C. A., & Hart, I. (2002). The lexical quality hypothesis. In L. Vehoeven, C. Elbro, & P. Reitsma (Eds.), *Precursors of functional literacy* (pp. 189–213). Amsterdam: John Benjamins.

Pinker, S. (1999). *Words and rules: Ingredients of language.* New York: HarperCollins.

Scott, J. A., & Nagy, W. E. (2004). Developing word consciousness. In J. F. Baumann & E. J. Kame'enui (Eds.), *Reading vocabulary instruction: Research to practice* (pp. 201–217). New York: Guilford Press.

Templeton, S. (1991). Teaching and learning the English spelling system: Reconceptualizing method and purpose. *Elementary School Journal, 92,* 183–199.

Part I
Teaching Specific Vocabulary

Chapter 2

Direct and Rich Vocabulary Instruction Needs to Start Early

Margaret G. McKeown
Isabel L. Beck
Cheryl Sandora

Since we wrote the original version of this chapter, recognition of the extent and enduring nature of the vocabulary gap between children of different socioeconomic (SES) groups has gained increased attention. With this attention has come a demand for more vocabulary development efforts and for a broadening of these efforts to include even the very youngest learners.

Recognition of the gap was promoted by Hart and Risley (1995), whose study and popular book, *Meaningful Differences*, captured attention for this phenomenon. These authors also illustrated the enduring nature of the gap, having tested the children they studied again at age 9 and finding that their status in vocabulary at age 3 predicted their reading ability 6 years later. Many other studies have found this same relationship for different ages and age spans: Cunningham and Stanovich (1997) found that students' first-grade vocabulary predicted their reading comprehension in 11th grade; Marchman and Fernald (2008) found that vocabulary size at 25 months accounted for unique variance in linguistic and cognitive skills at age 8; and Walker, Greenwood, Hart, and Carta (1994) found that the number of different words a child acquired by age 3 predicted vocabulary and language abilities through third grade.

FEATURES OF EFFECTIVE VOCABULARY INSTRUCTION: REVIEW AND UPDATE

A message that the field has taken from studies that show the long-term influence of early language and vocabulary experiences is that interventions aimed at upgrading students' vocabulary should begin early, even in preschool. Researchers have heeded this message, conducting studies that have examined the results of vocabulary teaching to children in kindergarten (e.g., Beck & McKeown, 2007; Coyne, Simmons, Kame'enui, & Stoolmiller, 2004; Coyne et al., 2010; Silverman, 2007), and even at the preschool level (Collins, 2009; Leung, 2008; Justice, Kaderavek, Fan, Sofka, & Hunt, 2009; Roskos et al., 2008).

Another message derived from vocabulary research and development (Coyne et al., 2004; Bos & Anders, 1990, 1992; Collins, 2009; Dole, Sloan, & Trathen, 1995; Medo & Ryder, 1993; National Reading Panel Report, 2000; Silverman, 2007) indicates a growing consensus about features of vocabulary instruction that are effective for enhancing vocabulary knowledge and comprehension for learners of all ages. The features, which initially emerged from reviews of vocabulary instructional studies conducted by Mezynski (1983) and Stahl and Fairbanks (1986), are (1) multiple exposures of the words being taught; (2) breadth of information—definitional and contextual; and (3) engagement of active or deep processing by getting students to think about the words and interact with them.

Recent research on readers' processes has shed light on how the instructional features identified lead to effective learning. Research by Wolf (2007) and by Perfetti and his colleagues (as cited in Perfetti, 2007; Reichle & Perfetti, 2003) has shown that when a learner acquires information about a word's meaning, connections form in the brain to other words and to experiences that are related to the new word. The connections developed from all the contexts in which a reader has encountered a word lead to the building of an abstract representation of the word's meaning. The abstract nature of a word's representation means that when the learner encounters the word in a new context, he or she is not dependent on specific information from an individual context that was met before, which might limit understanding of that new context. Rather, the representation is rich and nuanced, with many associated concepts, allowing the learner to bring the most relevant ones to the surface to help make the new context meaningful (Nagy & Scott, 2000; Perfetti, 2007).

Perfetti and colleagues' work in this area has led to the development of the lexical quality hypothesis (LQH; Perfetti & Hart, 2002), which holds that representations of word meaning that are of high quality are flexible and allow rapid retrieval of meaning when the word is met in context. It would seem that the goal of vocabulary instruction is to build this kind of high-quality word representation, given that such representations are a mark of successful comprehension (Perfetti, 2007). It would also seem that instruction that offers a variety of contexts around target words and opportunities to use the words is well positioned to provide the grist for developing such abstract, nuanced representations. The LQH also posits that differences between more and less successful comprehenders is more likely the result of knowledge differences—knowledge that, for poor comprehenders, has not been acquired or not practiced to a high-enough level. This possibility implies that we can help students become good comprehenders by providing high-quality practice with words and meanings.

WHICH WORDS TO TEACH

In addition to type of instruction, the types of words that are taught to students matter. Of course, there are too many words in the language to teach them all directly to students, so the goal is to select the most productive words to teach. That would be words that students are less likely to learn on their own and words that occur frequently enough in the types of texts students study to be of assistance to the comprehension process. That is, there is no need to teach easy words that students will hear and learn in conversation, and there is no need to teach words that are so rare that students may never encounter them. The notion of selecting the most productive words was the position from which we developed the heuristic of "word tiers" (Beck, McKeown, & Omanson, 1987; Beck, McKeown, & Kucan, 2002). Viewed through the lens of word tiers, the words that are the most frequent in the language, and which students encounter with great frequency on their own, are labeled Tier One. Words that are of very low frequency and apply to specific domains are labeled Tier Three. Tier Three, then, includes words from academic domains such as science, for example, *isotope* and *photosynthesis*, or government, for example, *inauguration* and *legislature*. But it also includes words such as *piano* and *dentist*, words that are much more familiar, but that meet the key criterion of belonging to a specific domain.

The words categorized as Tier Two are those that are less likely to be learned independently than Tier One words because they are the words that characterize text. Tier Two words are of general utility in that they label concepts that go across domains—concepts with which even young students are likely familiar. For example, *proficient* is a Tier Two word that labels the concept "being very good at doing something." We are frequently asked for lists of words for the three tiers. However, there really aren't lists of Tier One, Two, and Three words per se, because the concept of tiers is a heuristic for categorizing words. We have tried to avoid specific lists, also, because we don't want teachers to believe there is one set of "must-know" words. Having said that, we can point to lists that represent the properties of one tier or another. The General Services List (West, 1953), or certainly the first 1,000 words of it, represent Tier One words. Words on the Dale–Chall word list (Dale & Chall, 1948) would also represent Tier One words, except for those that are out of date. Coxhead's Academic Word List (Coxhead, 1998) to a great extent overlaps with Tier Two words. However, we find that we would categorize some of those words as Tier Three, for example, *chemical* and *ratio*. Tier Three contains content words, so words in the glossary of a science text that don't have scope beyond the science domain, for example, are representative of that tier.

From our perspective, the same rationale about word selection applies to young children. That is, their vocabulary instruction should target words that they are less likely to learn independently and that are more readily found in text, so that the potential for affecting literacy is greatest. The importance of learning the vocabulary of written language is captured by Corson's concept of the lexical bar (1985, 1995). According to Corson, a barrier—lexical bar—exists between everyday meaning systems and the meaning system created by academic, literate culture. The notion of a barrier between everyday language and text language reflects the findings of Hayes and Ahrens (1988), who noted the sharp distinctions between the word stock of informal oral language and that of written language. This distinction is such that everyday oral language—conversation—consists of a relatively small set of words that gets used with great frequency and redundancy, creating a limited but readily learnable vocabulary. After children master the bulk of those words, the words that are left to be learned are much less frequent in the language as a whole, and much more likely to be found in written language. Consequently, vocabulary learning must focus on the word stock of written language to be productive. Or in Corson's (1995) terms, individuals need to cross the lexical bar.

NEW RESEARCH ON DIRECT AND RICH INSTRUCTION

In our initial vocabulary research we created a program based on the notion of "rich instruction" (Beck, McCaslin, & McKeown, 1980). Our aim was to produce the kind of deep and facile word knowledge that we hypothesized was needed to affect comprehension. The aim of rich instruction was to engage students in active thinking about word meanings, about how they might use the words in different situations, and about the relationships among words. For example, students were asked to compare words by responding to questions such as, "What's the difference between *glimpsing* and *scrutinizing*?" To engage thinking about words that describe people, we asked how "*ambitious* Patricia" and "*obstinate* Bob" might work together on a project. We had students make associations to their new words by providing sentences such as "The man showed us a gold telephone and told us it was the only one like it in the world" to bring to mind *unique*, or "The material in Connie's dress had come all the way from Japan" for *exotic*.

In our research with fourth-grade students, we found that rich instruction led not only to growth in knowledge of word meanings but also to better comprehension of stories with those words (Beck, Perfetti, & McKeown, 1982; McKeown, Beck, Omanson, & Perfetti, 1983; McKeown, Beck, Omanson, & Pople, 1985) and to better integration of word meanings with context (McKeown et al., 1985). We have used a rich instruction approach to develop vocabulary for children as young as kindergarten. We conducted two studies with kindergarten and first-grade children from a low-achieving elementary school in which classroom teachers provided vocabulary instruction of Tier Two words selected from story read-alouds (Beck & McKeown, 2007). The first study compared the number of words learned by children who were directly taught the words and by children in the same school who received no instruction. Rich instruction was developed for several words from each of seven stories. The vocabulary instruction occurred after a story had been read, discussed, and concluded. Instruction took place after reading, because the goal for teaching the words was to enhance general vocabulary development and the primary role of the story was to provide rich contexts for the to-be-instructed words. As such, introducing words after the story took advantage of the story's use of the words with which to build initial understanding. We began each word introduction by contextualizing the role of the word in the story. For example, for the story *Burnt Toast on Davenport Street* (Egan, 1997), the word *familiar* was introduced as follows: "In the story it said that the smell of burnt toast every morning was *familiar*. That means it was something they were used to and something that happened a lot of times." The study found, as expected, that children in the experimental group learned significantly more words.

In the second study, reported in Beck and McKeown (2007), we used a within-subjects design to examine kindergarten and first graders' word learning under two different amounts of instruction; words were introduced and followed up for either 3 days or 6 days. The vocabulary gains for words that received more instruction were twice as large. In some ways, this may seem a rather obvious result—twice the instruction for twice the gains. But at the time we conducted the studies, some colleagues suggested that the gains we obtained in the first study might indicate ceiling levels for the learning of sophisticated words by young children.

For both studies, vocabulary learning was assessed using a picture task whose format was similar to the Peabody Picture Vocabulary Test (Dunn

students were asked to recall the stories and respond to open-ended questions. Results of the task showed no differences among the interactive, repetition, and control conditions for either recall or questions. On one hand, this result surprised us, because we have found differences in past research on recall tasks for interactive instruction (Beck et al., 1982; McKeown et al., 1985). On the other hand, we had never used a listening comprehension task on students as young as kindergarten. The requirements of such a task include, beyond vocabulary knowledge, ability to sequence ideas, knowledge of story structure, knowledge of syntax, short-term memory capacity, and referential understanding. Thus, any advantages to semantic processing may be overwhelmed or masked by these other requirements for students as young as kindergarten, who may be less likely to have these other aspects under control, relative to older students. Another possible factor in the results of this task is that the interventions were not long enough. In our previous work that found text comprehension effects, instruction had been carried out over most of the school year. In the current study, children participated in an intervention condition for only 7 days of instruction.

The production task explored students' ability to use newly learned vocabulary words in response to pictures that depicted features related to the words. For example, a sidewalk scene showed several centers of activity, including a man with a guitar sitting on a bench next to a boy who was grinning and waving his hands around, to represent being *gleeful*; two girls sitting on a bench nearby with their arms around each other, to represent *inseparable*; and a woman standing, *clutching* her purse. Students were not asked to label the pictures, but to talk about what they saw happening in them, as an attempt to capture spontaneous use of the words. The results for this task were similar to the context integration measure in that the interaction condition showed an advantage over the repetition condition.

Learning words well enough to express them is an important learning goal, and having words in one's productive vocabulary is generally viewed as a good measure of word ownership. Additionally, this task represents another aspect of processing that is related to comprehension: ease of access to word meanings. If a reader or listener is to understand a word within a stream of language—a context—he or she must be able to readily access a meaning for the word that fits the context. So being able to produce the word when seeing something that can be associated with the word suggests an ease of access that may make way for comprehension.

The results of the study confirm and extend the consensus about effective vocabulary instruction that has been reached over the past couple of decades: The most effective instruction for higher-order goals includes attention to deep or rich processing, instantiated as ample opportunities to think about and use words, and to interact with them in a variety of contexts. The extension is that processing-focused instruction allowed children as young as kindergarten to more successfully respond to tasks that tapped higher-order semantic processing, relative to instruction that offered repeated readings of stories and focus on word meaning practice or story reading only.

The impact of instruction that calls for deep processing was confirmed in a recent efficacy study conducted by the research organization McREL (Apthorp et al., 2011). The ongoing study involves the implementation of *Elements of Reading: Vocabulary* (Beck & McKeown, 2004), a commercial supplemental vocabulary program developed to provide the kind of instruction that would promote deep processing. The study examines gains in word knowledge and comprehension across two school years and four grades. Results from the first year of the study indicate both word knowledge and comprehension gains for all grades tested: kindergarten, first, third, and fourth grades (Apthorp et al., 2011). As part of that study, transcripts from randomly selected experimental and control classroom lessons at all grade levels were examined for depth-of-processing (McKeown, Beck, & Apthorp, 2010). The examination was based on a depth-of-processing taxonomy developed for the study, which included lower-level processing such as reading and recalling words or definitions, and higher-order processing that ranged from making associative connections between words and contexts or pictures, to integrating meaning and context by responding to questions such as "How could you help someone who felt *distraught*?", to explaining reasoning underlying word use such as "Why would you be *curious* if you heard lots of laughter from the classroom next door?" Treatment classrooms demonstrated substantially less lower-level processing and significantly more processing at the higher levels, including questions that called on students to explain the examples of words they provided or their reasons for choosing contexts as appropriate for new words. Control classrooms showed almost none of this higher-level processing.

CREATING OPPORTUNITIES FOR DEEP PROCESSING

What makes room for deeper processing to occur is providing ample opportunities for students not only to think and talk about words, but to be challenged to examine and articulate their thinking. How does that kind of instruction play out in classrooms? From our perspective and experience, inducing deep processing in students calls for some artful teaching that includes responding to students in ways that bring forth their reasoning to help them form connections to new words and make generalizations across contexts. In the section that follows, we share some examples of the kind of skillful teaching that comes from classrooms with which we have worked.

In this first example, the teacher is working with the word *deliver* and is asking the students to name people who might *deliver* something. Although the students are providing appropriate examples, the teacher recognizes the discussion has not included reasons for why these are good representations of the word. So he takes a "time out" to ponder that consideration:

TEACHER: Who do you know who might *deliver* something?

STUDENT: Pizza. The pizza guy.

TEACHER: Yes, the pizza guy might deliver something.

STUDENT: Mailman.

TEACHER: Okay, mailman.

STUDENT: Ah, like, the waiter that delivers your food.

TEACHER: The waiter that delivers your food. Yes. Hmm. Let's hold off . . . we're taking a time out right now. How do we know they're *delivering* us something? How do we know they're deliverymen?

STUDENT: Because, um, they are, like, taking the stuff to you.

The teacher's question of "How do we know they're deliverymen?" served to scaffold students' thinking toward making a generalization across contexts. In essence, the teacher's question allowed students to ferret out the key element of meaning in *deliver* that all the contexts shared. Thus, it was a much more effective question than simply asking for the meaning of *deliver*.

In this next example, the teacher clearly takes note of how a student is explaining a word and catches two aspects that she finds need clarification. First, the teacher makes sure that students are aware of the two elements of the word *exchange*—both giving and accepting. Then she checks that students are not restricting the word's use to the context of gifts.

TEACHER: What does *exchange* mean?

STUDENT: It means, like, um . . . if you're gonna . . . and um . . . like an exchange party and then you exchange your gifts to someone else.

TEACHER: Okay, so if you exchange something, do I just get to take something?

STUDENT: No, you, um . . . you have to give your gift to someone else, and then they give their gift to you.

TEACHER: Right. Does it always . . . is it always with gifts?

STUDENTS: No.

TEACHER: No. Let's see . . . Sophie, exchange something with me. All right, I'm going to give you this pen. I want you to exchange something with me out of your cubby. So, how would we do this? Okay, I'll give you my pen. Oh, and Sophie exchanged the pen for a pencil.

The final example is a further illustration of how skillful teaching of vocabulary entails being attentive to the interpretations students are making about word meanings. Students here are engaged and responsive in the discussion of *rummaging*. They offer good examples and respond well to why the character, Socrates, would be rummaging and why they themselves would rummage in their kitchens for a snack. But then, the teacher's persistent "why" uncovers a misconception about the word.

TEACHER: Okay, our next word is *rummage*. Now, in the story remember that Socrates *rummaged* through the garbage for food. And what did we say he was doing when he *rummaged* through the garbage cans?

STUDENT: Looking for food.

TEACHER: Okay, he was looking for food. Now, if you rummage through something, it means you look for something by moving things around . . . kinda carelessly. And why would Socrates be doing that quickly and carelessly?

STUDENT: 'Cause he was so hungry?

TEACHER: Yeah. He was so hungry. So when he rummaged through those garbage cans, he was doing it carelessly and quickly to try to get some food because he was really hungry. Now, if you were hungry and looking for a snack, you might rummage around in your kitchen. Can somebody tell me how you might do that?

STUDENT: Open the fridgerator.

TEACHER: Open the refrigerator. What else would somebody do if they're *rummaging* through their kitchen for a snack?

STUDENT: I'd look in the cabinet.

TEACHER: Oooohhh . . . in the cabinets. Why?

STUDENT: That's where we keep our food.

STUDENT: I'd look in the snack drawer.

TEACHER: Okay, everybody, listen to what we have. You're rummaging through the kitchen. You're looking in the refrigerator. You're looking in the cabinets. And you're looking in the snack bins. You all have different places where you are rummaging. Very good. And tell me what the word *rummage* means again.

STUDENT: You're moving things around quickly.

TEACHER: You're moving things around quickly. Why?

CLASS: Because you're hungry.

TEACHER: Uh-oh, hang on a minute. Does it have to be hungry?

STUDENT: Or thirsty.

STUDENT: Because you're trying to find something.

TEACHER: Thank you! Because you're trying to find something. It doesn't have to be food. Okay. Let me give you another example. Let's say you have your drawers filled with clothes, but you're looking for a special T-shirt. How would you rummage through your drawers to find that special T-shirt?

STUDENT: Like, taking stuff out real fast.

STUDENT: One time I had to rummage through my drawers because I couldn't find my Incredible Hulk shirt.

TEACHER: Okay, he gave a nice example. Rummaging for an Incredible Hulk shirt. And how were you looking for that shirt?

STUDENT: Like, just pulling everything out of my drawer and trying to find it in a hurry.

The common thread in the presented examples is that the teachers were using comments and questions to help students build a generalizable and flexible representation of the word, the kind of representation that will promote their understanding of novel contexts in which they encounter the word.

FIELDS LEFT TO CONQUER

What we have presented here—results from successful studies and thoughtful examples from classrooms—constitutes the good news. Now the bad news: Even when instruction is effective, it is probably not going to work to narrow the achievement gap, unless we dramatically increase the language interactions students experience. In the terms of Perfetti's LQH, students need "high-quality practice" in order to build rich, nuanced, flexible representations of word meaning. Developing these kinds of word representations requires ample opportunities to hear and respond to language. Effective instruction entails multiple encounters—our earlier research found comprehension advantages for 12 encounters, but not for 4 encounters, for example. The advantage showed for comprehension of text containing the taught words.

For the goal of enhancing general vocabulary and comprehenion ability, beyond the words taught, students need to use and respond to language beyond vocabulary class and beyond the school day. Evidence suggests that the amount and complexity of language to which children are exposed and in which they participate have significant and long-lasting consequences for literacy achievement. For example, the amount or complexity of caregiver talk has been found to be related to children's language comprehension scores (Tizard, Cooperman, & Tizard, 1972) and to predict differences in child's speech processing (Marchman & Fernald, 2008). Marchman and Fernald also found that 18-month-old children whose mothers produced more words and longer utterances were faster in orally recognizing words at 24 months. Huttenlocher, Vasilyeva, Cymerman, and Levine (2002) found that children's use of more complex sentences was related to the complexity of sentences in parent speech.

The implication is not only that students need to practice using the words they learn, but further, that students need to experience an abundance of language. The more language students hear and participate in, the more material they have for growing and refining their semantic networks, and the richer their semantic networks—the better equipped students will be to build meaning from future contexts they encounter. Just as vocabulary learning needs to be embedded in rich, interactive instruction, instruction needs to be embedded in broader ongoing language—talk! The goal of this ongoing language is not limited to prompting use of the "big words" that students are learning, but to create more language participation opportunities.

In their 2006 book, Stahl and Nagy talked about the importance of increasing talk in the classroom and provided some simple examples, such as modeling complete sentences with explicit references—for example, saying "Please put the marker in the box on the shelf" rather than "Put this over there." Stahl and Nagy also offer some ways to engage students in talk, such as having students teach each other something or practice giving directions.

To increase the amount of ordinary talk students experience, teachers might think about having some handy conversation starters that allow them to prompt talk during the school day. For example, a teacher might ask students about what they might have noticed in the morning, on the way to school, by asking:

- "How does the sky look today?"
- "What did you see on your way to school today?"
- "Was anyone asleep on the bus?"

The teacher might model this approach, beginning, for example, "Today I saw a chipmunk . . . " and describing that small event.

During the school day, as students prepare to move to other classes, to lunch, or leave for the day, talk can be inserted with questions such as:

- "What are you looking forward to in music today?"
- "What are you working on in art?"
- "What will taste best at lunch?"

KEEPING IT GOING: THEME AND VARIATIONS

In focusing on ordinary talk, we do not mean to discount creating opportunities for students to use their newly learned vocabulary beyond the classroom. That focus needs to remain an aim of a vocabulary program as well. We are still ardent proponents of a "Word Wizard" approach, in which students are encouraged to use and notice their vocabulary words outside of class and are rewarded for doing so. The specifics include challenging students to find their words outside of school, such as in books they read, on television programs, or in video games, or using the words themselves as they interact with family and friends. It can also be effective to ask students to look for possible uses of recently introduced words, such as identifying someone in a television program who can be described as *persistent* or who looks *dignified*.

There are many variations on the theme of keeping vocabulary going, and several have come to us from teachers we have worked with or communicated with over the years (Beck, McKeown, & Kucan, 2008). One is to post a list of the vocabulary words with which the class is currently working outside the door of the classroom. First of all, this serves to remind students of their words and to take those words with them, so to speak, as they go beyond the room. Second, it informs visitors, from parents to other teachers and administrators, of words that have some special status in the classroom. The result is often that a visitor will manage to work into his or her conversation with the class one or two of the words—which plays to much delightful recognition from the students!

Another idea we have seen implemented is to directly involve other school staff in vocabulary endeavors by giving them a list of words they can use when they encounter the students. We have seen this approach adopted by custodians, crossing guards, and lunch staff as well as other teachers. The result is an all-encompassing fervor for vocabulary! We have noted that teachers use a variety of classroom incentives for using words, such as points toward some kind of treat, extra recess time, homework release, and computer time, to name a few. All in all there are a myriad of creative ways that teachers can encourage ongoing attention to and enthusiasm for vocabulary.

In that same vein of vocabulary contagion and enthusiasm, we close by noting some striking advantages of working with the youngest school children. Young children so readily develop enthusiasm for words; they love having this new knowledge and sharing it! Also, there is nothing more irresistible than 5- or 6-year-olds wandering the school halls using words such as *distraught, ponder*, and *insist*. Witnessing this phenomenon, a school staff quickly becomes enamored of vocabulary! It is never too early to launch students on a lifelong language habit.

REFERENCES

Apthorp, H., Randel, B., Cherasaro, T., Clark, T., McKeown, M., & Beck, I. (2011). *Effects of a supplemental vocabulary program on word knowledge and passage comprehension.* Manuscript in review.

Beck, I. L., McCaslin, E. S., & McKeown, M. G. (1980). *The rationale and design of a program to teach vocabulary to fourth-grade students* (LRDC Publication No. 1980/25). Pittsburgh: University of Pittsburgh, Learning Research and Development Center.

Beck, I. L., & McKeown, M. G. (2004). *Elements of reading vocabulary.* Austin, TX: Steck-Vaughn.

Beck, I. L., & McKeown, M. G. (2007). Increasing young low-income children's oral vocabulary repertoires through rich and focused instruction. *Elementary School Journal, 107*(3), 251–271.

Beck, I. L., McKeown, M. G., & Kucan, L. (2002). *Bringing words to life: Robust vocabulary instruction.* New York: Guilford Press.

Beck, I. L., McKeown, M. G., & Kucan, L. (2008). *Creating robust vocabulary: Frequently asked questions and extended examples.* New York: Guilford Press.

Beck, I. L., McKeown, M. G., & Omanson, R. C. (1987). The effects and uses of diverse vocabulary instructional techniques. In M. G. McKeown & M. E. Curtis (Eds.), *The nature of vocabulary acquisition* (pp. 147–163). Hillsdale, NJ: Erlbaum.

Beck, I. L., Perfetti, C. A., & McKeown, M. G. (1982). Effects of long-term vocabulary instruction on lexical access and reading comprehension. *Journal of Educational Psychology, 74*(4), 506–521.

Bos, C. S., & Anders, P. L. (1990). Effects of interactive vocabulary instruction on the vocabulary learning and reading comprehension of junior-high learning disabled students. *Learning Disability Quarterly, 13*(1), 31–42.

Bos, C. S., & Anders, P. L. (1992). Using interactive teaching and learning strategies to promote text comprehension and content learning for students with learning disabilities. *International Journal of Disability, Development and Education, 39*(3), 225–238.

Collins, M. F. (2009). ELL preschoolers' English vocabulary acquisition from storybook reading. *Early Childhood Research Quarterly, 25*(1), 84–97.

Corson, D. J. (1985). *The lexical bar.* Oxford, UK: Pergamon Press.

Corson, D. J. (1995). *Using English words.* Dordrecht, The Netherlands: Kluwer Academic.

Coxhead, A. (1998). *An academic word list.* Wellington, NZ: Victoria University of Wellington.

Coyne, M. D., McCoach, D. B., Loftus, S., Zipoli, R., Ruby, M., Crevecoeur, Y., & Kapp, S. (2010). Direct and extended vocabulary instruction in kindergarten: Investigating transfer effects. *Journal of Research on Educational Effectiveness, 3*(2), 93–120.

Coyne, M. D., Simmons, D. C., Kame'enui, E. J., & Stoolmiller, M. (2004). Teaching vocabulary during shared storybook readings: An examination of differential effects. *Exceptionality, 12*(3), 145–162.

Cunningham, A. E., & Stanovich, K. E. (1997). Early reading acquisition and its relation to reading experience and ability 10 years later. *Developmental Psychology, 33*(6), 934–945.

Dale, E., & Chall, J. S. (1948). A formula for predicting readability. *Educational Research Bulletin, 27,* 37–54.

Dole, J. A., Sloan, C., & Trathen, W. (1995). Teaching vocabulary within the context of literature. *Journal of Reading, 38*(6), 452–460.

Dunn, L. M., & Dunn, D. M. (2007). *Peabody Picture Vocabulary Test—Fourth Edition.* Minneapolis, MN: NCS Pearson.

Egan, T. (1997). *Burnt toast on Davenport Street.* Boston: Houghton Mifflin.

Hart, B., & Risley, T. (1995). *Meaningful differences.* Baltimore: Brookes.

Hayes, D. P., & Ahrens, M. G. (1988). Vocabulary simplification for children: A special case of "motherese"? *Journal of Child Language, 15,* 395–410.

Huttenlocher, J., Vasilyeva, M., Cymerman, E., & Levine, S. (2002). Language input and child syntax. *Cognitive Psychology, 45,* 337–374.

Jenkins, J. R., Pany, D., & Schreck, J. (1978). *Vocabulary and reading comprehension: Instructional effects* (Tech. Rep. No. 100). Urbana, IL: University of Illinois, Center for the Study of Reading. (ERIC Document Reproduction Service No. ED 160 999)

Justice, L., Kaderavek, J., Fan, X., Sofka, A., & Hunt, A. (2009). Accelerating preschoolers' early literacy development through classroom-based teacher–child storybook reading and explicit print referencing. *Language, Speech, and Hearing Services in Schools, 40,* 67–85.

Kame'enui, E. J., Carnine, D. W., & Freschi, R. (1982). Effects of text construction and instructional procedures for teaching word meanings on comprehension and recall. *Reading Research Quarterly, 17*(3), 367–388.

Leung, C. (2008). Preschoolers' acquisition of scientific vocabulary through repeated read-aloud events, retellings, and hands-on science activities. *Reading Psychology, 29*(2), 165–193.

Marchman, V. A., & Fernald, A. (2008). Speed of word recognition and vocabulary knowledge in infancy predict cognitive and language outcomes in later childhood. *Developmental Science, 11*(3), F9–F16.

McKeown, M. G., & Beck, I. L. (2010). *Vocabulary instruction for kindergartners: Comparing two approaches.* Manuscript submitted for publication.

McKeown, M. G., Beck, I. L., & Apthorp, H. S. (2010). *Examining depth of processing in vocabulary lessons.* Manuscript in preparation.

McKeown, M. G., Beck, I. L., Omanson, R. C., & Perfetti, C. A. (1983). The effects of long-term vocabulary instruction on reading comprehension: A replication. *Journal of Reading Behavior, 15*(1), 3–18.

McKeown, M. G., Beck, I. L., Omanson, R. C., & Pople, M. T. (1985). Some effects of the nature and frequency of vocabulary instruction on the knowledge and use of words. *Reading Research Quarterly, 20*(5), 522–535.

Medo, M. A., & Ryder, R. J. (1993). The effects of vocabulary instruction in readers' ability to make causal connections. *Reading Research and Instruction, 33*(2), 119–134.

Mezynski, K. (1983). Issues concerning the acquisition of knowledge: Effects of vocabulary training on reading comprehension. *Review of Educational Research, 53*(2), 253–279.

Nagy, W. E., & Scott, J. A. (2000). Vocabulary processes. In M. L. Kamil, P. B. Mosenthal, P. David Pearson, & R. Barr (Eds.), *Handbook of reading research* (Vol. 3, pp. 269–284). Mahwah, NJ: Erlbaum.

National Reading Panel. (2000). *Teaching children to read: An evidence-based assessment of the scientific literature on reading and its implications for reading instruction* (NIH Publication No. 00-4754). Washington, DC: National Institutes of Health.

Perfetti, C. A. (2007). Reading ability: Lexical quality to comprehension. *Scientific Studies of Reading, 11*(4), 357–383.

Perfetti, C. A., & Hart, L. (2002). The lexical quality hypothesis. In L. Verhoeven, C. Elbro, & P. Reitsma (Eds.), *Precursors of functional literacy* (Published as Vol. 11 of the series Studies in Written Language and Literacy). Philadelphia: John Benjamin.

Reichle, E. D., & Perfetti, C. A. (2003). Morphology in word identification: A word-experience model that accounts for morpheme frequency effects. *Scientific Studies of Reading, 7*(1), 219–238.

Roskos, K., Ergul, C., Bryan, B., Burstein, K., Christie, J., & Han, M. (2008). Who's learning what words and how fast: Preschoolers' vocabulary growth in an early literacy program. *Journal of Research in Childhood Education, 22*(3), 275–290.

Silverman. R. (2007). A comparison of three methods of vocabulary instruction during read-alouds in kindergarten. *Elementary School Journal, 108*(2), 97–113.

Stahl, S. A., & Fairbanks, M. M. (1986). The effects of vocabulary instruction: A model-based meta-analysis. *Review of Educational Research, 56*(1), 72–110.

Stahl, S. A., & Nagy, W. E. (2006). *Teaching word meanings*. Mahwah, NJ: Erlbaum.

Tizard, B., Cooperman, O., Joseph, A., & Tizard, J. (1972). Environmental effects on language development: A study of young children in long-stay residential nurseries. *Child Development, 43*(2), 337–358.

Walker, D., Greenwood, C., Hart, B., & Carta, J. (1994). Prediction of school outcomes based on early language production and socioeconomic factors. *Child Development, 65*(2), 606–621.

West, M. (1953). *A general service list of English words*. London: Longman, Green.

Wolf, M. (2007). *Proust and the squid*. New York: HarperCollins.

Chapter 3

Teaching Vocabulary in the Primary Grades

Vocabulary Instruction Needed

Andrew Biemiller

THE RELATIONSHIP BETWEEN VOCABULARY AND COMPREHENSION

There is much evidence that vocabulary levels are strongly correlated with reading comprehension (Biemiller, 1999; Chall, Jacobs, & Baldwin, 1990; Hart & Risley, 1995; Cunningham & Stanovich, 1997; Scarborough, 2001; Stahl & Nagy, 2006; Lescaux & Kieffer, 2010). Chall et al. (1990) and Lescaux and Kieffer (2010) have shown that *vocabulary* is an increasingly important predictor of reading comprehension in higher grades. Thus, whereas vocabulary is a weak predictor of first grade-reading achievement, it is a much stronger predictor of fourth-grade reading achievement (Scarborough) and the main predictor by seventh or eighth grade (Lescaux & Kieffer, 2010). By the middle elementary grades, 95% of children can *read* more words than they *understand* (Biemiller, 2005). From third grade on, the main limiting factor for the majority of children is vocabulary, not reading mechanics (i.e., decoding print into words).

In the primary grades, the range between children with smaller and bigger vocabularies is already large (Biemiller & Slonim, 2001; Biemiller, 2005). By the end of grade 2, children in the lowest vocabulary quartile had acquired slightly more than 1.5 root words a day over 7 years, for a total of about 4,000 root word meanings. In contrast, children in the highest quartile had acquired more than 3 root words a day, for a total of about 8,000 root word meanings. Average vocabulary increases from an estimated 3,500 root word meanings at the beginning of kindergarten to 6,000 at the end of second grade (Biemiller, 2005). These estimates are consistent with findings by Anglin (1993) and my own work, as well as studies of root word knowledge by beginning college students (Hazenberg & Hulstijn, 1996; D'Anna, Zechmeister, & Hall, 1991; Goulden, Nation, & Read, 1990; Nation, 2001).

These large differences reflect many things: (1) levels of parental language support and encouragement, (2) other language sources (e.g., caregivers, day care, preschool, school), and (3) child constitutional differences in the ease of acquiring new words. However, after second grade, children in all vocabulary quartile groups may acquire new words at about the same rate, at least until the sixth grade (Biemiller & Slonim, 2001). Therefore, it seems likely that much of the important vocabulary differences before the third grade reflect differences in experiences as well as constitutional factors.

THE CURRENT LEVEL OF VOCABULARY FOCUS IN SCHOOLS

Unfortunately, in 2010, studies continue to suggest that current practice in primary education does little to promote vocabulary. Age but not necessarily school experience apparently affects vocabulary. Unlike early academic skills, vocabulary is affected by age but *not* by school experience in the primary years (Cantalini, 1987; Christian, Morrison, Frazier, & Massetti, 2000; Morrison, Smith, & Dow-Ehrensberger, 1995). Thus, the vocabulary of old kindergarten children and young-first grade children is similar. The vocabulary of old first-grade children and young second-grade children is also similar (Cantalini, 1987).

More than three decades ago, Becker (1977) suggested that the school emphasis on reading (word identification) skills in the early grades, without any emphasis on developing reasonably advanced vocabulary, results in problems of reading comprehension for many middle elementary children. Primary grade children with restricted oral vocabularies comprehend at lower levels. Other studies have shown that (1) developed vocabulary size in kindergarten is an effective predictor of reading comprehension in the middle elementary years (Scarborough, 1998, 2001; Silverman & Crandall, 2010); (2) orally tested vocabulary at the end of first grade is a significant predictor of reading comprehension 10 years later (Cunningham & Stanovich, 1997); and (3) children with restricted vocabulary by third grade have declining reading comprehension scores in the later elementary years (Chall et al., 1990; Lescaux & Kieffer, 2010). In each of these studies, observed differences in vocabulary were related to later comprehension.

In short, vocabulary levels diverge greatly during the primary years, and virtually nothing effective is done about this in schools. It is true that some children arrive in kindergarten with less vocabulary than others. Schools cannot change what happens before children start school. However, when children fall further behind while in the primary grades, it becomes less likely that they can later "catch up." Our chances of successfully addressing vocabulary differences in school are greatest in the preschool and early primary years.

In this chapter, I discuss the problem of assessing vocabulary in primary grades and briefly describe a new group method for assessing vocabulary of primary and preprimary children. I also discuss the problem of selecting vocabulary for instruction, including the listing available in my book, *Words Worth Teaching* (Biemiller, 2010a). Finally, I discuss types of vocabulary instruction, numbers of word meanings needed, and plausible methods of instruction and assessment for primary children. In addition, I briefly discuss vocabulary instruction in the upper elementary grades.

ASSESSING VOCABULARY IN THE PRIMARY GRADES: A MAJOR PROBLEM

A major barrier for including vocabulary in the primary curriculum is the difficulty of assessing vocabulary under classroom conditions. Testing children's vocabulary orally on a one-to-one basis is not difficult. The Peabody Picture Vocabulary Test (PPVT; Dunn & Dunn, 1997) and the Expressive Vocabulary Test (Williams, 1997) are well established. These and similar tests are predictive of later school achievement (Scarborough, 1998). However, none of these methods is feasible for classroom teachers, for such assessments typically take 10–15 minutes per student.

I believe that the inability to readily and directly assess vocabulary and vocabulary growth has been a major reason why vocabulary receives little attention in the primary grades. If vocabulary is to be taught in the primary grades, teachers will need to monitor children's acquisition of taught vocabulary. At present, the difficulty of assessing vocabulary with *preliterate* children (those who do not read at all or do not read well enough to be validly tested) is a real barrier for teachers. Practical methods for testing vocabulary with *groups* of preliterate children have not been available.

One Effective Group Vocabulary Assessment Method for This Age Group

Recently, Gail Kearns and I published a method for group assessment of vocabulary with preliterate children (i.e., students in kindergarten, first grade, and second grade), demonstrating that this "two-question" method yields results similar to the standard PPVT method, which requires one-on-one testing (Kearns & Biemiller, 2010). The method is based on "yes/no" questions used in curriculum by McKeown and Beck (1988) and Stahl (2005). Our method involves using two questions that could be answered by "yes" or "no" for each word meaning tested. Correct responses to both questions are required if the child is to be credited with knowledge of the word meaning. For example, a child could be asked "Are cherries and peaches *fruits?*" (*yes* or no). A child could also be asked, "Are carrots and beans *fruits?*" (yes or *no*). Correct answers to both questions would indicate that the child understood the meaning of the word *fruits*. The odds of *guessing* both questions correctly is 25%—the same as the odds of a correct response on standard four-alternative tests such as the PPVT. When constructing such tests, we mostly use *Living Word Vocabulary* "grade level 2" words in the test sentences, except for the target words (Dale & O'Rourke, 1981; "grade level 2" consists of words tested at grade 4 and known by more than 80% of students). In the future, we hope to restrict all other words in such tests to those known by 80% of beginning kindergartners.

We have used these test sentences with whole classes of kindergarten, first-grade, and second-grade children. Questions were given orally. Children responded on a sheet with *yes* (and a smile) and *no* (and a frown). Each item was cued with a small picture. Sample questions and a sample response sheet are shown in Figure 3.1.

Using a sample of 22 words from the PPVT, we compared group results of the two-questions test to full-scale PPVT results gained from individually administered tests. Using samples of about 80 children in each of the three grades, we found that children's scores on the two tests correlations ranged from .77 in kindergarten to .70 in grade 2. When word means from the two assessment methods were correlated, correlations in the three grades ranged from .76 in kindergarten to .94 in grade 2. The study included both less advantaged and more advantaged children. Details of this study are available in Kearns and Biemiller (2010). With regular use, this method can be used to test 20 word meanings in about half an hour. Although not perfect, we believe this level of accuracy is sufficient for monitoring children's progress in classroom vocabulary.

WHAT SEQUENCE OF WORD ACQUISITION EXISTS?

Any standardized test of vocabulary (e.g., the PPVT) identifies words learned early and words learned later. A child with a relatively large vocabulary will know more of the "later" words than a child with a small vocabulary, even if the children are the same age. Biemiller and Slonim (2001)

1. ALONE	Y	Can a person find interesting things to do when he or she is alone?
5. ALONE	N	Is someone with you when you are alone?
2. FRUIT	Y	Are peaches and cherries fruits?
6. FRUIT	N	Are carrots and beans fruits?
3. SIGNATURE	Y	Would you write your name if someone asked you for your signature?
7. SIGNATURE	N	Would a red traffic light be a signature?
4. LUXURIOUS	Y	Would a rich person live in a luxurious home?
8. LUXURIOUS	N	Would a luxurious suit of clothes be raggedy?

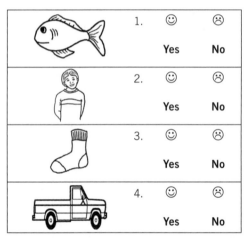

FIGURE 3.1. Sample test items for the Primary Group Vocabulary Test and sample student response page items. (Test items are sample items only; these words were not taken from the PPVT and were not used in the actual study.) Graphics courtesy of Slater Software, Inc., library of over 10,500 *Literacy Support Picture*™. *www. slatersoftware.com.*

showed that words known best by children from grades 1 to 5 are likely to be known even by children with relatively small vocabularies, whereas those with larger vocabularies know those words plus words known less well. Our data suggest that, at any given point in time, children are mainly adding words from an estimated 2,000–3,000 of the 17,500 root words known by average grade 12 students. Ideally, word meanings selected for classroom instruction or explanation should be drawn from the 2,000–3,000 meanings being learned at that point.

FINDING WORDS FOR ATTENTION AND INSTRUCTION

The existence of a sequence of already learned word meanings makes it possible to identify word meanings to be used and taught to children in primary and upper elementary grades. However, there are two problems. One problem is that children within a particular grade enter with different vocabulary sizes, and therefore, they are learning somewhat different words. Addressing the vocabulary needs of children with smaller vocabularies may not meet the needs of more advanced children, and vice versa. The other problem is that we have lacked an accurate, comprehensive listing of most word meanings known by children at different ages or by children with different sizes of vocabulary.

Words Worth Teaching

I recently published *Words Worth Teaching* (Biemiller, 2010a), which includes meanings that should be taught during the primary grades, as well as another set of meanings that should be acquired during the upper elementary grades. For the primary grades, a strategy for finding word meanings for instruction was to identify meanings known by *some* children by the end of grade 2. Meanings known by *most* children at this point would not require instruction in the primary grades. Similarly, meanings known by *few* children at the end of grade 2 would also not require instruction (unless the meaning was used in mandated curriculum). However, root word meanings known by *some* children are, in effect, meanings that are known by children with large vocabularies but that are less likely to be known by those with smaller vocabularies. For practical purposes, I identified these high-priority word meanings as those known by 40–79% of children at the end of grade 2.

To construct this list of "words worth teaching," I used a combination of direct testing of root word meanings with a representative sample of English-speaking children (3,000 meanings), and of rating another 3,000 word meanings. Words were rated as "probably known," "worth teaching," or "too difficult for primary students." Each word meaning was rated by two raters. If the raters didn't agree, the meaning was tested with students. Validity of ratings was assessed by having 100 meanings tested. Agreement between raters and test results was 80%. (Details are reported in Biemiller, 2010a.) Most of the word meanings were found in Dale and O'Rourke's (1981) *Living Word Vocabulary*, grade levels 4 and 6; a few were found at grade levels 8 or 10.

My colleagues and I found about 1,600 high-priority root word meanings that ought to be taught at some point in kindergarten, grade 1, or grade 2. The meanings can be explained as they are used in meaningful contexts (often stories). Acquisition of at least a sample of these priority meanings should be assessed. (In the previous section, I discussed the practical assessment of word meaning knowledge in groups of primary grade children.) Directly teaching or introducing 800+ word meanings per year—or about 20 per week—is not impossible. (Children won't need to learn 800 words; some words will already be known by some of the children. However, a review of the vocabulary studies that report word learning shows that not all meanings taught will be learned [Biemiller & Boote, 2006]). In the next main section of this chapter, I discuss teaching this vocabulary.

For *Words Worth Teaching* (Biemiller, 2010a) we also determined high-priority meanings for the upper elementary period, from grades 3 to 6. For this we included many of the meanings that were too difficult for primary children. In addition, we tested 3,000 more root word meanings and rated 2,000 meanings from in Dale and O'Rourke listed (1981) as known by half of children at grade 8 or grade 10. We used the same criteria for meanings: "known well," "known by some," and "difficult" at the end of grade 6. Overall, we found 2,900 high-priority meanings, based on meanings known at the end of grade 6.

Beck, McKeown, and Kucan's Tiers of Words

Beck, McKeown, and Kucan (2002) propose categorizing word meanings occurring in text as "Tier One" (likely to be known without any school instruction), "Tier Two" ("words . . . of high frequency for mature language users and are found across a variety of domains" [Beck et al., 2002, p. 8]), and "Tier Three" (rare, to be taught when needed as part of a specific discipline such as chemistry or biology). However, they do not provide a listing of such words and, in fact, object to generating such a list (Beck & McKeown, 2007). My approach to selecting word meanings is a variation of their "Tier" approach. Although I agree with the principle of three tiers of words, I differ in what meanings ought to be considered in Tiers One and Two, especially for the primary grades.

Tier One

Beck et al. base their conclusion on an estimate of 8,000 root words known by *average* children in grade 3. Unfortunately, there are many children in this grade who know 2,000–4,000 *fewer* word meanings. It is this smaller vocabulary that renders low-vocabulary children unable to understand typical third-grade texts. Furthermore, the missing meanings will likely be drawn from more recently learned words.

Tier Two

The Tier Two words that Beck et al. recommended for teaching are, for the most part, quite advanced. Example words include *coincidence, absurd, industrious,* and *fortunate* (Beck et al., 2002, p. 8). These are words that are typically learned between fourth and eighth grade (by half of students) (Dale & O'Rourke, 1981). They are similar to and overlap with what I have called "words worth teaching" *in the upper elementary grades.* However, for the *primary grades,* there are many other meanings that should probably be given higher priority. The existence of a strong sequence of meanings acquired suggests that many meanings probably need to be learned before these more advanced meanings are addressed.

Tier Three

I agree with Beck et al.'s conclusions regarding Tier Three word meanings—that is, because these words are generally rare words, they should be taught when needed as part of a specific discipline (e.g., chemistry or biology).

To summarize, when selecting word meanings to teach, there will be meanings that most children in a class know, words that will be unknown by some of the children and well worth teaching, and words that may not be important to teach in this class at this time. In the primary grades, there may be many meanings that Beck et al. would pass over, but I would recommend teaching.

Academic Word List

Averil Coxhead created a list of 570 useful root words and 3,000 derived words based on words appearing frequently in school text sources. Her "Academic Word List" can be accessed at *www.uefap.com/vocab/select/awl.htm.* This list overlaps with my list of words worth teaching, and includes many others that could be difficult for upper elementary students but needed by grade 8. Her text, *Essentials of Teaching College Vocabulary,* provides suggestions for teaching words in the Academic Word List (Coxhead, 2006).

Verbally Defined versus Concrete Meanings

Some word meanings refer to specific things or groups of things that can be pointed to and pictured; other words refer to actions that can be demonstrated or imitated. These are what are commonly called "concrete meanings." However, many word meanings require some verbal definition. Some verbally defined word meanings are called *abstract*—examples are the words *process* or *molecule*. However, many other verbally defined meanings are neither abstract nor concrete. Examples are *think, because,* or *animal.* These last examples may be understood by age 5, but are not concrete. I call all nonconcrete meanings *verbally defined.* I'm sure a more refined set of categories for verbally defined meanings will evolve.

I suspect that the verbally defined words may be the most important for later development. I recently reviewed data for advantaged students from the Biemiller and Slonim (2001) data and found that knowledge of verbally defined meanings was more predictive of reading comprehension a year later than knowledge of concrete meanings for children in kindergarten and grade 1. In the higher elementary grades, this was not true for this advantaged population. Much more data are needed to determine whether this distinction will prove to be useful when deciding what meanings to teach or address in school programs.

PROMOTING VOCABULARY IN THE PRIMARY YEARS

What is the magnitude of the task involved in teaching vocabulary in primary school grades? I have described the 2,000 root word meaning gap between average and the lowest 25% of children (Biemiller, 2005) in a sample of English-speaking children, who were from a range of economic backgrounds but mostly white. It is likely that gaps are even larger for seriously disadvantaged and second-language children.

My hope is that if children know root word meanings, they will be able to infer meanings of derived words (words with prefixes or suffixes or compound words) from context. There is evidence that this can happen when use of affixes (prefixes and suffixes) is taught (Baumann, Edwards, Boland, Olejnik, & Kame'enui, 2003; Bowers & Kirby, 2010).

Many children enter kindergarten with low vocabularies and continue to acquire new vocabulary at low rates during the primary grades (Biemiller, 2005; Hart & Risley, 1995). I estimate that at the beginning of kindergarten, *average low-vocabulary* children (i.e., those in the lowest 25th percentile) are about 1,200 meanings behind average classmates. To "catch up" to the average by the end of second grade, these children would have to acquire 1,200 root meanings each year, instead of 600 as they do now. Adding an additional 600 meanings to be learned per year may not be possible, and vocabulary support will likely need to start earlier and continue later.

There is now clear research showing that vocabulary instruction results in learning word meanings in the kindergarten and preprimary periods (Marulis & Neuman, 2010). Marulis and Neuman report "effect sizes" for the instruction (i.e., they compared word knowledge of instructed groups with control groups or with word knowledge before instruction). On average, gains in word knowledge for the instructed groups were about 0.9 standard deviations or almost a full standard deviation. Marulis and Neuman also note that whole-class lessons were as effective as tutoring or small-group instruction.

It's hard to translate effect sizes into words learned per week. However, in a shorter review of 11 studies, including 2 studies of ours (Biemiller & Boote, 2006), we found that acquiring up to 10–12 word meanings per week was plausible, using approximately 30 minutes of teacher reading and instruction each day. These studies, and most of the 67 studies that Marulis and Neuman reviewed, involved reading stories to children several times plus various levels of direct word meaning instruction. The few studies Marulis and Neuman (2010) included that omitted direct word meaning instruction resulted in substantially fewer word meanings being acquired.

In the past, most studies of vocabulary instruction have involved relatively short interventions, conducted for 1 or 2 weeks. Although the results were impressive, it was unclear whether such levels of gains could be sustained over half a year or a year. However, Marulis and Neuman (2010) report results for 29 studies that exceeded 42 days of instruction, and found that the effect size was about the same as for 30 shorter interventions. In short, it appears entirely possible to use vocabulary interventions for all or most of a school year and sustain a high level of word meaning acquisition.

There are good books available on word meaning instruction, including Graves's (2006) *The Vocabulary Book*, Stahl and Nagy's (2006) *Teaching Word Meanings*, and Beck et al.'s (2002) *Bringing Words to Life*. At present, the available data suggests that teaching *more* meanings per week *in less depth* (20–25 meanings) appears to result in the acquisition of more meanings than teaching *fewer* meanings *in greater depth* (5–10 meanings). Published results suggest that individual children typically learn one-third to one-half of previously unknown word meanings as a result of instruction. This finding holds whether many word meanings are taught (e.g., Biemiller & Boote, 2006) or few word meanings are taught in greater depth (e.g., Beck & McKeown, 2007). If it could be shown that teaching meanings in greater depth would result in learning *more* unknown meanings and/ or that teaching meanings in depth would significantly improve *inferring other unknown meanings*, there would be a strong case for teaching fewer meanings in greater depth.

I should acknowledge that at present, no study of vocabulary instruction in regular primary classrooms *for a full school year or more* has yet been conducted. Until this research is conducted, we won't know (1) if this level of instruction is adequate to meaningfully increase general vocabulary (as measured by the PPVT or other general vocabulary tests), or (2) if this level of instruction will significantly improve reading comprehension.

If a year-long program of instruction can consistently raise general vocabulary knowledge for kindergarten children, educators must understand that such a program would have to be continued in subsequent primary grades to bring students to average vocabulary levels by third grade, when vocabulary demands of texts become a major problem for low-vocabulary students.

Summary of Studies of Vocabulary Intervention in Primary Grades

All of the preschool or primary grade studies are remarkable for the magnitude of language gains produced from relatively short daily interventions with whole-class or less than whole-class interventions. In the long run, effective intervention will involve vocabulary work as a normal part of a primary curriculum. Interventions leading to the acquisition of 10 word meanings per week may appear to have a limited impact on overall vocabulary. However, over 150 days of school instruction (allowing that instruction does not occur every day), up to 300 words could be learned across a school year. If this gain proves to be largely *in addition* to words learned at home, many low-vocabulary children would have a serious chance of moving close to grade-level vocabulary.

PRACTICAL PROBLEMS IN PROMOTING VOCABULARY

Adding an oral teacher read-aloud component with some direct vocabulary and comprehension instruction should provide a significant opportunity to improve vocabulary. Although reading aloud to children is a common component of primary classroom programs, it is often used as a transition activity for changes of instruction or as a relaxation activity just after lunch (Lickteig & Russell, 1993). In my observation, books are rarely reread and rarely used in conjunction with any direct vocabulary or comprehension instruction. If teachers include a read-aloud component with some deliberate instruction, a number of practical issues need to be addressed that include, for example, choosing books, selecting words for explanations, reading with word explanations, keeping track of words taught, and assessing student progress.

Choosing Books

The first problem is choosing books to read to children. In my opinion, teachers should select books that are somewhat challenging for children in the less advanced half of the class *when read orally*. (You'll be able to tell how challenging the book is when you check children's knowledge of vocabulary you have targeted.) There should be a number of words not known by at least half of the class. *These books will have more advanced vocabulary than the beginning readers should be reading.*

It is not desirable to concentrate on words known by only a few of the children in a class, nor to select books that contain many little-known words. Allowing children with below-average vocabulary to acquire vocabulary known by children with above average-vocabulary will probably be most important. This progress will move these children up in the sequence of word meanings learned.

Selecting Words for Explanation

Which words in the book you've chosen should be selected for attention? We have found that our intuition is good but not perfect. We start simply by selecting words that we think will be challenging. We then check to see whether these words are on the list of "words worth teaching"—neither too well known nor too difficult (Biemiller, 2010a). (Word frequency in school books is another source [e.g., Zeno, Ivens, Millard, & Duvvuri, 1995]. However, print frequency is often a poor indicator of knowledge of word meanings [Biemiller & Slonim, 2001].) If we are selecting words for preschool or kindergarten children or for English language learners, even some of the "easy" meanings may need to be taught. You can only address a limited number of words, and although children may be able to learn rare word meanings, they will rarely encounter them in the primary grades. (Of course, if a rare word is to be used in the science curriculum, for example, the meaning should be taught.)

Reading with Word Explanations

Having established target word meanings that are not well known—at least by half of the class—we read the text several times, mostly with meaning explanations. In our experience, it is important to read the book *once* with minimal interruptions. After this initial reading, we find that we can interrupt up to 8 or 10 times to explain words while rereading a book, depending on its length. However, we try not to interrupt more than once every 75–100 running words while reading. With very young children, we try not to interrupt more than once a page in a specific reading. Books for very young children are typically short. Two such books may have to be read to be able to explain 10 words a day (Biemiller & Boote, 2006). It is possible that word explanations can be presented *after* story reading rather than during reading. The procedure would be similar.

We try to keep word explanations, which are given in a specific context, simple. We explain only what is needed to understand the content being read. For example, in kindergarten, the teacher reading *Clifford at the Circus* (Bridwell, 1977) comes to "A sign said the circus needed help." The teacher rereads this sentence and then explains, "*Help* in this story has a different meaning. *The circus needed help* means that the circus wants to hire some people to work at the show—to help put on the show." (Somewhat to our surprise, children have not had difficulty with the use of the word *means*.)

Keeping Track of Words Taught

As a teacher proceeds with reading and word explanations, it is very useful to keep a list of words introduced to the children and preferably some idea of whether the words were learned. I recommend keeping an alphabetical list of words introduced, brief notes on the books in which the words appeared, and an estimate of children's mastery of the words. It is rare for words to go from *unknown by all* to *known by all*. Rather, we can expect a significant increase in the percentage of children knowing a word.

Assessing Some Taught Meanings

I urge teaching 20 to 25 word meanings per week. Based on the studies reviewed in Biemiller and Boote (2006), and in our own experience, we can expect children to acquire 3–4 out of 10 words taught. Most meanings taught will already be known by some children. Some meanings will not be learned. These results have been reported both for studies teaching many words in less depth and in studies teaching fewer words in greater depth. If teachers test a sample of meanings taught during a month, both at the beginning of the month and again at the end, it will be possible to determine if half of words not known initially are learned by the end of the month. I recommend that a sample of 20 meanings taught during a month be assessed at the end of the month. In this chapter, I have described one method that can be used for assessing vocabulary with groups of primary grade children.

PROMOTING VOCABULARY IN THE UPPER ELEMENTARY YEARS

The need for vocabulary instruction changes once students become literate and because they can take greater responsibility for learning unfamiliar word meanings. By literate, I mean becoming able to understand text in print that students would understand if they heard it—typically somewhere between second and fifth grade. With guidance, literate students can become more sensitive to unfamiliar meanings—rather than just passing over them (Biemiller, 2010a, 2010b). Students can also be alerted to *appositions* (definitions supplied in texts) and other meanings that are available in texts (Edwards, Font, Baumann, & Boland, 2004). Skills for using affixes can be taught (Baumann et al., 2003; Graves, 2006). Stahl also recommended attention to Greek and Latin prefixes and roots (Stahl, 1999; Stahl & Nagy, 2006). While students can become more responsible for acquiring new meanings with various strategies, I recommend assessing vocabulary acquisition as new meanings appear in texts. (I list some 2,900 root meanings to be acquired in the grade 3 to grade 6 *period* [Biemiller, 2010a]. Of course, assessing vocabulary is much simpler with literate students *when* written vocabulary assessments can be used.)

CONCLUSION: USING CHILDREN'S LITERATURE TO TEACH VOCABULARY

The research literature suggests that children can acquire an average of 10 words per week, assuming that around 25 words per week are taught. Although this may not seem like a lot of words, vocabulary work over 40 weeks could add 300 root words to children's vocabularies. Marulis and Neuman's (2010) and our data suggest that children with initially smaller vocabularies (specific to the books instructed) have at least the same gains and sometimes larger gains. Those with relatively smaller vocabularies are most in need of added word meanings.

Increasing vocabulary gains by 400 words a year would have a measurable effect on vocabulary size. If vocabulary instruction were sustained over 3 years, this would add about two-thirds of the number of words needed to bring children from the lowest vocabulary quartile to average vocabulary levels, assuming that these children would continue to learn some words outside of school. However, I suggest that there is no magic bullet in vocabulary acquisition. Unlike early work with reading mechanics (e.g., Becker, 1977) or numbers (e.g., Griffin, Case, & Siegler, 1994), promoting vocabulary in the primary grades is not likely to increase self-learning of word meanings through inference. This is true of children who are not reading fluently or widely. (Among older children, especially in middle and high school, there is some evidence that active inference may help with vocabulary learning.) During the primary years, new root words are learned mainly from explanations by others.

Other vocabulary methods could be used in addition. A "word of the day" could be added (preferably a word that will be used in the classroom). If children can be encouraged to ask about unfamiliar words—and parents can be persuaded to encourage such questions—more gains could be achieved. However, total gains greater than three words per day have yet to be seen (or attempted!).

A classroom intervention along the lines described in this chapter would take about 30 minutes. I realize that asking for 30 minutes a day is a lot, as state and provincial curricula become ever more demanding. Some of the teachers I have worked with have complained that "they would not be able to complete the curriculum" (science, social studies, and art content) if they had to focus on stories and vocabulary 30 minutes a day. Their principal suggested that becoming literate was probably more important than some of the details in the prescribed curriculum. Curricula that result in children reaching grade 3 without the best possible vocabulary instruction and opportunities are curricula that probably hold disadvantaged children back. Some of the read-aloud and word-explanation activities can be conducted with specified curriculum materials related to social studies or science. However, in the primary grades, we should be more concerned with children acquiring an adequate normal vocabulary than mastering specific social studies or science facts. It is now widely accepted that children need basic academic skills—word identification, handwriting and spelling, and number skills. We will not begin to close the gaps between advantaged and disadvantaged children until we also succeed in ensuring adequate vocabulary development and use.

REFERENCES

Anglin, J. M. (1993). Vocabulary development: A morphological analysis. *Monographs of the Society for Research in Child Development, 58*(10, Serial No. 238).

Baumann, J. F., Edwards, E. C., Boland, E. M., Olejnik, S., & Kame'enui, E. J. (2003). Vocabulary tricks: Effects of instruction on morphology and context on fifth-grade students' ability to derive and infer word meanings. *American Research Journal, 40*(2), 447–494.

Beck, I. L., & McKeown, M. G. (2007). Increasing young low-income children's oral vocabulary repertoires through rich and focused instruction. *Elementary School Journal, 107,* 251–273.

Beck, I. L., McKeown, M. G., & Kucan, L. (2002). *Bringing words to life: Robust vocabulary instruction.* New York: Guilford Press.

Becker, W. C. (1977). Teaching reading and language to the disadvantaged: What we have learned from field research. *Harvard Educational Review, 47,* 518–543.

Biemiller, A. (1999). *Language and reading success.* Cambridge, MA: Brookline Books.

Biemiller, A. (2005). Size and sequence in vocabulary development: Implications for choosing words for primary grade vocabulary instruction. In E. H. Hiebert & M. L. Kamil (Eds.), *Teaching and learning vocabulary: Bringing research to practice* (223–242). Mahwah, NJ: Erlbaum.

Biemiller, A. (2010a). *Words worth teaching.* Columbus, OH: SRA/McGraw-Hill.

Biemiller, A. (2010b). Vocabulary development and implications for reading problems. In A. McGill-Franzen & R. Allington (Eds.), *Handbook of reading disabilities research* (pp. 208–218). New York: Routledge.

Biemiller, A., & Boote, C. (2006). An effective method for building meaning vocabulary in primary grades. *Journal of Educational Psychology, 98*, 44–62.

Biemiller, A., & Slonim, N. (2001). Estimating root word vocabulary growth in normative and advantaged populations: Evidence for a common sequence of vocabulary acquisition. *Journal of Educational Psychology, 93*, 498–520.

Bowers, P. N., & Kirby, J. R. (2010). Effects of morphological instruction on vocabulary acquisition. *Reading and Writing: An Interdisciplinary Journal, 23*, 515–537.

Bridwell, N. (1977). *Clifford at the circus.* New York: Scholastic.

Cantalini, M. (1987). *The effects of age and gender on school readiness and school success.* Unpublished doctoral dissertation, Ontario Institute for Studies in Education, Toronto, Canada.

Chall, J. S., Jacobs, V. A., & Baldwin, L. E. (1990). *The reading crisis: Why poor children fall behind.* Cambridge, MA: Harvard University Press.

Christian, K., Morrison, F. J., Frazier, J. A., & Massetti, G. (2000). Specificity in the nature and timing of cognitive growth in kindergarten and first grade. *Journal of Cognition and Development, 1*(4), 429–448.

Coxhead, A. (2006). *Essentials of teaching college vocabulary.* Boston: Houghton Mifflin.

Cunningham, A. E., & Stanovich, K. E. (1997). Early reading acquisition and its relation to reading experience and ability 10 years later. *Developmental Psychology, 33*, 934–945.

Dale, E., & O'Rourke, J. (1981). *The living word vocabulary.* Chicago: World Book/Childcraft International.

D'Anna, C. L., Zechmeister, E. B., & Hall, J. W. (1991). Toward a meaningful definition of vocabulary size. *Journal of Reading Behavior, 23*, 109–122.

Dunn, L. M., & Dunn, L. M. (1997). *Peabody Picture Vocabulary Test* (3rd ed.). Circle Pines, MN: American Guidance Service.

Edwards, E. C., Font, G., Baumann, J. E., & Boland, E. (2004). Unlocking word meanings: Strategies and guidelines for teaching morphemes and contextual analysis. In J. F. Baumann & E. J. Kame'enui (Eds.), *Vocabulary instruction: Research to practice* (pp. 159–178). New York: Guilford Press.

Goulden, R., Nation, P., & Read, J. (1990). How large can a receptive vocabulary be? *Applied Linguistics, 11*, 341–363.

Graves, M. F. (2006). *The vocabulary book: Learning and instruction.* New York: Teachers' College Press.

Griffin, S., Case, R., & Siegler, R. (1994). Rightstart: Providing the central conceptual prerequisites for first formal learning of arithmetic to students at risk for failure. In K. McGilly (Ed.), *Classroom lessons: Integrating cognitive theory and classroom practice* (pp. 25–50). Cambridge, MA: MIT Press.

Hart, B., & Risley, T. (1995). *Meaningful differences in the everyday experience of young American children.* Baltimore: Brookes.

Hazenberg, S., & Hulstijn, J. H. (1996). Defining a minimal receptive second-language vocabulary for non-native university students: An empirical investigation. *Applied Linguistics, 17*, 145–163.

Kearns, G., & Biemiller, A. (2010). Two-questions vocabulary assessment:

Developing a new method for group testing in kindergarten through second grade. *Journal of Education, 190*(1/2), 31–42.

Lescaux, N. K., & Kieffer, M. J. (2010). Exploring sources of reading comprehension difficulties among language minority learners and their classmates in early adolescence. *American Educational Research Journal, 47*(3), 596–632.

Lickteig, M., & Russell, J. (1993). Elementary teachers read-aloud practices. *Reading Improvement, 30,* 202–208.

Marulis, L. M., & Neuman, S. B. (2010). The effects of vocabulary on young children's word learning: A meta-analysis. *Review of Educational Research, 80*(3), 300–335.

McKeown, M. G., & Beck, I. L. (1988). Learning vocabulary: Different ways for different goals. *Remedial and Special Education (RASE), 9*(1), 42–52.

Morrison, F. J., Smith, L., & Dow-Ehrensberger, M. (1995). Education and cognitive development: A natural experiment. *Developmental Psychology, 31,* 789–799.

Nation, I. S. P. (2001). *Learning vocabulary in another language.* Cambridge, UK: Cambridge University Press.

Scarborough, H. S. (1998). Early identification of children at risk for reading disabilities: Phonological awareness and some other promising predictors. In B. K. Shapiro, P. J. Accardo, & A. J. Capute (Eds.), *Specific reading disability: A view of the spectrum* (pp. 75–119). Timonium, MD: York Press.

Scarborough, H. S. (2001). Connecting early language and literacy to reading (dis)abilities: Evidence, theory, and practice. In S. B. Neuman & D. Dickinson (Eds.), *Handbook of early literacy research* (pp. 97–110). New York: Guilford Press.

Silverman, R., & Crandall, J. D. (2010). Vocabulary practices in prekindergarten and kindergarten classes. *Reading Research Quarterly, 45*(3), 318–340.

Stahl, S. A. (1999). *Vocabulary development.* Cambridge, MA: Brookline.

Stahl, S. A. (2005). Four problems with teaching word meanings (and what to do to make vocabulary an integral part of instruction). In E. H. Hiebert & M. L. Kamil (Eds.), *Teaching and learning vocabulary: Bringing research to practice* (pp. 95–114). Mahwah, NJ: Erlbaum.

Stahl, S. A., & Nagy, W. E. (2006). *Teaching word meanings.* Mahwah, NJ: Erlbaum.

Williams, K. T. (1997). *Expressive Vocabulary Test.* Circle Pines, MN: American Guidance Service.

Zeno, S. M., Ivens, S. H., Millard, R. T., & Duvvuri, R. (1995). *The educator's word frequency guide.* Breward, NY: Touchstone Applied Science.

Chapter 4

Vocabulary Instruction for Young Children at Risk of Reading Difficulties

Teaching Word Meanings during Shared Storybook Readings

Michael D. Coyne
Ashley Capozzoli-Oldham
Deborah C. Simmons

Beginning reading research has converged on a profound and irrefutable finding: Children enter kindergarten with "meaningful differences" in early literacy experiences (Hart & Risley, 1995). Even at this early age, children are characterized by differences in skills, exposure, and opportunities with the form, functions, and conventions of language and print (National Research Council, 1998; Verhoeven, van Leeuwe, & Vermeer, 2011). For example, young children differ considerably in their understanding of, and familiarity with, the phonological features of language and the alphabetic nature of our writing system (Torgesen et al., 1999). Whereas some children begin school having already grasped the insight that language can be broken down into individual phonemes that map onto letters, many other children have only the most rudimentary awareness of sounds and their relation to print. A large body of research evidence suggests that these differences in phonological awareness and letter knowledge have important implications for learning to read and predicting success in acquiring beginning reading skills (National Reading Panel, 2000).

Similarly, young children possess vastly divergent vocabularies (Biemiller, 2001; Hart & Risley, 1995; National Early Literacy Panel, 2008). Whereas some children enter school with thousands of hours of exposure to books and a wealth of rich oral language experiences, other children begin school with very limited knowledge of language and word meanings. Like the research base on phonological awareness and alphabetic understanding, teachers and researchers have long recognized the important and prominent role that vocabulary knowledge plays in becoming a successful reader (Becker, 1977; Cunningham & Stanovich, 1998; RAND Reading Study Group, 2002).

The research evidence is unequivocal: Children enter kindergarten with significant differences in critical early literacy skills, and these differences place many children at serious risk for failing to learn how to read and understand text. As a result, early intervention matters, and it matters more for children who enter with less. These children not only begin school with limited skills and knowledge, but also these initial differences grow larger and more discrepant over time (Biemiller & Slonim, 2001; Stanovich, 1986). The goal of early intervention, therefore, is to target differences in early literacy skills and experiences at the outset of formal schooling before reading difficulties become entrenched and intractable (Coyne, Kame'enui, & Simmons, 2001). To this end, educators, policymakers, and researchers have actively and increasingly promoted prevention and early intervention efforts in beginning reading.

The results of early intervention have been largely encouraging. Over the past 20 years, researchers have engaged in a concerted and ever more successful effort to develop effective instructional strategies and interventions to increase the phonological awareness and word identification skills of young children at risk for reading difficulties and disability (e.g., Foorman, Francis, Fletcher, Schatschneider, & Mehta, 1998; Scammacca, Vaughn, Roberts, Wanzek, & Torgeson, 2007; Simmons et al., 2011; Torgesen et al., 1999). Yet, although the research community has concentrated its collective attention on helping children *read* words, there has been much less corresponding research conducted on helping children *understand* words or develop equally critical vocabulary knowledge (National Reading Panel, 2000). As Biemiller and Slonim (2001) asserted, "Although vocabulary development is crucial for school success, it has not received the attention and interest that work on identifying printed words and spelling have received" (p. 511).

Responding to this need, intervention studies have evaluated vocabulary instruction in kindergarten and first grade (Beck & McKeown, 2007; Biemiller & Boote, 2006; Coyne, McCoach, Loftus, Zipoli, & Kapp, 2009; Justice, Meier, & Walpole, 2005; Silverman, 2007). Results from this growing body of research have informed our understanding of how we can support the vocabulary development of students through intentional, teacher-directed instruction. For example, converging evidence from this research indicates that children learn new words when they are provided with a student-friendly definition in the context of either a storybook or a meaningful sentence (Elley, 1989; Justice et al., 2005; Penno, Wilkinson, & Moore, 2002) and that this word learning is further developed and deepened when children have multiple opportunities to interact with words across diverse contexts (Beck & McKeown, 2007; Biemiller & Boote, 2006).

In this chapter, we first summarize the research base on explicit vocabulary instruction and then describe and give examples of an experimental storybook vocabulary intervention designed for kindergarten children who are at risk for experiencing reading difficulties.

EXPLICIT VOCABULARY INSTRUCTION IN GRADES 3 AND ABOVE

Although there is less research on explicit vocabulary instruction in grades K–2 (Elleman, Lindo, Murphy, & Compton, 2009), there is a more extensive literature on direct vocabulary instruction in grades 3 and above (Baker, Kame'enui, & Simmons, 1998; Baumann, Kame'enui, & Ash, 2003). There is especially strong evidence on the effectiveness of explicitly teaching students the meanings of specific words and instructional principles that maximize vocabulary learning (National Reading Panel, 2000).

Explicit vocabulary instruction should teach directly the meanings of words that are important for understanding the text and of words that students will encounter often (Stahl, 1986). Effective strategies for directly teaching vocabulary include using both contextual and definitional information, providing multiple exposures to target words, and encouraging deep processing (Baumann et al., 2002; National Reading Panel, 2000; Stahl, 1986; Stahl & Fairbanks, 1986). Activities that encourage deep processing challenge students to move beyond memorizing simple dictionary definitions to understand words at a richer, more complex level by, for example, describing how they relate to other words and to their own experiences (Beck, McKeown, & Omanson, 1987; Kame'enui, Carnine, & Freschi, 1982).

Direct instruction of target words is also more effective when it adheres to validated principles of instructional and curricular design (Coyne, Kame'enui, & Carnine, 2007). For example, vocabulary instruction should be conspicuous (Baker et al., 1998). Conspicuous instruction is explicit and unambiguous and consists of carefully designed and delivered teacher actions. During vocabulary instruction, this conspicuous instruction would include direct presentations of word meanings using clear and consistent wording and extensive teacher modeling of new vocabulary in multiple contexts. Vocabulary instruction should also provide students with carefully scheduled review and practice to help them more firmly incorporate new vocabulary into their lexicon (Baker et al., 1998).

A program of research that evaluated the effectiveness of explicit vocabulary instruction was conducted by Beck, McKeown, and their colleagues with students in upper elementary grades (Beck, Perfetti, & McKeown, 1982; McKeown, Beck, Omanson, & Perfetti, 1983; McKeown, Beck, Omanson, & Pople, 1985). Their program of rich vocabulary instruction provided students with definitions of words but also extended instruction by providing experiences that promoted and reinforced deep processing of word meanings. Students were exposed to target words frequently within and across lessons and given opportunities to manipulate words in varied and rich ways. Results of these studies demonstrated that a carefully designed program of direct vocabulary instruction can have positive effects on both students' word learning and comprehension.

The vocabulary literature with older students has important implications for younger students at risk of reading difficulties. Previously, many researchers have argued that the number of words that children need to learn is so great that the role of direct instruction in helping students develop vocabulary knowledge is insignificant and inconsequential (Anderson & Nagy, 1992). Other researchers, however, have questioned this assertion. Lower estimates of the number of root word meanings that typical students acquire in a year suggest that direct instruction can, in fact, provide students with a significant proportion of the words they will learn, especially students with less developed vocabularies (Biemiller, 2001; Biemiller, Chapter 3, this volume; Stahl & Shiel, 1999).

VOCABULARY INSTRUCTION WITH YOUNG SCHOOL-AGE CHILDREN

Though most research on explicit vocabulary instruction has been carried out with older students in third grade and above (e.g., Baumann et al., 2003; Beck et al., 1982; Kame'enui et al., 1982), we know that waiting until third grade to systematically address vocabulary development may be too late for children who enter school with low vocabularies and at risk for experiencing reading difficulties. The urgency of targeting vocabulary development in the early grades was made acutely apparent in research conducted by Biemiller and Slonim (2001). Their findings revealed that most of the vocabulary differences between children occur before third grade, at which point children with high vocabularies know *thousands* more word meanings than children who are experiencing delays in vocabulary development.

Teaching Vocabulary within the Context of Storybook Reading

We know that older students acquire a great deal of new vocabulary through wide, independent reading (Anderson & Nagy, 1992), whereas younger students who have yet to become skilled readers must learn word meanings through a different medium (Becker, 1977). The primary way in which young nonreaders are exposed to new vocabulary is within the context of oral language experiences such as shared storybook reading. Storybook reading activities are an excellent means of developing language and vocabulary because of the opportunities for using decontextualized language during interactive discussion (Snow, 1991) and the relative rarity of the vocabulary encountered in storybooks compared with speech (Cunningham & Stanovich, 1998). For example, the complexity of vocabulary found in children's books is greater than in all of adult conversation, except for courtroom testimony (Hayes & Ahrens, 1988).

Researchers have begun to isolate factors that increase the likelihood that children will learn new vocabulary from listening to storybooks. In addition to engaging in rich dialogic discussion about the storybook, these factors include reading storybooks multiple times (Robbins & Ehri, 1994; Senechal, Thomas, & Monker, 1995), providing performance-oriented readings (Dickinson & Smith, 1994), and reading storybooks with small groups of students (Whitehurst, Arnold, et al., 1994). Finally, it is important to choose engaging storybooks with beautiful pictures and appealing stories that will capture and hold children's interest and attention.

The results of these studies suggest that shared storybook reading activities are a valuable way to support vocabulary development in young children.

Much of this research has been informed by an influential series of studies by Whitehurst and his colleagues (Whitehurst, Arnold, et al., 1994; Whitehurst, Epstein, et al., 1994; Whitehurst et al., 1999). These studies investigated the effects of a storybook reading intervention called "dialogic reading." In contrast to traditional storybook reading activities that typically consist of an adult reading and a child listening passively, dialogic reading actively involves the child in the overall literacy experience. According to Whitehurst et al. (1999), the

> adult assumes the role of an active listener, asking questions, adding information, and prompting the child to increase the sophistication of descriptions of the material in the picture book. The child's active engagement is encouraged through praise and repetition, and more sophisticated responses are encouraged by expansions of the child's utterances and by scaffolding by means of more challenging questions from the adult reading partner. (p. 262)

Results from studies evaluating dialogic reading with preschool children reported significant effects on young children's emergent literacy and language skills (Whitehurst et al., 1994; Whitehurst, Epstein, et al., 1999; see also Mol, Bus, De Jong, & Smeets, 2008). In a converging program of related research, Senechal and her colleagues similarly found that preschool children's active participation and engagement during shared storybook reading increased the likelihood that they would learn new vocabulary (Hargrave & Senechal, 2000; Senechal et al., 1995).

Although this research is encouraging, evidence from these studies reveals that these activities are not equally effective for all students. Children with lower initial vocabularies who are at risk for reading difficulties are less likely to learn unknown words from incidental exposure during storybook reading activities than their peers with higher vocabularies (Nicholson & Whyte, 1992; Robbins & Ehri, 1994; Senechal et al., 1995). In other words, with traditional storybook reading activities, the initial vocabulary differences among students grow larger over time (Stanovich, 1986; Penno et al., 2002).

Beyond Incidental Exposure

In response to this finding, researchers have called for more conspicuous, teacher-directed vocabulary instruction to complement traditional storybook reading activities for young children who are at risk of experiencing reading difficulties (Biemiller & Slonim, 2001; Simmons et al., 2007; Stahl & Shiel, 1999). For example, Robbins and Ehri (1994) concluded that "because children with weaker vocabularies are less likely to learn new words from listening to stories than children with larger vocabularies, teachers need to provide more explicit vocabulary instruction for children with smaller vocabularies" (p. 61).

One approach for directly teaching word meanings provides students with brief definitions of target words within the context of oral language experiences such as story read-alouds (e.g., Elley, 1989; Penno et al., 2002). This approach characterizes the research of Biemiller and his colleagues. Biemiller and Boote (2006) conducted two studies in which vocabulary learning among primary students improved when brief explanations of word meanings were provided during repeated storybook readings. Knowledge of word meanings was tested by rating verbal explanations of words presented in context sentences. Children demonstrated a 22% gain in instructed words compared to a 12% gain for noninstructed words, indicating that explicit explanations resulted in a statistically significant increase in word learning. In a second study, two reviews of each word meaning were provided, including an opportunity to review word meanings in new context sentences. Children in this study showed an average gain of 41%. Biemiller and Boote concluded that teaching many word meanings without in-depth discussion appeared to be an effective approach to direct vocabulary instruction.

Findings from studies such as these hold promise for improving early intervention efforts for young children with less developed vocabularies at risk of reading difficulties. By intensifying shared book reading activities with direct teaching of target vocabulary, these interventions increased the amount of vocabulary that children learned. Interventions that maximize learning are a critical component of prevention efforts because children who begin school with less require the most effective and efficient instruction to catch up to their peers who are not at risk (Coyne et al., 2001). Research suggests that providing a student-friendly definition or synonym during storybook reading or other rich oral language experiences is an efficient and effective way to teach new words to young school-age children (Biemiller & Boote, 2006; Elley, 1989; Justice et al., 2005; Penno et al., 2002). In addition, converging findings indicate that providing the definition to students during a read-aloud is more effective than relying on incidental exposure alone.

Rich or Extended Vocabulary Instruction

While introducing definitions to children in the context of storybook reading is one approach to direct instruction, an additional body of research has examined the effects of what has been referred to as extended or rich instruction. This instruction is characterized by Beck, McKeown, and Kucan (2002) as instruction that "offers rich information about words and their uses, provides frequent and varied opportunities for students to think about and use words, and enhances students' language comprehension and production" (p. 2). Research investigating this approach with young children suggests that word learning is enhanced through engaging this type of interaction around words in diverse contexts beyond that of storybook reading alone (Beck &McKeown, 2007; Coyne et al., 2009).

Beck and McKeown (2007) investigated the effects of this type of rich instruction on word-learning outcomes in kindergarten and first-grade students. They hypothesized that more and deeper exposure to words over the course of several days of instruction would lead to increases in word learning. They compared two instructional conditions that differed only in the amount of exposure to words across the week. Beck and McKeown observed word gains twice as large in the additional exposure condition, compared to the condition with less exposure to words. These findings suggest a connection between increased exposure to words and increased word learning.

In our 2009 study, we investigated the effects of two different types of vocabulary instruction on word learning in kindergarten students: embedded instruction and extended instruction (Coyne et al., 2009). In the *embedded instruction* condition, target words were introduced during storybook reading in a quick and efficient way. In the *extended condition*, instruction was more intensive and provided students with multiple opportunities to engage with words both within and outside of the story reading context. We found that the embedded instruction resulted in partial word learning, whereas the extended instruction condition resulted in deeper and more refined word knowledge. Our results converge with other findings suggesting that multiple diverse opportunities to engage with words enhance word learning (Beck & McKeown, 2007; Biemiller & Boote, 2006; McCoach & Kapp, 2007).

In summary, research highlights the need for early interventions that offer effective classroom-based vocabulary instruction for young children at risk of experiencing reading difficulties. The research literatures outlined previously provide a conceptual and empirical basis for developing such an intervention by incorporating validated principles of explicit and systematic vocabulary instruction from research conducted with students in grades 3 and above into storybook reading activities for young children in kindergarten through grade 2. In the following section, we describe and give examples of a vocabulary intervention informed by this conceptual framework.

LINKING RESEARCH TO PRACTICE

We recently completed a program of research designed to investigate the efficacy of explicit vocabulary instruction with kindergarten students (Coyne, McCoach, & Kapp, 2007; Coyne et al., 2009, 2010). As part of this research, we developed an 18-week program of direct and extended instruction designed to increase children's vocabulary knowledge. When designing the elements of the intervention targeting vocabulary development, we explicitly incorporated and integrated the instructional principles distilled from our review of the vocabulary research. To make the linkage between the research principles and their application more transparent, we outline these connections in Table 4.1. Findings from this study indicate that compared to controls, students who received vocabulary instruction had greater gains on both a measure of target word knowledge as well as measures of listening comprehension and generalized receptive vocabulary.

TABLE 4.1. Vocabulary Instruction Literature

Research principle	Application
Carefully selected target words	Three target words were chosen to teach directly from each storybook. Words were selected because they were important for understanding the story and likely to be unfamiliar to kindergarten students (i.e., Tier Two words).
Simple definitions within the context of the story	When introducing a new vocabulary word, teachers provided students with a simple definition or synonym when it was encountered in the story read-aloud. Teachers then used the definition within the context of the story.
Conspicuous instruction	Definitions of target words were presented through instruction that was direct and unambiguous. Definitions were explicitly modeled by teachers using clear and consistent wording.
Extended instruction	Teachers provided children with opportunities to discuss target words in extended discourse after stories. Additionally, teachers provided children with structured discrimination and generalization tasks that challenged them to process word meanings at a deeper and more complex level.
Multiple exposures to target words and carefully scheduled review and practice	Target vocabulary words were introduced during 1 week of instruction and then reviewed systematically during an average of 5 additional weeks.

KINDERGARTEN VOCABULARY INTERVENTION

We describe our approach to vocabulary instruction as "extended instruction" (see also Beck et al., 2002). Extended vocabulary instruction provides students with direct instruction of target words within the supportive context of a storybook reading as well as extended discussion and interaction with the target words beyond the storybook. The goal of this type of instruction is to move beyond simply memorizing definitions of unknown words to a deeper level of word processing that leads to a richer understanding of them.

In this section, we describe in more detail the vocabulary intervention evaluated in the kindergarten study (Coyne et al., 2010). The intervention consisted of 36 half-hour lessons developed to accompany 18 high-interest children's picture books (two lessons per week over 18 weeks). Three words were selected per story to be targeted for instruction (54 words total). We chose words according to Beck and McKeown's description of Tier Two words. These are words that are unknown to students, but have meanings that children are able to understand. Selected examples of picture books and target vocabulary are included in Appendix 4.1.

Storybook Reading

The teacher began each of the two storybook readings by introducing the target vocabulary words, referred to as "magic words," and having students pronounce them. Then the students were encouraged to listen for the magic words in the story and raise their hands when they heard one. The teacher then read the story and reinforced students when they raised their hands by saying, "Oh, good. Some of you raised your hands! What word did you hear? Yes, *apex*. This [pointing to picture] is a penguin standing at the *apex* of an iceberg." The teacher then provided students with a simple definition of the magic words (e.g., "*Apex* means the place at the very top of something."). Then the teacher reread the sentence and replaced the magic word with its definition or synonym (e.g., "Now I'll say the sentence again with words that mean *apex*. 'This is a penguin standing at the very top of an iceberg.'"). The teacher then reinforced the story context by referring to the illustration (e.g., "In the picture you can see that the penguin is standing at the very top, or the *apex*, of the iceberg."). Finally, students again pronounced the target word to strengthen phonological representations (e.g., "Everyone say *apex*.").

Postreading Discussion

In the postreading discussion, children engaged in an extended discourse about the target words. During this time, the teacher engaged students in activities that scaffolded interactions with words in rich and diverse contexts. For example, first, the teacher reintroduced students to each target word by reviewing how it was used in the story: "One of the magic words we learned in the story was *apex*. Everyone, say *apex*. An *apex* is the place at the very top of something. This [showing the anchor picture] is a penguin standing at the *apex* of an iceberg. In this picture, Tacky is standing at the *apex* of the iceberg—the place at the very top of the iceberg."

Next, the teacher provided students with examples of the target word used in other contexts—for example: "The *apex* of a tree would be the place at the very top of the tree. If you were at the *apex* of a mountain, you would be at the very top of the mountain. The *apex* of a house would be the very top of the roof."

Students then engaged in different interactive activities that focused on identifying examples and nonexamples of magic words in different contexts. For example: "Let's play a game about our magic word *apex*. I'll show you some pictures. If you think the picture shows an *apex*, or the place at the very top of something, put your thumbs up like this [demonstrating] and whisper 'That's an *apex*.' If the picture doesn't show an *apex*, put your thumbs down like this [demonstrating] and don't say anything." The teacher reinforced correct responses for both examples and nonexamples: "If you put your thumb up, like this, you're right! This picture shows an *apex*, or the place at the very top of a mountain. 'The sun shone down on the *apex* of the mountain.' " Or "If you put your thumb down, like this, you're right! This picture doesn't show an *apex*, it shows the trunk or the bottom of a tree. 'The trunk is at the bottom of the giant tree.' "). The teacher followed up with open-ended questions that encouraged students to extend and elaborate on their initial responses (e.g., "Why does/ doesn't this picture show an *apex*?"). Lastly, the intervention included systematic review of taught words. Review activities reinforced definitions and encouraged deep processing of word meanings. In addition, the teacher led students in exploring the relationships and connections between new words and previously learned words and concepts.

To illustrate this intervention, we provide examples of lessons that accompanied the two readings of the storybook *Lorenzo's Llama*, by Wendi J. Silvano (2003). The three target words selected from this picture book were *slope, regretful*, and *sprint*. Because children at risk of experiencing reading difficulties benefit from instruction that is highly explicit, we designed lessons with a considerable degree of instructional specificity (Simmons et al., 2007). For example, lessons were broken down into a series of specific instructional tasks, opportunities for corrective feedback were provided, and teachers were supplied with precise and consistent wording (Coyne, Kame'enui, & Carnine, 2007). (Note that suggested teacher wording in this and following lessons is shown in *italics*.)

STORY READING: LORENZO'S LLAMA

Story Introduction: Days 1 and 2

1. Point to the title on the cover. *The title of this story is **Lorenzo's Llama**. The story was written by Wendi J. Silvano. The pictures were drawn by Bruce Martin.*
2. *I want you all to be good listeners while I read the story. We'll talk about it after we finish. Listen to hear what happens with a boy named Lorenzo and his llama.*
3. *When I read this story, I am going to read and say a lot of words. I want you to listen for these magic words in the story. Here they are. **Slope.** Say it with me . . . slope. **Regretful.** Say it with me . . . regretful. **Sprint.** Say it with me . . . sprint. When you hear these*

words in the story, raise your hand. You might also hear some of our other magic words—when you hear those magic words, raise your hands.

The Reading: Days 1 and 2

Pause at the following breaks and ask these questions:

Slope: *Page 3*

Oh, good. Some of you raised your hands! What word did you hear? Yes, slope. "Then he would go outside and climb the slope to where the llamas grazed."

OR

I think I heard one of our magic words. Listen and raise your hands when you hear our magic word slope. "Then he would go outside and climb the slope to where the llamas grazed." What word did you hear? Yes, slope.

THEN ADD:

A slope is a hill. Now I'll say the sentence again with words that mean slope. "Then he would go outside and climb the hill to where the llamas grazed." (Point to the picture.) *In the picture you can see that Lorenzo is looking out at the hill, or slope. Everyone, say slope.*

Sprint: *Page 7*

Oh, good. Some of you raised your hands! What word did you hear? Yes, sprint. "He sprinted off in the other direction."

OR

I think I heard one of our magic words. Listen and raise your hands when you hear our magic word sprint. "He sprinted off in the other direction." What word did you hear? Yes, sprint.

THEN ADD:

Sprint means to run really fast. Now I'll say the sentence again with words that mean sprint. "He ran really fast off in the other direction." (Point to the picture.) *In the picture you can see that Oro is running really fast, or sprinting. Everyone, say sprint.*

Regretful: *Page 11*

Oh, good. Some of you raised your hands! What word did you hear? Yes, regretful. **"Lorenzo felt regretful about going so far up the mountain."**

OR

I think I heard one of our magic words. Listen and raise your hands when you hear our magic word regretful. **"Lorenzo felt regretful about going so far up the mountain."** *What word did you hear? Yes, regretful.*

THEN ADD:

Regretful means sorry. Now I'll say the sentence again with words that mean regretful. **"Lorenzo felt sorry about going so far up the mountain."** (Point to the picture.) *In the picture you can see that Lorenzo is sorry, or regretful, because he went too far up the mountain and got hurt. Everyone, say regretful.*

Postreading Discussion

During this section each activity would be completed with every targeted word. Here we illustrate the instruction only for the word *slope.*

Slope *(Picture Activity: Day 1)*

GROUP RESPONSES

One of the magic words we learned in the story was slope. Everyone, say slope.

A slope is a hill. (Show the anchor picture from the story.) **"Then he would go outside and climb the slope to where the llamas grazed."**

In the picture you can see that Lorenzo is looking out at the hill, or slope. You would see a slope outside and it could be grassy or snowy or even made out of dirt. You could do lots of fun things on a slope. You could climb up a slope, or go sledding or ski down a slope.

(Show the anchor picture again.) *Everyone, is this* (point to slope) *a flat piece of land?* (No.) *Is this a slope? Yes, that's right! This is a slope, or a hill.*

Let's play a game about our magic word slope. I'll show you some pictures. If you think the picture shows a slope, or hill, put your thumbs up, like this (demonstrating), *and whisper, "That's a slope." If the picture doesn't show a slope, put your thumbs down, like this* (demonstrating), *and don't say anything.*

(Show the following pictures to the group.)

- Picture 1 (people on slope): *Does this picture show a slope? If you put your thumb up, like this, you're right! This picture shows a slope, or a hill.* **"The children ran down the grassy slope to play with their mom."**
- Picture 2 (snowy slope): *Does this picture show a slope? If you put your thumb up, like this, you're right! This picture shows a slope, or hill.* **"The little girl was too scared to go sledding down the big, snowy slope."**
- Picture 3 (forest): *Does this picture show a slope? If you put your thumb down, like this, you're right! This picture shows a bunch of trees that are* **not** *on a slope, or hill.* **"In the winter, the trees lost all of their leaves."**
- Picture 4 (barn on slope): *Does this picture show a slope? If you put your thumb up, like this, you're right! This picture shows a little slope, or hill.* **"It is easy for the farmer to carry his basket of vegetables up the little slope."**
- Picture 5 (flat land): *Does this picture show a slope? If you put your thumb down, like this, you're right! This picture does* **not** *show a slope, or hill, it shows land that is flat.* **"People like to take walks on the sand."**

INDIVIDUAL TURNS

After going through all the pictures with the group, call on one or two individual students and show them one of the pictures. Call on students that may be having difficulty. Ask, *"Does this picture show a slope?"*

- If student answers *correctly*, say, *"Yes, that's right!* (and follow up) *Why does/doesn't this picture show a slope?"*
- If student answers *incorrectly*, say, *"This picture does/doesn't show*

a slope, because it does/doesn't show a hill. Does this picture show a slope?"

Everyone, say the magic word we've been talking about.

Slope *(Sentence Activity: Day 2)*

GROUP RESPONSES

(Show the anchor picture for slope.) **"Then he would go outside and climb the hill where the llamas grazed."** *Everyone, try to think about our magic word that means hill. (pause) Everyone, say the magic word together. That's right, slope means hill.* **"Then he would go outside and climb the slope where the llamas grazed."**

These are other pictures that show slopes. (Show the pictures for the three positive examples of slope and read these sentences.)

- Picture 1 (people on slope): **"The children ran down the grassy slope to play with their mom."**
- Picture 2 (snowy slope): **"The little girl was too scared to go sledding down the big, snowy slope."**
- Picture 4 (barn on slope): **"It is easy for the farmer to carry his basket of vegetables up the little slope."**

Let's play a game about our magic word slope. I'll tell you about some things and if you think they would be a slope, or hill, put your thumbs up, like this (demonstrating), *and whisper, "That's a slope." If you think they wouldn't be a slope, put your thumbs down, like this* (demonstrating), *and don't say anything.*

(Read the following examples to the group.)

- (Example 1) *"The kids went sledding at the park."* (That's a slope!) *If you put your thumb up like this, you're right! If kids were sledding, they would be going down a slope, or a hill.* **"The kids loved to go fast down the big slope."**
- (Example 2) *"The ball rolled down to the bottom of the backyard."* (That's a slope!) *If you put your thumb up, like this, you're right! If the ball rolled all the way to the bottom of the backyard, it must be on a slope or a hill.* **"The girl couldn't stop the ball before it rolled down the slope."**

- (Example 3) *"The team played on the soccer field."* (pause) *If you put your thumb down, like this, you're right! A soccer field has to be flat, so it could **not** be on a slope, or a hill.* *"The soccer players ran across the field toward the goal."*
- (Example 4) *"The bike riders had to rest after riding all the way up to the top of the street."* (That's a slope!) *If you put your thumb up, like this, you're right! If the bike riders were so tired that they had to rest at the top of the street, they would be on a slope, or a hill.* *"The bike riders could barely make it all the way to the top of the slope."*
- (Example 5) *"The woman climbed the stairs to her room."* (pause) *If you put your thumb down, like this, you're right! A woman going up the stairs would be climbing up something, but she **wouldn't** be on a slope, or a hill.* *"The woman went up the stairs to get a book from her room."*

INDIVIDUAL TURNS

After going through all the examples with the group, call on one or two students and read them one of the examples. Call on students who may be having difficulty. Say *"If this is a slope, say 'That's a slope:'"*

- If student answers *correctly*, say *"Yes, that's right!"* (and follow up) *Why is/isn't that a slope?*
- If student answers *incorrectly*, say *"That is/isn't a slope because it is/isn't a hill. Let's try another one."*

Everyone, say the magic word we've been talking about.

SUMMARY

In this chapter we outlined a conceptual and empirical framework for incorporating direct instruction of specific word meanings into storybook reading activities. To support this conceptual framework, we summarized research findings on shared storybook reading activities carried out with young children in preschool through grade 2 and the research on explicit vocabulary instruction conducted primarily with students in grade 3 and above.

We then illustrated how instructional components distilled from the results of vocabulary intervention research could be translated into instructional practice by providing examples of a storybook intervention designed to help kindergarten children at risk of experiencing reading difficulties increase their vocabulary knowledge. Results from a study evaluating this intervention demonstrated that these students can be taught the meanings of specific words within the context of storybook reading activities and that rich and extended vocabulary instruction can also support growth in listening comprehension and overall receptive vocabulary knowledge. Interventions that increase the effectiveness of storybook reading activities through explicit teaching of word meanings hold promise for decreasing the vocabulary differences among students in the primary grades.

REFERENCES

Anderson, R. C., & Nagy, W. E. (1992). The vocabulary conundrum. *American Educator, 16*(4), 14–18, 44–47.

Baker, S. K., Simmons, D. C., & Kame'enui, E. J. (1998). Vocabulary acquisition: Research bases. In D. C. Simmons & E. J. Kame'enui (Eds.), *What reading research tells us about children with diverse learning needs* (pp. 183–218). Mahwah, NJ: Erlbaum.

Baumann, J. F., Edwards, E. C., Font, G., Tereshinski, C. A., Kame'enui, E. J., & Olejnik, S. (2002). Teaching morphemic and contextual analysis to fifth-grade students. *Reading Research Quarterly, 37*, 150–176.

Baumann, J. F., Kame'enui, E. J., & Ash, G. E. (2003). Research on vocabulary instruction: Voltaire redux. In J. Flood, J. Jensen, D. Lapp, & J. R. Squire (Eds.), *Handbook of research on teaching the English language arts* (pp. 752–785). New York: Macmillan.

Beck, I. L., & McKeown, M. G. (2007). Increasing young low-income children's oral vocabulary repertoires through rich and focused instruction. *Elementary School Journal, 107*, 251–271.

Beck, I. L., McKeown, M. G., & Kucan, L. (2002). *Bringing words to life: Robust vocabulary instruction*. New York: Guilford Press.

Beck, I. L., McKeown, M. G., & Omanson, R. C. (1987). The effects and uses of diverse vocabulary instructional techniques. In M. G. McKeown & M. E. Curtis (Eds.), *The nature of vocabulary acquisition* (pp. 147–163). Hillsadale, NJ: Erlbaum.

Beck, I. L., Perfetti, C. A., & McKeown, M. G. (1982). Effects of long-term vocabulary instruction on lexical access and reading comprehension. *Journal of Educational Psychology, 74*(4), 506–521.

Becker, W. C. (1977). Teaching reading and language to the disadvantaged: What we have learned from field research. *Harvard Educational Review, 47*, 518–543.

Biemiller, A. (2001). Teaching vocabulary: Early, direct, and sequential. *American Educator, 25*, 24–28, 47.

Biemiller, A., & Boote, C. (2006). An effective method for building meaning vocabulary in primary grades. *Journal of Educational Psychology, 98*(1), 44–62.

Biemiller, A., & Slonim, N. (2001). Estimating root word vocabulary growth in normative and advantaged populations: Evidence for a common sequence of vocabulary acquisition. *Journal of Educational Psychology, 93*(3), 498–520.

Coyne, M. D., Kame'enui, E. J., & Carnine, D. W. (2007). *Effective teaching strategies that accommodate diverse learners* (3rd ed.). Columbus, OH: Merrill.

Coyne, M. D., Kame'enui, E. J., & Simmons, D. C. (2001). Prevention and intervention in beginning reading: Two complex systems. *Learning Disabilities Research and Practice, 16,* 62–72.

Coyne, M. D., McCoach, D., & Kapp, S. (2007). Vocabulary intervention for kindergarten students: Comparing extended instruction to embedded instruction and incidental exposure. *Learning Disability Quarterly, 30*(2), 74–88.

Coyne, M. D., McCoach, D. B., Loftus, S., Zipoli, R., & Kapp, S. (2009). Direct vocabulary instruction in kindergarten: Teaching for breadth vs. depth. *Elementary School Journal, 110,* 1–18.

Coyne, M. D., McCoach, D. B., Loftus, S., Zipoli, R., Ruby, M., Crevecoeur, Y., et al. (2010). Direct and extended vocabulary instruction in kindergarten: Investigating transfer effects. *Journal of Research on Educational Effectiveness, 3,* 93–120.

Cunningham, A. E., & Stanovich, K. E. (1998). What reading does for the mind. *American Educator, 22*(1–2), 8–15.

Dickinson, D. K., & Smith, M. W. (1994). Long-term effects of preschool teachers' book readings on low-income children's vocabulary and story comprehension. *Reading Research Quarterly, 29,* 104–122.

Elleman, A. M., Lindo, E. J., Morphy, P., & Compton, D. L. (2009). The impact of vocabulary instruction on passage-level comprehension of school-age children: A meta-analysis. *Journal of Research on Educational Effectiveness, 2,* 1–44.

Elley, W. B. (1989). Vocabulary acquisition from listening to stories. *Reading Research Quarterly, 24,* 174–187.

Foorman, B. R., Francis, D. J., Fletcher, J. M., Schatschneider, C., & Mehta P. (1998). The role of instruction in learning to read: Preventing reading failure in at-risk children. *Journal of Educational Psychology, 90,* 37–55.

Hargrave, A. C., & Senechal, M. (2000). A book reading intervention with preschool children who have limited vocabularies: The benefits of regular reading and dialogic reading. *Early Childhood Research Quarterly, 15,* 75–95.

Hart, B., & Risley, R. T. (1995). *Meaningful differences in the everyday experience of young American children.* Baltimore: Brookes.

Hayes, D. P., & Ahrens, M. (1988). Vocabulary simplification for children: A special case of "motherese." *Journal of Child Language, 15,* 395–410.

Justice, L., Meier, J., & Walpole, S. (2005). Learning new words from storybooks: An efficacy study with at-risk kindergartners. *Language, Speech, and Hearing Services in Schools, 36*(1), 17–32.

Kame'enui, E., Carnine, D., & Freschi, R. (1982). Effects of text construction and instructional procedures for teaching word meanings on comprehension and recall. *Reading Research Quarterly, 17*(3), 367–388.

Keats, E. J. (1976). *A snowy day.* New York: Puffin Books.

Lane, E. (2003). *Anansi and the Seven Yam Hills.* Menlo Park, CA: Electronic Education.

Lee, H. B. (2003). *While we were out.* La Jolla, CA: Kane/Miller.

Lester, H. (1988). *Tacky the penguin.* Boston: Houghton Mifflin.

Lester, H. (1989). *A porcupine named Fluffy.* Boston: Houghton Mifflin.

Marshall, J. (1996). *The three little pigs.* New York: Puffin Books.

Marshall, J. (1998). *Goldilocks and the three bears.* New York: Puffin Books.

McKeown, M. G., Beck, I. L., Omanson, R. C., & Perfetti, C. A. (1983). The effects of long-term vocabulary instruction on reading comprehension: A replication. *Journal of Reading Behavior, 15,* 3–18.

McKeown, M. G., Beck, I. L., Omanson, R. C., & Pople, M. T. (1985). Some effects of the nature and frequency of vocabulary instruction on the knowledge and use of words. *Reading Research Quarterly, 20,* 482–496.

Mol, S. E., Bus, A. G., De Jong, M. T., & Smeets, D. J. H. (2008). *Added value of dialogic parent–child book readings: A meta-analysis. Early Education and Development, 19,* 7–26.

National Early Literacy Panel. (2008). *Developing early literacy: Report of the National Early Literacy Panel.* Washington, DC: National Institute for Literacy.

National Reading Panel. (2000). *Teaching children to read: An evidence-based assessment of the scientific research literature on reading and its implications for reading instruction: Reports of the subgroups.* Bethesda, MD: National Institute of Child Health and Human Development.

National Research Council. (1998). *Preventing reading difficulties in young children.* Washington, DC: National Academy Press.

Nicholson, T., & Whyte, B. (1992). Matthew effects in learning new words while listening to stories. In C. K. Kinzer & D. J. Leu (Eds.), *Literacy research, theory, and practice: Views from many perspectives: Forty-first yearbook of the National Reading Conference* (pp. 499–503). Chicago: National Reading Conference.

Penno, J. F., Wilkinson, I. A. G., & Moore, D. W. (2002). Vocabulary acquisition from teacher explanation and repeated listening to stories: Do they overcome the Matthew effect? *Journal of Educational Psychology, 94,* 23–33.

RAND Reading Study Group. (2002). *Reading for understanding.* Washington, DC: Author.

Ringgold, F. (1996). *Tar beach.* New York: Dragonfly Books.

Robbins, C., & Ehri, L. C. (1994). Reading storybooks to kindergartners helps them learn new vocabulary words. *Journal of Educational Psychology, 86,* 54–64.

Roos, M. (2000). *The city mouse and the country mouse.* Sunnyvale, CA: Electronic Education.

Scammacca, N., Vaughn, S., Roberts, G., Wanzek, J., & Torgesen, J. K. (2007). *Extensive reading interventions in grades K–3: From research to practice.* Portsmouth, NH: RMC Research Corporation, Center on Instruction.

Senechal, M., Thomas, E., & Monker, J. (1995). Individual differences in 4-year-old children's acquisition of vocabulary during storybook reading. *Journal of Educational Psychology, 87,* 218–229.

Silvano, W. J. (2003). *Lorenzo's llama.* Salt Lake City, UT: Waterford Institute.

Silverman, R. D. (2007). Vocabulary development of English-language and English-only learners in kindergarten. *Elementary School Journal, 107,* 365–383.

Simmons, D. C., Coyne, M. D., Hagan-Burke, S., Kwok, O., Simmons, L., Johnson, et al. (2011). Effects of supplemental reading interventions in authentic contexts: A comparison of kindergarteners' response. *Exceptional Children, 77*, 207–228.

Simmons, D. C., Kame'enui, E. J., Harn, B., Coyne, M. D., Stoomiller, M., Santoro, L., et al. (2007). Attributes of effective and efficient kindergarten reading intervention: An examination of instructional time and design of instruction specificity. *Journal of Learning Disabilities, 40*, 331–347.

Snow, C. E. (1991). The theoretical basis for relationships between language and literacy in development. *Journal of Research in Childhood Education, 6*, 5–10.

Stahl, S. A. (1986). Three principles of effective vocabulary instruction. *Journal of Reading, 29*(7), 662–668.

Stahl, S. A., & Fairbanks, M. M. (1986). The effects of vocabulary instruction: A model-based meta-analysis. *Review of Educational Research, 56*, 72–110.

Stahl, S. A., & Shiel, T. G. (1999). Teaching meaning vocabulary: Productive approaches for poor readers. In *Read all about it!: Readings to inform the profession* (pp. 291–321). Sacramento: California State Board of Education.

Stanovich, K. E. (1986). Matthew effects in reading: Some consequences of individual differences in the acquisition of literacy. *Reading Research Quarterly, 21*, 360–406.

Torgesen, J. K., Wagner, R. K., Rashotte, C. A., Rose, E., Lindamood, P., Conway, T., et al. (1999). Preventing reading failure in young children with phonological processing disabilities: Group and individual responses to instruction. *Journal of Educational Psychology, 91*, 1–15.

Verhoeven, L., van Leeuwe, J., & Vermeer, A. (2011). Vocabulary growth and reading development across the elementary school years. *Scientific Studies of Reading, 15*, 8–25.

Wasik, B. A., & Bond, M. A. (2001). Beyond the pages of a book: Interactive book reading and language development in preschool classrooms. *Journal of Educational Psychology, 93*, 243–250.

Wells, R. (2001). *Yoko's paper cranes.* New York: Hyperion.

Wells, R. (2005). *McDuff moves in.* New York: Hyperion.

Whitehurst, G. J., Arnold, D. H., Epstein, J. N., Angell, A. L., Smith, M., & Fischel, J. E. (1994). A picture book reading intervention in day care and home for children from low-income families. *Developmental Psychology, 30*, 679–689.

Whitehurst, G. J., Epstein, J. N., Angell, A. L., Payne, A. C., Crone, D. A., & Fischel, J. E. (1994). Outcomes of an emergent literacy intervention in Head Start. *Journal of Educational Psychology, 86*, 542–555.

Whitehurst, G. J., Zevenbergen, A. A., Crone, D. A., Schultz, M. D., Velting, O. N., & Fischel, J. E. (1999). Outcomes of an emergent literacy intervention from Head Start through second grade. *Journal of Educational Psychology, 91*, 261–272.

APPENDIX 4.1. Selected Storybooks and Target Vocabulary

Book	Vocabulary taught
Helen Lester (1988), *Tacky the Penguin*. Boston: Houghton Mifflin.	*Peculiar* *Apex* *Plummet*
Helen Lester (1989), *A Porcupine Named Fluffy*. Boston: Houghton Mifflin.	*Slender* *Drenched* *Sprawl*
James Marshall (1998), *Goldilocks and the Three Bears*. New York: Puffin Books.	*Cycling* *Scalding* *Parlor*
James Marshall (1996), *The Three Little Pigs*. New York: Puffin Books.	*Sturdy* *Weep* *Festival*
Elizabeth Lane (2003), *Anansi and the Seven Yam Hills*. Menlo Park, CA: Electronic Education.	*Irritated* *Plot* *Exclaim*
Wendi J. Silvano (2003), *Lorenzo's Llama*. Sunnyvale, CA: Electronic Education.	*Slope* *Regretful* *Sprinted*
Ezra Jack Keats (1976), *A Snowy Day*. New York: Puffin Books.	*Grin* *Saunter* *Glum*
Rosemary Wells (2005), *McDuff Moves In*. New York: Hyperion.	*Terrace* *Thrash* *Serene*
Rosemary Wells (2001), *Yoko's Paper Cranes*. New York: Hyperion.	*Voyage* *Gaze* *Soar*
Maryn Roos (2000), *The City Mouse and the Country Mouse*. Sunnyvale, CA: Electronic Education.	*Cautions* *Devour* *Metropolis*
Faith Ringgold (1996), *Tar Beach*. New York: Dragonfly Books.	*Boulevard* *Hoist* *Immense*
Ho Baek Lee (2003), *While We Were Out*. La Jolla, CA: Kane/Miller Book Publishers.	*Grasp* *Minute* *Weary*

Chapter 5

Young Word Wizards!

Fostering Vocabulary Development in Preschool and Primary Education

Katherine A. Dougherty Stahl
Steven A. Stahl

Consider the power that a name gives a child—"This is a *table* and that is a *chair*." No longer are they merely things that one must crawl around. Having a name for something means that one has some degree of control, because naming words engenders a cause-and-effect relationship with the environment. The child can say *eat* and, in response, receive a cracker or some baby food. As children acquire more words, they gain more control over their environment. To move from *eat* to *cracker* or *cookie* or *fruit*, from *bottle* to *milk* or *juice*, allows the child to better communicate wants and needs, and to have a better chance of having them fulfilled.

As children learn new words, they can further classify the environment. They progress from gross categories—things that sit on the floor, things that children can get nourishment from—to more precise labels. Children's ability to name things establishes their ability to form categories (Nelson, 1996). As knowledge about the named item increases, that word can be transferred to related situations. This pattern is true for first vocabulary and extends to each new or expanding knowledge domain. Language and reading both act as the tools of thought to bring representations to a new level of awareness and to allow the formation of new relationships and organizations.

Vocabulary development does not end in early childhood, but goes on and on as long as we continue to learn (Kintsch, 1998; Paris, 2005).

To follow the *juice* example from *orange juice* to the various kinds of juice available (*fresh-squeezed, no pulp, from concentrate, organic*) in your local supermarket may seem absurd, but a good deal of the process of knowing about the world is learning the categories and subcategories of objects and actions within that world.

Having access to more word meanings enables us to think more precisely about our environment and to manipulate that environment. Classification, the basic mental process underlying naming is important not only in naming, but also in summarizing (Kintsch, 1998; Kintsch & van Dijk, 1978) and inferencing (Anderson & Pearson, 1984), among other cognitive operations. To expand a child's vocabulary is to teach that child to think about the world, and in a reciprocal fashion, more refined vocabulary indicates that child's degree of knowledge about his or her world. For example, generate a mental image in response to the three statements below.

- "Place the ingredients in a pot."
- "Place the ingredients in a Dutch oven."
- "Place the ingredients in a saucier."

Certainly, each sentence creates a different mental image. However, a person's knowledge base and cooking experiences will inform other broader inferences based solely on the type of pot being used.

This chapter discusses the teaching of word meanings to children from prekindergarten to grade 2. The vocabulary foundation that is established in the primary grades is vitally important to comprehensive literacy development across the years.

THE DEVELOPMENT OF WORD KNOWLEDGE

Knowing a word involves more than knowing a word's definition (Anderson & Pearson, 1984; Nagy & Scott, 2000); knowing a word is not an all-or-nothing phenomenon (Dale, 1965). Word learning happens incrementally, with each additional encounter with a word expanding the depth of understanding. With each exposure, the child learns a little about the word, until he or she develops a full and flexible knowledge of the word's meaning. This knowledge will include definitional aspects, such as the category to which it belongs and how it differs from other members of the category, but this knowledge will be implicit, informal, and not conventionalized, as in a dictionary definition. It will also contain information about the various contexts in which the word was found and how the meaning differed in the different contexts. The process of word learning also requires moving from a process of overgeneralization to a more constrained and particular usage. As the word is encountered repeatedly in different contexts, the child will acquire a refined understanding of the boundaries and nuances of that particular word.

Over time vocabulary knowledge generally expands from receptive to generative usage. As children develop and enter formal educational settings, acquiring knowledge about word meaning might include replications of *motherese* and conversational exchanges that replicate early language learning as well as learning from both reading and listening in instructional settings (Hayes & Ahrens, 1988).

VARIATION IN VOCABULARY KNOWLEDGE

It is important to recognize the diversity of vocabulary knowledge among children entering formal educational settings. These variations are evident in the preschool years and persist through the elementary school years, and probably beyond. For example, Hart and Risley (1995) found that children from advantaged homes (i.e., mostly children of college professors) had receptive vocabularies that were as much as five times larger than children from homes receiving Aid to Families with Dependent Children (AFDC). They found that children in AFDC homes had concomitantly fewer words spoken to them, with more words spoken in imperative sentences and fewer in descriptive or elaborative sentences. Hart and Risley's research points to students from well-off versus poor families—a gap that threatens to grow with time in the absence of instructional interventions.

These differences in vocabulary knowledge, even in the young years, can influence children's reading throughout the elementary years. Dickinson and Tabors (2001) found that children's word knowledge in preschool still had significant correlations with their comprehension in upper elementary school. Stanovich (1986) suggests that children who are more proficient readers tend to read more, and to read more challenging materials, than children who struggle in reading. Because most words that children acquire are learned from reading them in context (Kuhn & S. A. Stahl, 1998) and because proficient readers read more challenging materials that contain rarer or more difficult words, they tend to learn more of those words, enabling them to read yet more challenging materials. Thus, without instructional interventions, the gap between proficient and struggling readers grows each year.

Another study of elementary school students exemplifies differences in vocabulary acquisition persisting through the elementary years. White, Graves, and Slater (1990) examined the reading and meaning vocabularies of children in first through fifth grades in three schools—a largely European American suburban school, an inner city school with mainly African American students, and a semirural school enrolling largely Pacific Island children. They found that both reading and meaning vocabularies grew rapidly over the school years, with meaning vocabularies growing at an estimated average of 3,000 words per year. This average, though, concealed large variations, with estimated vocabulary growth ranging from 1,000 to 5,000 words per year. The reading and meaning vocabularies of children in the suburban school grew more rapidly than those in the two schools serving disadvantaged children.

In contrast, Biemiller and Slonim (2001), who examined children's growth in word meanings between grades 2 and 5, found that children in the bottom quartile learned more words per day (averaging 3 root words) than did children in the upper quartile (averaging 2.3 root words per day). They suggest that children in the lower quartile had more words to learn, so, given the same exposure to words in school, were able to learn more. However, children in the lowest quartile still knew only as many word meanings by the fifth grade as a typical fourth grader, because they started so far behind in second grade. Biemiller and Slonim suggest that vocabulary instruction should begin earlier to close the gap.

THE ROLE OF EXPERIENCES IN VOCABULARY DEVELOPMENT

Hart and Risley (1995) also found that professional parents not only spoke more words than parents of lower socioeconomic (SES) children but also exhibited different discourse patterns. Although both groups of parents engaged in similar talk around functional daily routines, professional parents incorporated more elaborated explanations than did the lower-income parents. The discourse patterns may have reflected the more limited resources available to the lower-income parents to provide vocabulary rich experiences for their children. Families with professional salaries and schedules can more easily afford vacations, museum visits, and leisurely conversations around the dinner table about the day's events than can families coping with economic stresses.

To expand children's vocabularies, then, one must provide not only more words for children to learn, through expanding the number of words used when speaking to them, but also expand their experiences. After all, words are mere labels for things and ideas. These experiences do not have to be first-hand ones; we know many things without ever having seen them directly. For example, we have a clear idea of what dinosaurs look like (or at least what scientists have posited that they look like), and we had this idea even before seeing the movie *Jurassic Park*. Children learn from television, the movies, the Internet, and descriptions in books—and today's technology makes it possible for students to have vicarious virtual experiences (Silverman & Hines, 2009). What is important is that children *experience* a wide variety of concepts.

TALKING TO CHILDREN

One aspect of expanding the vocabulary of children should be obvious: Talk to them! There are wide variations in how much adults talk to children at home as well as at school (Hart & Risley, 1995; Schwanenflugel et al., 2010). For children to develop rich vocabularies, they need to have many interactions with adults who converse with them beyond the barest routine management of the day's schedule. It is from these interactions that they will develop the words they need to negotiate their world. Huttenlocher, Haight, Bryk, Seltzer, and Lyons (1991) found that both the total amount of words and the number of different words mothers spoke to children significantly influenced the children's vocabulary learning.

"Goldilocks" Words

It is not enough to just throw big words into conversations with children. This does not seem to be effective in improving children's vocabularies. Beck and McKeown (2001, 2003, 2007) suggest teaching what they call Tier Two words—that is, words for known concepts that are used by sophisticated language users. Children are familiar with these concepts, but they are likely to use a more general term (e.g., *yellow* rather than *amber*). Tier One words are common words, such as common sight words, and simple nouns and verbs. Tier Three words are rare, limited to a single discipline, or represent concepts that young children might not have yet developed, such as *cogitate, anarchy,* or *photosynthesis.* Tier Two words include words such as *dome, beret, wade, chef, amble,* and *bellow.* We call these Tier Two words "Goldilocks" words—words that are not too difficult, not too easy, but just right.

There is evidence that children learn words in a similar order. Biemiller and Slonim (2001) found that the order of vocabulary acquisition seemed similar between children, with high correlations in word knowledge between children. Words vary in their complexity, and children cannot learn a more complex word without learning the simpler word. Thus, we should make sure that the words we are teaching are of appropriate complexity. This sounds harder than it is. In natural conversation, for example, mothers and teachers often seem able to manage the right level of communication, if they keep their ears open to how the children are responding to them.

Talk Around Words

The type of talk that takes place around is important. Motherese is a good example of what effective teachers, including parents, do to expand their children's vocabulary. Motherese might be demonstrated in dialogues that start with what a child knows and expand that knowledge through a series of questions. This type of expansion through questioning seems effective in helping older children learn new words encountered in context. The work of De Temple and Snow (2003) and Beck and McKeown (2003, 2007) indicates that nonimmediate and cognitively challenging talk is effective in helping both preschool and primary grade children develop word meanings.

Nonimmediate or decontextualized talk is talk that goes beyond what is in front of the child and enables him or her to make connections to past experiences, to analyze information or draw inferences, or to discuss the meaning of words. Mothers' use of this type of talk was found to relate to their children's later performance on vocabulary measures (De Temple, 1994). De Temple and Snow (2003) use storybook reading for examples of this type of talk, but it can be done when talking about things that one encounters on a walk or on a trip. In cognitively challenging talk, the adult tries to get the child to extend his or her thinking about the topic. Such talk not only expands vocabulary knowledge, in terms of the numbers of words known, but also expands the depth of that knowledge. For example:

MOTHER: That's a tusk, see? It's white. Know what, Domingo [child, age 5 years, 11 months]?

CHILD: Hmm?

MOTHER: Hunters kill these elephants for that.

CHILD: Why?

MOTHER: Because they want it for, um, well, they use it for different things. I think, um, some museums buy them, and I don't know about museums, but I know that they kill the elephants for this white, um.

CHILD: There's no tusk on these elephants, though.

MOTHER: See? That one's bigger so some of them die because of that. That is sad.

CHILD: I wish there was not such things as hunters and guns.

MOTHER: I know. Me too. Oh, there's a herd. That's a lot of them. See how they walk?

CHILD: Ma, here's one that's dead.

MOTHER: I don't think he's dead! Well, we'll find out. "They use their tusks to dig." Oh, see he's digging a hole! "They use their tusks to dig for salt. . . . "

CHILD: Hmm.

MOTHER: Let's look and see if there's another page you might like.

It's ivory! The tusks are made of ivory. And they can make things with these tusks and that's why some animals, they die, hunters kill them.

CHILD: No wonder why they have hunters.

MOTHER: Yeah, that's sad.

CHILD: I'm never gonna be a hunter when I grow up. (De Temple & Snow, 2003, pp. 23–24)

The talk in this excerpt shows how a mother can use target vocabulary as the entrée to broader conceptual development. In this case, the mother begins by pointing out the tusk, then she expands it to the uses of the tusk by the elephant and by the hunters, finally ending on an emotional reaction to hunting. The richness of the language expands the child's knowledge of the word *tusk* by connecting it to *hunting, digging,* and so forth.

Just talking is important. However, it is equally important to have something to talk *about*. This means that adults (teachers and parents) need to consciously provide experiences that expand children's horizons. These experiences might include trips around the neighborhood, to the grocery store (to talk about all those varieties of orange juice), to the park, the zoo, or any other place that gives the child new experiences or a chance to expand on previous experiences.

WHERE THE WORDS ARE

The maximum vocabulary learning, however, comes from reading books. Storybook reading is the most powerful source of new vocabulary, including those academic words that are valued in school discourse. Books are literally "where the words are." Hayes and Ahrens (1988) examined the vocabulary used in a variety of sources. The average difficulty in a typical children's book ranks above that of either a children's or an adult television program, and even above that of a typical conversation between two college-educated adults. The number of rare words per 1,000 in children's books also ranks above that of television programs, adult conversation, and cartoon shows. Even a book like *Curious George Gets a Job* (Rey, 1947), intended for first graders to read and younger children to listen to, contains relatively rare words. These include not only *curious* but also *cozy, dizzy, wound, scold,* and *attention*, and these words are from just the first 20 pages.

Stanovich (2000) and Cunningham and Stanovich (1991) have found that exposure to books, as measured by author recognition or title recognition measures, can account for a great deal of the variation in vocabulary knowledge among children and adults. In their studies, they examined exposures specifically to books, but language acquisition studies seem to indicate that the same effect holds true for exposure to all verbal language, written or spoken.

Neuman and Celano (2001) examined the availability of print resources in low- and middle-income communities and found striking differences in the availability of print resources between these communities. For example, in one middle-class community there were 13 venues selling children's books, with 358 titles available. In a contrasting low-income community there were 4 venues with only 55 titles available. Thus, the gap between socioeconomic communities that are well off and those that struggle may begin with differences in the richness of language usage, but continues through economic differences in the availability of print resources.

If we are to decrease the vocabulary knowledge gaps between children, we must respond when the differences begin to appear: in the preschool or at least the primary grades. By addressing the differences early, intentional efforts to foster vocabulary development can bridge, rather than perpetuate, gaps in vocabulary knowledge, allowing more children to succeed in school.

THE LANGUAGE OF SCHOOL

All words are not valued equally. Instead, what we want children to learn is the language of school. For many children, this is literally a foreign language (S. A. Stahl & Nagy, 2006). This language of school includes words that are used in school, but not necessarily in children's homes or neighborhoods.

Olson (1977) makes a useful distinction between *utterance* and *Text*. *Utterance* refers to the conversational language that often contains sentence fragments, reliance on deixis ("over there") and other contextualized referents, a reduced vocabulary and a shared knowledge base between speaker and hearer. Utterance tends to be a relatively restricted form of language, capable of communicating in the here and now, but dependent on a shared context for communication. This contextualization is in contrast to the nonimmediate or decontextualized talk encouraged by De Temple and Snow (2003), Beck and McKeown (2003), and others. *Text*, on the other hand, is relatively autonomous, contains more complex sentence forms, uses a more complex and exact vocabulary, and makes fewer assumptions about a shared knowledge base. It is this Text[1] that is the language of school.

---

[1] *Text*, when capitalized, refers to Olson's usage of that term. When used in lower-case letters, "text" refers to the conventional meaning.

Although we use the term *text* usually to refer to written text, in Olson's (1977) notion, Text could be written or oral, as long as it contains the autonomous and elaborated language typical of written text. One could argue that the college professor parents in Hart and Risley's (1995) study were speaking in Text, with more full sentences and rarer, more academic words, even to their preschoolers. Children's books also are Text, containing more formal language, especially rarer vocabulary words. This *academic vocabulary* is the vocabulary of school. To learn the language of schooling, children need to be exposed to Text, both spoken Text, as in the rich utterances of Hart and Risley's (1995) professor parents, and by reading written children's books.

Children who are not exposed to Text can be predicted to have difficulties in learning academic vocabulary. And, again, there are wide disparities in the amount of Text to which children are exposed. Adams (1990) estimated that she spent at least 1,000 hours reading storybooks to her son prior to his entrance in first grade. In contrast, Teale (1984) observed children from low-income homes engaged in reading storybooks an average of 2 minutes per day with a projected average of 60 hours prior to first grade. Teale did not observe any storybook reading in the majority of homes in which he observed. The differences between the exposures given to the children studied by Teale, and that of Adams's own child, can be assumed to have profound effects on children's learning, including the learning of word meanings.

Reading storybooks to children is a good starting point, but this is not the only solution. Storybook reading might occur 45 minutes to an hour per day. Children need to be in an environment rich in vocabulary in order to learn words. In such an environment, children experience elaborated interactions that involve academic vocabulary. Silverman and Crandell's (2010) study of prekindergarten and kindergarten classes determined that teachers' attention to vocabulary instruction during non-read-aloud time had a strong positive relationship to children's vocabulary learning. In addition to reading storybooks, some direct teaching of word meanings will help.

DIRECT TEACHING IN EARLY CHILDHOOD CLASSES

S. A. Stahl and Fairbanks (1986) found that, for older children teaching word meanings significantly improved children's vocabulary knowledge, as well as improving their comprehension of texts containing the taught words. Such vocabulary teaching is often completed before reading for older children. For younger children, in contrast, the teaching might take place before reading a book, in a picture walk (Fountas & Pinnell, 1996), but also after reading a book (Beck & McKeown, 2001) or apart from reading entirely (Silverman & Crandell, 2010). Several activities can be used to teach word meanings in classroom settings.

Structured Conversations

Recent research has found that classrooms that build time into the day for small-group or one-on-one conversations yielded greater levels of vocabulary growth and growth in overall emergent reading skills (Schwanenflugel et al., 2010) than classrooms with no such talk. Whether one-on-one conversations between teachers and students are scheduled a few days a week or whole-class teacher read-alouds are followed with small discussion groups, children's vocabulary growth is fostered by engaging in talk with adults. Small-group conversations provide a smaller, safer space in which shy children and English learners can more easily exercise their language skills. Additionally, providing the time for all children to express themselves equals the playing field, unlike whole-group discussions that tend to be dominated by a few of the most expressive children. Theme-based or content-area discussions provide a forum for using new terminology in response to a conversational or activity prompt. Small-group conversations also provide a setting for assessing which children have gained ownership of target words (K. A. D. Stahl & Bravo, 2010).

Teacher Read-Alouds: Text Talk

Beck and McKeown (2001, 2003, 2007) suggest an interchange with young children they call Text Talk, an approach to read-alouds that is designed to promote comprehension and language development. One of the primary purposes of Text Talk is to help young children make sense of decontextualized language or Text. It involves the *selection* of texts that exhibit an event structure and enough complexity to prompt discussion and higher-level thinking. The strategic use of open-ended *questioning* encourages children to explain, elaborate, and formulate their own questions surrounding the text. Salient features of Text Talk include the way *background knowledge* and *vocabulary* are addressed as part of the read-aloud. Only background knowledge that has specific ties to the text is encouraged. "Birdwalking"—encouraging elaborations that are only tangentially related to the text—have been found to disrupt the comprehension process and distract students from the text itself. Children are encouraged to use the text to create their own mental images or representations of story events before seeing the illustrator's representation.

Extensive vocabulary work follows each story. The meaning of three or four words is given with examples of how each word is used. Children are encouraged to orally generate their own sentences for each word immediately after the reading, and an incentive chart is used to record each child's use of the words over time. This discussion extends the meaning of the word as encountered in the story. From a single encounter, it is unlikely that children would gain much information about the word. Using this protocol, teachers provide a child-friendly definition for the word and extend its use into other contexts. Including both types of information was found to be characteristic of vocabulary instruction that improved children's comprehension (S. A. Stahl & Fairbanks, 1986). In addition, the discussion requires children not only to listen, but to generate new knowledge about the word (e.g., "I would like everyone to stand up and show me what it looks like to amble" or "Who can give an example of a time that he or she *ambled*?"). Generating new understandings is also important in word learning. Through the generative process, words become more memorable, and multiple contexts for use are instantiated. All of these proposed interactions, as with the interactions around storybooks described earlier, lead to increased vocabulary learning.

Early Guided Reading: Picture Walk

A *picture walk* is an introduction to a guided reading book in which the teacher goes through the pictures methodically, carefully supporting children's predictions about the text. In this section, we stress the use of picture walks for vocabulary development, but they are used more broadly than just for vocabulary. Picture walks are based on the work of Marie Clay and her descriptions of an effective book introduction for novice readers (Clay, 1991, 1993; see Fountas & Pinnell, 1996, for more explicit descriptions). These conversations typically occur as the teacher and students preview each page or few pages of the new book before reading. The pictures are used as a catalyst for discussion of what the book is likely to be about. The picture walk is conducted with early readers who have limited knowledge of the alphabetic writing system and are, therefore, still heavily reliant on meaning, language and predictable story structures to propel their reading. The exchange during a picture walk serves as a scaffold from vernacular utterance to Text. The picture walk does not have a specific set of procedures. It is used flexibly and in response to the students' needs and the challenges of a particular text. Teachers can follow several guidelines to ensure that students have a successful, independent first reading of the text.

- The introduction is conducted as a conversational, social interaction around the text.
- The conversation prompts student engagement in activating background knowledge and experiences that relate to the text.
- The teacher provides an overview of the plot, theme, or important ideas.

- Children's attention is directed to text structure and language structure.
- Teachers use the book's language structure and vocabulary in the conversation about the book.
- Teachers may direct attention to using letter–sound relationships in one or two places in the text.

The extensiveness of the introduction depends on the expected challenges of the content or text readability. A few vocabulary words may be introduced during the story introduction and conversation. The teacher selects vocabulary that the particular group of students may need introduced or developed. Unlike a prereading vocabulary workbook page, the discussion and the illustrations help situate the vocabulary in the story context. After reading, the students and teacher might include the new vocabulary in their discussion or writing activity.

Teaching Children to Classify

As discussed in the beginning of the chapter, classification is a basic mental process that underlies vocabulary knowledge as well as other cognitive processes. A study of second graders exposed the difficulties that novice readers often experience when attempting to categorize the vocabulary found in simple informational texts (K. A. D. Stahl, 2008). Therefore, it is wise to provide specific attention to the categorization of conceptual vocabulary in the earliest formal educational settings.

Sorting and Venn Diagrams

Teaching children to classify can be done as early as preschool. Simply asking a question such as "Which one does not belong?" forces children to think about concepts in terms of their attributes. For example, you can give children as young as preschool age pictures of a bird, an airplane, a cat, and a kite, and ask them which one does not belong. Then ask them why they chose the answer they did. In this case, you want children to verbalize the shared attribute of flying: Bird, airplane, and kite fly or are often found in the air, whereas cats do not (usually) fly.

A little more advanced activity is a type of sorting game. A teacher can take a flannel board divided into two sections and ask a group of children to sort the pictures into two groups. Sample categories might be farm animals versus zoo animals, things found in a kitchen versus things found in a living room, and the like. This activity can be an opportunity to introduce words that refine existing knowledge, such as *sofa, couch, stool,* and *spatula*. It is important to ask children to verbally label the pictures and explain their sorting justifications. As often as possible, teachers should avoid using sorting as an independent station activity that lacks opportunities for children to use expressive language to explain the sort.

Venn diagrams can be used to show children that some items can be part of more than one category of things. A Venn diagram consists of two intersecting circles. You might label one circle "Things with Fur" and the other "Things That Fly." On the "Fur" side, you might include a cat, dog, lion, ocelot, leopard, and so on, taking care to *include animals that might not be known to children*. The other side might include a bird, a butterfly, a bee, an owl, a hornet, and so on. You might put a picture of a bat in the middle, since it fits in both categories. Remember the goal here is to stretch vocabulary and conceptual knowledge with scaffolding provided by a more knowledgeable other. So these words might show up at other times of the day as part of a unit on animals.

Although we have used a fairly simple set of categories in this example, Venn diagrams can be used with many sets of concepts. We have used it with the terms *rebellion* and *protest* to discuss concepts surrounding the American Revolution. Venn diagrams can be a fast and easy way to talk about many different concepts.

Semantic Maps

Another activity that extends the child's ability to classify is the creation of semantic maps. These have been used in vocabulary instruction for a long time (e.g., Heimlich & Pittelman, 1986; Johnson, Toms-Bronowski, & Pittelman, 1982; S. A. Stahl & Vancil, 1986), especially in content-area instruction. However, they adapt very easily for use with young children, even prereaders. In general, a semantic mapping lesson has four parts:

1. *Brainstorming.* The teacher and the class brainstorm ideas that relate to a topic. For example, for the topic of "weather," a class might come up with *rain, snow, wind, hot, thermometer, hurricane, blizzard,* and so on. The teacher might stop and explain some of the terms that the students generate. The teacher might also add some terms, again explaining what they mean. These terms can be written on the board or pictured for young children.
2. *Mapping.* These terms can be drawn into a map. To draw the map, children (with the aid of the teacher) would come up with three or four categories that describe the terms on the board. These are arranged into a map.
3. *Reading.* After the map is completed, the students and teacher read a book or selection about that topic. For younger children, the teacher can read the text aloud; children who can read might read in partners or by themselves. An alternative might be an observation.

For a lesson on weather, this might involve going outside to discuss the current weather. A lesson on plants might involve growing a plant.

4. *Completing the map.* After the reading, teacher and children discuss what they have learned from the book as a group. At this time, students might change categories or add another category to reflect what they have learned.

It is important that semantic maps *not* be used as an end in themselves; instead, they should be connected to a book, an observation, or some ongoing part of the curriculum. Novice readers who participate in teacher think-alouds and the collaborative sorting of conceptual vocabulary found in small informational texts are creating mental structures that replicate the process used in recalling and representing informational texts (K. A. D. Stahl, 2008). For example, creating the semantic map shown in Figure 5.1 leads to summarizing the information found in each chapter in a book about spiders.

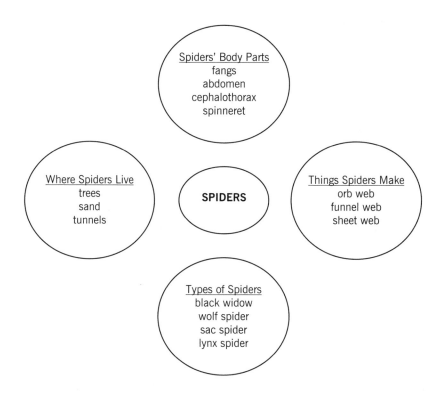

FIGURE 5.1. Semantic map for spider vocabulary.

Consolidating and Assessing Word Knowledge

Vocabulary Word Walls

While high-frequency word walls are commonly found in primary class-rooms, conceptual vocabulary word walls can also play an important role. Conceptual vocabulary word walls are not likely to be organized alphabetically. Rather words are added as they are encountered in read-alouds or shared reading. They might be used in conjunction with the Word Wizard activity described below. Conceptual vocabulary word walls serve as a reminder and model for children to use the words in their own speech and writing, and they also serve as a powerful reminder for teachers to use those words in their own classroom talk. Multiple exposures are required for children to truly own words that they encounter, and the word wall helps facilitate usage and ownership.

Additionally, a bulletin board with the vocabulary from themed units or disciplinary content units is useful as a reference point for children when reading and spelling the targeted words in a unit of study. Unlike older readers who can read content words but need multiple exposures for increasing knowledge about the word, young readers are likely to need more support recognizing the words in print. Again, having the words easily accessible makes it more likely that the children will read and write the words correctly as they engage in creating written products throughout the unit. Sometimes this is as simple as duplicating the semantic web that may have been created on a whiteboard to a large piece of butcher paper for display throughout the duration of the unit.

Word Wizard

The Word Wizard activity was designed by Beck, Perfetti, and McKeown (1982) to sensitize children to a wide range of words and to provide encouragement and incentive for the repeated use of new vocabulary. Individual classroom teachers apply the Word Wizard ideas in a variety of ways.

In some classrooms, interesting words from class read-alouds are posted on a vocabulary word wall. A class poster contains the children's names along the side and the words along the top. When the children use the vocabulary in their conversations or written products, they receive a check on the poster. They may also receive a check for noticing the word in a new book, conversation, or elsewhere. The student with the most checks at the end of a designated time period becomes the Word Wizard.

For example, in a second-grade class, Wednesday was word day and each child brought in an unfamiliar or interesting word that he or she had heard or read during the previous week. The word-of-the-week (WOW) sheet included the interesting word, where it had been heard or seen, the meaning, and the word in a sentence. The words were posted on a vocabulary word wall. Again, a poster was used to track the students' names and the weekly words. Checks were given, as in the original example. Each Wednesday, the children who had received the most checks and the children who had contributed the words with the most checks since the previous Wednesday ate lunch with the teacher in a special section of the cafeteria. Rewarding the contributors resulted in a wider range of student participants receiving the special lunch. It also resulted in the selection of sophisticated words that were likely to be used in conversation, rather than obscure words that were difficult to apply in classroom conversations.

Documenting Growth in Vocabulary Development

Most standardized measures are not sensitive to the growth of a selective list of words that might be targeted for instruction in a primary-level classroom. Therefore, teachers should feel comfortable developing assessments based on their own curriculum (National Institute of Child Health and Human Development [NICHD], 2000). Teachers might list words that have been targeted for instruction and document their students' usage of those words. For example, teachers can chart students' use of target vocabulary during a small-group conversation or content-area center activity.

More formally, novice readers might be assessed using the vocabulary recognition task (VRT; K. A. D. Stahl, 2008; K. A. D. Stahl & Bravo, 2010). The VRT is a teacher-constructed yes/no task that requires children to read and select words that are associated with a particular theme or unit of study. Typically, the list includes 18 content-related words and 7 foils (see Figure 5.2). A pretest and posttest administration can be used to gauge growth during the course of an instructional unit. Children are required to read and identify the theme-related words. Although the VRT might seem more appropriate for older readers, evidence indicates that the reinforcement of vocabulary instruction with attention to the graphophonemic representation of the word actually supports vocabulary learning (Rosenthal & Ehri, 2008; Silverman, 2007; Silverman & Crandell, 2010). Additionally, Anderson and Freebody (1983) determined that a yes/no task is a valid and reliable measure of vocabulary assessment. Particularly for younger readers, they determined that it was a better measure of vocabulary knowledge than a multiple-choice task. As a posttest, students would also be asked to categorize the words that they select on a semantic map or web.

Teachers can use simple calculations in classrooms or apply a correction formula to adjust for guessing (Anderson & Freebody, 1983). A student scores a "hit" (H) when a word is circled correctly or a "false alarm" (FA) if an unrelated word is incorrectly circled. When using the VRT in the classroom, a simple score

$$H - FA = Score$$

or a proportional (P) score

$$(H) - P (FA) = Score$$

may be determined. Using the correction formula, the proportion of words truly known, P (K), is determined by calculating

$$P (K) = P (H) - P (FA) / 1 - P (FA)$$

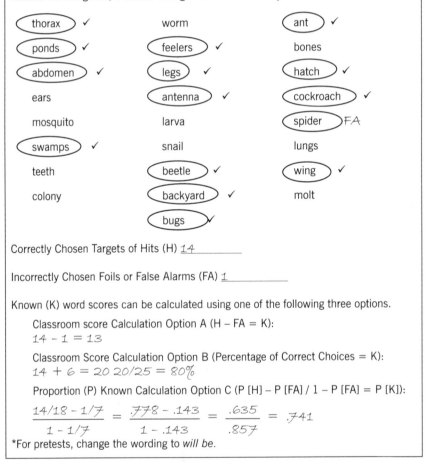

We *have been** learning about insects. Below you see a list of words. Put a circle around the words that you are able to read and are sure have something to do with insects. Do not guess, because wrong answers will lower your score.

thorax ✓   worm   ant ✓

ponds ✓   feelers ✓   bones

abdomen ✓   legs ✓   hatch ✓

ears   antenna ✓   cockroach ✓

mosquito   larva   spider FA

swamps ✓   snail   lungs

teeth   beetle ✓   wing ✓

colony   backyard ✓   molt

          bugs ✓

Correctly Chosen Targets of Hits (H) 14

Incorrectly Chosen Foils or False Alarms (FA) 1

Known (K) word scores can be calculated using one of the following three options.

Classroom score Calculation Option A (H – FA = K):
14 – 1 = 13

Classroom Score Calculation Option B (Percentage of Correct Choices = K):
14 + 6 = 20 20/25 = 80%

Proportion (P) Known Calculation Option C (P [H] – P [FA] / 1 – P [FA] = P [K]):

$$\frac{14/18 - 1/7}{1 - 1/7} = \frac{.778 - .143}{1 - .143} = \frac{.635}{.857} = .741$$

*For pretests, change the wording to *will be*.

FIGURE 5.2. VRT—insects (pretest and posttest). From Stahl and Bravo (2010). Copyright 2010 by the International Reading Association. Reprinted by permission.

Types of Insects	*Places* Insects Live
beetle	ponds
bugs	swamps
ant	backyards
cockroach	
spider	
Insects' *Body Parts*	Other Insect Words
thorax	hatch
abdomen	
feelers	
legs	
antenna	
wing	

Words correct _14/18_

Percentage of correctly categorized hits _100%_

FIGURE 5.3. VRT—Web (posttest only). From Stahl and Bravo (2010). Copyright 2010 by the International Reading Association. Reprinted by permission.

Figure 5.2 demonstrates each scoring formula on a VRT example. The web score is simply the total number of words placed correctly in each category (see Figure 5.3).

TEACHING WORD MEANINGS IN PRESCHOOL AND EARLY ELEMENTARY CLASSROOMS

This chapter contains techniques that can be useful for teaching word meanings in early education, but what is more important is maintaining a dialogue about words. This dialogue should be cognitively challenging, pushing students to expand their knowledge about the world by expanding the words they use to describe that knowledge. There should be an interplay between what the student knows and this ongoing dialogue. Words should not be too difficult, or they will be beyond the child's ability to learn, nor should they be too easy. Instead, they should be "Goldilocks" words; that is, words that are *just right*. Finding the right level is not hard—it comes from the kinds of interactions we have illustrated in this chapter.

Further, effective vocabulary teaching in the early years should make children curious about words. To be a good word learner, one must be hungry for words. Learning (and using) new words can be exciting, because a new word not only is a sign of growing up, but it also is a sign of greater control in one's world. Effective instruction should make children seek out words, to be sensitive to hearing and learning more about new words. It is not enough to fill children up with words as if they were an empty vessel. Instead, teachers should create an environment wherein children go out and seek new words as well. Good vocabulary teaching in the primary grades involves talking about words when you find them in books, on trips, or in the classroom and bringing them in and sending children out to find more.

REFERENCES

Adams, M. J. (1990). *Beginning to read: Thinking and learning about print.* Cambridge, MA: MIT Press.

Anderson, R. C., & Freebody, P. (1983). Reading comprehension and the assessment and acquisition of word knowledge. *Advances in Reading/Language Research, 2,* 231–256. Greenwich, CT: JAI.

Anderson, R. C., & Pearson, P. D. (1984). A schema-theoretic view of basic processes in reading. In P. D. Pearson (Ed.), *Handbook of reading research* (pp. 255–292). White Plains, NY: Longman.

Beck, I. L., & McKeown, M. G. (2001). Text talk: Capturing the benefits of read-aloud experiences for young children. *The Reading Teacher, 55,* 10–35.

Beck, I. L., & McKeown, M. G. (2003). Taking advantage of read-alouds to help children make sense of decontextualized language. In A. van Kleeck, S. A. Stahl, & E. B. Bauer (Eds.), *On reading books to children: Parents and teachers* (pp. 159–176). Mahwah, NJ: Erlbaum.

Beck, I. L., & McKeown, M. G. (2007). Increasing young low-income children's oral vocabulary repertoires through rich and focused instruction. *Elementary School Journal, 107*(3), 251–271.

Beck, I. L., Perfetti, C. A., & McKeown, M. (1982). Effects of long-term vocabulary instruction on lexical access and reading comprehension. *Journal of Educational Psychology, 74,* 506–521.

Biemiller, A., & Slonim, N. (2001). Estimating root word vocabulary growth in normative and advantaged populations. *Journal of Educational Psychology, 93,* 498–510.

Clay, M. M. (1991). Introducing a new storybook to young readers. *The Reading Teacher, 45,* 264–273.

Clay, M. M. (1993). *Reading recovery: A guidebook for teachers in training.* Portsmouth, NH: Heinemann.

Cunningham, A. E., & Stanovich, K. E. (1991). Tracking the unique effects of print exposure in children: Associations with vocabulary, general knowledge, and spelling. *Journal of Educational Psychology, 83,* 264–274.

Dale, E. (1965). Vocabulary measurement: Techniques and major findings. *Elementary English, 42*(8), 895–901.

De Temple, J. (1994). *Book reading styles of low-income mothers with preschoolers and children's later literacy skills.* Unpublished doctoral dissertation, Harvard Graduate School of Education, Cambridge, MA.

De Temple, J., & Snow, C. E. (2003). Learning words from books. In A. van Kleeck, S. A. Stahl, & E. B. Bauer (Eds.), *On reading books to children: Parents and teachers* (pp. 15–34). Mahwah, NJ: Erlbaum.

Dickinson, D. K., & Tabors, P. O. (2001). *Beginning literacy with language: Young children learning at home and school.* Baltimore: Brookes.

Fountas, I. C., & Pinnell, G. S. (1996). *Guided reading: Good first teaching for all children.* Portsmouth, NH: Heinemann.

Hart, B., & Risley, T. R. (1995). *Meaningful differences in the everyday experiences of young American children: The everyday experience of one- and two-year-old American children.* Baltimore: Brookes.

Hayes, D. P., & Ahrens, M. G. (1988). Vocabulary simplification for children: A special case of "motherese." *Journal of Child Language, 15,* 395–410.

Heimlich, J. E., & Pittelman, S. D. (1986). *Semantic mapping: Classroom applications.* Newark, DE: International Reading Association.

Huttenlocher, J., Haight, W., Bryk, A., Seltzer, M., & Lyons, T. (1991). Early vocabulary growth: Relation to language input and gender. *Developmental Psychology, 27*(2), 236–248.

Johnson, D. D., Toms-Bronowski, S., & Pittelman, S. D. (1982). *An investigation of the effectiveness of semantic mapping and semantic feature analysis with intermediate grade children* (Program Report 83-3). Madison, WI: Wisconsin Center for Educational Research, University of Wisconsin.

Kintsch, W. (1998). *Comprehension: A paradigm for cognition.* Cambridge, UK: Cambridge University Press.

Kintsch, W., & van Dijk, T. A. (1978). Toward a model of text comprehension and production. *Psychological Review, 85,* 363–394.

Kuhn, M. R., & Stahl, S. A. (1998). Teaching children to learn word meanings from context: A synthesis and some questions. *Journal of Literacy Research, 30,* 119–138.

Nagy, W. E., & Scott, J. A. (2000). Vocabulary processing. In M. L. Kamil, P. B. Mosenthal, P. D. Pearson, & R. Barr (Eds.), *Handbook of reading research* (Vol. 3, pp. 269–274). Mahwah, NJ: Erlbaum.

National Institute of Child Health and Human Development (NICHHD). (2000). *Report of the National Reading Panel. Teaching children to read: An evidence-based assessment of the scientific research literature on reading and its implications for reading instruction.* (NIH Publication No. 00–4769). Washington, DC: Author.

Nelson, K. (1996). *Language in cognitive development: Emergence of the mediated mind.* Cambridge, UK: Cambridge University Press.

Neuman, S. B., & Celano, D. (2001). Access to print in low-income and middle-income communities: An ecological study of four neighborhoods. *Reading Research Quarterly, 36*(1), 8–26.

Olson, D. R. (1977). From utterance to text: The bias of language in speech and writing. *Harvard Educational Review, 47,* 257–281.

Paris, S. G. (2005). Reinterpreting the development of reading skills. *Reading Research Quarterly, 40,* 184–202.

Rey, H. (1947). *Curious George gets a job*. New York: Houghton Mifflin.

Rosenthal, J., & Ehri, L. C. (2008). The mnemonic value of orthography for vocabulary learning. *Journal of Educational Psychology, 100*(1), 175–191.

Schwanenflugel, P. J., Hamilton, C. E., Neuwirth-Pritchett, S., Restrepo, M. A., Bradley, B. A., & Webb, M. Y. (2010). PAVEd for success: An evaluation of a comprehensive preliteracy program for four-year-old children. *Journal of Literacy Research, 42*, 227–275.

Silverman, R. (2007). A comparison of three methods of vocabulary instruction during read-alouds in kindergarten. *Elementary School Journal, 108*(2), 97–113.

Silverman, R., & Crandell, J. D. (2010). Vocabulary practices in prekindergarten and kindergarten classrooms. *Reading Research Quarterly, 45*, 318–340.

Silverman, R., & Hines, S. (2009). The effects of multimedia enhanced instruction on the vocabulary of English-language learners and non-English-language learners in pre-kindergarten through second grade. *Journal of Educational Psychology, 101*(2), 305–314.

Stahl, K. A. D. (2008). The effects of three instructional methods on the reading comprehension and content acquisition of novice readers. *Journal of Literacy Research, 40*, 359–393.

Stahl, K. A. D., & Bravo, M. A. (2010). Contemporary classroom vocabulary assessment for content areas. *The Reading Teacher, 63*, 566–579.

Stahl, S. A., & Fairbanks, M. M. (1986). The effects of vocabulary instruction: A model-based meta-analysis. *Review of Educational Research, 56*, 72–110.

Stahl, S. A., & Nagy, W. E. (2006). *Teaching word meanings*. Mahwah, NJ: Erlbaum.

Stahl, S. A., & Vancil, S. J. (1986). Discussion is what makes semantic maps work. *The Reading Teacher, 40*, 62–67.

Stanovich, K. E. (1986). Matthew effects in reading: Some consequences of individual differences in the acquisition of literacy. *Reading Research Quarterly, 21*, 360–407.

Stanovich, K. E. (2000). *Progress in understanding reading: Scientific foundations and new frontiers*. New York: Guilford Press.

Teale, W. H. (1984). Reading to young children: Its significance for literacy development. In H. Goelman, A. Oberg, & F. Smith (Eds.), *Awakening to literacy* (pp. 110–121). Portsmouth, NH: Heinemann.

White, T. G., Graves, M. F., & Slater, W. H. (1990). Growth of reading vocabulary in diverse elementary schools: Decoding and word meaning. *Journal of Educational Psychology, 82*, 281–329.

Part II

Teaching Vocabulary-Learning Strategies

Chapter 6

Teaching Prefixes

Making Strong Instruction Even Stronger

Michael F. Graves
Melanie Ruda
Gregory C. Sales
James F. Baumann

In the first edition of *Vocabulary Instruction: Research to Practice*, one of us (Graves, 2004) authored a chapter titled "Teaching Prefixes: As Good as It Gets?" in which he provided a rationale for prefix instruction, reviewed prior research on prefix instruction, and described a specific method of teaching prefixes in some detail. He concluded by posing the question of whether the instruction described is as good as prefix instruction is likely to get and answered that question with a definite "no," saying that there is always the potential for improving instruction.

As we write this chapter for the second edition of *Vocabulary Instruction*, the four of us are working on an Institute of Education Sciences/Small Business Innovation Research (IES/SBIR) grant from the U.S. Department of Education to develop an instructional program for teaching word-learning strategies. IES/SBIR grants provide funds to small businesses to produce educational materials and programs. Gregory Sales is the Principal Investigator on the project, Melanie Ruda is the lead instructional designer, and Michael Graves and James Baumann are consultants. The purpose of the grant is to develop and test a comprehensive program to teach fourth and fifth graders a set of practical, research-based, and theoretically sound strategies for inferring the meanings of unknown words they encounter while reading. The strategies to be taught include using context, word parts (compound words, inflectional suffixes, prefixes, and derivational suffixes), and dictionaries. Additionally, Spanish-speaking English learners (ELs) will receive instruction in using cognates, and all ELs will receive instruction in recognizing idioms. The final product will be a comprehensive supplementary program to teach word-learning strategies.

We have been working on the project for about 2 years and still have about a year's work left. We have, however, completed most of the prefix instruction and tested a partial version of that instruction. In this chapter, we describe the instruction detailed in the original chapter, note the major changes we have made to that instruction in the present project, and comment on the extent to which we believe we have strengthened it.

THE 2004 APPROACH TO TEACHING PREFIXES

Space does not allow us to present our rationale for prefix instruction or review the research on prefix instruction. For that information, we recommend reading the original chapter (Graves, 2004). What we do include here, however, is a description of our general approach to instruction, other influences on the instruction, and a fairly detailed description of 5 days of instruction.

A General Approach to Instruction

The general approach used is explicit instruction (Pearson & Gallagher, 1983; Duke & Pearson, 2002), which includes these components:

- An explicit description of the strategy and when and how it should be used.
- Teacher and/or student modeling of the strategy in action.
- Collaborative use of the strategy in action.
- Guided practice using the strategy with gradual release of responsibility.
- Independent use of the strategy (Duke & Pearson, 2002, pp. 208–210).

Other Influences on the Instruction

Overhead transparencies have played a major part in several studies of strategy instruction, and they are used in the instruction described here. They serve two particular functions: They focus students' attention, and they free teachers from the task of writing on the board and in doing so let them better attend to students and their presentation.

A good deal of strategy instruction has included what Rosenshine and Meister (1994) refer to as "concrete prompts," brief summaries of the actions students undertake in using the strategies. In the approach suggested here, students are given a set of concrete prompts that are prominently displayed on a poster that is frequently referred to during the instruction and that remains up after the instruction.

The instruction described here includes elements from four studies (Baumann et al., 2002; Ess, 1979; Graves & Hammond, 1980; Nicol, 1980; White, Sowell, & Yanagihara, 1989) that have a good deal in common. However, because the information on Nicol's approach is the most detailed (a 150-page master's thesis), we rely primarily on her approach. The instruction also follows the three-part framework employed by Baumann and his colleagues: an introduction and examples of the lesson content; verbal explanations, modeling, and guided practice; and independent practice. Additionally, the approach includes one component that has not been a part of previous studies: deliberate and systematic review.

Day 1: Introduction, Clarification, Motivation, and Overview

On day 1, the teacher introduces the concept of prefixes and the strategy of using prefixes to unlock the meanings of unknown words, attempts to motivate students by stressing the value of prefixes, and gives students an overview of the unit. As Stotsky (1977) has shown, there has been a good deal of confusion about prefixes and prefix instruction, and thus it is particularly important to be sure that students understand just what prefixes and prefixed words are.

To alert students to what they will be studying and as a continuing reminder throughout the prefix unit, on the first day of instruction, the teacher displays a poster advertising the instruction, perhaps something like: "Prefixes—One Key to Building Your Vocabularies." Then, the teacher might say something like this:

> "Over the next few days, we're going to be looking at how you can use prefixes to help you figure out the meanings of words you don't know. If you learn some common prefixes and how to use your knowledge of these prefixes to understand words that contain those prefixes, you're going to be able to figure out the meanings of a lot of new words. And, as you know, figuring out the meanings of words you don't know in a passage is an important step in understanding the passage."

Next, the teacher asks students what they already know about prefixes, reinforcing correct information students provide and gently suggesting that any incorrect information they give is not quite on target.

The purpose here is to get students thinking about prefixes and to get them actively involved in the session. However, it is critical that students have a clear understanding of prefixes, and for this reason, the teacher follows the discussion with a presentation supported by an overhead transparency. Below is the transparency, which the teacher reads aloud to students.

A prefix is a group of letters that goes in front of a word. *Un-* is one prefix you have probably seen. It often means "not."

- Although you can list prefixes by themselves, in stories or other things that we read, prefixes are always attached to words. They don't appear by themselves. In *unhappy*, for example, the prefix *un-* is attached to the word *happy*.

- When a prefix is attached to a word, it changes the meaning of the word. For example, when the prefix *un-* is attached to the word *happy*, it makes the word *unhappy*, which means "not happy."

- It's important to remember that, for a group of letters to really be a prefix, when you remove them from the word, you still have a real word left. Removing the prefix *un-* from the word *unhappy* still leaves the word *happy*. That means that *un-* in the word *unhappy* is a prefix. But if you remove the letters *un* from the word *uncle*, you are left with *cle*, which is not a word. This means that the *un* in *uncle* is not a prefix.

This is a lot for students to remember, too much, in fact. For this reason, the teacher constructs a shortened version of these points on a "Basic Facts about Prefixes" poster, puts that up next to the poster on the unit, and tells students that the poster will stay up for them to refer to throughout the unit and even after that.

At this point, the teacher asks students if they know any additional prefixes, being generally accepting of their answers, but (assuming that some responses are incorrect) noting afterward that some of the elements given are not actually prefixes and that the class will continue to work on what is and what is not a prefix as the unit progresses.

Finally, the teacher introduces the three prefixes for study the next day: *un-* (not), *re-* (again), and *in-* (not)—putting them on an overhead, asking students to copy them down and asking students to each bring in a word beginning with one of the prefixes the next day. These three prefixes are taught at the beginning of the program because they are used in large numbers of words.

Day 2: Instruction on the First Three Prefixes

At the beginning of the session, the teacher refers to the "Basic Facts" posters and briefly reminds students of what prefixes are, where they appear, and why it is important to know about them. Then, the teacher calls on some students to give the prefixed words they have located, jotting down those that are indeed prefixed words on the board and gently noting that the others are not actually prefixed words and that they will discuss words of this sort later.

After this, the teacher begins the standard instructional routine for teaching prefixes and prefix removal. This standardized routine is used for three reasons. First, there is experimental evidence that it works. It is basically the one validated in Nicol's (1980) study, with some additions from the Baumann et al. (2002) study. Second, using the same routine for teaching all the prefixes to be taught means that students can soon learn the procedure itself and then concentrate on learning the prefixes and how to work with them. Third, this routine can serve as a model for teachers to use in creating a complete set of materials for teaching prefixes and the strategy of prefix removal and replacement.

Next, the teacher tells students that today they will be working with the three prefixes introduced the day before and how to use them in unlocking the meanings of unknown words. Again, the three prefixes are *un-* meaning "not," *re-* meaning "again," and *in-* also meaning "not." In teaching these three prefixes, the teacher will use several types of materials: transparencies introducing each prefix, worksheets with brief exercises requiring use of the prefix just taught, transparencies of these worksheets, exercise sheets requiring additional use and manipulation of each prefix, and review sheets on which students manipulate the three prefixes and the words that were used in illustrating the prefixes for the day. On the back of the worksheets, exercise sheets, and review sheets are check sheets (answer keys) so that students can immediately check their efforts.

Each introductory transparency presents one prefix, illustrates its use with two familiar words and two unfamiliar words, and uses each of the four words in a context-rich sentence. Below each sentence, the word and its definition are shown, and below these sample sentences is a fifth sentence that gives students a root word and requires them to generate the prefixed form of the word.

Instruction begins with the teacher displaying the first sentence on the introductory transparency and leading students from the meaning of the familiar prefixed word to the meaning of the prefix itself, as illustrated below:

TEACHER: If Tom were asked to *retake* a test, what must he do?

STUDENTS: He has to take it over. He has to take it again.

TEACHER: That's correct. Using your understanding of the word *retake*, what is the meaning of the prefix *re-*?

STUDENTS: Again. Over again.

The process is repeated with the next three sentences on the transparency. With some prefixes, students are likely to be able to volunteer the response without difficulty. With other prefixes, students may need further prompting, in which case the teacher rephrases the sentence to add more clues. If students are still unable to respond after the prompting, the teacher gives the definition. After going through the first four sentences on the *re-* introductory overhead, the teacher presents the fifth sentence, which defines the unknown root word and asks students to define the prefixed word.

After completing introductory instruction on the first prefix, students individually complete their check sheets, while a student volunteer completes the check sheet on a transparency. As soon as students complete their check sheets, the volunteer puts the transparency on the overhead so that all students receive immediate feedback on their work. If the volunteer has made an error, the teacher corrects it at this time.

These same procedures are then completed with the two remaining prefixes for the day: *un-* and *in-*. Following initial instruction on the three prefixes, the students complete a review sheet and immediately receive feedback by checking the answers on the back of the sheet. While students are completing the review sheet, the teacher monitors their work and provides assistance when requested. This concludes the second day of the unit.

Day 3: Review, the Prefix Strategy, and the Remaining Three Prefixes

Day 3 begins with the teacher reviewing the basic facts about prefixes. Then students complete a review sheet on the three prefixes taught the previous day and immediately correct their work.

Next comes another crucial part of the instruction—instruction in the prefix strategy. The teacher introduces the strategy by telling students that now that they have worked some with the strategy and understand how useful prefixes can be in figuring out the meanings of unknown words, she is going to teach a specific strategy for working with unknown words. The teacher titles the procedure "Prefix Removal and Replacement," emphasizing that they are using a big name for an important idea.

The teacher then puts up the following transparency, which is reproduced on a prominently displayed "Prefix Removal and Replacement Strategy" poster, which is shown below, and talks students through the procedure with one or two sample prefixed words.

THE PREFIX REMOVAL AND REPLACEMENT STRATEGY

When you come to an unknown word that may contain a prefix:

- Remove the "prefix."
- Check that you have a real word remaining. If you do, you've found a prefix.
- Think about the meaning of the prefix and the meaning of the root word.
- Combine the meanings of the prefix and the root word and infer the meaning of the unknown word.
- Try out the meaning of the "unknown" word in the sentence and see if it makes sense. If it does, read on. If it doesn't, you'll need to use another strategy for discovering the unknown word's meaning.

Following this explicit description of the strategy and modeling of its use, the teacher tells students that they will continue to work on learning the meanings of prefixes and learning to use the strategy today, tomorrow, and in future review sessions. Finally, the teacher teaches and reviews the remaining three prefixes (*dis-*, *en-*, and *non-*) using procedures and materials that exactly parallel those used on day 2. This concludes the third day of the unit.

Day 4: Review of the Information about Prefixes, the Prefix Strategy, and the Prefixes Taught

Day 4 begins with the teacher reviewing the four facts about prefixes, again using the "Basic Facts" poster in doing so. As part of the review, the teacher asks students a few questions about these facts to be sure that they understand them and answers any of their questions.

Next, the teacher reviews the prefix removal and replacement strategy. After this, the teacher continues with the explicit instruction model, first modeling use of the strategy with two of the six prefixes taught and then collaboratively using the strategy in a whole-class session with two more of the six prefixes. Then, the teacher divides students into small groups and provides guided practice by having the groups use the strategy with the final pair of six prefixes. The teacher also has some of the groups share their work and their findings.

As the final activity of the initial instruction, small groups of students work together on a quiz that requires them to state the four facts about prefixes, state the steps of the prefix removal and replacement strategy, and give the meanings of the six prefixes taught. As soon as students complete the quiz, they correct it in class so that they get immediate feedback on their performance and hand the corrected quizzes in so that the teacher has this information to plan reviews.

Reviewing, Prompting, and Guiding Students to Independence

At this point, the instruction is far from complete. If we really want students to remember what a prefix is, recognize and know the meanings of some prefixes, and use the prefix removal and replacement strategy when they come to unknown words in their reading, reviewing what has been taught, prompting students to use the strategy in materials they are reading, and generally continuing to nudge them toward independence are crucial.

By *reviewing*, we mean formal reviews. It seems reasonable to have the first review about a month after the initial instruction, a second review something like 2 months after that, and a third review, if necessary, several months after that. Each review might last 30–45 minutes. Two somewhat conflicting considerations are important in undertaking these reviews. The first is that it does no good, and in all probability does some harm, to spend time "teaching" students things they already know. Thus, if at the beginning of a review it is apparent that students already know the material well, then the review should be kept very brief. The second consideration is that we need to do our best to ensure that all students understand prefixes and the prefix removal and replacement strategy. It is not enough if only average and better readers get it.

Prompting refers to briefly reminding students about prefixes and the prefix strategy at appropriate points. Thus, when students are about to read a selection that contains some unknown prefixed words, the teacher might say something like, "In looking through today's reading, I noticed some pretty hard words that begin with prefixes. Be on the lookout for these, and if you don't know them, try using the prefix strategy to figure out their meanings." This sort of prompting should be fairly frequent, for it can do a lot to move students toward independent use of the strategy.

Instruction in Additional Prefixes and Additional Review and Prompting

During this week, students have been taught six prefixes. It seems reasonable to teach the 20 most frequent prefixes (see White et al., 1989, for a list of them) over a 3-year period. Thus, six or so additional prefixes might be taught in fifth grade and another six or so in sixth grade. Such instruction would be similar to that used with the initial six prefixes, with one very important exception. Students will have already been taught the basic facts about prefixes and the prefix removal and replacement strategy; thus, the instruction can be briefer than the initial instruction.

Finally, reviewing and prompting are still important during fifth and sixth grades. Again, two reviews—cumulative reviews of all the prefixes taught as well as the basic facts about prefixes and the prefix strategy—seem likely to be sufficient. And again, it is important to keep in mind that the goal is to ensure that all students know the prefixes and can use the strategy without boring them by teaching them what they already know.

CHANGES IN THE CURRENT INSTRUCTION

In this section of the chapter, we describe a number of changes to the 2004 instruction that we have made in the current instruction in the hope of making it stronger. We first note a change to the instructional approach and a change in the authors of the instruction. After that, we describe a number of enhancements to the instruction, some major and some minor. Finally, we describe what we see as the biggest difference between the final product of the 2004 chapter and the final product of the IES/SBIR work.

A General Approach to Instruction 2011

As we have noted, the general approach underlying the 2004 work was explicit instruction as defined by Pearson and Gallagher (1983) and Duke and Pearson (2002). We still believe that explicit instruction can be a very powerful approach. However, we also believe that, used by itself, explicit instruction can be a rather sterile and uninteresting approach, the sort of teaching that does not grab kids' attention, and the sort that does not lead as much as it should to transfer. We have, therefore, adopted some elements of constructivist instruction, drawing particularly from the position advanced by Pressley, Harris, and Marks (1992), who suggest the following constructivist elements:

- Give students opportunities to construct knowledge rather than explicitly teaching them everything.
- Make motivation a prime concern.
- Explain and discuss the value of strategies.
- Provide lots of collaborative discussion of the thinking behind the strategies.
- Extend practice, encouragement, and feedback over considerable time.
- Continually work on transfer.
- Encourage student reflection and planning.

Taken together, the instructional principles we derive from these two lines of thinking—explicit instruction and constructivist elements—that we follow in our current prefix instruction are these:

- Provide a description of the strategy and information on when, where, and how it should be used.
- Model use of the strategy for students on a text the class can share.
- Work with students in using the strategy on a text the class can share.
- Discuss with students how the strategy is working for them, what they think of it thus far, and when and how they can use it in the future.
- Guide and support students as they use the strategy over time. At first, provide a lot of support; later, provide less and less.
- Give students opportunities to construct knowledge.
- Motivate students to use the strategy by explaining and discussing its value.
- Work over time to help students use the newly learned strategy in various authentic in-school and out-of-school tasks.
- Review the strategy and further discuss students' understanding of it and responses to it from time to time.

Our Author Team 2011

The author "team" for the instruction described in the 2004 chapter was Michael Graves. All four of us writing the current chapter, as well as several others on the development team, have had a hand in the development of the instruction. Michael Graves (a former secondary English teacher and retired professor of literacy education) does the general planning of the instruction. Melanie Ruda (a former elementary teacher with a master's in instructional design, who now works as a full-time instructional designer) creates the day-to-day instruction. Gregory Sales (a former elementary teacher and university professor with a doctorate in instructional design and currently the CEO of an instructional design and development company) sets general parameters such as how many weeks of instruction we can create and what sort of nonprint materials we can create. And James Baumann (a former elementary teacher who currently holds an endowed chair in reading education) both provides advice as we plan instruction and critiques the instruction we create. Several other people have also had a hand in the effort. These include an editorial and content strategist, who is producing the teacher's guide; a graphic artist, who develops characters and produces posters, manual covers, and interface graphics; a videographer, who is producing video to be used in teacher training; and programmers, who are producing supplementary online lessons.

Literature on Prefix Instruction Available in 2010

In designing the instruction described in the 2004 chapter, we considered seven sources on teaching prefixes: Otterman (1955), Thompson (1958), Ess (1978), Graves and Hammond (1980), Nicol (1980), White et al. (1989), and Baumann et al. (2002). In designing and analyzing the 2010 instruction, we had five additional sources available: Baumann, Edwards, Boland, Ojejnik, and Kame'enui's (2003) instruction in morphology and context, used with fifth-grade students; Baumann, Font, Edmonds, and Boland's (2005) summary and teaching suggestions based on the Baumann et al. 2002 and 2003 studies; Carlisle's (2010) review of morphological awareness instruction; Kieffer and Lesaux's (2007, 2010) suggestions for morphology instruction, based on their research with urban classrooms and ELs; and Baumann, Blachowicz, Graves, Olejnik, and Manyak's (2008) ongoing IES-funded research on a multifaceted vocabulary program for the upper elementary grades. We have also profited from our experience developing an IES-sponsored program to teach reading comprehension strategies (Graves, Sales, Lawrenz, Robellia, & Richardson, 2010) and have found that much of what we learned about teaching comprehension strategies is also relevant to teaching word-learning strategies.

Motivation: A Central Thought Underlying Everything We Do

If you asked a group of fourth- or fifth-grade students what really interested and excited them and they said instruction in how to use prefixes to infer the meanings of unknown words, you'd almost certainly be speechless. Yet again and again we see educational materials that are dull and make no attempt to motivate young learners. In designing the 2011 instruction, we made motivation a number-one priority.

As one motivational element, we emphasize the notion of student empowerment, using as the subtitle of the Word-Learning Strategies program "Power to Unlock Word Meanings." Playing off the notion of power, we have designed a superhero theme and superheroes with a science fiction flavor. The science fiction flavor has allowed us to create superheroes with a sophisticated look that we think will make them appealing to fourth and fifth graders. Each word-learning strategy—including using prefixes—is represented by a superhero avatar, a colorful figure that represents the strategy and assists students in learning to use it. The avatar for the prefix strategy is Enfracta, whose image is shown in Figure 6.1. Students read a story about Enfracta and learn of her exploits on the planet Barrage—a story filled with

Enfracta
and her robot assistant

FIGURE 6.1. Enfracta, the prefix avatar who breaks words into parts. Reprinted with permission from Seward Incorporated.

prefixed words. Enfracta relies on her strength, the use of gadgets, and the assistance of robotic characters in breaking words into parts.

Other motivational elements include the use of posters, games, contests, and group work. The prefix power poster shown in Figure 6.2, for example, is displayed a week before instruction begins to stimulate students' interest and anticipation of the unit, and it stays up throughout the prefix instruction as a constant and colorful reminder of what the class is studying. The prefix matching game is another example of a motivational element. In this game—played with the game cards shown in Figure 6.3—a pair of students compete to gain the largest number of cards as they try to match the white cards, which contain prompts, with the gray ones, which contain the correct responses to each prompt.

Constructivist Elements

Constructivist instruction has many tenets, but certainly one of the most basic tenets is that learners need to create their own information rather than being given information by the teacher. One constructivist element comes near the beginning of the prefix unit when students learn the meaning of several prefixes. Students are not directly told the meanings of the prefixes. Rather, the instruction follows a process that leads them to infer the meanings on their own. Whether students are working as a class or in small groups, the instruction follows the same sequence:

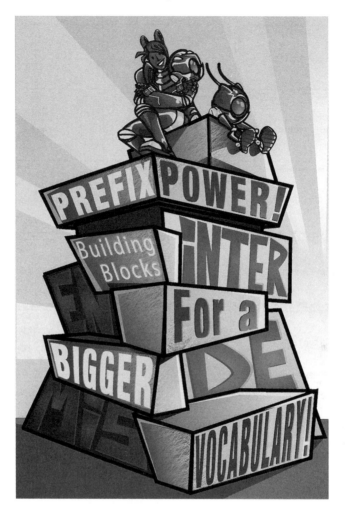

FIGURE 6.2. The prefix power poster to stimulate interest and anticipation. Reprinted with permission from Seward Incorporated.

1. Students answer multiple-choice questions about the meanings of familiar prefixed words.
2. They analyze the answers to look for common meaning.
3. They make an inference about the prefix meaning.
4. They apply their inference to an unfamiliar prefixed word.

The activity sheet students use in inferring the meaning of the prefix *un-* is shown in Figure 6.4. *Un-* is the first prefix to be learned, and in this lesson

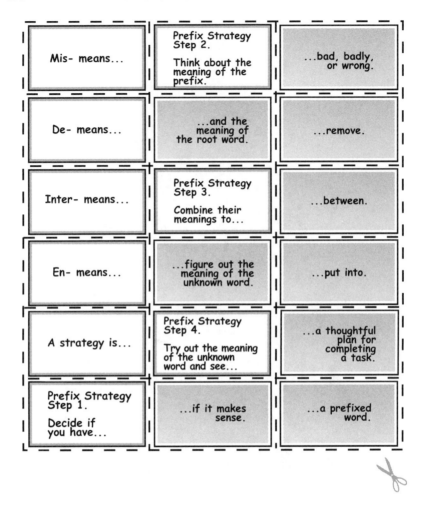

FIGURE 6.3. Prefix matching game cards in which the white cards contain prompts and the gray cards contain correct responses. Reprinted with permission from Seward Incorporated.

the teacher guides students through the questions; in later lessons on prefix meanings, students work in small groups.

Other constructivist activities students engage in include discussing why prefixes and the prefix strategy are important, working on stories rather than isolated sentences as a step toward working with prefixes in authentic situations, and searching for prefixes in materials they are reading in other subjects.

The Prefix Un-

Purpose

When you're finished with this page, you should be able to:

- Give the meaning for the prefix **un-**
- Use the meaning of the prefix to infer the meaning of an unknown word

For Questions 1-2, circle the answer that best completes the sentence.

1. If a pie is cut into **unequal** pieces, ____.
   a. the pieces are the same size
   (b.) the pieces are not the same size

2. If the knight is **unafraid**, that means ____.
   a. the knight is scared
   (b.) the knight is not scared

Write the answer to Question 3.

3. What does **un-** mean? _not, do the opposite of_

*Use your knowledge of the prefix **un-** to infer the meaning of the word in bold. Write the answer to Question 4.*

The girl made an **unwise** choice.

4. If wise means smart, **unwise** means _not wise, not smart_.

Word Parts   **Activity 3**

FIGURE 6.4. Activity sheet for learning the prefix *un-*. Reprinted with permission from Seward Incorporated.

Embedding Prefix Instruction in a Program That Teaches Other Word-Learning Strategies

Of course, when students come to unknown words as they are reading, making use of prefixes to unlock their meaning is just one of a set of word-learning strategies they need at their disposal. Consequently, the Word-Learning Strategies program provides instruction in several strategies for inferring the meaning of unknown words and includes work with compound words, various word parts (prefixes, inflectional suffixes, and derivational suffixes), context clues, the dictionary, cognates (for Spanish-speaking students), and idioms (for all ELs). Importantly, once a strategy is taught, work with that strategy is embedded in work with each additional strategy taught, so that by the end of the program students have had many experiences in working with multiple strategies.

Supplementary Online Remedial Instruction

Certainly, no educator believes that all students learn at the same rate. Yet much of school operates as if they do. All too often, teachers are forced to present a concept or skill to be learned, spend a certain amount of time with it, and then go on to the next topic or skill. As Bloom (1981) argued so cogently, most students can learn much of what we need to teach them, *but they will learn it at very different rates.* To quote Eisner (2000) in his UNESCO tribute to Bloom and his accomplishments:

> The variable that needed to be addressed, as Bloom saw it, was time. It made no pedagogical sense to expect all students to take the same amount of time to achieve the same objectives. There were individual differences among students, and the important thing was to accommodate those differences in order to promote learning rather than to hold time constant and to expect some students to fail. (p. 4)

The problem, of course, is that teachers have classes of 30 or so students and only so much time. Although it is not impossible to give those students who have learned what has been taught some independent work and provide additional instruction for those who have not learned, doing so is difficult; and often no instructional differentiation or remediation is provided. In the Word-Learning Strategies program, we provide individualized, web-based remedial instruction on the prefix strategy (as well as on the other strategies taught). The remediation on prefixes will contain six lessons, each of which a learner should be able to complete independently in 15–30 minutes. Each lesson will be self-paced and will consist of three parts: Strategy Steps (SS, where the strategy is explained), Strategy Training (ST, where the student practices using the strategy with short stories),

FIGURE 6.5. Online remediation on prefixes. Reprinted with permission from Seward Incorporated.

and Strategy Power (SP, where the student tests his or her skills and knowledge in a game-like setting). We have tried to make each lesson as enticing and motivating as possible by including colorful graphics, animation, the Enfracta avatar, text, audio, and learner control features. In the ST example shown in Figure 6.5, the story is read to a student, he or she clicks on the "yes" button to get questions on whether *overgrown* and *refuge* are prefixed words and their meanings, and he or she gets immediate feedback.

Supplementary Online Instruction for English Learners

Two additional strategies that are useful for ELs but not for English-only students are the use of cognates (for Spanish-speaking ELs) and recognizing and dealing with idioms (for all ELs). We have yet to complete this instruction, but our plan is to make it much like the online remedial work, including, of course, more actual instruction because this is initial instruction rather than review. Like the remediation, this will be individualized. The work on cognates will include 12 lessons and the work on idioms 6 lessons, with each lesson taking a learner 15–30 minutes to complete. Each of the lessons will be self-paced and will consist of the same three parts as the remediation lessons: In the SS section, the steps we plan to present for cognates include (1) decide if the unknown word might have a Spanish cognate, (2) think about the meaning of the Spanish word, and (3) try the meaning in the sentence to see if it makes sense. The steps we plan to present for idioms include (1) decide if you have found an idiom, (2) ask a native speaker what it means, and (3) try the meaning in the sentence to see if it makes sense.

In the ST section, the student will practice using the strategy following a gradual release-of-responsibility model in which he or she receives less and less support in using the strategy as he or she proceeds through the lessons. As part of this gradual release, each student will initially work with cognates or idioms at the individual word or phrase level, advance to the working with them in sentences, and in the end work with them in paragraphs and brief stories or articles. And in the SP section, the student will test his or her knowledge and skills. Finally, as with the remedial online work, we will strive to make each lesson as enticing as possible, including animation, an avatar for each strategy, text, audio, and learner control.

Final Product of Our 2011 Work

The final product of our 2004 work—what we could provide teachers to assist them in teaching prefixes—was the 2004 chapter, 25 pages on how to create prefix instruction. The final product of our 2011 work will be something quite different, a complete set of procedures and materials for teaching prefixes and other word-learning strategies. Student materials will include student activity books, pretests, and posttests. Teacher materials will include online tutorials with videos modeling best teaching practices, a detailed teacher manual, and presentation materials such as slides and posters. To provide extra assistance for students, the final product will also include web-based remedial instruction on each of the strategies, web-based instruction on using cognates for Spanish-speaking ELs, and web-based instruction on recognizing idioms for all ELs. For up-to-date information on the Word-Learning Strategies program, see *sewardreadingresources. com.*

CONCLUDING COMMENTS

Forty years ago, Richard Shutes, then chairperson of the Department of Educational Psychology at Arizona State University, offered an insight into what he saw as a huge chasm in the U.S. educational enterprise. In most fields—medicine, business, industry, and the like—Shutes observed that there is a relatively small research arm, a much larger development arm, and an even larger production arm. In education, however, Shutes saw a relatively small research arm, a much larger production arm, and virtually no development arm. In education, we most frequently go—or at least expect to go—directly from research to production. It doesn't work. The end product of research is knowledge, not a product; and without the development phase, production cannot really be research based; it is disconnected from the research.

IES/SBIR grants such as the one that is funding our work on Word-Learning Strategies represent an attempt to build a development arm in education. IES Goal Two Development grants, which put the emphasis on developing an educational innovation rather than on testing its efficacy, represent another attempt. Both, we strongly believe, are very fortunate funding for education and have the potential to create much better instruction for students.

As we noted, our development team includes eight or nine individuals. Thus far, this team has put about 1,500 hours into the design and development of our prefix instruction, and we anticipate another 300 hours of additional work. Cleary, a teacher who sets out to develop prefix instruction can put in only a very small fraction of that time, probably only a handful of hours; and a handful of hours is highly unlikely to produce instruction as strong as that produced in 1,800 hours. Equally clearly, very few teachers have the expertise and experience of our author team.

The 2004 version of this chapter concluded by posing the question of whether the instruction described is as good as prefix instruction is likely to get and answered that question with a definite "no," saying that there is always the potential for improving instruction. The same is undoubtedly true of the present instruction; there will always be room for improvement in our instruction. Still, we believe that we have created some very strong instruction.

Although we have yet to complete our testing of the efficacy of this instruction, preliminary results appear promising. As part of the development process, we evaluated the effect of 1 week of our prefix instruction on teachers and students. Three teachers completed a pretest of their knowledge about prefixes and prefix instruction, taught three 30-minute classes on prefixes and the prefix strategy, and took a posttest similar to the pretest. The teacher test included eight multiple-choice questions and four matching questions for a total of 12 items. Questions focused on the nature of word-learning strategies, how to use the prefix teaching strategy, and the meanings of the selected prefixes. In addition to the three teachers, 71 students in these teachers' classrooms were pre- and posttested on their knowledge and skills related to prefixes. The 17-item student test included four true–false items about prefixes, one multiple-choice item about what a strategy is, four fill-in-the-blank items about the meanings of prefixes, four items in which students read a sentence containing a target word and were asked if that word contained a prefix and to write the meaning of the word, and four fill-in-the-blank items about the prefix strategy.

As would be expected, teachers knew a good deal about prefixes and teaching prefixes prior to the training and consequently did very well on the pretest, averaging 9.7 on the 12-item pretest. However, the training still improved teachers' knowledge, and all three teachers scored a perfect 12 on the posttest. This difference was statistically significant at $p < .05$. Examination of the items show that most of the teachers' gains were in increased knowledge about word-learning strategies. The results with students were

TABLE 6.1. *t*-Test Results and Student Pretest and Posttest Mean Scores

Class	Pretest mean (*SD*)	Posttest mean (*SD*)	*t*	*p*
All three classes	6.08 (2.10)	14.60 (5.52)	13.19	< .001
Class 1	5.72 (1.86)	14.08 (4.82)	7.95	< .001
Class 2	6.08 (2.02)	14.85 (5.35)	7.82	< .001
Class 3	6.46 (2.40)	14.90 (5.14)	6.91	< .001

also very positive. As shown in Table 6.1, students overall showed a statistically significant gain, more than doubling their scores from pretest to posttest; and each class also showed a statistically significant gain, again more than doubling their scores from pretest to posttest. Although there is, as we have said, undoubtedly room for improvement, the effects of our current approach are certainly positive.

ACKNOWLEDGMENTS

The research reported in this chapter was supported by a contract titled Word-Learning Strategies, awarded to Seward Incorporated through the Small Business Innovation Research program of the Institute of Education Sciences, U.S. Department of Education, under Contract No. ED-IES-09-C-0013. The opinions expressed are those of the authors and do not necessarily represent the views of the Instute or the U.S. Department of Education.

REFERENCES

Baumann, J. F., Blachowicz, C. L. Z., Graves, M. F., Olejnik, S., & Manyak, P. C. (2008). *Development of a multi-faceted, comprehensive vocabulary instructional program for the upper-elementary grades.* Project funded by the Institute of Education Sciences, Washington, DC.

Baumann, J. F., Edwards, E. C., Boland E., Olejnik, S., & Kame'enui, E. J. (2003). Vocabulary tricks. Effects of instruction in morphology and context on fifth grade students' ability to derive and infer word meaning. *American Educational Research Journal, 40,* 447–494.

Baumann, J. F., Edwards, E. C., Font, G., Tereshinski, C. A., Kame'enui, E. J., & Olejnik, S. (2002). Teaching morphemic and contextual analysis to fifth-grade students. *Reading Research Quarterly, 37,* 150–176.

Baumann, J. F., Font, G., Edwards, E. C., & Boland, E. (2005). Strategies for teaching middle-grade students to use word-part and context clues to expand reading vocabulary. In E. Hiebert & M. L. Kamil (Eds.), *Bringing scientific research to practice: Vocabulary* (pp. 179–205). Mahwah, NJ: Erlbaum.

Bloom, B. (1981). *All our children learning.* New York: McGraw-Hill.

Carlisle, J. F. (2010). Effects of instruction in morphological awareness on literacy achievement: An integrative review. *Reading Research Quarterly, 45,* 464–487.

Duke, N. K., & Pearson, P. D. (2002). Effective practices for developing reading comprehension. In S. J. Samuels & A. E. Farstrup (Eds.), *What research has to say about reading instruction* (3rd ed., pp. 203–242). Newark, DE: International Reading Association.

Eisner, E. W. (2000). Benjamin Bloom 1913–99. *Prospects: The Quarterly Review of Comparative Education, 30*(3). Retrieved October 2010, from *www.ibe. unesco.org/publications/ThinkersPdf/bloome.pdf*

Ess, H. K. (1978). *The transfer value of teaching prefixes to increase vocabulary.* Unpublished master's thesis, University of Minnesota, Minneapolis.

Graves, M. F. (2004). Teaching prefixes: As good as it gets? In J. F. Baumann & E. B. Kame'enui (Eds.), *Vocabulary instruction: Research to practice* (pp. 81–99). New York: Guilford Press.

Graves, M. F., & Hammond, H. K. (1980). A validated procedure for teaching prefixes and its effect on students' ability to assign meaning to novel words. In M. L. Kamil & A. J. Moe (Eds.), *Perspectives on reading research and instruction.* Washington, DC: National Reading Conference.

Graves, M. F., Sales, G. C., Lawrenz, F., Robellia, B., & Richardson, J. W. (2010). Effects of technology-based teacher training and teacher-led classroom implementation on learning reading comprehension strategies. *Contemporary Educational Technology, 1*(2), 160–174. Available at *cedtech.net*

Kieffer, M. J., & Lesaux, N. K. (2007). Breaking down words to build meaning: Morphology, vocabulary, and reading comprehension in the urban classroom. *The Reading Teacher, 61,* 134–144.

Kieffer, M. J., & Lesaux, N. K. (2010). Morphing into adolescents: Active word learning for English-language learners and their classmates in middle school. *Journal of Adolescent and Adult Literacy, 54,* 47–56.

Nicol, J. E. (1980). *Effects of prefix instruction on students' vocabulary size.* Unpublished master's thesis, University of Minnesota, Minneapolis.

Otterman, L. M. (1955). The value of teaching prefixes and root words. *Journal of Educational Research, 48,* 611–616.

Pearson, P. D., & Gallagher, M. C. (1983). The instruction of reading comprehension. *Contemporary Educational Psychology, 8,* 317–344.

Pressley, M., Harris, K. R., & Marks, M. G. (1992). But good strategy instructors are constructivists! *Educational Psychology Review, 4,* 3–31.

Rosenshine, B., & Meister, C. (1994). Reciprocal teaching: A review of the research. *Review of Educational Research, 64,* 479–531.

Stotsky, S. L. (1977). Teaching prefixes: Facts and fallacies. *Language Arts, 54,* 887–890.

Thompson, E. (1958). The "Master Word" approach to vocabulary training. *Journal of Developmental Reading, 2,* 62–66.

White, T. G., Sowell, J., & Yanagihara, A. (1989). Teaching elementary students to use word-part clues. *The Reading Teacher, 42,* 302–308.

Chapter 7

The Vocabulary–Spelling Connection and Generative Instruction

Morphological Knowledge at the Intermediate Grades and Beyond

Shane Templeton

Years ago, the noted literacy researcher and educator Edgar Dale and his colleagues pointed out that "Organizing spelling lessons to coincide with the study of morphology gives the students a contextual structure for the study of spelling" (Dale, O'Rourke, & Bamman, 1971, p. 172). Several years later, Templeton (1983) described this relationship in terms of the *spelling–meaning connection* and offered a general sequence according to which derivational relationships can be explored. Later still, the linguist Mark Aronoff observed that "From a teacher's point of view, *morphology is important for two major reasons: spelling and vocabulary.* . . . Unfortunately, very little time is spent in school on systematic learning of morphology" (1994, pp. 820–821; emphasis added). In recent years, however, the relationship among morphological knowledge, spelling, and vocabulary has been explored more widely and with greater precision (e.g., Bowers & Kirby, 2010; Larsen & Nippold, 2007; Nagy, 2007; Nagy, Berninger, & Abbott, 2006; Nunes & Bryant, 2006, 2009). A very substantive rationale for attaining the instructional alignment between spelling and morphology for which Dale called is available, and the consequent implications for vocabulary development to which Aronoff referred are quite significant.

116

With most educators and lay professionals, the term *spelling* invokes a range of reactions and perceptions. Generations of English-speaking and English-learning individuals have bemoaned what they believe to be the inconsistency, incoherence, and incomprehensibility of the English spelling system (Templeton, 2003; Templeton & Morris, 2000). Spelling or orthographic systems, however, can be considered as falling along a phonemic-to-morphological continuum; English falls more toward the morphological end of this continuum, but, as a number of individuals have noted over the years, English spelling is far more logical at both the level of sound and at the level of meaning than it is usually credited (Chomsky, 1970; Cummings, 1988; Templeton, 1983, 2010; Venezky, 1999). It is the latter feature that this chapter addresses, for it is the tendency of the writing system of the English language to represent meaningful word elements consistently and straightforwardly that captures the *morphology* of the language. Morphological awareness—identifying prefixes, suffixes, bases, and Greek and Latin roots and understanding *how* they combine to form words—is facilitated by attention to the *spelling* of words. Spelling *visually* preserves these meaning or morphological relationships among words. Templeton (1979) first framed this position in terms of "the degree to which knowledge of orthographic [spelling] structure influences the psychological reality of words. . . . The question is an important one, for it is part of a broader concern involving *the way in which individuals organize information about the vocabulary of English*" (p. 255; emphasis added). To explore the support for this perspective, the reader is referred to this chapter in the first edition (Templeton, 2004) and to Bowers and Kirby (2010) and Seymour (1997).

Most words in the English language have been created through morphological processes. A classic study by Nagy and Anderson (1984) concluded that over 60% of English vocabulary is generated through the combination of Latin and Greek roots and affixes; for more technical, domain-specific vocabulary, this figure exceeds 90% (Green, 2008). Why is attention to morphology so important? Knowledge of word formation processes involving affixes, bases, and word roots is the *generative* engine that can drive students' independent word learning from the intermediate grades and beyond (Baumann, Edwards, Boland, & Olejnik, 2003; Stahl & Nagy, 2006). This knowledge enables students to problem-solve and determine the meaning of most of the unfamiliar words they encounter (Anglin, 1993; Bowers & Kirby, 2010). Morphological knowledge provides a unique and significant contribution to the development of reading ability from the intermediate grades at least through ninth grade (Nagy et al., 2006), and Carlisle (2010) suggested that morphological awareness may deepen "students' understanding of the morphemic structure, spelling, and meaning of written words" (p. 464).

Linguists describe morphology in either one of two perspectives: (1) Morphemes are elements that combine with each other to produce words; or (2) morphemes are the end product of a process—what counts are the relations or contrasts that morphemes create (Spencer, 1991). In the real world of literacy and vocabulary instruction, we needn't feel the need to choose between one or the other perspective: Our teaching needs to address and support students' growth in *both* of these areas. And students' orthographic knowledge—the knowledge about printed word structure that underlies their ability to read and to write words—is advanced as the foundation for the study of morphology and vocabulary.

Just as directing beginning readers' attention to printed words and the letters that comprise them helps to objectify or concretize the concept of a phoneme (Olson, 1994; Templeton & Bear, 2011), so too may directing older students' attention to orthographic patterns of meaning concretize the concept of morphemes within words and between semantically related words. This chapter explores the implications of this position, because with few exceptions (e.g., Bear, Invernizzi, Templeton, & Johnston, 2008; Bowers & Kirby, 2010; Henry, 1989; Flanigan et al., 2011; Templeton, 1992; Templeton, Bear, Invernizzi, & Johnston, 2010), there has been no focused investigation of the particulars involved in the integration of spelling, morphology, and vocabulary instruction at the intermediate grades and beyond.

Students' spelling knowledge should anchor and guide the study of particular types of morphological patterns as represented in the orthography. Once the nature of these morphological patterns as they occur in the spelling of known words is understood, these patterns can be extended to unfamiliar words. Spelling knowledge provides the basis for understanding morphological processes, which in turn may guide the systematic growth of vocabulary knowledge. Simply put, attending to spelling is how we identify the morphemes or meaningful parts within words—these visual aspects are more constant than the pronunciation. This aspect of orthographic representation of morphology is referred to as the *spelling–meaning connection:* "Words that are related in meaning are often related in spelling as well, despite changes in sound" (Templeton, 1991, p. 194). Spellings that appear illogical from a letter–sound perspective become quite understandable when considered from the perspective of morphology or *spelling–meaning* relationships; "Orthography *clarifies*, where pronunciation may obscure, relationships among words" (Templeton, 1979, p. 257). For example, the roll of the "silent" *g* in *resign* makes sense when the word *resignation* is pointed out; the spelling visually preserves the meaning relationship between the words. *Autumn* is spelled with a final silent *n* to preserve its visual identity with *autumnal*, in which the *n* is pronounced. As Venezky (1999) summarized with respect to the spelling of most words in English, "Visual identity of word parts takes precedence over letter–sound simplicity" (p. 197).

ORTHOGRAPHIC KNOWLEDGE: THE FOUNDATION OF SPELLING, READING, AND MORPHOLOGICAL AWARENESS

A growing body of research suggests that systematic attention to the ways in which spelling provides visual cues of word meaning and to the semantic relationships among words also support students' vocabulary growth and understanding (Bowers & Kirby, 2010; Leong, 2000; Smith, 1998). The convergence of two lines of research—development of morphological knowledge and development of spelling or orthographic knowledge—helps to identify when students may benefit from (1) simply exposure to, or (2) more systematic instruction in, morphology that explores this relationship between the spelling or visual representation of words and their meaning. Studies have documented the striking growth in children's derivational morphological knowledge beginning in third grade (e.g., Anglin, 1993; Berninger, Abbott, Nagy, & Carlisle, 2009; Bowers & Kirby, 2010; Bowers, Kirby, & Deacon, 2010; Carlisle, 1988; Carlisle & Fleming, 2003; Derwing, Smith, & Wiebe, 1995; Fowler & Liberman, 1995; Leong, 2000; Mahony, Singson, & Mann, 2000). Interestingly, and importantly, students whose *spelling instructional level* (Morris, Blanton, Blanton, Nowacek, & Perney, 1995) is at least third grade are able to begin explicit exploration of simple derivational morphological patterns; their lexical organization and representations accommodate simple two-syllable words and enable them to apply this knowledge to encode and decode polysyllabic words (Templeton, 1992). For the classroom teacher, therefore, a qualitative inventory of spelling knowledge can be a relatively quick and valid indicator of students' level of vocabulary and morphological knowledge (Templeton, Smith, Moloney, VanPelt, & Ives, 2009). Studies using the Academic Vocabulary Spelling Inventory (Templeton et al., 2010; Townsend, Bear, & Templeton, 2009; Townsend, Burton, Bear, & Templeton, 2010) have found that, among middle school students, morphological knowledge of academic words significantly predicts achievement in math, social studies, and science above and beyond breadth of vocabulary knowledge.

In a classic summation, Perfetti (1997) observed that the process of spelling and the process of reading draw upon the same lexical or orthographic representation; spelling, therefore, is "the purest indicator of lexical quality" (p. 30). More recently, Perfetti (2007) has elaborated on this observation in his *lexical quality hypothesis*; the perspective offered in this chapter is that over time, with development, orthographic knowledge is the "glue" that binds together phonological, semantic, and morphological information about individual words and their relationships with other words. Developmental spelling research has offered insight into the nature and content of this lexical quality, also referred to as *orthographic knowledge* (e.g., Bourassa & Treiman, 2008; Ehri, 1997; Larkin & Snowling, 2008; Perfetti, Rieben, & Fayol, 1997; Templeton & Bear, 1992), as well as how this knowledge is applied in both the encoding and decoding of print. The nature and content of orthographic knowledge determine the types of printed information the reader perceives and processes, and therefore the rate and degree of accuracy with which the words are recognized. For this reason, the work of Morris and his colleagues, addressing spelling instructional level, is significant (e.g., Morris, Nelson, & Perney, 1986; Morris et al., 1995; see also, Bear, Templeton, & Warner, 1991; Ganske, 1999). Determining a spelling instructional level reveals the zone of proximal *orthographic* development within which students can most productively examine words and abstract spelling patterns, thus being more likely to learn, retain, and apply these patterns in their writing, in their perception of familiar words, and in decoding unfamiliar words in reading. As orthographic knowledge advances, so too does the literate lexicon. (For a fuller discussion of this relationship between the recognition and the production of orthographic patterns, see Bear et al., 2008; Bear & Templeton, 1998, 2000; Templeton & Bear, 2011.)

Orthographic knowledge, therefore, is placed as the fulcrum for instruction in morphology and vocabulary. Beginning in the intermediate school years, a significantly larger proportion of words occurring in print than in spoken language reflects derivational morphological processes (Aronoff, 1994; Bertram, Baayen, & Schreuder, 2000; Carlisle & Katz, 2006; Chomsky, 1970; Nagy & Anderson, 1984). Words that reflect these patterns tend to be spelled more in accordance with their meaning than with their sound (Taft, 2003; Templeton & Scarborough-Franks, 1985; Venezky, 1999). In order to have access to a sufficient number of examples that reflect these morphological processes, a student's reading and spelling instructional level should probably be, as noted earlier, at least third grade. Through reading at both independent and instructional levels, students encounter words several times that later are selected for spelling study. The examination of these known words in reading ensures that the structure of the words will more likely be learned. This in turn strengthens the abstraction of particular orthographic *patterns*, which in the lexicon provide an orthographic frame that guides the perception of words in reading. In this regard, Perfetti (1997) noted that attention given to spelling is of more benefit to reading than is reading to spelling. Working within the spelling instructional level—within the zone of proximal orthographic development—affords the lexicon the optimal conditions for growth.

A necessary preliminary to effective, integrated spelling and vocabulary instruction through the exploration of morphological features and processes is the administration of a qualitative spelling inventory (Bear et al., 2008; Ganske, 1999; Masterson, Apel, & Wasowicz, 2002; Townsend et al., 2009). To illustrate the relationship between underlying orthographic knowledge and the acquisition of new orthographic patterns, consider the following spelling errors on an elementary spelling inventory by three students in the same fifth-grade classroom:

	Student A	Student B	Student C
drive	driev	drive	drive
float	flote	float	float
hurry	hery	hurry	hurry
striped	stipt	stripped	striped
mental	mintul	mentle	mental
competition		computishun	compitition
amusement		amusemint	ammusement

As revealed through his spelling errors, Student A's orthographic knowledge indicates that he is sensitive to the orthographic pattern in which silent letters are used to indicate long-vowel sounds (*driev, *flote). His failure to double consonants at syllable junctures (*hery) and to represent past tense with -*ed* indicate that these features are not yet part of his orthographic knowledge; requiring him to memorize spelling words traditionally found at fifth-grade level would lead inevitably to frustration—his orthographic knowledge is not sufficient to support the retention of such words in long-term memory. Although Student A, as a fifth grader, may pick up some information while listening to a teacher walking through a discussion of concrete Greek roots such as -*therm*- and -*photo*-, his word study for purposes of encoding and decoding will not include systematic examination of words that include these forms. On the other hand, Student B's spelling errors reveal that her underlying orthographic knowledge *would* benefit from spelling instruction that includes systematic examination of polysyllabic words, notably the addition of inflectional endings to base words. She would also benefit from exploring simple Greek and Latin word roots and from learning a number of new vocabulary words that include these elements, though with a few exceptions such words would not be part of her spelling words. Student C's underlying orthographic knowledge would support a more systematic and extensive exploration of spelling–meaning patterns as part of her instruction as well as of Greek and Latin word roots and the affixes with which they combine. To the degree that an individual's underlying orthographic knowledge supports an understanding of morphological patterns and processes, as represented in the spelling of words—the visual representation of sound and meaning—the decoding and encoding of these patterns becomes easier, more facile, and increasingly automatic.

Given the significance of orthographic knowledge in the development of the literate lexicon, it is not surprising that a number of researchers have consistently found that older struggling readers and spellers do not process morphological information well (e.g., Bourassa & Treiman, 2008; Leong, 2000; Smith, 1998). They do not possess the underlying orthographic knowledge and organization that would support learning and retaining words that reflect these processes. More simply expressed, such students are attempting to process and remember words that are at their spelling *frustration* level (Morris et al., 1995). Though these students may indeed study and remember how to spell new polysyllabic vocabulary words on a Friday test, they will most likely misspell those words when they return to writing because their underlying orthographic knowledge will not support the retention of these words in long-term memory. This does not mean that teachers should avoid discussion of spelling–meaning relationships with such students—such "mentioning" alerts the students to the existence of these elements (Templeton, 1989)—but the systematic spelling instruction these students require should focus on simpler and developmentally appropriate orthographic patterns.

THE NATURE AND COURSE OF STUDENTS' KNOWLEDGE OF DERIVATIONAL MORPHOLOGICAL PATTERNS IN ORTHOGRAPHY

Taken together with the research into students' knowledge of derivational morphology, developmental spelling research provides some guidance by which a general scope and sequence for morphologically based spelling and vocabulary instruction can be developed (see Bear et al., 2008; Templeton, 2004; Templeton et al., 2010). Although grounded in research, it is important to note that the sequence should not be considered lockstep, but rather a general guide and point of reference for teachers. Beginning exploration can be focused on what linguists term *external* derivational morphology. A number of studies investigating the development of derivational morphology have focused on this aspect (e.g., Anglin, 1993): Adding the suffix *-ly* to the adjective *glad* yields the adverb *gladly*; there is no change in the pronunciation of the base when the suffix is added. Much of the initial learning in derivational morphology involves this process of simply combining morphemic elements. As students move through the intermediate grades and beyond, however, words that reflect processes of *internal* derivational morphology are encountered with increasing frequency. These are words in which the addition of suffixes often causes a phonological shift within the base or root; note the different pronunciation of the letter string *defin-* in the words *define*, *defin*ition, and *defin*itive, and of the letter string *-jud-* in pre*jud*ice and ad*jud*icate. The vocabulary–spelling connection applies most productively to internal derivational morphological processes. Usually these words also include Greco-Latin roots that underlie most specialized or academic vocabulary. Word roots are those elements that remain at the core or "root" of the word after all affixes have been removed but which, in contrast to base words, usually do not stand alone as words: for example, *-dic-* ("to speak") in *dic*tate, pre*dic*t, and in*dic*t and *-spec-* ("to look, see") in *spec*tator, *spec*tacle, and *circum*spect.

Before exploring the specific Greco-Latin roots and the processes that apply to them, a foundation should be established that firmly anchors this exploration in students' awareness of *familiar* words and the ways in which they reflect spelling–meaning patterns (Templeton, 2003). Investigation of the nature, course, and complexity of the development of certain derivational morphological patterns offers guidelines for the construction of this spelling–meaning foundation (see Templeton, 2004, for a discussion of this development).

IMPLICATIONS FOR SELECTION OF PATTERNS AND WORDS

Based on a synthesis of the developmental spelling research and the research investigating the development of derivational morphological knowledge, the following two criteria emerge for designing an integrated spelling and vocabulary curriculum: (1) the ratio of occurrence of concrete to more abstract derivational morphological patterns in orthography and phonology (Carlisle & Katz, 2006; Templeton, 1989); and (2) the degree of semantic transparency among the words that represent these patterns (Corson, 1997; Elbro & Arnbak, 1996; Nagy & Anderson, 1984).

Two examples illustrate these criteria. To develop an awareness of the vocabulary–spelling connection, we can "walk through" with students those word formation processes involving (1) the straightforward process in semantically transparent words in which no phonological shift occurs, then (2) relationships in semantically transparent words that do involve phonological shifts (long-vowel to short-vowel alternation such as w*i*se/w*i*sdom, s*a*ne/s*a*nity and consonant alternation such as bom*b*/bom*b*ard, *sign*/s*ign*ature). In these examples involving phonological shift, the sound changes are easily discriminable in the familiar words that we use to illustrate the processes. Several examples of these usually lead to students' explicit realization of the role of meaning in spelling, and thus, why the spelling of the related words does not change significantly. With respect to Greek and Latin word elements, the combinatorial process first explored is straightforward, as are the meanings of the elements that are studied: Introduce, examine, and apply knowledge of affixes and roots using words in which the combination of these morphemes results in concrete and consistent meanings— for example, an affix or two combining with a root, the meaning of which is concrete, as with *pre-* + *-dict-* and *pre-* + *-dict-* + *-ion*; *in-* + *-spect-* and *in-* + *-spect-* + *-ion*. The function of *-dict-* in more abstract words such as bene*dict*ion and *inter*dict and the function of *-spect-* in intro*spect*ion and circum*spect* would be examined later; in these instances the meaning has often evolved from the literal and more concrete to the more abstract—a phenomenon that should in time be discussed with students. For example, the word *circumspect* is a combination of two roots—combining *spect* (to look) with *circum* (around) literally means "to look around." The word has grown metaphorically to mean that one is cautious in what one does and says, and does not take risks. When you behave in a "circumspect" manner you "look around," so to speak, and are careful. This process is more common in literary texts; notably, as students advance through the grades, the meanings of less frequently occurring unfamiliar words may be quite reliably inferred by analyzing the combination of affixes and roots. This is because the meanings of words that have entered the language more recently—most often in specific academic domains—are more straightforwardly the sum of their morphemic parts. *Dehydrogenate*, for example, literally means "the act (*-ate*) of removing (*de-*) hydrogen."

Teachers can find words that reflect appropriate derivational morphological patterns and semantic transparency in Bear et al. (2008), Flanigan et al. (2011), Ganske (2000), Fresch and Wheaton (2002), and Templeton, Johnston, Bear, and Invernizzi (2009). In addition, some published spelling and spelling–vocabulary programs for the intermediate and middle grades have been constructed with these criteria in mind. It is still important, however, that such materials be used developmentally. Most such materials have a grade-level designation, but because of the variability of students they are probably not appropriate for all students at a particular grade level, and accommodating below- and above-level students is important. These criteria can guide instruction in reading/English classes at the intermediate and middle levels (Templeton, 2002), as well as in other content areas such as mathematics, science, and social studies. Teachers who are able to plan cross-curricular units or work together to do so are in the best position to optimize spelling and vocabulary integration. In *social studies*, terms such as *democracy, plutocracy, oligarchy*, and *monarchy* can be related by examining their constituent parts: The form of government or rule is by the people, the wealthy, the few, or one. The confusion between *immigrant* and *emigrant* can be explained by noting the prefix in each word: *im-* means "into"; *immigrants* migrate *into* a country; *e-* means "out"; *emigrants* migrate *out of* or leave a country. When selecting vocabulary words that represent important concepts and ideas in a content area, teachers should think about words that are related orthographically and semantically to the focused terms, and which students are already likely to know but perhaps have not analyzed.

In math, as an example, the concept of *fraction* gets lost, even for many intermediate and middle grade students, in the complexities of manipulating numbers in numerators and denominators; students do not realize that *fraction* literally deals with *breaking* something down into parts. Teachers can relate the term to the word *fracture*, which has most likely been experienced by at least one student in the class, and point out that both words contain the Latin word root *fract*, which means "to break." *Fractions*, in other words, involve breaking things down into parts and manipulating those parts.

In science, many terms are created by combining Greek and Latin roots; science offers one of the richest domains for students' to appreciate the role and importance of these elements. Moreover, the meaning of the combined elements is usually very precise. Students can be asked about a *hydroplane*—the noun or the verb; they're likely to know one or both. Then ask about a fire *hydrant*—what does it have in common with a *hydroplane*? If students do not come to the realization themselves as a consequence of teacher questioning, the teacher then points out *hydr-* in both words and tells students that it is a Greek root meaning *water* or liquid, fluid. Then move to *hydrology* and *hydraulic*. This would also be the perfect time to share an etymological narrative (Stahl & Nagy, 2006): The root *hydr* came from the Greek legend of Herakles, whose twelve labors included slaying the snakelike, multiheaded monster who lived under the water, who was called the *Hydra*.

Such narratives serve to ground and enrich the semantic network that binds the words that share this particular root (Templeton et al., 2010). C. S. Lewis wrote of the *semantic biographies* of words (1990) to convey a sense of where the words come from, what they have meant, and how that history may determine their present-day use. Even the dean of American behaviorists, B. F. Skinner, observed that, if we attend closely enough, words may reveal nothing less than "the archaeology of thought" (as cited in Bear & Templeton, 2000). This is a fairly sophisticated level of insight, of course, and is a type of resonance with words that arguably most literate adults have not attained. It is encouraging to realize, however, that with guidance from us, most older students may indeed develop this degree of insight.

INSTRUCTION

Put succinctly, students should be actively engaged in examining words from a *variety* of perspectives (Bear et al., 2008; Templeton, 2003, 2011). The contexts in which this examination occurs include direct teacher "walk-throughs" with guided discussion, which lead to more independent student engagements and exploration. When teachers help students develop an inquisitive attitude toward words and their structure, students are motivated to compare and contrast words, looking for patterns that apply to larger families of words. *Word sort* activities, in which words are categorized according to sound, spelling, and meaning criteria (Bear et al., 2008; Ganske, 2000; Templeton, 2002), are particularly effective. Teachers can establish categories according to which students sort words, and students can establish their own criteria. For example, students can sort words according to common word roots, type of sound–spelling alternation pattern, or other conceptual categories. In addition to sorting the words that have been written on cards into categories, students at other times should *write* the words as they are being categorized. Once students become aware of and understand how *absorbed prefixes* work, for example, they often become intrigued by the idea of keeping lists of words with assimilated prefixes. Students can also be encouraged to set up and maintain *word study notebooks*, in which they record new words encountered in their reading, along with the sentence in which the words occurred, appropriate dictionary definitions, and any related words occurring to students that share structural features with the target word.

The quality and appropriate mix of teacher-guided and student-exploratory aspects most likely depends on four teacher factors: first, a knowledge base in the form and function of English orthography, in particular, those features of English word morphology; second, a general understanding of a logical instructional sequence to be followed; third, knowledge of how to assess where students fall along a developmental continuum of word knowledge; and fourth, an awareness of and facility with providing appropriate types of activities and strategies for learning words. This chapter offers additional resources that can help establish and develop these factors.

Teacher "Walk-Throughs"

The examples in this section flow from the more concrete to the more abstract. In this first example, the teacher models a walk-through in which students are first guided toward an explicit awareness of the vocabulary–spelling connection. The teacher begins with words the students know:

> Writing the word *sign* on the board, the teacher talks about what happens when you *sign* a letter and comments, "I wonder why there's a *g* in the word *sign*." Then, the teacher mentions that we refer to someone's signed name as his or her *signature*, and writes the word directly underneath *sign* so that the letters *s-i-g-n* line up. "Hmmm . . . that's interesting. We hear the *g* pronounced in *signature*, even though we don't hear it in *sign*. Are these two words related in *meaning*? I wonder if that might have something to do with why the spelling *s-i-g-n* doesn't change?
>
> "Let's try a couple of other words. Several of you have taken turns writing a *column* for our class newspaper. [Writes the word *column* on the board.] What did we call ourselves when we wrote a column? Right, a *columnist*. [Writes the word directly under

column.] That's interesting—we don't hear the *n* in *column* pronounced, but we do hear it in *columnist*. Are these two words related in meaning? Might that have something to do with why the spelling doesn't change?"

This walk-through and subsequent discussion helps students revisit words they already know but have not explicitly realized the spelling–meaning connections that they share. Students will encounter a large number of words in their reading that follow this type of pattern; when teachers explicitly walk through these patterns with students, the students are more likely to notice and remember such relationships on their own.

After several long- to short-vowel alternation patterns are examined (e.g., n*a*ture/n*a*tural, st*u*dent/st*u*dy), students can explore in depth the process of vowel reduction, in which sound is not a clue to the spelling of the *schwa* or least-accented vowel; misspellings such as *resadent, *confadence, and *oppisition are common. Pairing appropriate base words together with their derivatives should provide a clue to the spelling of the schwa sound: res*i*de/res*i*dent, conf*i*de/conf*i*dence, oppose/opposition. The awareness of the spelling–meaning connection should evolve into a strategy for learning and remembering the spelling of words: *If you're uncertain about how to spell a word, try to think of a word that is related in spelling and meaning*—very often, it will provide a clue. Remembering *oppose*, for example, will help in remembering *opposition*. Remembering *confide* will help in remembering *confidence*.

Once students are aware of and understand how the relationship between spelling and meaning functions in *known* words, this relationship can be extended to *unknown* words. In the following example, the teacher begins with words students have misspelled:

> After writing the misspellings *locle, presadent*, and *autum* on the board, the teacher explains: "These are some misspellings I've noticed in your writing recently. For each of them, there is a word that is similar in spelling and meaning and which will help you remember the correct spelling. Let's take the first word. [Writes *locality* on the board.] Who's heard of it? [Several hands raise.] Any idea what it means? Or is it one of those words we've heard but we're not quite sure about the meaning? Well, it can help us with the spelling of this word [pointing to *locle*]. What do you think the base of *locality* is? Good! [Underlines *local*.] Might this give us a clue to the spelling of *local*? That's right—you've figured me out by now! Sure—*local* [writes *local* underneath *locality*] is related to *locality*. And what does *local* mean? [Students respond.] Good! So *locality* has to do with or describes something that is *local*, and it helps us remember the spelling of the /el/ sound in *local*. Why? We hear that strongly accented second syllable in

loCALity, don't we, and because words that are related in meaning are often related in spelling, that's our clue for remembering
the *-al* spelling in *local*.

"We've done two things: First, we've cleared up the spelling of *local*, and second, we've just expanded our vocabulary by
learning the word *locality*." The teacher proceeds with the other
words, discussing how a president *presides* over a country and
how *autumnal* describes something that characterizes or happens
in *autumn*. In each case, he or she points out how the problematic
spelling in the *known* word is explained by the sound and spelling in the *new* word: The *long-i* spelling in pres*i*de explains the
spelling of the schwa sound in pres*i*dent; the pronounced *n* at the
end of *autumnal* explains the silent *n* in *autumn*. Beginning with
its focus on spelling, this lesson has become a vocabulary lesson,
which in turn has reinforced spelling. The teacher concludes with
the following observation:

"You know what's neat about all of this? More and more
often, you're going to notice words when you read that you don't
know but which remind you of words you *do* know because of
their similarity in spelling. This similarity in spelling is a very
important clue to the meaning of an unknown word, because as
we've learned, words that are related in meaning are also often
related in spelling. Knowing *local*, for example, would help you
with *locality*; knowing *autumn* helps you with *autumnal*."

In contrast to earlier developmental levels, in which unfamiliar words are
used sparingly as part of spelling study, at this level, unfamiliar words can
indeed be part of spelling study, provided that they are orthographically
and semantically related to the familiar words—as in the cases of *preside,
locality*, and *autumnal*.

Exploring internal derivational morphological processes as they apply
in base words and derivatives should lay a secure foundation for exploring
these processes as they apply to word roots. The consistent spelling of word
roots is the key to identifying them and studying how they function within
words; students' understanding of spelling–meaning relationships extends
to perceiving the kinship among words that at first glance may appear quite
different. The following example illustrates a beginning lesson addressing
the concept of word roots.

The teacher begins by reviewing briefly how base words and pre-
fixes/suffixes combine, then moves on: "In literally thousands of
words, there is a 'root' to which prefixes and suffixes attach. This
word root is the most important part of the word, but unlike a
base word, it usually can't stand alone as a word. Let's check one
out." [Points to the words *inspect, inspection*, and *spectator* written on the board.]

"Let's think about the words *inspect* and *inspection*. What do you do when you *inspect* something? [Student responds, describing how you "look real close at something."] Good! So, what would an *inspection* be? [Inspecting something.] All right! Now, let's think about *spectator*. What does a *spectator* do? [Watches something.] Good; a spectator watches or *looks* at something, like at a basketball game. Now, these three words all have *spect* in them. Is *spect* a word? You're right; it isn't, but it's a very important part of each of these words. We call *spect* a word *root*; it comes from Latin and means 'to look.' Let *us* look at these words and think about how the root works in each one.

"*Inspect* has the prefix *in-*, meaning 'into,' so when we put *spect* together with *in-* [pointing to *spect* and then to *in-*] we get 'to look into.' And with *inspection*, we have the *-ion* suffix, which means 'the act of doing something'—in this case [pointing to *ion*, then to *spect*, then to *in*] 'the *act* of *looking into*.'

"Now let's think about these words [writes *dictate, dictation,* and *predict* on the board]. What's the same in these three words? [Students reply that they all have *d-i-c-t* in them.] Right! Those letters spell the word root. Take a minute and talk to your partner about the meaning of each word and what you think that root might mean. [Students' responses indicate that they have a sense of 'talking.'] Very good! When you dictate something, you are talking or speaking; you can 'dictate' a 'dictation,' a written record of what you've said. '*Dict*' comes from a Latin word that means 'to say or speak.' That certainly makes sense in the words *dictate* and *dictation*, but what about *predict*? Remember what *pre-* means? [Student responds 'before.'] Okay! So, let's put *dict*, meaning 'to say or speak,' together with *pre*, meaning 'before,' and we literally get the meaning 'to say or speak before.' Do you see how that works—when you *predict* something will happen, you are *saying* that it will happen before it occurs?"

The teacher then writes the following sentence containing the unfamiliar word *contradict*: *No matter what Eric says, his little brother always contradicts him.* The teacher engages the students in a discussion of what they know about this word (the root *dict* and what it means) and how it might help them determine the meaning of the word in the context of the sentence and what they know about younger brothers and sisters. Through a number of such examples, the teacher helps students develop the understanding of how a knowledge of word roots can usually help them get an approximate meaning of an unfamiliar word; they can then check this approximate meaning in the context of the sentence, paragraph, or even entire text to determine if it makes sense.

The following example illustrates how a teacher walks students through an exploration of *prefix assimilation*, or absorbed prefixes. This feature of spelling has wide applicability and is remarkably consistent but is conceptually more advanced, in that it depends upon an awareness of, and familiarity with, more advanced derivational morphological relationships:

> The teacher asks the students if they've ever wondered why the prefix *in-* winds up being spelled so many different ways; when they look it up in the dictionary they find that it is also spelled *il-*, *im-*, and *ir-*. "What's going on here?" the teacher asks. He or she continues by discussing the word *immobile* and its meaning with the students, telling the students that this word was chosen because a number of them have spelled it and similar words with only one *m*:
>
> "In the dictionary, we see that *immobile* is made up of the prefix *in-* and the word *mobile*—literally, 'not mobile.' Why did it change? Why don't we still have the word *inmobile*?
>
> "Try saying the word *inmobile* . . . now say *immobile*. Which word is easier to pronounce? Now think about it: Our tongue and lips have to move around more in order to pronounce *inmobile*. With *immobile*, however, there's less movement going on. Now try it with *immortal* . . . that's easier to say than *inmortal*, right?
>
> "Let's try another one: If something is 'not legible,' do we say it is '*inlegible*'? No, we say it is '*illegible*' instead. How about if someone is 'not responsible'; do we say that he or she is '*inresponsible*'? Right! We say '*irresponsible*' instead. Why? Right—because it's easier!
>
> "Let's look at the words *immobile, illegible,* and *irresponsible*. In each word, the spelling of the prefix changed from *in-*. Why did *in-* change to *im-* in *immobile*? Why did it change to *il-* in *illegible*? Why did it change to *ir-* in *irresponsible*? [The teacher gets the students talking about this; it may be helpful to write additional examples such as *illegal* and *irreversible* for students to consider.] The teacher leads the students to the realization that the letter *n* changed to match the first letter of the base word.
>
> "This process began a long time ago. We say that the sound of the *n* was 'absorbed' into the sound at the beginning of the word onto which the prefix was added. So, when *in-* is changed into *im-*, *il-*, or *ir-*, we say that the *n* has been 'absorbed.' Let's try this out: How would you spell the word that means 'not measurable'? 'Not logical'? 'Not rational'?"

Later, after students have explored other prefixes and how they have been "absorbed" into base words (e.g., *ad-* + *count* = *account*; *ad-* + *locate* = *allocate*; *con-* + *respond* = *correspond*; *sub-* + *port* = *support*), the teacher explains what happens when prefixes are added to word roots; for example, *ad-* + *tract* = *attract*; *con-* + *mit* = *commit*. In each case, it is important to talk explicitly about how the meaning of the word parts—base word or word root and prefix—combine to result in the meaning of the word. For example: "What happens when you are *attracted* to someone? The word *attracted* contains the root *tract*, meaning 'draw or pull,' and the absorbed prefix *at-* was originally *ad-*, meaning 'to or toward.' So, when you are *attracted* to someone, you are 'pulled toward' him or her!"

On occasion, words that are orthographically similar do not seem to be related, as, for example, *design* and *designate*. This is a good opportunity to refer students to the etymological information for *design* and *designate* in the dictionary; they both come from a Latin term that means "to mark." When someone is *designated* as a spokesperson, for example, he or she is, in a sense "marked" to perform this duty. When an architect *designs* a house, he or she is "marking" how the house will be laid out and how it will look.

Cognates provide the opportunity to engage students in exploring vocabulary–spelling or morphological connections across languages. Cognates are words in different languages that are spelled the same or similarly and have the same or similar spellings. Cognate study can occur right along with our other vocabulary–spelling and morphological investigations. Cognate study has considerable potential for English learners as well as for monolingual English students who would benefit from exploring another language or languages (Kiefer & Lesaux, 2008; Templeton, 2010). In the following example, the teacher asks students to pair the words that they think go together and align them vertically:

abbreviation	*creation*	*anticipation*	*imitation*	*declaration*
abreviación	*creación*	*anticipación*	*imitación*	*declaración*
vegetation	*elevation*	*vocation*		
vegetación	*elevación*	*vocación*		

She then asks, "What do you notice? How are these words alike? Different?" If students do not point out the similarity in suffixes between English and Spanish, the teacher would ask if the students they think that the *-ción* suffix in Spanish might have the same meaning as the *-tion* suffix in English.

Over time, as students realize and come to understand a number of roots and the processes of formation with affixes, they can explore those instances in which the spellings of roots within related words *do* change— an apparent "violation" of the vocabulary–spelling connection. Even in such instances, however, there is an underlying logic at work. For more advanced middle school students, and for most secondary students at some point, the following type of exploration would be very productive (Templeton et al., 2010).

The teacher reminds the students that, up to this point, they have learned how *suffixes* can affect the pronunciation of a base or root in spelling–meaning families. Usually the spelling does not change significantly—it visually preserves the meaning—but on occasion, the spelling of the base *does* change. As examples, he or she reminds them of the patterns in related words such as *explain–explanation* and *retain–retention*. She tells them that today they'll explore situations in which the spelling within *roots* changes. She then writes the following, underlining the letters that represent the appropriate roots:

sacred	*factory*	*aptitude*	*sedentary*
sacrament	*affect*	*adapt*	*preside*
consecrate	*suffice*	*inept*	

Four different roots are illustrated here, and in each, the spelling of the vowel changes: *sac/sec*, *fac/fec/fic*, *apt/ept*, and *sed/sid*. Rather than suffixes affecting the spelling of the roots, in these cases *prefixes* exerted an influence. In Latin, when these prefixes were affixed to a root, the spelling changed to reflect this.

The teacher next talks about each "root group" and how the meaning of the root contributes to the meaning of each word: *sac/sec* mean "holy"; *fac/fec/fic* mean "make" or "do"; *apt/ept* mean "fit"; and *sed/sid* mean "sit." The teacher then shares that, depending on the root and the prefix that was added in Latin, the following "rule" applied: An *a* changed to an *e*, and an *e* changed to an *i*.

The teacher reminds the students that the purpose in looking at these words and their roots is to illustrate that, even when the spelling *does* change among related words and their roots, the changes are usually not haphazard—there is an explanation. The teacher also is able to reinforce the awareness that, when they run into an unfamiliar word, this is an additional skill that will help students figure out its meaning *and* remember the meaning more efficiently. For example, in a news article about the visit of the pope, the sentence "A new group of priests will be *consecrated* tomorrow" provides both contextual and morphological clues to the meaning of the unfamiliar word. The teacher points out that, because we're now aware that a root may, on occasion, have different spellings, it is possible to determine that *consecrated* may have something to do with a sacred act or event. Checking the dictionary, we confirm this possible meaning.

To summarize this more "advanced" lesson: The teacher's objective is (of course) *not* to teach students the finer points of Latin word formation. Rather, he or she wishes to (1) reinforce the understanding that when spelling *does* change among related words, it does so for a reason—enough letters will remain after the spelling change to preserve the root relationship (e.g., *s-cr* in *sac*red/con*sec*rate, *f-c* in *fac*tory/af*fec*t/suf*fic*e, and so forth); (2) help students understand how this type of examination affords deeper insight into the core semantic relationships that these words share; and (3) guide students in further applying their increasingly deeper funds of underlying orthographic knowledge.

The digital revolution affords considerably greater access to information about the content of morphology—there are innumerable online dictionary and etymology websites, and new apps for smartphones, iPads, and related digital devices are continually appearing that both search for and provide definitions of classic roots and affixes. These developments are exciting and may indeed help to revolutionize students' understanding of and growth in vocabulary. What they have yet to do, however, is walk a particular group of students through how these elements "work" and engage students in consequential conversations about that work. It would be naïve to assume that this type of engagement online is far off; the design, however, will probably not be by a classics scholar or a linguist but by knowledgeable teachers.

CONCLUSION

To return to linguists' two competing perspectives on morphology: Morphemes are (1) things or (2) the result of a process. Yes, our students certainly need to learn how morphemes combine, but they also need to learn and appreciate that this combination and the meaning that results is so often more than the sum of the morphemic parts. To suggest an analogy between morphological structure and narrative structure: We guide our students' exploration of narratives so that they ultimately become aware of and understand that stories are so much more than the sum of their parts—their beginnings, episodic structure, and resolutions are means to deeper insights and understandings. Similarly, we guide our students' exploration of *words*—their affixes, bases, and roots—so that students use this insight to explore and understand the relationships and contrasts among underlying concepts and their connotations.

As this chapter has suggested, we now have a better understanding of how the relationship between spelling and vocabulary can be addressed more systematically. There continues to be a need for sustained research efforts that investigate the effects of the type of integrated spelling and vocabulary approach advanced in this chapter, but such an approach is promising. Moreover, this approach should be part of an overall instructional context for vocabulary development that emphasizes a range of activities and strategies for learning particular words (Beck, McKeown, & Kucan, 2008; Blachowicz & Fisher, 2009; Graves & Watts-Taffe, 2003; Lubliner & Scott, 2008; Templeton et al., 2010; Whitaker, 2008). There now exists the potential for considerably more students to develop the excitement, curiosity, and inquisitiveness about words that characterize the true wordsmiths—with payoffs not only in better spelling and vocabulary knowledge, but because of that knowledge, more efficient and insightful reading and writing as well.

REFERENCES

Anglin, J. M. (1993). Vocabulary development: A morphological analysis. *Monographs of the Society for Research in Child Development, 58*(10, Serial No. 238).

Aronoff, M. (1994). Morphology. In A. C. Purves, L. Papa, & S. Jordan (Eds.), *Encyclopedia of English studies and language arts* (Vol. 2, pp. 820–821). New York: Scholastic.

Baumann, J. F., Edwards, E. C., Boland, E. M., & Olejnik, S. (2003). Vocabulary tricks: Effects of instruction in morphology and context on fifth-grade students' ability to derive and infer word meanings. *American Educational Research Journal, 40*(2), 447–494.

Bear, D. R., Invernizzi, M., Templeton, S., & Johnston, F. (2008). *Words their way: Word study for phonics, spelling, and vocabulary development* (4th ed.). Boston: Pearson/Allyn & Bacon.

Bear, D. R., & Templeton, S. (1998). Explorations in developmental spelling: Foundations for learning and teaching phonics, spelling, and vocabulary. *The Reading Teacher, 52*, 222–242.

Bear, D., & Templeton, S. (2000). Matching development and instruction. In N. Padak & T. Rasinski (Eds.), *Distinguished educators on reading: Contributions that have shaped effective literacy instruction* (pp. 363–376). Newark, DE: International Reading Association.

Bear, D. R., Templeton, S., & Warner, M. (1991). The development of a qualitative inventory of higher levels of orthographic knowledge. In J. Zutell & S. McCormick (Eds.), *Learner factors/teacher factors: Issues in literacy research and instruction* (Fortieth yearbook of the National Reading Conference; pp. 105–110). Chicago: National Reading Conference.

Beck, I., McKeown, M. G., & Kucan, L. (2008). *Creating robust vocabulary.* New York: Guilford Press.

Berninger, V. W., Abbott, R. D., Nagy, W., & Carlisle, J. (2009). Growth in phonological, orthographic, and morphological awareness in grades 1 to 6. *Journal of Psycholinguistic Research—Online First.* Retrieved October 16, 2009, from *www.springerlink.com.innopac.library.unr.edu/content/gpu4572318l52242*

Bertram, R., Baayen, R. H., & Schreuder, R. (2000). Effects of family size for complex. *Journal of Memory and Language, 42*, 390–405.

Blachowicz, C., & Fisher, P. J. (2009). *Teaching vocabulary in all classrooms* (4th ed.). Boston: Allyn & Bacon.

Bourassa, D. C., & Treiman, R. (2008). Morphological constancy in spelling: A comparison of children with dyslexia and typically developing children. *Dyslexia, 14*(3), 155–169.

Bowers, P. N., & Kirby, J. R. (2010). Effects of morphological instruction on vocabulary acquisition. *Reading and Writing: An Interdisciplinary Journal, 23*(5), 515–537.

Bowers, P. N., Kirby, J. R., & Deacon, S. H. (2010). The effects of morphological instruction on literacy skills: A systematic review of the literature. *Review of Educational Research, 80*(2), 144–179.

Carlisle, J. F. (1988). Knowledge of derivational morphology and spelling ability in fourth, sixth, and eighth graders. *Applied Psycholinguistics, 9*, 247–266.

Carlisle, J. F. (2010). Effects of instruction in morphological awareness on literacy achievement: An integrative review. *Reading Research Quarterly, 45*(4), 464–487.

Carlisle, J. F., & Fleming, J. (2003). Lexical processing of morphologically complex words in the elementary years. *Scientific Studies of Reading, 7*(3), 239–253.

Carlisle, J. F., & Katz, L. A. (2006). Effects of word and morpheme familiarity on reading of derived words. *Reading and Writing, 19*, 669–693.

Chomsky, C. (1970). Reading, writing, and phonology. *Harvard Educational Review, 40*, 287–309.

Corson, D. (1997). The learning and use of academic English words. *Language Learning, 47*, 671–718.

Crutchfield, R. *English vocabulary quick reference: A comprehensive dictionary arranged by word roots.* Leesburg, VA: LexaDyne.

Cummings, D. W. (1988). *American English spelling.* Baltimore: Johns Hopkins University Press.

Dale, E., O'Rourke, J., & Bamman, H. (1971). *Techniques of teaching vocabulary.* Palo Alto, CA: Field Educational Enterprises.

Derwing, B. L., Smith, M. L., & Wiebe, G. E. (1995). On the role of spelling in morpheme recognition: Experimental studies with children and adults. In L. B. Feldman (Ed.), *Morphological aspects of language processing* (pp. 3–27). Hillsdale, NJ: Erlbaum.

Ehri, L. C. (1997). Learning to read and learning to spell are one and the same, almost. In C. A. Perfetti, L. Rieben, & M. Fayol (Eds.), *Learning to spell: Research, theory, and practice across languages* (pp. 237–269). Mahwah, NJ: Erlbaum.

Elbro, C., & Arnbak, E. (1996). The role of morpheme recognition and morphological awareness in dyslexia. *Annals of Dyslexia, 46*(1), 209–240.

Flanigan, K., Hayes, L., Templeton, S., Bear, D. R., Invernizzi, M., & Johnston, F. (2011). *Words their way with struggling readers: Word study for reading, spelling, and vocabulary instruction, grades 4–12.* Boston: Pearson/Allyn & Bacon.

Fowler, A. E., & Liberman, I. Y. (1995). The role of phonology and orthography in morphological awareness. In L. B. Feldman (Ed.), *Morphological aspects of language processing* (pp. 157–188). Hillsdale, NJ: Erlbaum.

Fresch, M., & Wheaton, A. (2002). *Teaching and assessing spelling.* New York: Scholastic.

Ganske, K. (1999). The Developmental Spelling Analysis: A measure of orthographic knowledge. *Educational Assessment, 6*, 41–70.

Ganske, K. (2000). *Word journeys*. New York: Guilford Press.

Graves, M. F., & Watts-Taffe, S. M. (2003). The place of word consciousness in a research-based vocabulary program. In A. E. Farstrup & S. J. Samuels (Eds.), *What research has to say about reading instruction* (3rd ed., pp. 140–165). Newark, DE: International Reading Association.

Green, T. M. (2008). *The Greek and Latin roots of English* (4th ed.). Lanham, MD: Rowman & Littlefield

Henry, M. K. (1989). Children's word structure knowledge: Implications for decoding and spelling instruction. *Reading and Writing, 1*, 135–152.

Kiefer, M. J., & Lesaux, N. J. (2008). The role of derivational morphology in the reading comprehension of Spanish-speaking English language learners. *Reading and Writing, 21*, 783–804.

Larkin, R. F., & Snowling, M. J. (2008). Morphological spelling development. *Reading and Writing Quarterly, 24*(4), 363–376.

Larsen, J. A., & Nippold, M. A. (2007). Morphological analysis in school-age children: Dynamic assessment of a word learning strategy. *Language, Speech, and Hearing Services in Schools, 38*, 201–212.

Leong, C. K. (2000). Rapid processing of base and derived forms of words and grades 4, 5, and 6 children's spelling. *Reading and Writing: An Interdisciplinary Journal, 12*, 277–302.

Lewis, C. S. (1990). *Studies in words* (2nd ed.). London: Cambridge University Press.

Lubliner, S., & Scott, J. (2008). *Nourishing vocabulary: Balancing words and learning*. Thousand Oaks, CA: Corwin Press.

Mahony, D., Singson, M., & Mann, V. (2000). Reading ability and sensitivity to morphological relations. *Reading and Writing: An Interdisciplinary Journal, 12*, 191–218.

Masterson, J. J., Apel, K., & Wasowicz, J. (2002). *SPELLs: Spelling performance evaluation for language and literacy*. Evanston, IL: Learning by Design.

Morris, D., Blanton, L., Blanton, W. E., Nowacek, J., & Perney, J. (1995). Teaching low-achieving spellers at their "instructional level." *Elementary School Journal, 96*, 163–178.

Morris, D., Nelson, L., & Perney, J. (1986). Exploring the concept of "spelling instructional level" through the analysis of error-types. *Elementary School Journal, 87*, 181–200.

Nagy, W. (2007). Metalinguistic awareness and the vocabulary-comprehension connection. In R. K. Wagner, A. Muse, & K. Tannenbaum (Eds.), *Vocabulary acquisition: Implications for reading comprehension* (pp. 52–77). New York: Guilford Press.

Nagy, W., & Anderson, R. C. (1984). How many words are there in printed school English? *Reading Research Quarterly, 19*, 304–330.

Nagy, W., Berninger, V. W., & Abbott, R. D. (2006). Contributions of morphology beyond phonology to literacy outcomes of upper elementary and middle-school students. *Journal of Educational Psychology, 98*, 134–147.

Nagy, W., Berninger, V., Abbott, R., Vaughan, K, & Vermeulen, K. (2003). Relationship of morphology and other language skills to literacy skills in at-risk second-grade readers and at-risk fourth-grade writers. *Journal of Educational Psychology, 95*(4), 730–742.

Nunes, T., & Bryant, P. (2006). *Improving literacy by teaching morphemes.* London: Routledge.

Nunes, T., & Bryant, P. (2009). *Children's reading and spelling: Beyond the first steps.* Chichester, UK: Wiley-Blackwell.

Olson, D. (1994). *The world on paper: The conceptual and cognitive implications of writing and reading.* New York: Cambridge University Press.

Perfetti, C. A. (1997). The psycholinguistics of spelling and reading. In C. A. Perfetti, L. Rieben, & M. Fayol (Eds.), *Learning to spell: Research, theory, and practice across languages* (pp. 21–38). Mahwah, NJ: Erlbaum.

Perfetti, C. A. (2007). Reading ability: Lexical quality to comprehension. *Scientific Studies of Reading, 11,* 357–383.

Perfetti, C. A., Rieben, L., & Fayol, M. (Eds.). (1997). *Learning to spell: Research, theory, and practice across languages.* Mahwah, NJ: Erlbaum.

Seymour, P. H. K. (1997). Foundations of orthographic development. In C. A. Perfetti, L. Rieben, & M. Fayol (Eds.), *Learning to spell: Research, theory, and practice among languages* (pp. 319–337). Hillsdale, NJ: Erlbaum.

Smith, M. L. (1998). *Sense and sensitivity: An investigation into fifth-grade children's knowledge of English derivational morphology and its relationship to vocabulary and reading ability.* Unpublished doctoral dissertation, Harvard University, Cambridge, MA.

Spencer, A. (1991). *Morphological theory.* Oxford, UK: Blackwell.

Stahl, S. A., & Nagy, W. (2006). *Teaching word meanings.* Mahwah, NJ: Erlbaum.

Taft, M. (2003). Morphological representation as a correlation between form and meaning. In E. G. H. Assink & D. Sandra (Eds.), *Reading complex words: Cross language studies* (pp. 113–137). New York: Kluwer Academic.

Templeton, S. (1979). Spelling first, sound later: The relationship between orthography and higher order phonological knowledge in older students. *Research in the Teaching of English, 13,* 255–264.

Templeton, S. (1983). Using the spelling/meaning connection to develop word knowledge in older students. *Journal of Reading, 27,* 8–14.

Templeton, S. (1989). Tacit and explicit knowledge of derivational morphology: Foundations for a unified approach to spelling and vocabulary development in the intermediate grades and beyond. *Reading Psychology, 10,* 233–253.

Templeton, S. (1991). Teaching and learning the English spelling system: Reconceptualizing method and purpose. *Elementary School Journal, 92,* 183–199.

Templeton, S. (1992). Theory, nature, and pedagogy of higher-order orthographic development in older students. In S. Templeton & D. R. Bear (Eds.), *Development of orthographic knowledge and the foundations of literacy: A memorial Festschrift for Edmund H. Henderson.* Hillsdale, NJ: Erlbaum.

Templeton, S. (2002). Effective spelling instruction in the middle grades: It's a lot more than memorization. *Voices from the Middle, 9,* 8–14.

Templeton, S. (2003). Spelling. In J. Flood, D. Lapp, J. R. Squire, & J. M. Jensen (Eds.), *Handbook of research on teaching the English language arts* (2nd ed., pp. 738–751). Mahwah, NJ: Erlbaum.

Templeton, S. (2004). The vocabulary–spelling connection: Orthographic development and morphological knowledge at the intermediate grades and beyond.

In J. F. Baumann & E. J. Kame'enui (Eds.), *Vocabulary instruction: Research to Practice* (pp. 118–138). New York: Guilford Press.

Templeton, S. (2010). Spelling-meaning relationships among languages: Exploring cognates and their possibilities. In L. Helman (Ed.), *Literacy development with English learners: Research-based instruction in grades K–6* (pp. 196–212). New York: Guilford Press.

Templeton, S. (2011). Teaching spelling in the English/language arts classroom. In D. Lapp & D. Fisher (Eds.), *The handbook of research on teaching the English language arts* (3rd ed., pp. 247–251). New York: Routledge.

Templeton, S., & Bear, D. R. (Eds.). (1992). *Development of orthographic knowledge and the foundations of literacy: A memorial Festschrift for Edmund H. Henderson.* Hillsdale, NJ: Erlbaum.

Templeton, S., & Bear, D. R. (2011). Phonemic awareness, word recognition, and spelling. In T. Rasinski (Ed.), *Developing reading instruction that works* (pp. 153–178). Bloomington, IN: Solution Tree Press.

Templeton, S., Bear, D. R., Invernizzi, M., & Johnston, F. (2010). *Vocabulary their way: Word study with middle and secondary students.* Boston: Pearson/Allyn & Bacon.

Templeton, S., Johnston, F., Bear, D., & Invernizzi, M. (2009). *Words their way: Word sorts for derivational relations spellers* (2nd ed.). Boston: Pearson/Allyn & Bacon.

Templeton, S., & Morris, D. (2000). Spelling. In M. Kamil, P. Mosenthal, P. D. Pearson, & R. Barr (Eds.), *Handbook of reading research* (Volume 3, pp. 525–543). Mahwah, NJ: Erlbaum.

Templeton, S., & Scarborough-Franks, L. (1985). The spelling's the thing: Older students' knowledge of derivational morphology in phonology and orthography. *Applied Psycholinguistics, 6,* 371–389.

Templeton, S., Smith, D. L., Moloney, K., VanPelt, J., & Ives, B. (2009, December). *Generative vocabulary knowledge: Learning and teaching higher-order morphological aspects of word structure.* Symposium presented at the annual conference of the National Reading Conference, Albuquerque, NM.

Townsend, D., Bear, D. R., & Templeton, S. (2009, December). *The role of orthography in academic word knowledge and measures of academic achievement for middle school students.* Paper presented at the annual meeting of the National Reading Conference, Albuquerque, NM.

Townsend, D., Bear, D. R., & Templeton, S. (2010). Academic Vocabulary Spelling Inventory. In S. Templeton, F. Johnston, D. Bear, & M. Invernizzi *Vocabulary their way: Word study for middle and secondary students* (p. 171). Boston: Pearson/Allyn & Bacon.

Townsend, D., Burton, Bear, D. R., & Templeton, S. (2010, May). *The role of morphological awareness of academic words for academic achievement.* Paper presented at the annual meeting of the American Educational Research Association, Denver, CO.

Venezky, R. L. (1999). *The American way of spelling: The structure and origins of American English orthography.* New York: Guilford Press.

Whitaker, S. R. (2008). *Word play: Building vocabulary across texts and disciplines, grades 6–12.* Portsmouth, NH: Heinemann.

Chapter 8

Teaching Word-Learning Strategies

James F. Baumann
Elizabeth Carr Edwards
Eileen Boland
George Font

One important component of vocabulary teaching and learning is word-learning strategies, which involve instruction in using the linguistic textual clues (contextual analysis) to infer the meanings of unfamiliar words and instruction in using word-part clues (morphemic analysis). Although it is important for primary grade teachers to provide basic instruction in word-learning strategies, in this revised chapter we focus on the content and nature of instruction appropriate for students in grades 4–6.

We begin by situating word-learning strategies instruction within the broader realm of vocabulary teaching and learning. Next, we discuss why instruction on contextual analysis and morphemic analysis is important for developing readers, followed by an explication of the content of word-learning strategy instruction. We conclude by presenting a sample lesson in contextual and morphemic analysis.

PUTTING CONTEXTUAL ANALYSIS AND MORPHEMIC ANALYSIS IN THEIR PLACE

Complexity of Vocabulary Learning

Vocabulary development is a lifelong endeavor (Nagy, 2005), and there are multiple aspects to word knowledge. Nagy and Scott (2000) argued that vocabulary acquisition is challenging because of the complexity of word knowledge, which they stated involved five dimensions: (1) *incrementality:* learning a word's meaning occurs in bits and pieces over time; (2) *multidimensionality:* there are different types of knowledge one must acquire to truly know a word; (3) *polysemy:* most words have more than one meaning; (4) *interrelatedness:* knowing the meaning of a word is typically related to knowledge of other words; and (5) *heterogeneity:* words vary in type or form class (i.e., speech parts) and thus convey different types of information. Given this complexity, students and teachers face a challenging task when it comes to acquiring and teaching word meanings at a deep, complex level.

Vocabulary Processes and Models

Another way to think about the teaching and learning of vocabulary is with regard to the processes and modes involved. Vocabulary processes include *receptive vocabulary* (comprehending words heard and read) as well as *expressive vocabulary* (producing words in speech and writing). Likewise, we can consider two vocabulary modes: *written vocabulary* (words read or written down) and *oral vocabulary* (words heard or spoken). Crossing these processes and modes results in reading vocabulary, writing vocabulary, speaking vocabulary, and listening vocabulary (see Figure 8.1).

Typically, these vocabularies develop at different times and rates (Chall, Jacobs, & Baldwin, 1990; White, Graves, & Slater, 1990). For example, an average preschool child may have a rather extensive speaking and listening vocabulary in his or her home language when compared to the child's typically more limited reading and writing vocabulary. On the other hand, the gap between the four vocabularies narrows in an average literate adult (Kamil & Hiebert, 2005), although it is likely that the adult's receptive vocabulary exceeds his or her expressive vocabulary, and one

		Vocabulary Processes	
		Receptive (comprehension)	Expressive (production)
Vocabulary Modes	Written	READING VOCABULARY	WRITING VOCABULARY
	Oral	LISTENING VOCABULARY	SPEAKING VOCABULARY

FIGURE 8.1. Four types of vocabulary.

might surmise that native-language vocabulary size for many adults would be ordered from largest to smallest as follows: listening vocabulary > reading vocabulary > speaking vocabulary > writing vocabulary.

In this chapter, we focus on *reading vocabulary*—understanding the meanings of words in printed and electronic texts—but we acknowledge that knowing the meaning of a word that is read is not isolated from the other three vocabularies. Furthermore, instruction in reading vocabulary is likely to enhance development of speaking, listening, and writing vocabularies, and reading vocabulary instruction typically does—or at least ought to—include speaking, listening, and writing (Beck, McKeown, & Kucan, 2008)

Comprehensive Vocabulary Instruction

There are several theoretical perspectives (e.g., Anderson & Nagy, 1991; Beck & McKeown, 1991; Stahl & Fairbanks, 1986; Nagy & Scott, 2000) and considerable research on instructional approaches (e.g., Baumann, Kame'enui, & Ash, 2003; Blachowicz & Fisher, 2000; Farstrup & Samuels, 2008). Additionally, there is no shortage of resources for vocabulary instructional techniques and strategies for teachers that build on this theoretical and empirical base (e.g., Beck et al., 2002; Blachowicz & Fisher, 2010; Block & Mangieri, 2006; Graves, 2006; Hall, Burns, & Edwards, 2011; Hiebert & Kamil, 2005; Stahl & Nagy, 2006).

The instructional perspective that has guided our own vocabulary research (Baumann et al., 2011; Baumann, Font, Edwards, & Boland, 2005; Baumann, Ware, & Edwards, 2007) is the four-part structure provided by Michael Graves (2000, 2006). Graves (2006) argued that effective vocabulary instruction should include "(1) providing rich and varied language experiences; (2) teaching individual words; (3) teaching word-learning strategies; and (4) fostering word consciousness" (p. 5). Research indicates that each component contributes to children's and adolescents' vocabulary growth. We have adopted and operationalized Graves's (2006) framework in our own research and writing as follows:

1. *Provide rich and varied language experiences.* We know that students learn words incidentally by reading independently (Cunningham, 2005; Cunningham & O'Donnell, Chapter 13, this volume; Swanborn & de Glopper, 1999), by listening to texts read aloud (Albright & Ariail, 2005; Elley, 1989), and through exposure to enriched oral language (Dickinson, Cote, & Smith, 1993). In this component, teachers structure the classroom literacy environment such that students acquire words from context by engaging in considerable independent reading, listening to materials read aloud, exploring word meanings in written compositions, and engaging in

peer conversations about words in order to co-construct vocabulary knowledge (Stahl & Nagy, 2006).

2. *Teach individual words.* Words that teachers identify in texts as being difficult and essential for reading comprehension should be taught directly to students. Specific words can be taught directly through a variety of instructional strategies (Beck & McKeown, 1991; Beck et al., 2002; Blachowicz & Fisher, 2010; Graves, 2009; Jitendra, Edwards, Sacks, & Jacobson, 2004). We know further that teaching the meanings of specific words is particularly effective when both definitions and context are provided (Stahl & Fairbanks, 1986) and when instruction involves deep processing and multiple encounters with instructed words (Beck, McKeown, & Omanson, 1987; Mezynski, 1983; Nagy & Scott, 2000). In this component, teachers provide instruction in (a) specific, high-utility, grade-level words (Graves, 2009); and (b) words that are central to understanding narrative and subject-matter texts (see Hiebert & Cervetti, Chapter 16, this volume).

3. *Teach word-learning strategies.* A number of studies have demonstrated that when students are taught the meanings of prefixes, suffixes, and word roots, and a strategy for how to use word-part knowledge when encountering unfamiliar words, they acquire the ability to infer word meanings from morphemic clues (Baumann et al., 2011; Baumann, Edwards, Boland, Olejnik, & Kame'enui, 2003; Baumann, Edwards, Font, Tereshinski, Kame'enui, & Olejnik, 2002; White, Sowell, & Yanagihara, 1989). Moreover, additional work indicates positive effects of teaching students to recognize and use context clues (Baumann et al., 2002, 2007; Baumann, Edwards, et al., 2003; Blachowicz & Zabroske, 1990; Buikema & Graves, 1993; Fukkink & de Glopper, 1998). In this component, teachers provide instruction in how to identify and use linguistic context clues to infer word meanings by teaching students how to identify and use (a) high-frequency prefixes, suffixes, and Latin and Greek word roots (morphemic analysis); and (b) different types of linguistic context clues to infer word meanings (contextual analysis).

4. *Foster word consciousness.* Word consciousness includes "various aspects of words—their meanings, their histories, relationships with other words, word parts, and most importantly, the way writers use words effectively to communicate" (Nagy, 2005, p. 30). Students develop word consciousness by engaging in playful language activities and by developing word awareness or metacognitive knowledge (Beck et al., 1987; Graves & Watts-Taffe, 2002; Scott & Nagy 2004). This component includes techniques and activities to (a) pique students' interest in words and the nuanced ways literate individuals use them; (b) develop an awareness of words in oral and written texts in school and out-of-school experiences; (c) engage

in word and language play activities to experience the joy in using the just-right word in oral and written compositions; and (d) motivate students to become self-aware of interesting, colorful words.

We have used this four-component approach successfully in a yearlong study that was conducted in a single classroom (Baumann et al., 2007), and we are currently employing this framework in a 3-year, federally funded research study, which we refer to as the multifaceted, comprehensive, vocabulary instructional program (MCVIP; Baumann, Blachowicz, Manyak, Grave, & Olejnik, 2009; Baumann et al., 2011). Although word-learning strategies are an integral part of the MCVIP, it is important that we put them in their place. In other words, teaching students about morphemic analysis and contextual analysis and how to use them is just *one* aspect of a balanced vocabulary instruction program. We refer readers to other chapters in this volume for further explication of the other three components of Graves's (2006) approach.

WHY TEACH CONTEXTUAL ANALYSIS AND MORPHEMIC ANALYSIS

Definitions

In applying *contextual analysis*, the reader infers the meaning of a word by scrutinizing surrounding text for syntactic and semantic cues provided by preceding and succeeding words, phrases, and sentences. Instruction in contextual analysis, as we have implemented it, involves (1) teaching students that writers provide readers different types of clues to the meaning of a low-frequency or "hard" word (e.g., Synonym context clues); (2) providing examples and modeling the use of context clue types (e.g., the synonym clue for *intrepid* in *The **intrepid** firefighter went into the burning building to find the little boy. She later was given an award for how **brave** she was at the burning house.*); and (3) providing guided and independent practice in the use of a context clue type in short texts written to include rich context clues and in natural, extended texts with context clues of varying intensities. In short, contextual analysis involves using the between-word, or *interword*, linguistic information with which to infer a word's meaning.

Morphemic analysis, which is also referred to as *structural analysis*, involves deriving the meaning of a word by examining its meaningful parts (morphemes), such as root words (or base words), prefixes and suffixes (collectively, affixes), inflected endings, and Latin and Greek word derivatives (word roots). Instruction in morphemic analysis, as we conceptualize it, involves teaching students to (1) disassemble words into roots and affixes (*indecipherable* = *in-* + *decipher* + *-able*); (2) acquire the meanings of roots and affixes (*in-* = not; *decipher* = to decode or understand; *-able* = able to do so); and (3) reassemble the meaningful parts to derive word meanings (*indecipherable* means to not be able to decode or understand something). In short, morphemic analysis involves the use of within-word, or *intra-word*, linguistic information to derive a word's meaning.

Rationale for Instruction in Contextual Analysis and Morphemic Analysis

Based on an analysis of vocabulary in materials students encounter in school, Nagy and Anderson (1984) asserted that "for every word a child learns, we estimate that there are an average of one to three additional related words that should also be understandable to the child" (p. 304). They qualified this estimate, however, by stating that this kind of vocabulary growth depends upon "how well the child is able to utilize context and morphology to induce meanings" (p. 304). In other words, students skilled in contextual and morphemic analysis have the potential to increase their vocabulary breadth and depth substantially.

Given the logic for teaching students to use context and morphology, curriculum developers include lessons on contextual and morphemic analysis in reading and language arts programs (e.g., Afflerbach et al., 2011). Additionally, curriculum standards, particularly the Common Core State Standards for English Language Arts (CCSS-ELA, 2010), include many standards that recommend instruction in contextual and morphemic analysis within a K–12 language arts program. The CCS-ELA are especially significant in that, as of this writing, all but 5 of the 50 U.S. states have adopted them.

Research on Teaching Contextual Analysis and Morphemic Analysis

Contextual Analysis

There is considerable research supporting instruction in context clues as a means to promote students' independent vocabulary learning (Buikema & Graves, 1993; Carnine, Kame'enui, & Coyle, 1984; Jenkins, Matlock, & Slocum, 1989; Patberg, Graves, & Stibbe, 1984; Sternberg, 1987). Although several researchers and writers (e.g., Schatz & Baldwin, 1986; Beck et al., 2002; Kuhn & Stahl, 1998) have cautioned educators about the reliability of context clues and the efficiency of instruction in them, a meta-analysis by Fukkink and de Glopper (1998) of 21 intervention studies revealed a moderate effect size (mean d = 0.43) for teaching students to use context clues.

Morphemic Analysis

Likewise, there is considerable research that suggests that students can be taught various morphemic elements as a means to derive the meanings of novel words (Graves & Hammond, 1980; Kirk & Gillon, 2009; Parel, 2006; White, Sowell, & Yanagihara, 1989; Wysocki & Jenkins, 1987). Additionally, two recent research syntheses or meta-analyses have documented the positive impact of teaching students morphological analysis as a means to learn the meanings of new words (Carlisle, 2010; Reed, 2008). There is also evidence suggesting that instruction in morphemic analysis may be especially appropriate for students in grade 4 and above (Nagy, Diakidoy, & Anderson, 1993; White, Power, & White, 1989).Thus, there is ample evidence for teaching morphological analysis to enhance vocabulary development.

Combined Instruction in Contextual Analysis and Morphemic Analysis

Dale and O'Rourke (1986) argued that "students need to make use of context clues in relation to other methods of vocabulary study [that include] the process of word formation by means of roots, prefixes, suffixes, and compounds" (p. 72). Several studies have combined instruction in context clues and morphology and reported positive results on vocabulary learning. For example, Tomesen and Aarnoutse (1998) reported that fourth-grade Dutch students who were taught contextual and morphemic analysis were able to derive the meanings of unfamiliar words. Investigations by Block and Mangieri (2006) and Lubliner and Smetana (2005) have explored the combination of instruction in both contextual and morphemic analysis in English language contexts.

We addressed combined instruction in contextual and morphemic analysis in three studies with grade 5 students in diverse U.S. public elementary school classrooms. In our first quasi-experiment (Baumann et al., 2002), we found that students who received instruction in contextual and morphemic analysis—either individually or in combination—outperformed instructed controls on a series of measures of the ability to infer word meanings from morphemic or contextual information. In a follow-up quasi-experiment (Baumann et al., 2003), we found that students who received instruction in contextual and morphemic analysis embedded within social studies lessons outperformed students who received explicit instruction on specific words on measures of contextual and morphemic analysis. In a yearlong formative experiment (Baumann et al., 2007), we employed Graves's (2006) four-part framework that included instruction in word-learning strategies. Results demonstrated significant growth from the beginning to the end of the year on multiple measures of vocabulary knowledge.

Research with English Learners

Several recent studies have documented that students for whom English is not their primary language can benefit from instruction in word-learning strategies (e.g., Carlo et al., 2004; Lesaux, Kieffer, Faller, & Kelley, 2010). For example, Carlo et al. (2004) provided multifaceted vocabulary instruction that included teaching use of context and morphology to fifth-grade students working on a social studies unit. Results on tests of target vocabulary revealed that English learners in the intervention classrooms outperformed English learners in comparable classrooms who received the standard curriculum.

In summary, a theoretical rationale and empirical base exist for teaching contextual and morphemic analysis. We now turn to the content of and instruction in contextual and morphemic.

THE CONTENT OF CONTEXTUAL ANALYSIS
AND MORPHEMIC ANALYSIS INSTRUCTION

Contextual Analysis

Context clues in print or electronic texts may involve graphic (e.g., tables, maps), pictorial (e.g., photos, illustrations), or typographic (e.g., bold, italic) information, and it is important to provide instruction in the use of these cues to students. We focus here, however, on *linguistic* context clues: syntactic and semantic clues. *Syntactic clues* involve using word order, which is potentially powerful because English relies heavily on word order to convey meaning, and the position of words in a sentence affects meaning. For example, *Alex hit the ball* has a meaning different from *The ball hit Alex*.

Semantic clues involve the use of meaning-based information in a text that enables a reader to infer the sense of a word or at least limit alternate meanings (Johnson & Pearson, 1978). For example, whereas *Alicia ate the tangerine* is a semantically acceptable sentence, *Alica ate the Golden Gate Bridge* is not. Both sentences are syntactically correct (i.e., subject–verb–object structure), but only the former is semantically acceptable.

Although we are not aware of any empirically based typology for context clues, there exist many descriptions and syntheses of them (e.g., Dale & O'Rourke, 1986; Drum & Konopak, 1987; Johnson & Pearson, 1978; Sternberg & Powell, 1983; Suttles & Baumann, 1991). We have synthesized these extant context clue typologies into a short list that we have used in our own research (Baumann et al., 2002, 2007; Baumann, Edwards, et al., 2003), which has demonstrated success in sensitizing students to the presence, importance, and utility of context for inferring the meaning of an unknown word. Drawing from extant typologies and our own work, we recommend teaching the five context clue types shown in Table 8.1.

TABLE 8.1. Types of Context Clues

Context clue type	Example
1. **Definition:** The author explains the meaning of the word right in the sentence or selection.	When Sara was hiking, she accidentally walked through a patch of **brambles,** *prickly vines and shrubs,* which resulted in many scratches to her legs.
2. **Synonym:** The author uses a word similar in meaning.	Josh waked into the living room and accidentally tripped over the **ottoman.** He then mumbled, "I wish people would not leave the *footstool* right in the middle of the room. That's dangerous!"
3. **Antonym:** The author uses a word nearly opposite in meaning.	The supermarket manager complained, "Why do we have such a **plethora** of boxes of cereal on the shelves? In contrast, we have a real *shortage* of pancake and waffle mix. We've got to do a better job ordering."
4. **Example:** The author provides one or more example words or ideas.	There are many members of the **canine** family. For example, *wolves, foxes, coyotes,* and pets such as *collies, beagles,* and *golden retrievers* are all canines.
5. **General:** The author provides several words or statements that give clues to the word's meaning.	It was a **sultry** day. The day was very *hot and humid.* If you moved at all, you would *break out in a sweat.* It was one of those days to *drink water* and *stay in the shade.*

Note. Words in *italic* provide context clues for **bold** words. From Baumann, Font, Edwards, and Boland (2005). Copyright 2005 by Taylor & Francis Group LLC-Books. Reprinted by permission.

It is important to point out that the objective of context clue instruction is to teach students to be aware of and to *use* syntactic and semantic clues to assign a logical meaning to an unknown or partially known word, rather than being able to *label* the specific context clue type that was present in the text. In other words, our ultimate goal is to have students rely on available syntactic and semantic information to assign a logical meaning to an unknown or unfamiliar word encountered in text rather than necessarily being able to assign a type to the context clue.

Morphemic Analysis

The key instructional elements of morphemic analysis are roots and affixes. A *root* is "the basic part of a word that usually carries the main component of meaning and that cannot be further analyzed without loss of identity" (Harris & Hodges, 1995, p. 222). When roots stand alone as words, they are referred to as *free morphemes* or simply *root words* (e.g., *car, run, blue*).

When roots are meaningful parts of words that cannot stand alone, they are referred to as *bound morphemes* or simply *word roots* and often take the form of Latin or Greek roots (e.g., *scribe*, as in *transcribe* and *inscribe*).

An *affix* is "a bound (nonword) morpheme that changes the meaning or function of a root or stem to which it is attached" (Harris & Hodges, 1995, p. 5). Affixes that come before a root are called *prefixes* and alter meaning (*un*happy, *over*heat). Affixes that follow roots are called *suffixes* and come in two varieties: (1) *Inflectional suffixes*, or simply *inflections*, change the meaning of a word slightly but not its part of speech; these include verb forms (jump, jump*ed*, jump*ing*), noun plurals (cow, cow*s*), and adjectival comparatives and superlatives (bright, bright*er*, bright*est*). (2) *Derivational suffixes* are like prefixes in that they alter a word's meaning slightly (e.g., kind*ness*, the quality of being kind; power*less*, the lack of power).

Like many researchers and writers, we recommend teaching both common affixes and roots (Irwin & Baker, 1989; Johnson & Pearson, 1978; Templeton, Bear, Invernizzi, & Johnston, 2010; White, Sowell, & Yanagihara, 1989). Regarding affixes, Graves and Hammond (1980) argued that prefixes are worth teaching because they are relatively few in number and most have consistent meanings and spellings. White, Sowell, and Yanagihara (1989) reported that 20 prefixes accounted for 97% of prefixed words that appear in school reading materials (Carroll, Davies, & Richman, 1971), and four (*un-, re-, in-, dis-*) accounted for 58% of all prefixes. We believe that it is sensible to teach the most commonly occurring prefixes—those at the highest frequency—and select others at moderate levels of frequency.

We also recommend that teachers spend time teaching derivational suffixes because, like prefixes, they are fairly regular in meaning and can lead to useful word building and vocabulary expansion. Because inflectional suffixes do not alter a word's root meaning (e.g., the meaning of the root word *jump* in *jumps, jumped*, and *jumping* is basically unchanged) and because they have been addressed intensively in virtually all primary grade curricula, they are not as helpful in deriving word meanings, so we recommend less instructional emphasis on them.

Students at the middle grades will also benefit from instruction in the meanings of commonly occurring Greek and Latin word roots (Templeton, personal communication, February 29, 2008). These are useful in general vocabulary acquisition but especially because they tend to occur often in words in subject-matter areas such as science, mathematics, and social studies. There are many lists of roots and affixes that are suggested for instruction. Our recommended list draws from these lists but includes frequency as a primary criterion for selection of affixes and roots. Our recommended list of morphemic elements is presented in Table 8.2, and comes from two sources (Baumann et al., 2005, for the affixes, and Templeton, personal communication, February 28, 2008, for the word roots).

TABLE 8.2. Word-Part Families

Family	Prefix or suffix	Meaning	Sample words
"Not" prefix family	*dis-*	not, opposite	*dislike, disloyal, disentangle, disparity, disrepute*
	un-	not, opposite	*unafraid, unhappy, undefeated, unsympathetic*
	in-	not, opposite	*invisible, incurable, inappropriate, inedible, infallible*
	im-	not, opposite	*imperfect, impolite, imprecise, immobile, immortal*
	il-	not, opposite	*illogical, illegal, illiterate, illegible, illimitable*
	ir-	not, opposite	*irresponsible, irreplaceable, irresistible, irrelevant*
	non-	not, opposite	*nonfiction, nonstop, nonliving, nonviolent, nonverbal*
"Position" prefix family	*pre-*	before	*preview, predawn, prehistoric, prepublication*
	fore-	before	*forewarn, foreleg, forenoon, forethought, foreshadow*
	mid-	middle	*midnight, midair, midland, midlife, midterm*
	inter-	between, among	*intercity, intermix, interaction, international, intergalactic*
	post-	after	*postwar, posttest, postdate, postoperative*
"Over/under" prefix family	*super-*	over, high, big, extreme	*superheat, superhuman, superdeluxe, supercompetitive*
	over-	more than, too much	*oversleep, overload, overheat, overqualified, overexert*
	sub-	under, below	*subset, substation, subcontinent, subtropical*
"Together" prefix family	*com-*	together, with	*compress, composition, compatriot, compassion*
	con-	together	*conform, concentric, conjoin, configure*
	co-	together, with	*coauthor, cosign, coequal, cooperate*

(cont.)

TABLE 8.2. *(cont.)*

Family	Prefix or suffix	Meaning	Sample words
"Bad" prefix family	*mis-*	bad, wrong, not	*misuse, misread, misunderstand, mismanage, misquote*
	mal-	bad, ill	*maltreat, malodor, malnourished, maladjusted*
"Against" prefix family	*anti-*	against	*antifreeze, antibiotic, antisocial, antipollution*
	contra-	against, opposite	*contraband, contradict, contraindicate, contravene*
"Number" prefix family	*uni-*	one	*unicycle, unicorn, unidirectional, unicellular*
	mono-	one	*monorail, monosyllable, monogram, monotone, monocle*
	bi-	two	*bicycle, biweekly, bicolor, biplane, binomial*
	tri-	three	*triangle, tricycle, tricolor, triathlon, tripod*
	quad-	four	*quadrilateral, quadruplets, quadrennial, quadrangle*
	penta-	five	*pentagon, pentameter, pentagram, pentathalon*
	dec-	ten	*decagon, decade, decapod, decibel*
	cent-	hundred	*centimeter, centipede, centennial, centigram*
	semi-	half, part	*semicircle, semiyearly, semiprivate, semiretired*
Other useful prefixes	*re-*	again, back	*redo, reorder, rearrange, reposition, reconnect*
	trans-	across, through	*transport, transatlantic, transmit, transfusion*
	de-	take away	*defrost, deforest, deodorize, deflate, deactivate*
	ex-	out of, away from	*export, exhale, extinguish, exclude, excise*
	under-	low, too little	*underweight, underachieve, underestimate, underappreciated*

(cont.)

TABLE 8.2. *(cont.)*

Family	Prefix or suffix	Meaning	Sample words
"Person" suffix family	*-ee*	person who	*employee, referee, trainee, interviewee*
	-er	person/thing that does something	*writer, teacher, composer, reporter, consumer*
	-or	person/thing that does something	*actor, governor, dictator, juror, donor*
Other useful suffixes	*-ful*	full of, characterized by	*joyful, beautiful, successful, delightful, pitiful*
	-able, -ible	can be, worthy of, inclined to	*valuable, comfortable, dependable, impressionable, terrible, responsible, reversible, compatible*
	-less	without, free of	*helpless, hopeless, bottomless, expressionless*
Commonly occurring Latin and Greek roots	*aud*	to hear	*audiology, auditorium, audio, audition*
	bio	life	*biology, biometrics, biome, biosphere*
	dic, dict	to speak or say	*dictation, dictionary, dictate, dictator, Dictaphone, edict, predict, verdict, contradict, benediction*
	fract	to break	*fracture, infraction, fragile, fraction, refract*
	geo	earth	*geometry, geography, geocentric, geology*
	graph, gram	to write or draw	*graph, graphic, autograph, photography, graphite, telegram*
	micro	small	*microscope, microfilm, microcard, microwave, micrometer*
	phon	sound	*phonograph, phonetic, symphony, homophone*
	photo	light	*photograph, photoelectric, photogenic, photosynthesis*
	port	to carry	*porter, portable, transport, report, export, import, support, transportation*
	rupt	to break	*rupture, interrupt, abrupt, disrupt, reputable*

(cont.)

TABLE 8.2. *(cont.)*

Family	Prefix or suffix	Meaning	Sample words
Commonly occurring Latin and Greek roots *(cont.)*	*scop*	to see or watch	*telescope, microscope, kaleidoscope, periscope, stethoscope*
	spec, spect	to look at	*specimen, specific, spectator, spectacle, aspect, speculate, inspect, respect, retrospective, introspective*
	struct	to build	*construe* (build in the mind, interpret), *structure, construct, instruct, obstruct, destruction, destroy*
	tele	far	*telephone, telegraph, telegram, telescope, television, telephoto, telecast, telepathy*
	tract	to pull or draw	*tractor, attract, traction, subtract, tractable, abstract*
	vis, vid	to see or look	*video, evident, provide, providence, visible, revise, supervise, vista, visit, vision*

Note. Prefix and suffix entries from Baumann, Font, Edwards, and Boland (2005). Copyright 2005 by Taylor & Francis Group LLC-Books. Reprinted by permission. Latin and Greek roots from Shane Templeton (personal communication, February 29, 2008).

Cognates

For children whose first language is not English, another aspect of morphemic analysis may involve *cognates*, which are "words descended from a common ancestor; that is, words having the same linguistic family or derivation" (Molina, 2011, Preface). For example, the English word *activate* has cognates in Spanish (*activar*), Portuguese (*ativar*), Italian (*attivare*), and French (*activer*) (*www.cognates.org*). A speaker of one of these languages is likely to recognize the cognate in another language due to its similar pronunciation and spelling, with the speaker then logically assigning the meaning in her or his first language to the cognate in the other language.

The most helpful use of cognates is with English learners who speak or read Spanish to some degree. It is especially useful for Spanish speakers to learn the corresponding English words for Spanish cognates, given how common it is for Spanish-speaking students to be enrolled in U.S. English-only classrooms, and given that there are many close Spanish–English cognates that often have similar spellings and pronunciations (e.g., *artist/ artista, simplify/simplificar*) (*www.cognates.org*).

Morphemes in "Families"

To help students acquire meanings, we have grouped most morphemic elements in Table 8.2 into "Families" whose members contain semantic likenesses. The table contains 41 affixes and 17 word roots, totaling 58 items. This is an ambitious curriculum, but our experience tells us that when students begin to understand the meaning of one or two elements in a family, it helps them generalize meanings to other family members. Much like a reading teacher not needing to teach every consonant cluster (e.g., *st, bl, spr*) separately because the students begin to generalize across clusters, students typically make generalization with regard to morphemic elements.

SAMPLE LESSON FOR TEACHING CONTEXTUAL ANALYSIS AND MORPHEMIC ANALYSIS

Following is the introductory lesson to word-learning strategies that we have used in one of our recent studies (Baumann et al., 2011). It provides students with an overview of contextual and morphemic analysis and explains how the strategies can work in tandem to help them infer the meanings of previously unknown words. It should be noted that this lesson provides just an overview and that there is a series of lessons that follow on specific types of context clues and the various morphemic families. Understanding and using contextual and morphemic analysis effectively to learn the meanings of new words takes considerable intensive instruction, review, and practice.

Given that we had quite a few English learners with Spanish as their first language in our study, we included information on cognates, when appropriate, in our lessons. If you have no or few Spanish–English learners in your classroom, or English learners whose home languages do not have many English cognates, then we suggest omitting that portion of the lesson.

Finally, although the lesson presented here contains directions to the teacher and some possible teacher wording, our lessons were not scripted in the sense that our teacher-participants were expected to read aloud instructional texts verbatim. Rather, the instructional text was provided to help teachers prepare for the lesson and to refer to it as needed as they taught the lesson. Teachers were encouraged to use their own wording and to modify the instructional text as needed to clarify information for students, to rephrase or provide the information in another way if necessary, or to embellish on the instructional text.

In the following example, we use Roman (standard) font to denote the instructional text that accompanied the lessons. These statements are in the second person, as we were speaking directly to the teachers. *Italic text* denotes possible teacher wording for modeling aspects of contextual and structural analysis for students. Again, this text is to exemplify what a teacher might say in his or her own words when thinking aloud for students; it is not a teacher script.

Slide 1: Use the Vocabulary Rule

- This is just a title slide. Tell your students that today they will begin learning about strategies that they can use to help them figure out the meanings of many unknown words they encounter when they are reading or when they are listening to someone speak.

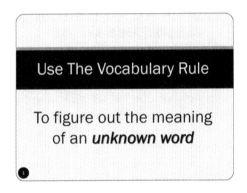

Slide 2: The Vocabulary Rule–1

- Present the vocabulary rule (VR) slide, which shows the short form of the VR. The VR is also duplicated on a classroom wall chart and may be displayed either today or in a later lesson, so that you can refer students to it conveniently. Use this slide to give the students an overview of the four-part strategy or rule. You can read the text or invite selected students to read portions of it.

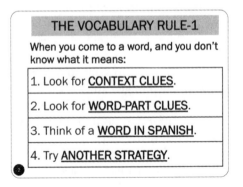

Slide 3: The Vocabulary Rule–2

- Explain that this slide gives details of the VR. You can read the steps or invite students to read each step. Be sure to clarify, rephrase, or respond to questions as needed about any of the steps. This slide is also provided to you as a wall chart.

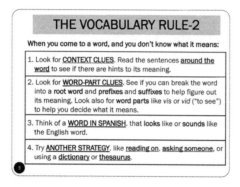

Slide 4: The Vocabulary Rule: Try It Out!–1

- Tell the students that you will now demonstrate how the VR works, step by step, and that this slide begins with Step 1. Read Step 1 and think aloud in a manner such as the following:

  It says to read the sentences around the word to see if there are hints. This means that I should probably read the whole paragraph.

- Read aloud the first sentence of paragraph, after which you might say:

  *Here is the hard word, which I think is pronounced **in-ter-con-tin-en-tal**. The sentence says that Mr. Alexander is leaving on an **intercontinental** airplane at 6:00 in the evening. I suppose that an **intercontinental** airplane must be some special kind of airplane. Maybe it's one that flies really fast or is really large. What do you think?*

- Allow a few students to offer their initial thoughts and then read the rest of the sentences, thinking aloud as you proceed. For example, you might read the next two sentences and say:

  It says that Mr. Alexander fell asleep and when he woke up he was landing in London, England. I know that England is across the Atlantic Ocean, so this must have been a pretty long flight! Do you agree?

- Allow a few quick student responses, but keep the pace of the lesson moving! Then read to the end of the paragraph, after which you might say:

  Here is says that London is in Europe, which is a continent across the Atlantic Ocean, and the author reminds us that New York is in the continent of North

America. So, an intercontinental airplane still could be large or fast, but it might have something to do with flying across the Atlantic Ocean between two continents. What are you thinking?

- Ask pairs of students to discuss their ideas briefly and provide responses to the class.

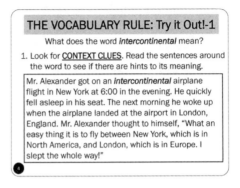

THE VOCABULARY RULE: Try it Out!-1

What does the word *intercontinental* mean?

1. Look for <u>CONTEXT CLUES</u>. Read the sentences around the word to see if there are hints to its meaning.

Mr. Alexander got on an *intercontinental* airplane flight in New York at 6:00 in the evening. He quickly fell asleep in his seat. The next morning he woke up when the airplane landed at the airport in London, England. Mr. Alexander thought to himself, "What an easy thing it is to fly between New York, which is in North America, and London, which is in Europe. I slept the whole way!"

Slide 5: The Vocabulary Rule: Try It Out!–2

- Continue to think aloud as you explain how context clues help a reader make a logical prediction about what **intercontinental** means. Do this by rereading the paragraph and commenting how the underlined words when put together give you a good idea of what **intercontinental** means. If you use a smart board, you could either do this by underlining the context clue on Slide 4, or you could circle the context clues on Slide 5 *during* the think-aloud.

    *Now let's see if we can spot some specific words that are context clues that give us hints to the meaning of **intercontinental**. It says in the paragraph that the plane went from New York to London, England, which seem to be impor-tant clues, so I'll underline them. Does anyone see some other context clues that might help us figure out the meaning of intercontinental?*

- Students may offer **North America** and **Europe**, for example, and if so, underline them.

    Does anyone see any other words that might be context clues?

- Students might say **fly between,** and the teacher underlines these words.

    *So, put the clues together. Listen to them as I read the underlined words: New York, London England, fly between, North America, and Europe. Does anyone have an idea what **intercontinental** means?*

- A student may offer that **intercontinental** might be a special jet that can fly long distances over water.

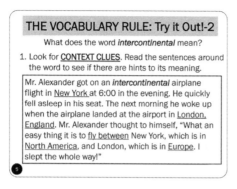

Slide 6: The Vocabulary Rule: Try It Out!–3

- Explain that you will now move on to word-part, or structural analysis, clues. Read the sentence after #2 to the students. Keep the information in the box on the bottom half of Slide 6 covered for now.

  This is Step 2 of the vocabulary rule, which tells us to look for parts of a word that might give clues to its meaning. It reminds us what a root word, a prefix, and a suffix is.

- If necessary, briefly review the meanings of these word parts. You could use the root word **happy** and the prefix **un-** and the suffix **-ness** (i.e., **un-happy-ness**) to review what these word parts involve.

  *Does anyone find any word parts in the word **intercontinental**?*

- Student responds that **inter-** is probably a prefix and that **-al** is probably a suffix with **continent** being the root word.

  Excellent! Now does anyone know what these word parts mean?

- If necessary, guide the students to remember that they learned in social studies that continents are large land masses like North America and Europe. Another student might say that **inter-** means *between*; for example, when a Girl Scout troop has a meeting with another troop, they call it an *intertroop*, or *between-troop*, meeting.

  Good thinking. Let's look at this box.

- Teacher removes screen from smart board slide.

  *You were right that **inter-** means between and **continent** is one of the largest land areas on Earth. It also tells us that **-al** means the process of. If we put all this together, we get the idea of the process of going between continents. So, what would an intercontinental airplane be?*

- One or more students are likely to respond that it is an airplane that flies between continents like North America and Europe.

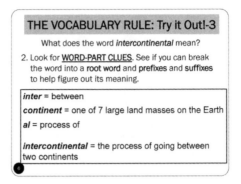

Slide 7: The Vocabulary Rule: Try It Out!–4

- Read Step 3 and ask if anyone knows a word in Spanish that looks like or sounds like **intercontinental**. A Spanish-speaking student may respond that the word **continente** in Spanish can mean a large piece of land.

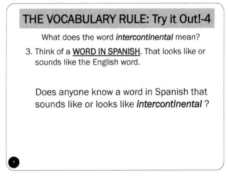

Slide 8: The Vocabulary Rule: Try It Out!–5

- Let's look at the rest of this slide. We were correct. The word **continente** in Spanish means just about the same as the word **continent** does in English. Therefore, if you know Spanish or are studying it in school, you might be able to think of a word in Spanish that helps you figure out the meaning of an unfamiliar word in English.

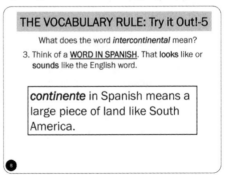

Slide 9: The Vocabulary Rule: Try It Out!–6

- Display this slide and explain:

    *Sometimes we just cannot figure out the meaning of a word in something we are reading. When that happens, we should ask, "Does this word seem to be important to understanding the selection?" If you answer "No," then you might skip the word and read on. When you do this, sometimes authors use the same word again. If you see the hard word again, look for context clues nearby the word. However, if you think that knowing the meaning of the word is important for you to understand what you are reading, then you can use other strategies such as asking someone or using a dictionary or a thesaurus. You'll see in the box a dictionary definition for **intercontinental**. This shows that the way we used context clues, word-part clues, and a word in Spanish that sounds like or looks like the root word helped us understand very well what **intercontinental** means.*

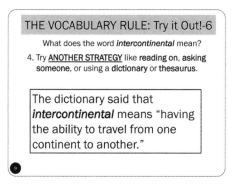

Slide 10: Practice the Vocabulary Rule–1

- Use Slide 10 to provide practice in using the VR. Slide 10 is provided as a handout for students. See if the students can use the four steps to try to figure out the meaning of the word **unstable**. If students need help, you can guide them to work through the VR individually or as a whole class. Students should be able to find and use the following clues:

- **Step 1: Look for context clues.** Have students look for context clues and underline them. They might underline **tower**, **building blocks**, **taller**, **toppled over**, or **big pile.** Then see if they can make a reasonable prediction for the meaning of **unstable.**

- **Step 2: Look for word-part clues.** Have the students examine **unstable** for word parts, which in this case include a root word (**stable**) and the prefix **un-**. See if they know what each word part means and how they can work together to predict a meaning.

- **Step 3: Think of a word in Spanish.** If one or more students know Spanish, they may be able to connect the Spanish word **instable,** which means something that can easily tip over, to **unstable.**

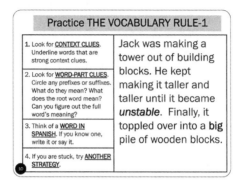

Slide 10: Practice the Vocabulary Rule–2

- After the students complete the work paper independently, with a partner, or with some teacher guidance, reveal Slide 11, which illustrates the VR as it applies to the word **unstable.**

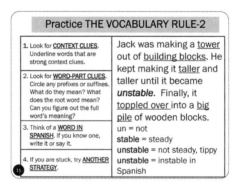

Lesson Extension

To provide students with practice in using the VR, you may see if they can determine the meanings of some words you point out that are likely to be familiar to them in reading and language arts instruction texts or in textbooks used in science, social studies, or math.

The preceding sample lesson is just the first in a series of lessons on teaching students word-learning strategies. Following this lesson, we taught a series of lessons on the specific types of context clues contained in Table

8.1. We then taught a series of lessons on learning the meanings of the word parts shown in Table 8.2, as we reviewed the use of context clues.

As noted above, within the contextual and morphemic analysis lessons, and subsequent to them, we gave students opportunities to review and practice the VR in actual texts they were reading in their curriculum or self-selected books and stories they were reading independently. It is important to understand that one solid introductory lesson is insufficient for students to acquire and use word-learning strategies in natural reading situations. Instead, teachers need to teach the separate parts of the rule explicitly and then provide ongoing attention and opportunities to practice the rule as they engage in teacher-assigned or student-selected reading opportunities.

CONCLUSION

During the past 25 years, many researchers have called for promoting independent vocabulary-learning strategies that will enable students to access the sheer volume of vocabulary they are likely to encounter in school texts (e.g., Baumann, Kame'enui, & Ash, 2003; Nagy, 1988; Nagy & Anderson, 1984). Teaching students how to apply interword (contextual) and intraword (morphemic) cues separately and in tandem is important so that they can add to their repertoire of vocabulary skills the ability to rely on contextual and morphemic analysis when words and texts provide such clues. Thus, teaching students to understand and use word-learning strategies independently is one important component of a balanced, comprehensive vocabulary program (Graves, 2000).

ACKNOWLEDGMENTS

The preparation of this chapter was supported in part by the Institute of Education Sciences, U.S. Department of Education, through Grant No. R305A090163 to the University of Missouri, the University of Wyoming, and National Louis University. The opinions expressed are those of the authors and do not represent views of the Institute or the U.S. Department of Education.

REFERENCES

Afflerbach, P., Blachowicz, C. L. Z., Boyd, C. D., Izquierdo, E., Juel, C., Kame'enui, E. J., et al. (2011). *Scott Foresman reading street.* Upper Saddle River, NJ: Pearson Education.

Albright, L. K., & Ariail, M. (2005). Tapping the potential of teacher read-alouds in middle schools. *Journal of Adolescent and Adult Literacy, 48,* 582–591.

Anderson, R. C., & Nagy, W. (1991). Word meanings. In R. Barr, M. Kamil, P. Mosenthal, & P. D. Pearson (Eds.), *Handbook of reading research* (Vol. II, pp. 690–724). New York: Longman.

Baumann, J. F., Blachowicz, C. L. Z., Manyak, P. C., Graves, M. F., & Olejnik, S. (2009). *Development of a multi-faceted, comprehensive, vocabulary instructional program for the upper-elementary grades* (No. R305A090163). Washington, DC: U.S. Department of Education, Institute of Education Sciences, National Center for Education Research.

Baumann, J. F., Edwards, E. C., Boland, E., Olejnik, S., & Kame'enui, E. J. (2003). Vocabulary tricks: Effects of instruction in morphology and context on fifth-grade students' ability to derive and infer word meaning. *American Educational Research Journal, 40,* 447–494.

Baumann, J. F., Edwards, E. C., Font, G., Tereshinski, C. A., Kame'enui, E. J., & Olejnik, S. (2002). Teaching contextual and morphemic analysis to fifth-grade students. *Reading Research Quarterly, 37,* 150–176.

Baumann, J. F., Font, G., Edwards, E. C., & Boland, E. (2005). Strategies for teaching middle-grade students to use word-part and context clues to expand reading vocabulary. In E. H. Hiebert & M. L. Kamil (Eds.), *Teaching and learning vocabulary: Bringing research to practice* (pp. 179–205). Mahwah, NJ: Erlbaum.

Baumann, J. F., Kame'enui, E. J., & Ash, G. (2003). Research on vocabulary instruction: Voltaire redux. In J. Flood, D. Lapp, Squire, J. R., & Jensen, J. (Eds.), *Handbook of research on teaching the English language arts* (2nd ed., pp. 752–785). New York: Macmillan.

Baumann, J. F., Manyak, P. C., Blachowicz, C. L. Z., Bates, A., Cieply, C., Graves, M. F., et al. (2011, April). *A formative experiment on vocabulary instruction in grades 4 and 5.* Paper presented at the annual meeting of the American Educational Research Association, New Orleans, LA.

Baumann, J. F., Ware, D., & Edwards, E. C. (2007). "Bumping into spicy, tasty words that catch your tongue": A formative experiment on vocabulary instruction. *The Reading Teacher, 62,* 108–122.

Beck, I. L., & McKeown, M. G. (1991). Conditions of vocabulary acquisition. In R. Barr, M. Kamil, P. Mosenthal, & P. D. Pearson (Eds.), *Handbook of reading research* (Vol. III, pp. 789–814). New York: Longman.

Beck, I. L., McKeown, M. G., & Kucan, L. (2002). *Bringing words to life: Robust vocabulary instruction.* New York: Guilford Press.

Beck, I. L., McKeown, M. G., & Kucan, L. (2008). *Creating robust vocabulary: Frequently asked questions and extended examples.* New York: Guilford Press.

Beck, I. L., McKeown, M. G., & Omanson, R. C. (1987). The effects and uses of diverse vocabulary instructional techniques. In M. G. McKeown & M. E. Curtis (Eds.), *The nature of vocabulary acquisition* (pp. 147–163). Hillsdale, NJ: Erlbaum.

Blachowicz, C. L. Z., & Fisher, P. (2000). Vocabulary instruction. In M. L. Kamil,

P. B. Mosenthal, P. D. Pearson, & R. Barr (Eds.), *Handbook of reading research* (Vol. III, pp. 503–523) Mahwah, NJ: Erlbaum.

Blachowicz, C. L. Z., & Fisher, P. (2010). *Teaching vocabulary in all classrooms* (4th ed.). Englewood Cliffs, NJ: Merrill/Prentice Hall.

Blachowicz, C. L. Z., & Zabroske, B. (1990). Context instruction: A metacognitive approach for at-risk readers. *Journal of Reading, 33*, 504–508.

Block, C. C., & Mangieri, J. (2006). *The effects of powerful vocabulary for reading success on students' reading vocabulary and comprehension achievement.* Research Report 2963-005 of the Institute for Literacy Enhancement. Retrieved June 15, 2008, from *teacher.scholastic.com/products/powerfulvocabulary/pdfs/1521-PVfRS_eff_rep.pdf.*

Buikema, J. L., & Graves, M. F. (1993). Teaching students to use context cues to infer word meanings. *Journal of Reading, 36*, 450–457.

Carlisle, J. F. (2010). Review of research: Effects of instruction in morphological awareness on literacy achievement—an integrative review. *Reading Research Quarterly, 45*(4), 464–487.

Carlo, M., August, D., McLaughlin, B., Snow, C., Dressler, C., Lippman, D., et al. (2004). Closing the gap: Addressing the vocabulary needs of English-language learners in bilingual and mainstream classrooms. *Reading Research Quarterly, 38*, 188–215.

Carnine, D. W., Kame'enui, E., & Coyle. G. (1984). Utilization of contextual information in determining the meaning of unfamiliar words. *Reading Research Quarterly, 19*, 188–204.

Carroll, J. B., Davies, P., & Richman, B. (1971). *The American heritage word frequency book.* Boston: Houghton Mifflin.

Chall, J. S., Jacobs, V. A., & Baldwin, L. E. (1990). *The reading crisis: Why poor children fall behind.* Cambridge, MA: Harvard University Press.

Common Core State Standards Initiative. (2010). *Common Core State Standards for English language arts and literacy in history/social studies, science, and technical subjects.* Washington, DC: National Governors Association Center for Best Practices and the Council of Chief State School Officers.

Cunningham, A. E. (2005). Vocabulary growth through independent reading and reading aloud to children. In E. H. Hiebert & M. L. Kamil (Eds.), *Teaching and learning vocabulary: Bringing research to practice* (pp. 45–68). Mahwah, NJ: Erlbaum.

Dale, E., & O'Rourke, J. (1986). *Vocabulary building: A process approach.* Columbus, OH: Zaner-Bloser.

Dickinson, D. K., Cote, L., & Smith, M. W. (1993). Learning vocabulary in preschool: Social and discourse contexts affecting vocabulary growth. In D. Daiute (Ed.), *The development of literacy through social interaction* (New Directions for Child Development, No. 61, pp. 67–78). San Francisco: Jossey-Bass.

Drum, P. A., & Konopak, B. C. (1987). Learning word meanings from written context. In M. G. McKeown & M. E. Curtis (Eds.), *The nature of vocabulary acquisition* (pp. 73–87). Hillsdale, NJ: Erlbaum.

Elley, W. B. (1989). Vocabulary acquisition from listening to stories. *Reading Research Quarterly, 24*, 174–187.

Farstrup, A. E., & Samuels, S. J. (Eds.). (2008). *What research has to say about vocabulary instruction*. Newark, DE: International Reading Association.

Fukkink, R. G., & de Glopper, K. (1998). Effects of instruction in deriving word meaning from context: A meta-analysis. *Review of Educational Research, 68*, 450–469.

Graves, M. F. (1986). Vocabulary learning and instruction. In E. Z. Rothkopf (Ed.), *Review of research in education* (Vol. 13, pp. 49–89). Washington, DC: American Educational Research Association.

Graves, M. F. (2000). A vocabulary program to complement and bolster a middle-grade comprehension program. In B. M. Taylor, M. F. Graves, & P. van den Broek (Eds.), *Reading for meaning: Fostering comprehension in the middle grades* (pp. 116–135). Newark, DE: International Reading Association.

Graves, M. F. (2006). *The vocabulary book: Learning and instruction*. New York: Teachers College Press.

Graves, M. F. (2009). *Teaching individual words: One size does not fit all*. Newark, DE: International Reading Association.

Graves, M. F., & Hammond, H. K. (1980). A validated procedure for teaching prefixes and its effect on students' ability to assign meaning to novel words. In M. L. Kamil & A. J. Moe (Eds.), *Perspectives on reading research and instruction: Twenty-ninth yearbook of the National Reading Conference* (pp. 184–188). Washington, DC: National Reading Conference.

Graves, M. F., & Watts-Taffe, S. M. (2002). The place of word consciousness in a research-based vocabulary program. In S. J. Samuels & A. E. Farstrup (Eds.), *What research has to say about reading instruction* (3rd ed., pp. 140–165). Newark, DE: International Reading Association.

Hall, L. A., Burns, L. D., & Edwards, E. C. (2011). *Empowering struggling readers: Practices for the middle grades*. New York: Guilford Press.

Harris, T. L., & Hodges, R. E. (Eds.). (1995). *The literacy dictionary: The vocabulary of reading and writing*. Newark, DE: International Reading Association.

Hiebert, E. H., & Kamil, M. L. (Eds.). (2005). *Teaching and learning vocabulary: Bringing research to practice*. Mahwah, NJ: Erlbaum.

Irwin, J. W., & Baker, I. (1989). *Promoting active reading comprehension strategies: A resource book for teachers*. Englewood Cliffs, NJ: Prentice-Hall.

Jenkins, J. R., Matlock, B., & Slocum, T. A. (1989). Approaches to vocabulary instruction: The teaching of individual word meanings and practice in deriving word meaning from context. *Reading Research Quarterly, 24*, 215–235.

Jitendra, A. K., Edwards, L. L., Sacks, G., & Jacobson, L. A. (2004). What research says about vocabulary instruction for students with learning disabilities. *Exceptional Children, 70*, 299–322.

Johnson, D. D., & Pearson, P. D. (1978). *Teaching reading vocabulary*. New York: Holt, Rinehart & Winston.

Kamil, M. L., & Hiebert, E. H. (2005). Teaching and learning vocabulary: Perspectives and persistent issues. In E. H. Hiebert & M. L. Kamil (Eds.), *Teaching and learning vocabulary: Bringing research to practice* (pp. 1–23). Mahwah, NJ: Erlbaum.

Kirk, C., & Gillon, T. G. (2009). Integrated morphological awareness intervention as a tool for improving literacy. *Language, Speech, and Hearing Services in Schools, 40,* 341–351.

Kuhn, M. R., & Stahl, S. A. (1998). Teaching children to learn word meanings from context: A synthesis and some questions. *Journal of Literacy Research, 30,* 119–138.

Lesaux, N., Kieffer, M., Faller, S. E., & Kelley, J. (2010). The effectiveness and ease of implementation of an academic vocabulary intervention for linguistically diverse students in urban middle schools. *Reading Research Quarterly, 45,* 196–228.

Lubliner, S., & Smetana, L. (2005). The effects of comprehensive vocabulary instruction on Title I students' metacognitive word-learning skills and reading comprehension. *Journal of Literacy Research, 37,* 163–200.

Mezynski, K. (1983). Issues concerning the acquisition of knowledge: Effects of vocabulary training on reading comprehension. *Review of Educational Research, 53,* 253–279.

Molina, R. M. (2011). *The dictionary of cognates: English–Spanish* [Kindle ed.]. *www.cognates.org*

Nagy, W. E. (1988). *Teaching vocabulary to improve reading comprehension.* Newark, DE: International Reading Association.

Nagy, W. E. (2005). Why vocabulary instruction needs to be long-term and comprehensive. In E. H. Hiebert & M. L. Kamil (Eds.), *Teaching and learning vocabulary: Bringing research to practice* (pp. 27–44). Mahwah, NJ: Erlbaum.

Nagy, W. E., & Anderson, R. C. (1984). How many words are there in printed school English? *Reading Research Quarterly, 19,* 303–330.

Nagy, W. E., Diakidoy, I. N., & Anderson, R. C. (1993). The acquisition of morphology: Learning the contribution of suffixes to the meanings of derivatives. *Journal of Reading Behavior, 25,* 155–170.

Nagy, W. E., & Scott, J. A. (2000). Vocabulary processes. In M. L. Kamil, P. B. Mosenthal, P. D. Pearson, & R. Barr (Eds.), *Handbook of reading research* (Vol. III, pp. 269–284) Mahwah, NJ: Erlbaum.

Parel, R. (2006). The impact of training in morphological analysis on literacy in the primary grades. *International Journal of Learning, 13,* 119–128.

Patberg, J. P., Graves, M. F., & Stibbe, M. A. (1984). Effects of active teaching and practice in facilitating students' use of context clues. In J. A. Niles & L. A. Harris (Eds.), *Changing perspectives on research in reading/language processing and instruction: Thirty-third yearbook of the National Reading Conference* (pp. 146–151). Rochester, NY: National Reading Conference.

Reed, D. K. (2008). A synthesis of morphology interventions and effects on reading outcomes for students in Grades K–12. *Learning Disabilities Research and Practice, 23*(1), 36–49.

Schatz, E. K., & Baldwin, R. S. (1986). Context clues are unreliable predictors of word meanings. *Reading Research Quarterly, 21,* 439–453.

Scott, J. A., & Nagy, W. E. (2004). Developing word consciousness. In J. F. Baumann & E. J. Kame'enui (Eds.), *Vocabulary instruction: Research to practice* (pp. 201–217). New York: Guilford Press.

Stahl, S. A., & Fairbanks, M. M. (1986). The effects of vocabulary instruction: A model-based meta-analysis. *Review of Educational Research, 56,* 72–110.

Stahl, S. A., & Nagy, W. E. (2006). *Teaching word meanings.* Mahwah, NJ: Erlbaum.

Sternberg, R. B. (1987). Most vocabulary is learned from context. In M. G. McKeown & M. E. Curtis (Eds.), *The nature of vocabulary acquisition* (pp. 89–105). Hillsdale, NJ: Erlbaum.

Sternberg, R. B., & Powell, J. S. (1983). Comprehending verbal comprehension. *American Psychologist, 38,* 878–893.

Suttles, W. C., & Baumann, J. F. (1991, December). *A review and synthesis of descriptive, theoretical, and empirical definitions of context clues: A classification scheme for researchers and practitioners.* Paper presented at the annual meeting of the National Reading Conference, Palm Springs, CA.

Swanborn, M. S. L., & de Glopper, K. (1999). Incidental word learning while reading: A meta-analysis. *Review of Educational Research, 69,* 261–285.

Templeton, S., Bear, D. R., Invernizzi, M., & Johnston, R. (2010). *Vocabulary their way: Word study with middle and secondary students.* Boston: Pearson Education.

Tomesen, M., & Aarnoutse, C. (1998). Effects of an instructional programme for deriving word meanings. *Educational Studies, 24*(1), 107–128.

White, T. G., Graves, M. F., & Slater, W. H. (1990). Growth of reading vocabulary in diverse elementary schools. *Journal of Educational Psychology, 82*(2), 281–290.

White, T. G., Power, M. A., & White, S. (1989). Morphological analysis: Implications for teaching and understanding vocabulary growth. *Reading Research Quarterly, 24,* 283–304.

White, T. G., Sowell, J., & Yanagihara, A. (1989). Teaching elementary students to use word-part clues. *The Reading Teacher, 42,* 302–308.

Wysocki, K., & Jenkins, J. R. (1987). Deriving word meanings through morphological generalization. *Reading Research Quarterly, 22,* 66–81.

Part III

Teaching Vocabulary through Word Consciousness and Language Play

Chapter 9

Developing Word Consciousness

Lessons from Highly Diverse Fourth-Grade Classrooms

Judith A. Scott
Tatiana F. Miller
Susan Leigh Flinspach

> Really knowing a word . . . always means being able to apply it flexibly but accurately in a wide range of new contexts and situations. Thus it can be argued that there is no knowledge addressed in school in which application is more crucial than knowledge of word meanings. The challenge for educators is to provide instruction of the sort that will lead to flexible application of word knowledge.
> —ANDERSON AND NAGY (1991, p. 721)

Vocabulary instruction that nurtures the flexible application of word knowledge goes beyond the typical practices of giving weekly word lists and quizzes, teaching key words for a new unit, or discussing the highlighted terms in a textbook. It centers on strategic and motivational aspects of word learning, rather than on the set of words to be taught. In 2004, we (Scott & Nagy, 2004) discussed the importance of generative word knowledge—the knowledge and dispositions that will transfer to and enhance students' learning of other words—and conceptualized *word consciousness* as a cluster of rather diverse types of knowledge and skills that lead to an awareness of words and a flexible engagement with their use. Although the research community has become increasingly aware of the important role of word consciousness in vocabulary development (Baumann, Kame'enui, & Ash, 2003; Blachowicz, Fisher, Ogle, & Watts-Taffe, 2006; Graves, 2000; Graves & Watts-Taffe, 2002; RAND Reading Study Group, 2002; Scott, Nagy, & Flinspach, 2008), the concept is still relatively unknown among teachers. We believe, and have evidence that, thorough grounding in word consciousness encourages teachers to offer "instruction of the sort that will lead to flexible application of word knowledge" (Anderson & Nagy, 1991, p. 721).

In this chapter, we report on our recent intervention with elementary teachers, VINE (Vocabulary Innovations in Education), which helped teachers develop word-conscious instruction. In doing so, we revisit the discussion regarding the development of word consciousness in the first edition of this book (Baumann & Kame'enui, 2004). We propose a new conceptual framework explaining how word consciousness affects vocabulary development, and we illustrate the framework with empirical data about instruction and teacher change from VINE.

THE VINE INTERVENTION AND ITS EFFECTIVENESS

We are pleased to report that the VINE intervention resulted in changes in teachers' instruction and in enhanced student achievement in vocabulary learning. The VINE project was funded by the United States Department of Education, as a Reading/Writing Development Grant (Grant No. R305G060140) from the Institute of Education Sciences, National Center for Educational Research. The goal of this scientific and experimental intervention project was to explore the development and efficacy of fourth- and fifth-grade students' word consciousness through building their teachers' awareness of, knowledge of, and dispositions toward learning words.

We collected data for the 3-year study from over 1,400 students in culturally and linguistically diverse classrooms found in rural, suburban, and urban communities. The first year was a pilot year during which we developed both the intervention model and instruments to study and assess its effects. In the second year of VINE, approximately 32% of the 381 participants were English learners (ELs) that came from backgrounds representing over 20 home languages. More than half of the students (52%) spoke a language other than English at home, with Spanish being the most common heritage language. In addition, approximately 40% qualified for free and reduced-price lunch programs. In the third year, the demographics were approximately the same for our 663 students, with 29% ELs and students from backgrounds representing 34 home languages. More than half of the students (54%) spoke a language other than English at home, with Spanish again as the most common heritage language.

The 3-year VINE project involved a team of researchers and 34 teachers from 19 schools in nine districts. VINE built on the Gift of Words project (Henry et al., 1999; Scott, 2004; Scott, Skobel, & Wells, 2008), a teacher–researcher collaboration designed to develop word-rich reading and writing strategies for teaching vocabulary. The research design for VINE involved both control and intervention teachers who were drawn from a wide range of the teacher population. In year 1 of VINE, teachers were randomly assigned to the intervention and control groups, and the intervention took place through six 3-hour dinner meetings evenly spaced throughout the school year. In years 2 and 3, the control teachers were invited to join the intervention group, and a new control group was recruited. In those years the intervention began with a one-to-two day professional development institute followed by the six dinner meetings. VINE teachers could thus be part of the intervention group for 1, 2, or 3 years.

Teachers in the VINE intervention ranged from first-year teachers to veterans. Some favored teacher-directed instruction, some preferred child-centered instruction, and most drew from both approaches. They had diverse backgrounds, and two were bilingual. The intervention was designed to support the diversity of teachers found in California's elementary classrooms.

The VINE intervention provided teachers with two basic mechanisms to promote changes in instruction. First, it raised the word consciousness of the teachers. VINE was based on the premise that teachers who are more word conscious teach in ways that help students become more word conscious, which accelerates vocabulary development.

A longitudinal analysis of responses on VINE teacher questionnaires demonstrates that VINE raised intervention teachers' word consciousness and that greater word consciousness affected their vocabulary instruction. Teachers made references to VINE and VINE activities as triggers to growth in word consciousness. Teachers told us about becoming more aware of words, beginning to reflect on their own knowledge and use of words and connecting their own process of word learning to how their students were learning. For example, when asked about VINE, one teacher wrote:

> "V.I.N.E. has been the force that has set my consciousness regarding words in motion. At first it was rather annoying, always thinking about words. Now, however, it's fun playing with words."

The longitudinal analysis of teacher questionnaires also revealed that the sophistication with which teachers spoke about word consciousness increased the longer they participated in the intervention. One teacher who exemplified this growth said that she wanted to learn more about word consciousness and how to teach it in her first-year VINE questionnaire. In year 3, however, she wrote all of her answers to the questionnaire in haikus, telling us:

> Gaining confidence;
> seeing words in a new light;
> I think I get it!

Another teacher, also in her third year of VINE, wrote:

> "I feel that my word consciousness is constantly growing. Now that I am aware of my own learning of words, I catch myself in moments of discovery. I'll look at a word with a different purpose, or [I] think about the strategies I use when I come across words I'm unfamiliar with."

Through exposure to word-learning theories, rich literature, instructional strategies, word play and games, and materials promoting vocabulary learning across the curriculum, VINE intervention teachers tended to grow both in their own engagement with words and in their reflection on that engagement (Flinspach, Miller, Zeamer, Gage-Serio, & Scott, 2010).

In addition to making statements about their own word consciousness, the teachers reported designing and using specific classroom activities to raise word consciousness in their students. During her second year in the VINE intervention, for instance, another teacher converted her language arts period on Fridays into "Word Play Friday." Early in the year she introduced students to word consciousness explicitly, and they agreed to do activities focused on word appreciation, descriptive language, word choice, word play, poetry, and creative writing. During "Word Play Friday," the class produced two class books, and the teacher said that word consciousness was "trickling down into their [students'] writing drafts."

The second mechanism through which VINE promoted classroom change was its multiple supports for teachers to create, share, and adapt strategies that increase students' word consciousness. During intervention meetings, vocabulary researchers and classroom teachers worked together as a single community whose members brought different expertise to the table. In this "think-tank" model of professional development (Henry et al., 1999), all members of the VINE community were learning and teaching. VINE intervention teachers frequently praised the community support and sharing, and, like this teacher, they urged VINE to "Keep the conversation going; I think we learn so much from each other." The wealth of sharing and cooperation was designed to help teachers expand the amount of time they spent on vocabulary and to motivate them to try out new ideas for vocabulary instruction. The seven teachers who participated in the VINE intervention two consecutive years or more did both of these. That group of teachers reported spending much more time on vocabulary development in 2008–2009 than previously, with five of the seven estimating they had doubled, or more than doubled, the class time dedicated to vocabulary. One noted, "I tried to keep words and vocabulary near the front of our thinking throughout the day, whether with math vocabulary, science and social studies vocabulary, or the big idea words in reading and writing." VINE data from classroom observations, teacher journals, interviews, and questionnaires document some of the many ways that these teachers changed their practices based on the sharing of ideas at intervention meetings. Their adopted innovations ran the gamut from reading aloud a book introduced at one of the meetings to developing word-inquiry strategies across the curriculum. One teacher acknowledged that "Sharing with other intervention teachers kept me motivated." Another said, "The thing that helps me most is hearing ideas from people [at VINE meetings]. I think about it for awhile and then sometimes apply it in my teaching." She added a request that VINE keep providing "opportunities for teachers to openly share." VINE teachers repeatedly singled out the sharing and sense of community as high points of the intervention and as effective ways to support instructional change (Flinspach et al., 2010).

By nurturing the word consciousness of teachers and by building a collaborative, supportive community, the VINE intervention facilitated changes in teachers' vocabulary instruction that translated into improved student achievement (Scott, Flinspach, Miller, Gage-Serio, & Vevea, 2009; Miller, Gage-Serio, & Scott, 2010; Scott, Vevea, & Flinspach, 2010). In both the 2007 and 2008 school years, intervention students significantly outperformed control students on the VINE vocabulary tests described below.

The VINE vocabulary tests were based on a conceptual understanding of vocabulary acquisition and addressed several issues identified as problematic areas of vocabulary assessment by Pearson, Hiebert, and Kamil (2007). The words used in test items were drawn from grade-level textbooks and novels commonly used in the school districts and region. The VINE team of teachers and researchers first identified words in the texts that we thought might be new or unfamiliar to typical fourth- and fifth-grade students. Then, words for test items were chosen from a subset of those words that appeared in at least two source texts across subject areas, building on the idea of incremental word learning (Nagy & Scott, 2000; Stahl, 2003). The assessment also tested multiple domains of students' word knowledge, including knowledge of definitions, parts of speech, and words with a shared semantic field. The high marginal reliability and face validity of the tests (Scott, Hoover, Flinspach, & Vevea, 2008) resulted in the opportunity to refine this tool statewide with additional federal funds[1] in order to establish a new standardized and norm referenced assessment. Neither control nor intervention teachers in the VINE project were privy to the assessment tool or were aware of which words would be tested; thus, the assessment instruments we used were not measures of instruction on

[1] We gratefully acknowledge funding from the Institute of Education Sciences Reading and Writing Measurement Grant No. R305A090550 (2009–2012).

specific words; rather, they assessed words that students may or may not have encountered through exposure to grade-level materials.

Growth estimates from fall to spring in 2007–2008 indicated that students in intervention classrooms improved significantly over the control group on VINE vocabulary tests. Of particular interest is that these results also held for the ELs. This pattern of results was essentially replicated in 2008–2009. In sum, all students, including the ELs, acquired enough generative knowledge of words and word-learning strategies through the VINE intervention to significantly outperform a comparison group of students on a vocabulary test comprised of words that were not explicitly taught (see Scott, Hoover, et al., 2008; Scott, Flinspach, Miller, Vevea, & Gage-Serio, 2009; Scott et al., 2010, for further details). While more substantive analyses are ongoing, we have found strong evidence that participation in the VINE intervention accelerated the growth of students' vocabulary knowledge, particularly for ELs, on the multitude of words found throughout the fourth-grade curriculum.

HOW WORD CONSCIOUSNESS AFFECTS VOCABULARY DEVELOPMENT

In our previous work (Nagy & Scott, 2000; Scott & Nagy, 2004; Scott, Skobel, & Wells, 2008), we emphasized types of metalinguistic awareness that can contribute to word consciousness: helping students recognize the differences between the spoken and written registers of English, and creating classroom environments wherein students are actively engaged in the word-learning process and encouraged to take linguistic risks. Drawing lessons from our close, collaborative work with VINE intervention teachers over three years, we have now expanded our framework and suggest that word-conscious instruction influences vocabulary development by encouraging growth in three domains: (1) *metacognitive knowledge* and awareness of words and word learning, (2) *metalinguistic knowledge* and awareness, and (3) the *affective aspects* of word learning, which we define as an appreciation for, and enjoyment of, words. Students learned more vocabulary in the VINE intervention classrooms than in the control classrooms, and evidence from our teacher questionnaires, interviews, and case studies documents many examples of intervention teachers' word-conscious instruction—instruction that often targeted one or more of these domains. We propose that word-conscious instruction can lead to accelerated word learning by encouraging greater growth in the metacognitive, metalinguistic, and affective domains of word knowledge. In the next section, we describe instruction designed to encourage such growth from the VINE intervention classrooms.

The Metacognitive Domain of Word-Conscious Teaching

According to Anderson and Nagy (1991), word-learning processes that develop students' metacognitive and metalinguistic awareness, particularly the flexible use and application of word knowledge, are very important in learning vocabulary. These researchers emphasize that students gain insight into the complexity and multidimensionality of word meanings through class discussions and by making vocabulary knowledge, and processes explicit. In VINE classrooms, students often engaged in metacognitive discussions about how people learn new words, why words are important (see Figure 9.1), how words make people feel, how words are used (see Figure 9.2), and how we know if we "really know" a word. For example, after a presentation at an intervention meeting by one of us (T. F. M.) describing a study in which fourth graders investigated their own theories of word learning (Miller, 2009), three teachers developed a "Word Consciousness Launch Unit." Their unit was designed to engage students in explicit metacognitive discussions about word-learning processes, making connections to students' background knowledge. It included activities linked to children's literature that encouraged active cognitive engagement and depth of processing. We use a composite case study drawn from several classrooms[2] to illustrate the word-conscious instruction that intervention teachers used to develop students' metacognitive knowledge and skills.

A Unit on Word Consciousness

On the first day of this unit, the fourth-grade class discussed how learning new words was similar to learning other things, like beginning to ride a bike or trying out a new skateboarding trick. This elicited a conversation about how people learn new words. Students responded that they learned new words by reading books or other materials; looking up words in dictionaries; using computers; asking parents and other family members; going on field trips; listening to songs; seeing subtitles on TV shows; and by utilizing more than 15 additional sources. Interestingly, not one student mentioned school vocabulary lists as a source for learning new words!

The next day of the unit, the teacher continued this metacognitive discussion of word learning by reading *Max's Words* (Banks, 2006). In this story, Max has a brother, Benjamin, who collects stamps, and another brother, Karl, who collects coins, and neither will share with Max. So, Max decides to collect words. This delightful picture book created the context for a discussion about why words are important. In the book, Max

---

[2] The composite case study is taken from interviews and journals by six VINE teachers in spring 2009 and from a booklet of best practice produced by VINE teachers.

Why Words Are Important

- need words to talk
  - advertisements
    ads
- to make sense
- singing (lyrics)
- tell us location
  - name of city
  - driving
  - directions
- Communicate
  - read   - speech
  - write   - details
  - speak   - describe
            - letters
- Language
- names

- vocabulary
  - learn new words
- Think
- Make you smarter
- Interview
- Reading Signs
- Help People
- feelings, emotions
- Solve Problems

FIGURE 9.1. Classroom chart recording metacognitive conversation about words.

How Do We Use Words?

- remind people or yourself
- as commands
- you want to say it
- Sometimes you use words to hurt people
- use it to compliment or to show respect.
- You have to think about it first.
- express our feelings
- translate
- to communicate

"What would God say?"
"Stop!"
"You mean it."
"Like the bullies sometimes."
"use kind words."
"Like greeting Mr. Keegan or say 'good morning'."
- To persuade people
- To change the world

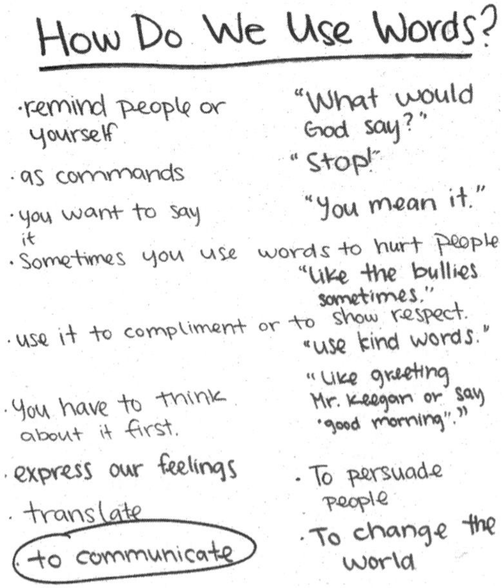

FIGURE 9.2. Classroom chart recording another metacognitive conversation about words.

realizes that when Benjamin looks at his collection, he has a set of stamps, and when Karl looks at his collection, he has a pile of coins, but when Max looks at his collection, he has thoughts and stories—and the thoughts and stories change depending on word choice and word order.

After reading the story, the teacher asked students to recall the collection of presidential memorabilia she had brought to the class earlier in the year. She told them about how she collected presidential figurines that used to come in cereal boxes, and how excited she had been to find a whole set on eBay. This led to a discussion about why she liked the figurines and why she decided to collect them, transitioning into a conversation about what would make a word worth collecting (e.g., its rarity, its sound, its prospects for use in speaking or writing), and reasons why people would want to collect words. Pairs of students worked together to identify "at least one reason to collect words and phrases," all of which were posted at the end of the lesson.

In the third lesson, which focused on how words make students feel, students contributed to a chart of positive and negative words connected to "I can't do it" and "I can do it" phrases. The unit continued with the book *The Boy Who Loved Words* (Schotter, 2006). Students were then sent out with notebooks to collect their own interesting or powerful words. The teacher introduced the notion of "juicy words." Using the analogy of a tasty tangerine, a juicy word is one that bursts full of flavor as opposed to a word that is dried out, shriveled, and desiccated. She asked students to use sticky notes to collect juicy words for a community chart.

These collections of words served as the foundation for numerous activities, including an exploration of words borrowed from other languages, discussions of synonyms and shades of meaning, the writing of poetry and a play, creating a poster/drawing of favorite words, and acting out the meanings of words. Throughout the unit, the teacher focused on overt discussions of words through think-alouds, explicit connections to multiple subject areas, and processes for scaffolding student writing. For instance, before students wrote a narrative, the teacher talked to them about reasons they might want to use more descriptive words and why they would want people to see and feel exactly how the character felt.

This activity then led to class discussions of the relative value of different words, particularly words expressed as variations of a particular concept along a continuum or "shades of meaning" (Scott, Skobel, & Wells, 2008). Figure 9.3 is a chart that the class developed to identify more sophisticated word choices for common words such as *mad, big*, and *pretty*. The idea of using dollar amounts to express value served as effective shorthand for the teacher, who often reminded students to use $100 words in their writing. We were particularly impressed to find that other students, in addition to the teacher, challenged their classmates to use these "juicy words"

$1	$2	$50	$100
Mad	Angry	Furious	Livid
Big	Large	Huge	Enormous
Pretty	Beautiful	Outstanding	Gorgeous

FIGURE 9.3. A chart used to emphasize more sophisticated word choice.

in their writing. As students engaged in peer editing of the narratives, the teacher overheard comments such as, "Oh, what's a better word choice for that?" or "Look, you used *superfluous* in your writing!"

THE METALINGUISTIC AND AFFECTIVE DOMAINS OF WORD-CONSCIOUS TEACHING

Word-conscious instruction in VINE often involved more than one of our proposed avenues for vocabulary development—enhancing students' metacognitive abilities, metalinguistic skills, and affective engagement with words. In this section, we present an example of word-conscious instruction designed to increase metalinguistic awareness, especially in Spanish-speaking ELs, through the recognition of Spanish–English cognates. Although metalinguistics is at the core of instructional strategies involving cognates, Spanish-speaking students also received an affective boost through the public recognition that such instruction placed on their bilingual knowledge. Similarly, several VINE intervention teachers loved word play, and they used word games both to get students more interested in words and to teach them metalinguistic and other word skills. Examples and discussion of the affective domain appear at the end of this section.

Cognates are word pairs with the same meaning and similar spelling patterns that are derived from a common origin, such as Latin. Analyses suggest that Spanish and English share between 10,000 to 15,000 cognates (Nash, 1997), offering bilingual Spanish speakers a productive source for acquiring new English vocabulary (Lubliner & Hiebert, 2011). Elsewhere we found that teachers were largely unaware of, or felt unable to capitalize on, the value of cognates as potential sources of vocabulary knowledge (Flinspach, Scott, Samway, Miller, & Vevea, 2008). Our research agrees with other findings (Garcia, 1991; Garcia & Nagy, 1993; Nagy, Garcia, Durgunoglu, & Hancin-Bhatt, 1993; Hancin-Bhatt & Nagy, 1994) that fourth-grade students did not often reflect on their knowledge of Spanish to infer meanings of English words. In fact, one EL fourth grader told us that she "throws out [her] Spanish" when speaking English at school. Despite the fact that 31% of VINE students came from Spanish-speaking homes in the first year of the intervention, only two of the 13 teachers taught about cognate connections beyond a few incidental instructional asides.

After a VINE intervention meeting in which teachers and researchers discussed the value of helping students see how words could be related to each other through their common roots, several teachers developed activities to enhance students' Spanish–English cognate awareness. A number of intervention teachers created classroom charts through discussion, such as the one in Figure 9.4. They then sent their students on "cognate searches" to find words to add to the chart. Through this activity, Spanish speakers were valued as experts in their classrooms. For example, one teacher reported that her Spanish speakers felt empowered because they had access to a special set or "bank" of words from another language. Spanish words are ubiquitous in California, so cognate searches became a game-like activity accessible for students of all languages. In fact, one teacher reported that two students, one Spanish speaking and one who knew only English, had spent a play date coming up with new words for the cognate list. The VINE exploration of cognates invited Spanish-speaking students to use their knowledge to help others form metalinguistic links, underscoring

Cognates: Same or similar meaning + spelling	
Spanish	English
no	no
capitán	captain
chocolate	chocolate
teléfono	telephone
minuto	minute
aguacate	avocado
fruta	fruit
vegetales	vegetables
atención	attention
contento	content
cero	zero
invitación	invitation
jirafa	giraffe
importante	important
carro	car
montaña	mountain
suéter	sweater
chaqueta	jacket
número	number
California	California
silencio	silence

FIGURE 9.4. Cognate chart developed to highlight Spanish–English connections.

the value of making connections between morphologically related words (Scott, Nagy, et al., 2008; Flinspach et al., 2008). Teachers, even those who knew little Spanish, were able to draw on students' home language as a resource to help bridge the language gap and provide a powerful form of word learning in the classroom.

Although Spanish-speaking students are at an advantage for learning Spanish–English cognates, all students benefit from growth in metalinguistic awareness. Studies have shown that metalinguistic awareness contributes to achievement in both reading comprehension and vocabulary (Nagy, Beringer, & Abbott, 2006). Anglin's (1993) findings suggest that metalinguistic awareness makes an important contribution to the explosive increase from first to fifth grade in the number of words with known prefixes and suffixes that children can explain. Carlisle (2000) found that measures of morphological awareness (structural knowledge and meaning) and the ability to read derived forms contribute significantly to reading comprehension, especially for fifth graders. In her review of the effects of instruction on children's metalinguistic knowledge, Carlisle (2000) concluded that "students generally do become more able to infer the meanings of unfamiliar words after receiving instruction in morphological awareness" (p. 478).

Carlisle (2000, 2010) also found that game-like activities designed simply to heighten students' interest in morphology are valuable as a starting point in stimulating greater metalinguistic awareness. Vocabulary scholars have documented and described the importance of the affective domain in word learning, especially engagement with words through word play, games, puzzles, and word choice activities. They have recognized that games create a playful and motivating context for word learning. For students with less developed knowledge of English vocabulary, games and word play also provide a safe environment to ask about words and a low-stakes setting, as they try out and experiment with new words with few consequences for mistakes (Blachowicz & Fisher, 2004; Blachowicz & Obrochta, 2005; DaSilva Iddings & McCafferty, 2005; Baumann, Ware, & Edwards, 2007; Cumming, 2007; Graves & Watts-Taffe, 2008; Scott, Skobel, et al., 2008).

Many of the VINE intervention teachers liked to use word play and games to enhance students' metalinguistic awareness and to boost their interest in and enthusiasm for words. One of the games they created, Root Relay, combined physical activity and cooperative team effort to build words from the word parts that students were learning in class (see Figure 9.5).

In the game, teams of students competed to construct a word from a pile of roots, a pile of prefixes, and a pile of suffixes similar to those shown in Figure 9.6. When a group came up with words such as *defrosting*,

Root Relay: The object of this game is to help students become more familiar with different word parts and how they fit together to create new words.

Time: 20–30 minutes

Materials: Roots, prefixes, and suffixes on word strips. A large room or outside area.

Step-by-step directions:
1. Groups of three or more race against other groups.
2. First person runs and chooses a prefix, suffix, or a root word and brings it back to the group.
3. Next person runs and chooses another word part.
4. Third person chooses a final word part.
5. The group then makes a word, and participants raise their hands to signal to the teacher. They say the word and talk about the meaning. If the created word is not correct, it is a great opportunity to point out rules of morphological combinations.

Notes for success: Have students make the word cards for extra practice and to enhance ownership of the game. Put the word parts in separate piles and have more than one copy of them.

FIGURE 9.5. Root Relay, a game using morphemes.

Prefixes	Roots	Suffixes
un-	*employ*	*-ment*
de-	*frost*	*-er*
re-	*view*	*-ing*
bi-	*week*	*-ly*
de-	*odor*	*-ize*
bio-	*graph*	*-y*
dis-	*appear*	*-ing*
re-	*pay*	*-able*
dis-	*agree*	*-s*
re-	*record*	*-ing*

FIGURE 9.6. Sample word parts for the Root Relay game.

defrosts, or *defroster*, they gained a point. No points were given for invented or nonsense words such as *biofrostize*. However, invented words often led to interesting discussions about the meaning of affixes and of possible word meanings. Students examined their invented words to arrive at appropriate meanings by following the conventions of English morphology (e.g., *biofrostize* could be *"to cause one's body to become frostbitten"; he was biofrostized after his 6-hour ordeal in the meat locker*).

Although not a VINE invention, Word Wizzle was another popular game in intervention classrooms. In this "guess my rule" game, the teacher or another student became the Word Wizzle and set a rule. Students tested their understanding of the rule by offering a word for acceptance or rejection by the Word Wizzle. At the very end of one school day, for instance, an intervention teacher, whose last name began with *R*, assumed the role of Word Wizzle and issued this challenge to her class (who were already familiar with the game): "I'm going on a trip, and I'm bringing a rhinoceros." At first, few students figured out the rule. By trial and error, gradually most of the class figured out the rule, getting to accompany their teacher on her trip (at the head of the classroom) by saying that they were bringing along an animal that started with the first letter of their own last name. Variations of the game included giving explicit examples and nonexamples of the rule, using the game to explore multiple word meanings or spellings, and using the game to reinforce and expand shades of meaning. One advantage was the ability to play it anywhere and at any time. Another teacher wrote the following about this game in her journal:

> "I have written about how I play the [Word Wizzle] game with my students while in line for lunch. I now have students who are starting us off and leading the game. I don't even have to initiate it—they just start playing, and I get to be on the other end with trying to guess the rule . . . "

Word Wizzle helped these VINE students understand the rule-governed nature of language and explore word categorization in English; it was also fun. Figure 9.7 provides additional information about the Word Wizzle game.

The VINE intervention teachers found that their growing appreciation for word learning was contagious; it sparked their students' own interest and excitement about words. In her journal, one teacher wrote: "I think another important part of trying to promote word consciousness in your class is also having an enthusiasm about it all. I feel when my class sees me fascinated by words, then they are also finding word play fascinating. . . ." This teacher added that, as she taught her class about puns, oxymorons, anagrams, and palindromes, she "had kids on the lookout for puns in their

---

Word Wizzle: The easiest way to identify the Word Wizzle rule is to give students contrasting words from the same semantic domain that either fit or do not fit the rule. A simple rule is that the word needs to start with a particular letter.

"I like *apples*, but I don't like *bananas*."
"I like *asparagus*, but I don't like *green beans*."
"I like *airplanes*, but I don't like *trains*."

Word Wizzle pairs can be used for categorization (e.g., nouns vs. verbs: "I like going to *plays*, but I don't like to *play*"), to look at spelling patterns (e.g., words with double consonants: "I like *drizzle*, but I don't like *rain*"); or to focus on particular types of words (e.g., words that describe slow motion: "I like *jogging*, but I don't like *sprinting*").

Showing the words that fit and don't fit the rule on the board, and adding the words accepted from students, provides a visual aid to help students see the patterns of the rule without having to remember all the examples.

More difficult wizzles use different meanings of words or challenge students to consider alternatives in their word schemas:

"I like *springs*, but I don't like *falls*."
"I like *deltas*, but I don't like *omegas*."
"I like *bays*, but I don't like *palominos*."

[Rule = words that describe types of natural water features.]

FIGURE 9.7. Word Wizzle, a game of cognitive connections.

reading." Her students "liked the challenge of being pushed to think of words; it was like a game for them." Another teacher wrote that using word consciousness seemed "to impact how the students feel as young authors and how they happily explore the world of words. . . . There is more joy in words this year." Teachers' attitudes toward words, word play, and games sparked students' motivation and enjoyment. As a result, another teacher said, "They really enjoy finding words that have shades of meaning and are more complex. They are even using the words when I don't expect it. I had a student describe the character from a book as *gregarious*, and two students used *plethora* at science school. I saw one of my students use *tenacious* as a hangman word, and she had to explain what it meant to the other student. So, not only are students using these more sophisticated words but also they are using them correctly and showing that they really understand the meaning."

Word-conscious instruction in the VINE intervention classrooms was not standardized or prescribed. In the VINE collaborative community, each teacher adapted and invented strategies that made his or her approach to teaching word consciousness unique. Not surprisingly, over the 3 years of the intervention, teachers and researchers discussed hundreds of instructional activities and strategies for many purposes. Important aspects of the VINE vocabulary intervention included (1) nurturing greater student interest in words; (2) using generative vocabulary-learning strategies, such as cognates and knowledge of morphology; (3) teaching students to recognize the differences between everyday language and the language of schooling; (4) helping students adopt a literate identity; (5) orchestrating opportunities to try out new words in a safe environment; (6) boosting student competency in using academic language; and (7) cultivating the ability of students to use words to communicate ideas. We think that these seven components can be subsumed under the tripartite understanding of word-conscious instruction as instruction that focuses on building metacognitive awareness, metalinguistic knowledge, and affective interest in words. The research team was theoretically driven by this tripartite understanding of word-conscious instruction, but it was never explicitly presented to the teachers. This conceptual framework has further evolved as the researchers learned about the ways that the VINE intervention teachers decided to teach word consciousness in their classrooms. Based on the VINE intervention, we propose that word-conscious classrooms feature instruction that fosters growth in students' metacognitive and metalinguistic knowledge and skills and that enhances their affective engagement with words.

FINAL THOUGHTS

According to Nagy and Anderson (1995), "It is the youngest, least advantaged, least able children who will benefit most from instruction that helps them become aware of the structure of their writing system and its relationship to their spoken language" (p. 6). The task of helping the "youngest, least advantaged, and least able" students learn vocabulary is enormous. There are approximately 300,000 key word entries in the *Oxford English Dictionary*. In one of our recent studies, a group of experienced teachers identified over 6,000 words that they thought would be conceptually difficult or unfamiliar for students in widely used science and math textbooks in both fourth and fifth grades. A similar examination of Newbery Award winning novels yielded a count more than three times as large. While the type of in-depth focus on specific words found in many core reading programs is useful, the sheer volume of the task of learning new words is overwhelming.

The examples of activities and strategies described in this chapter offer illustrations of the metacognitive, metalinguistic, and affective components of students' word consciousness that were developed within the VINE project. These components alone do not constitute a complete vocabulary program, but we think that fostering students' generative knowledge and dispositions within these components is a valuable addition to normal classroom practice and vocabulary instruction. Each teacher in the VINE intervention took the principles of word consciousness gleaned from the professional development sessions, along with shared strategies and activities, and transformed his or her practice across the curriculum and content areas. And, we found that word-conscious instruction made a difference in students' knowledge of vocabulary on an assessment that covered words not explicitly taught by the teachers. In other words, these teachers' principled practices seem to have fostered students' ability to generalize vocabulary knowledge beyond a specific set of words.

Teachers in the VINE intervention were excited and pleased by the growth they saw in their students and in their own understanding of vocabulary instruction. As one teacher said:

> "At first, I thought word consciousness was just knowing lots of words. Now word consciousness means so much more to me. It's like a key was given to me that unlocked new understandings about words. Word consciousness is not just about definitions of words, but how they are used, how they make you feel, what you think about words and how they are related to other words."

Intervention teachers reported that their students were looking at cognates on play dates, playing word games independently, and using sophisticated language in conversation—so we were not surprised that their instruction translated into the increased vocabulary knowledge captured on the VINE vocabulary tests. Using metacognitive, metalinguistic, and affective domains to relay information about words to students is like the well-known aphorism of teaching students to fish instead of giving them a prepared serving of fish. VINE intervention teachers met the challenge described by Anderson and Nagy (1991) at the opening of this chapter; that is, the instruction they provided enabled their students to apply their word knowledge flexibly and successfully.

ACKNOWLEDGMENTS

We gratefully acknowledge the support of our colleagues, the school districts, the schools, the teachers, and the students involved in the VINE project. The research described in this chapter was funded in part by an Institute of Education Sciences National Center for Educational Research Reading and Writing Development Grant (Grant No. R305G060140) from the U.S. Department of Education. Although the contents of the chapter do not necessarily reflect the position or policies of the federal government, we are also grateful for this support.

What we know and what we need to know. *Reading Research Quarterly*, 42(2), 282–296.

RAND Reading Study Group. (2002). *Reading for understanding: Toward a research and* development *program in reading comprehension.* Washington, DC: U.S. Department of Education.

Schotter, R. (2006). *The boy who loved words.* New York: Schwartz & Wade.

Scott, J. A. (2004). Scaffolding vocabulary learning: Ideas for equity in urban settings. In D. Lapp, C. Block, J. Cooper, J. Flood, N. Roser, & J. Tinajero (Eds.), *Teaching all the children: Strategies for developing literacy in an urban setting* (pp. 275–293). New York: Guilford Press.

Scott, J. A., Flinspach, S., Miller, T., Gage-Serio, O., & Vevea, J. (2009). An analysis of reclassified English learners, English learners and native English fourth graders on assessments of receptive and productive vocabulary. In Y. Kim, V. Risko, D. Compton, D. Dickinson, M.Hundley, R. Jimenez, et al. (Eds.), *58th annual yearbook of the National Reading Conference* (pp. 312–329). Oak Creek, WI: National Reading Conference.

Scott, J. A., Flinspach, S., Miller, T., Vevea, J., & Gage-Serio, O. (2009, December). *Vocabulary growth over time: Results of a multiple level vocabulary assessment based on grade level materials.* Paper presented at the annual meeting of the National Reading Conference, Albuquerque, NM.

Scott, J. A., Hoover, M., Flinspach, S. L., & Vevea, J. L. (2008). A multiple-level vocabulary assessment tool: Measuring word knowledge based on grade-level materials. In Y. Kim, V. Risko, D. Compton, D. Dickinson, M. Hundley, R. Jimenez, et al. (Eds.), *57th annual yearbook of the National Reading Conference* (pp. 325–340). Oak Creek, WI: National Reading Conference.

Scott, J. A., & Nagy, W. E. (2004). Developing word consciousness. In J. Baumann & E. Kame'enui (Eds.), *Vocabulary instruction: From research to practice* (pp. 201–217). New York: Guilford Press.

Scott, J. A., Nagy, W. E., & Flinspach, S. L. (2008). More than merely words: Redefining vocabulary learning in a culturally and linguistically diverse society. In A. E. Farstrup & S. J. Samuels (Eds.), *What research has to say about vocabulary instruction* (pp.182–210). Newark, DE: International Reading Association.

Scott, J. A., Skobel, B., & Wells, J. (2008). *The word conscious classroom: Building the vocabulary readers and writers need.* New York: Scholastic.

Scott, J. A., Vevea, J., & Flinspach, S., (2010, December). Vocabulary growth in fourth grade classrooms: A quantitative analysis. In K. Moloney (Chair), *The VINE Project: A three-year study of word consciousness in fourth-grade classrooms.* Symposium conducted at the meeting of the National Reading Conference, Fort Worth, TX.

Stahl, S. (2003). How words are learned incrementally over multiple exposures. *American Educator, 27*(1), 18–19.

Chapter 10

Keep the "Fun" in Fundamental

*Encouraging Word Consciousness and Incidental
Word Learning in the Classroom through Word Play*

Camille L. Z. Blachowicz
Peter Fisher

The title of this chapter comes from a teacher, participating in a staff development activity on word play, who noted, "Well, this puts some of the 'fun' back in fundamental. Vocabulary instruction can be pretty grim sometimes." This comment dovetailed with our own experiences in working with reluctant readers in clinics and classrooms where word play proved to be a powerful learning and motivation tool, particularly for children whose home experiences do not involve linguistic play. These two observations helped us set the first goal of this chapter: to link word play and the development of word consciousness in students with the research on metacognition and vocabulary instruction. In this age of evidence-based practice, such a link is needed for teachers to ground the inclusion of word play in the curriculum. Our stimulus came from reviews of vocabulary instruction and development that emphasized the importance of vocabulary (Baumann, Kame'enui, & Ash, 2003), suggested that researchers address the application of vocabulary research to teachers' practical problems (Blachowicz & Fisher, 2001), and that vocabulary learning should be emphasized as a metacognitive activity (Nagy & Scott, 2001). On the basis of the work we reviewed, we propose research-based principles for using word play in the classroom. Our second goal is to share some examples of instruction consistent with these principles and to discuss the ways in which these principles offer guidance in the development of effective strategies, good habits, and the love of words in learners.

THE RESEARCH BASE FOR WORD PLAY IN THE CLASSROOM

We believe that the evidence base supports using word play in the classroom. Our belief relates to these four research-grounded principles about word play:

- Word play is a motivating and important component of the word-rich classroom.
- Word play calls on students to reflect metacognitively on words, word parts, and context.
- Word play requires students to be active learners and capitalizes on possibilities for the social construction of meaning.
- Word play develops domains of word meaning and relatedness as it engages students in the practice and rehearsal of words.

Word Play, Motivation, and the Language- and Word-Rich Classroom

All teachers know the motivational value of play. Things we enjoy and view as sources of pleasure stay with us throughout our lives. The motivated learner is the engaged learner who has a personal sense of self-confidence in participating in learning activities (Au, 1997), participates in a knowledgeable and strategic fashion, and is socially interactive (Casey, 2009; Guthrie et al., 2006). This engagement and enjoyment are highly correlated with achievement in all areas of literacy (Campbell, Voelkl, & Donahue, 1997), including vocabulary learning. In one highly controlled study of vocabulary learning in the middle grades (Beck, Perfetti, & McKeown, 1982), a curious phenomenon surfaced. Out of all the classrooms involved in the research project, students in one classroom learned more incidental vocabulary—words no one was attempting to teach. When trying to locate the source of this learning, the researchers were unable to come up with any instruction or materials that could account for the difference. Then one researcher noted a poster of interesting words in the classroom. When the teacher was asked about it, she noted that it was the "word wall"—a place where students could write new words that they encountered in reading, in conversation, on TV, or in their daily experiences. If they could write the word, talk about where they heard or saw it, and use it, they received points in a class contest. Very little expense, instructional time, or effort was involved, but the students became "tuned in" to learning new words in a way that positively affected their learning. They actively watched and listened for new words and shared them with their peers. They were motivated word learners.

Self-direction is an important component of motivation. With students who are English learners, some degree of choice about word learning is important. Jiminez (1997) found that middle school readers were more motivated and learned more vocabulary when they could have a say in selecting some of the words they were to learn. Using the Vocabulary Self-Collection Strategy (Haggard, 1982), a strategy that helps students develop selection and learning strategies, motivated students to say, "I used to only think about vocabulary in school. The whole world is vocabulary" and "I hear words everywhere that would be good to use" (Ruddell & Shearer, 2002, p. 352). Self-selection does not water down vocabulary learning in the classroom. Rather, the opposite often occurs. For example, fourth-grade students allowed to choose words to learn from a novel study unit chose words of greater difficulty than graded word lists would have provided them. Importantly, they learned the words they selected (Fisher, Blachowicz, & Smith, 1991). Personal interest and choice are powerful aids to vocabulary learning.

Word play is also one element of the word-rich classroom so critical to the development of word consciousness in students (Lubliner & Scott, 2008)—the same consciousness that leads to greater incidental word learning. There is a significant research base for creating a word-rich environment in the classroom and for the development of word-aware learners. The need to increase student exposure to vocabulary is well established. Students from families entering preschool who have many opportunities for oral interactions have larger vocabularies than children who have limited interactions (Hart & Risley, 1995). The latter often lag behind in reading so that by third grade their exposure to new vocabulary through reading has been impoverished as well (Cunningham & Stanovich, 1998). All these gaps result in learners who, by fourth grade, have much smaller vocabularies than their peers (Becker, 1977).

All students need to be surrounded by words and motivated to learn them. Reading to students is a must to expose them to vocabulary that they would not encounter on their own. Just as teachers have begun to use the term "flood of books" to talk about situations where students have many and varied opportunities to read (Anderson, Wilson, & Fielding, 1988), so too is creating a "flood of words" an important hallmark of general vocabulary development. Wide reading is another characteristic of word learning, with many studies suggesting that word learning occurs normally and incidentally during normal reading (Anderson, 1996; Nagy, Herman, & Anderson, 1985). Reading to children has been shown to have an effect not only on their recognition knowledge of new words but also on their ability to use these words in their own retellings (Dickinson & Smith, 1994); so a wide variety of materials used for reading to children and for their own reading is necessary to develop the word-rich classroom. Word play can round out the word-rich classroom by providing another way for young learners to encounter, practice, and become interested in these building blocks of literacy.

Metacognition and Word Play

Question: What vehicle do you use to take a pig to the hospital?
Answer: A *ham*bulance, of course!

Corny? Yes. Metacognitive? Definitely. Anyone who understands the pun has performed a metacognitive act. First, there must be the association of *ham* with *pig*, the segmenting of the first syllable of *ambulance* and replacing it with the syllable *ham*, and then recognizing and using the meaning of *ambulance* as a vehicle for hospital transport. The groan or laugh that results is our metacognitive check. We get the joke and we exhibit cognitive flexibility, the ability to look at the same thing in different ways. Many children, however, don't get it. Watch a child react to a book such as *The King Who Rained* (Gwynne, 1970), which focuses on humorous interpretations of various expressions. Some students interpret the expressions literally; they don't have the knowledge to draw on for word meaning, nor do they have the flexibility to think about words and word parts in more than one way. So a joke about having a "frog in my throat" is horrifying rather than funny. Creating and sharing jokes, riddles, and puns can help develop this flexibility.

Traditionally, vocabulary instruction has focused on helping students learn meanings of words (Watts, 1995). In this long-entrenched approach, words are considered individually, not in a domain or context, and the learning is typically receptive, not constructive. Students are either given a definition or asked to look one up, often resulting in hilarious mistakes, as the young girl who described an *acute angle* as "a very good looking angle." An alternative approach is to consider vocabulary instruction as metalinguistic development (Nagy & Scott, 2001). The ability to reflect on, manipulate, combine, and recombine the components of words is an important part of vocabulary learning (Tunmer, Herriman, & Nesdale, 1988). Phonological awareness (being able to segment speech sounds, such as removing *am* from *ambulance*), morphological awareness (the awareness of word-part meanings), and syntactic awareness (how a word functions in language) all play important parts in word learning (Carlisle, 1995). There is also evidence that this type of learning is developmental over the school years (Anglin, 1993; Roth, Speece, Cooper, & De la Paz, 1996).

Using morphology along with context is the most effective way to unravel the meanings of new words. Syntax is needed to determine if the letters *t-e-a-r* mean a *tear* in the eye or a *tear* in fabric. You can't phonologically decode those letters without a context. Context enables you to check your understanding by reading further to see if your choice makes sense (Tunmer, 1990). Indeed, the learning of definitions is often hampered by the failure to use a word's part of speech to help understand what a word really means and how it is used (Fischer, 1990; Scott, 1991). It has been proposed that the greater metacognitive ability of children functioning in two languages is the result of their operating on words as objects and examining words and word parts in an analytical way (Taeschner, 1983; Carlo, 2009). Word play, punning, joking, and other forms of word manipulation can make this metacognitive operation happen. So, developing an environment in which word play and word consciousness are integral is an appropriate goal for the classroom teacher. Later in this chapter, we share ideas for word play in order to develop flexible ways of thinking about words.

Word Play and Active Social Construction of Meaning

In addition to immersion in words, talk is critical to word play and word learning. Discussion in the classroom (Stahl & Vancil, 1986) and around the dinner table (Snow, 1991) is another correlate of incidental word learning. Although this type of learning through exposure cannot guarantee the learning of specific words, it does develop a wide, flexible, and usable general vocabulary, as well as the opportunity to learn from others. "Two heads are better than one" is especially true in vocabulary learning. There is rarely any word presented in a classroom context that does not elicit some meaning, association, or idea from some member of the class.

As in all learning situations, having learners actively attempt to construct their own meanings is a hallmark of good instruction. Learning new words as we have new experiences is one of the most durable and memorable ways to develop a rich vocabulary. Words such as *thread, needle, selvage, pattern*, and *dart* are naturally learned in the context of learning to sew, just as *hit, run, base*, and *fly* take on special meanings for the baseball player. Answering and asking questions that invite students to evaluate different features of word meaning or different issues of a text are other ways to actively engage students in discovering meaning (McKeown, Beck, & Worthy, 1993). For example, answering and explaining one's answer to the question, "Would a recluse enjoy parties?" helps students focus on the important features of the word *recluse*. This discussion makes the process of figuring out meanings visible to learners.

Teachers can also make word meanings and relationships visible for students by having them actively construct word meaning. Chart games, collections, pen-and-paper games, manipulative category games, and art and drama not only physically display attributes of meanings but also provide memory organizers for later word use. For example, in coining the word *inoculatte*—the first shot of coffee that gets you through the day—the student who drew the picture (see Figure 10.1) provided a pun with the attendant actual word meanings for memory.

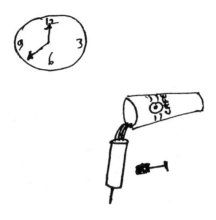

FIGURE 10.1. Inoculatte.

Word Play, Semantic Relatedness, Practice, and Rehearsal

Many studies have shown the efficacy of putting word meaning into graphic form, such as a map or web, a semantic feature chart, or advanced organizer (Johnson, Toms-Bronowski, & Pittelman, 1982). It is critical to note, however, that mere construction of such graphics without discussion is not effective (Stahl & Vancil, 1986). Other approaches that stress actively relating words to one another are clustering strategies that call for students to group words into related sets. These include brainstorming, grouping, and labeling (Marzano & Marzano, 1988); designing concept hierarchies; constructing definition maps related to concept hierarchies (Bannon, Fisher, Pozzi, & Wessell, 1990; Schwartz & Raphael, 1985); and mapping words according to their relation to story structure categories (Blachowicz, 1986). All these approaches involve student construction of maps, graphs, charts, webs, or clusters that represent the semantic relatedness of words under study to other words and concepts.

In word play, category games such as Scattergories are the "play" versions of these techniques. Word picture games such as Pictionary that use art to display meaning, acting-out games such as Charades, and synonym games such as Password and Taboo all emphasize semantic categories and relatedness and provide for practice and rehearsal. In addition to the obvious active learning involved, word play also provides a vehicle for use and rehearsal; the creation of a personal record, including visualization in graphics and drawing (Pressley & Woloshyn, 1995); and kinesthetic representations in drama (Duffelmeyer, 1980). Discussion, sharing, and use of the words are necessary components of active involvement, as is feedback and scaffolding on the part of the teacher.

In summary, we ground word play in the classroom in the research base that suggests that it develops word consciousness by engaging learners in learning and wanting to learn new words and developing their metacognitive ability. The evidence base suggests that, for effective word play in the classroom, teachers should (1) create a word-rich environment; (2) call on students to reflect metacognitively on words, word parts, and context; (3) encourage active engagement with discussion; and (4) emphasize relatedness in rehearsal and practice. We now present examples of word play that achieve these objectives.

PRACTICE: MAKING IT HAPPEN

Creating a Word-Rich Environment

Materials

A classroom full of materials is essential for exposing all growing readers to a wide selection of vocabulary (Cunningham & Stanovich, 1998). Variety in levels of materials and topics is a *must*. Literacy materials should be chosen for motivational as well as instructional value. In addition to books, materials such as newspapers, magazines, reference works, and technological references such as CD ROMs are necessary to meet the needs of all readers. A variety of excellent magazines is available for young children (e.g., *Lady Bug, Ranger Rick, National Geographic for Kids*) and for upper elementary or adolescent students (e.g., *BMX, Skateboarder, Guitar*). Subscriptions to daily newspapers and weekly newsmagazines provide ongoing connections to current events and an introduction to adult reading. Magazines in content areas such as science (*Contact*) or history (*Cobblestone*) or regional magazines such as *Illinois History* or *Merlin's Pen* provide current and motivating material related to the curriculum. Internet news groups and topical forums also require reading and give a "hot-off-the-press" feel to the reading curriculum. Classrooms should also have small-group and large-group sets of books, novels, anthologies, short stories, and magazines. Teachers often like to create sets of related books centering around one topic. For example, for a unit on the sea, a third-grade teacher collected books on several different levels. As part of the unit, she included a book about whale rescue, one about the life cycle of whales, and a third about whale habitats. The first book was about at grade level, the second a bit easier, and the third a bit more difficult. She used these as core books for the unit and then allowed students to seek out related materials. As the students engaged in small- and large-group discussions, the teacher listed thematic vocabulary that crossed all the books (e.g., *baleen, blowhole, spout, sound*).

Students with easy access to books read more and encounter more vocabulary than students who have to go down the hall at fixed periods to a school library or fetch books from high shelves. A comfortable place to read; a collection of good books, magazines, and newspapers; and the ability to develop a personal collection through book orders all increase the number of new words students encounter and practice on a daily basis.

Games

Games are useful for vocabulary practice and rehearsal. We suggest a variety of card, board, and other games to promote vocabulary development.

CARD GAMES

Cards emphasize semantic relationships by working on the pairing principle. A pair is made when you match a word with a synonym, a definition, an antonym, a cloze sentence in which the word makes sense, a picture symbolizing the word's meaning, or an English translation. Have students prepare a deck of at least 40 word-card pairs from words across their curriculum. For example, you might emphasize synonyms such as:

altitude		height

Cards are shuffled, and seven are dealt to each player. Each player can choose a card and discard one card in turn. Pairs can be placed on the table. The first player to pair all cards wins.

The same decks of word cards can be used to play more traditional games. For "Go Fish," all the cards are dealt, and players pick one card from the player on their left in turn. Pairs can be placed on the table. The first player to pair all cards wins. For "Old Teacher," a variation of Old Maid, an extra card is prepared with a drawing of the teacher—or a generic teacher. This is played like Go Fish. The person who is left with this card is the "Old Teacher."

In all card games, students must read their pairs and can be challenged by another student if the group does not agree with the pair. The dictionary settles disputes. If the challenger is correct, she or he can take an extra turn; if the challenger is incorrect, the player gets an extra turn.

RACE-AND-CHASE BOARD GAMES

Race-and-chase games require a poster board game board and moving pieces. Many teachers like to construct generic race-and-chase boards that can be used with many sets of cards. A 2" × 3" index card cut in half or thirds is an excellent size for word cards. Moving pieces can be commercially purchased at teacher stores or taken from garage sale games. In addition, dice or spinners are useful.

One of the easiest race-and-chase formats is "Synonym Match." The stack of word cards is placed in the center of the board, and the synonym cards are arranged face up. Each student rolls a die and picks up a word card. If the student can correctly locate the synonym match, he or she can move the number of spaces on the die. The group and the dictionary again serve as the check. A harder version requires the students to use words in original sentences.

MEMORY GAMES

Like commercial memory games, word memory, or "Concentration," involves finding matches and remembering cards. Play this game with about 25 cards—12 word cards, 12 match cards, and 1 wild card. All the cards are shuffled and placed face down. In each turn, a student turns up and reads two cards. If the cards are a match, the student takes the cards. If they are not a match, they are turned over and left in the same place. Students may use the wild card only if they can supply a suitable match orally. This can be checked at the end of the game by looking at the remaining card. The student with the most cards wins.

BINGO

This popular game can be played by any size group. Students have sets of word cards from which they construct a 5 × 5 (25-space) bingo card. They lay out their cards in any manner they choose, placing a "free" card in the space of their choice. The caller chooses definitions from the definition pile and reads them out. Students can place markers on the words that match. The first student to mark an entire row, column, or diagonal wins. Students check by reading the words and definitions. The cards are reshuffled, each student's cards are rearranged, and the winner becomes the caller for the next game. There are also many versions of Spanish–English cognate activities, including bingo available on-line (e.g., *www.eslprintables.com*).

ADAPTING COMMERCIAL GAMES

Besides teacher-made games (*teachers.net/lessons/posts/1399.html*), many commercial games can be adapted for class use. For general word learning, Scrabble, Probe, Pictionary, Pictionary Junior, Bananagrams, Apples to Apples, and Boggle are excellent. Teachers can add dictionary use as a component of play. Facts in Five, and Scattergories are variations of the category game and can build general word learning. Outburst and Outburst Junior help develop networks by association. All are worthwhile for general vocabulary development.

CROSSWORDS AND OTHER PUZZLES

Browsing any newsstand or bookstore will emphasize the popularity of word puzzles. Involvement in creating and doing puzzles can build a lifelong interest in words for students. Crossword puzzles are among the most popular type of word puzzle for adults. They are so familiar that we won't go into detail about them here. One point for teachers to note is that, although crosswords are familiar to most adults, the process is not familiar to most children. Take the time to work through puzzles with your students until they get the general idea of how they are completed. Keeping blank grids in your classroom for creating puzzles is also a wonderful way to stimulate thinking about words and definitions.

CODES

Students love secret codes. Decoding a word, phrase, or sentence demands a substantial use of context and inference. Many books of coded and encrypted messages can be purchased at bookstores, supermarkets, and newsstands.

JUMBLES

Jumbles, or anagrams, call for readers to unscramble words and letters to match a clue, sometimes in cartoon form. Most newspapers run a daily jumble that can provide good classroom material—as well as an incentive to browse the paper each day. This can be a good starter in middle school or high school homeroom periods.

Media Resources

Modern media offer many opportunities for providing a variety of differentiated learning and practice activities.

TV/VIDEO

The PBS series *WordGirl* (*pbskids.org/wordgirl*) stars WordGirl, an alien with superpowers whose secret identity is Becky Botsford, a 10½-year-old fifth-grade student. WordGirl was born on the fictional planet Lexicon (also a term referring to the vocabulary of a language or to a dictionary) but was sent away after sneaking onto a spaceship and sleeping there. Each episode deals with two or more target words in the context of an entertaining program. The site also offers ideas for parents and teachers and links to archived programs.

ONLINE

Teachers and students can consult a number of vocabulary websites. For example:

- *www.vocabulary.com.* This website can be used by both teachers and students in middle school or above. It links to Visual Thesaurus, the Online Etymological Dictionary, and other useful sites.
- *www.wordsmith.org/awad.* A.Word.A.Day (AWAD) has a theme of the week, such as words of German origin or words related to Halloween.
- *www.randomhouse.com/features/rhwebsters/game.html.* The game on this website is called "Beat the Dictionary," and it is basically a version of online "Hangman."
- *rhyme.lycos.com.* This website contains a rhyming dictionary and thesaurus program.
- *www.wordexplorations.com.* This site describes itself as an advanced English vocabulary site that will expand visitors' vocabulary by focusing on Latin and Greek elements used in English.
- Facebook and other social networking sites also offer vehicles for playing interactive word games online both in real time and asynchronously.

Computer Play and Exploration

Many commercial programs are available for word play. For example, some create crosswords, semantic maps, or word clusters, and there are electronic dictionaries and thesauruses. Handheld programs, such a Wordiac and others, are available for word practice.

Word Play Emphasizing Metacognitive Manipulation of Words and Word Parts

Students become interested in riddles and jokes in the early grades, and "pun-o-mania" hits in the middle grades. Riddle and joke books abound and quickly circulate in most classrooms. Creating riddles, jokes, and puns is one way to stimulate exploration of words and to build interest and flexibility in word learning.

Word Riddles

Mike Thaler (1988), a prolific author and conference speaker, has collected many ideas for riddle and joke making. One way to make word riddles that are questions with pun-like responses is to choose a subject and generate a list of related terms. For example, if your subject is *pig*, your list might contain *ham, pork, pen, grunt, hog,* and *oink.* You take the first letters off one of the words and make a list of words that begin with that letter pattern. For example, if you chose *ham,* you would make a list that began with *am,* such as *ambulance, amnesia, amphibian,* and *America.* Then you put back the missing letter and get *hambulance, hamnesia, hamphibian,* and *hamerica.* Then you make up riddles for the words.

> *Riddle:* How do you take a pig to a hospital?
> *Answer:* In a *ham*bulance!
>
> *Riddle:* What do you call it when a pig loses its memory?
> *Answer: Ham*nesia!

Taking students through five steps ensures that the process is transparent to them: (1) shared experience, (2) think-aloud through the riddle, (3) group creation, (4) independent scaffolded creation, and (5) independent practice. Students can be supported further by providing many books of jokes, riddles, and puns that give them pleasurable practice as they become "riddlers."

Name Riddles

Thaler (1988) also suggests name riddles. Look for names with the related word part. For example, remaining in the "pig mode":

> *Riddle:* What pig discovered the theory of relativity?
> *Answer:* Albert *Swine*stein!

Hink Pink

Hink Pink asks students to come up with a pair of rhyming words to match a defining phrase. Each word in the pair should have the same number of syllables. The person who creates the phrase clues the guesser with the term Hink Pink (two one-syllable words), Hinky Pinky (two two-syllable words), Hinkety Pinkety (two 3-syllable words), and so forth. For example:

> *Clue:* Hink Pink—an angry father. (Answer: mad dad)
> *Clue:* Hinkety Pinkety—an evil clergyman. (Answer: sinister minister)

Hink Pinks are fun, and often students can come up with more than one answer for a clue. Any meaningful answer is acceptable. The trick to understanding Hink Pinks is to learn to write them. Start with the answer, which is usually an adjective paired with a noun. These words must share the same number of syllables and rhyme, for example, *mad dad* from above. To write the question, brainstorm synonyms for each word (e.g., synonyms for *mad* = *angry, irritated, upset*; synonyms for *dad* = *father, pop, pater*). Pick one from each set to make the riddle (e.g., What's an angry father, an irritated pater, or an upset pop?).

Encouraging Active Engagement with Discussion

Many activities we have described call upon students to speak with others to clarify thinking. There are other playful ways in which talk can be encouraged in word play, such as playing guessing games and engaging in drama and drawing games.

20 Questions

This game can be adapted to help students think about words they are learning. The student who is "it" selects a word card from a prepared stack. Other students ask up to 20 yes/no questions. A turn ends with a "no." If one correctly guesses the word, that player becomes "it" for the next round. If students do not guess the word, "it" gets another turn.

Categories

One of the most popular pencil-and-paper games is Categories. Draw a suitable size grid (e.g., 2 × 2 for young students; 5 × 5 for older students), and label each row with a category. Then choose a word whose number of letters matches the number of columns. For example, students in a ninth-grade study hall working on the Civil War constructed the grid shown in Figure 10.2. Players are given a designated time limit to fill in as many squares as they can, after which points are totaled. Taking each student's card individually, players get 5 points for every category square they fill in

	A	R	M	I	E	S
Specific Confederacy Words		Rebel				
Specific Union Words						Sherman
Military Words		Rifle		Infantry		Sniper
Battles and Places	Atlanta					

FIGURE 10.2. Categories grid for the Civil War.

that no other player has filled; 2 points for every category square filled in that others have filled in, but with other words; and 1 point for every category square filled in where someone else has the same term. Inappropriate entries can be challenged and carry no point totals if they are not suitable.

Word Challenge

Word Challenge is another category game in which the categories are established to focus on particular word characteristics. For example, categories might include synonyms, antonyms, or related words (see Figure 10.3). The rules for Word Challenge are the same as for Categories.

Word	Antonym
hard	*soft*
sensible	*silly*
healthy	*sick*
neat	*sloppy*
praise	*scold*
friendly	*spiteful*

FIGURE 10.3. Word Challenge grid—alphabet antonyms (students have to choose antonyms that all begin with the same letter).

Word Fluency

Word Fluency is a technique that encourages students to use categorization to learn vocabulary (Readence & Searfoss, 1980). It is especially useful in a one-to-one or small-group situation. The task is to name as many words as possible in 1 minute. The teacher or a student chosen to be monitor tallies the words as the student says them. If the student hesitates for 10 seconds or more, the teacher suggests looking around the room or to think about an activity he or she recently completed. After the student's initial effort, the teacher models naming words in *categories*, which is much easier and faster than choosing random words. The rules for scoring are (1) no repetitions, no number words, no sentences; (2) 1 point for each word; and (3) 1 point for each category of four words or more.

Students see this game as a challenge and enjoy it—they want to try to beat their own score. Once a student is familiar with the activity, the tutor can provide categories from topics that have been studied recently: animals, science, or families, for example. The student must name only those words that could be in these categories. Recently a tutor in our reading center wrote in her log about using Word Fluency with her student, Serge: "The word fluency was so much fun. Serge left it until last, but he had so much fun with it, I think he will choose it much earlier tomorrow." She felt that this activity provided a good review of the vocabulary for Serge and, more importantly, demonstrated to him that he knew "lots of words."

Drama

Drama can be used in three games to promote word play: Synonym String, Situations, and charades. First, use drama to build a set of related words, the Synonym String. Divide the class into two teams and present each team with a starter word, such as *walk*. The groups need to come up with as many synonyms as they can and illustrate each dramatically. For example, they might *stroll, saunter, sashay, amble*, and so forth. A thesaurus can be helpful, or the teacher can present a list of words. Synonym Strings can lead to a discussion of denotative and shades-of-word meanings.

Second, students can dramatize words to create meaningful Situations that clarify word meaning (Duffelmeyer, 1980). Prepare a set of word cards, each containing a word, its meaning, an example of a situation, and a question. For example, the word might be *irate*; the situation might be to act out an irate father talking with a son who came in late for curfew; and the question might be, "When have you been *irate?*" Form groups of students and give one card to each group. The actors have time to discuss the word and plan a skit (limit to 5 minutes). They can use the situation on the card or plan their own. When presenting their skit, one member of the group writes the word on the board and pronounces it. The skit is acted out, and a cast member asks the audience the question and meaning of the word. At this point, the teacher can provide feedback, and all class members enter the word in a vocabulary file along with the meaning and some personal context.

Third, charades can be played with phrases or single words. Words or phrases are written on word cards and placed in a stack. Students are divided into teams. One member of a team draws a card and attempts to act out each word or syllable of the word using a series of signals. A timekeeper from the other team keeps track of the time, and the team with the lowest time score after a full round wins. The related game Guesstures is a playful form of acting out words that older students love.

Art

Students love to play with words using art and drawing to create visual riddles. Not only does art provide a multisensory way to provide keys to word learning, but it also can provide a playful way for students with nonverbal talents to relate to word learning. For example, for high school students studying word parts, a drawing activity was a natural way to show learning. If students are studying Latin forms (e.g., *tri* = three, *ped* = feet, *bi* = two, *corn* = horned, *optis* = eye), they can create and label their own original animals. For example, a bicornoptistriped (two-horned, three-footed animal with an eye) was drawn, as shown in Figure 10.4.

FIGURE 10.4. A bicornoptistriped triped.

Emphasizing Relatedness in Rehearsal and Practice

Most school curricula focus on common word categories such as synonyms, antonyms, similes, and metaphors. But what about acronyms, portmanteau words, imported words, slang, collective words, and other creative categories of words?

Consider portmanteau words. When you pack a suitcase, or portmanteau, sometimes you scrunch things together to make room. For example, you might put your socks in your shoes. *Portmanteau* words are packed words formed by merging portions of one word with another. For example, *smog* is a common portmanteau word based on a combination of *smoke* and *fog*. English has a rich history of creating new words in this way, a tendency readily picked up by Madison Avenue, journalists, and comic book writers. Advertising has given us the *motel* (*motor* + *hotel*), cartoons *zap* (*zip* + *slap*), science the *beefalo* (*beef* + *buffalo*), and political journalism *insinuendo* (*insinuation* + *innuendo*) (McKenna, 1978). Include these in your investigation of words to help build broad categories of vocabulary. Teachers often have students build bulletin board lists or word walls of these fascinating types of words, such as the following categories:

- Acronym: a word formed from the initial letters of other words (e.g., *scuba* = self-contained underwater breathing apparatus).
- Anagram: a word or phrase formed by scrambling the letters of a word (e.g., *lake*<cstyle:TextItalic>kale).
- Borrowed words: words used in English from other countries (e.g., *café, lariat, pretzel*).
- Collective words: words that label a group, typically of animals (e.g., *a gaggle* of geese, a pride of lions).
- Malapropism: use of an incorrect word for a similar sounding one (e.g., "My gramma has very close veins").
- Onomatopoeia: a word whose sound relates to its meaning (e.g., *buzz, gulp*).
- Oxymoron: a phrase composed of words that seem contradictory (e.g., *plastic silverware*).
- Palindrome: words or phrases that read the same forward or backward (e.g., *mom, dad*, "Able was I ere I saw Elba").
- Spoonerism: an unintentional transposition of sounds (e.g., "Please pass the salt and *shecker papers*").

Students also like to make collections of personal-interest words, such as "All the Words about . . . " books. In these books, students collect words related to a topic, a hobby, a person of interest, and so forth, and soon the class library has such collections as "All the Words about Baseball," "All the Words about Ferrets," and "All the Words about Denzel Washington." Students are fascinated by other students' collections, and these books, many illustrated or collaged, circulate widely.

A FINAL WORD

In this chapter, we have presented a research base for using word play in the classroom. This grounding supports four goals for classroom word play: (1) create a word-rich environment; (2) call on students to reflect metacognitively on words, word parts, and context; (3) encourage active engagement with discussion; and (4) emphasize relatedness in rehearsal and practice. There is convincing evidence that classroom practice reflecting these principles will encourage students' incidental word learning as well as developing their word consciousness and interest. In addition, our own experience working with struggling readers, in particular, is that, almost universally, they have not participated in word games either at home or at school. When we invite them to do so, they often become animated and motivated. They look forward to those parts of our sessions together and frequently take games home to play with parents and siblings. We have found that parents who are eager to improve their child's literacy rarely think of word games as something that can be done at home. However, when they try them and see the joy that they can bring to a previously reluctant learner, they ask for more. Consequently, we view games and word play as valuable activities in the curriculum and as an effective way to encourage links between home and school. Games and word play are vehicles for putting the "fun" back in one of the most fundamental aspects of learning during the school years—vocabulary development.

ACKNOWLEDGMENTS

The preparation of this chapter was supported in part by the Institute of Education Sciences, U.S. Department of Education, through Grant No. R305A090163 to the University of Missouri, the University of Wyoming, and National Louis University. The opinions expressed are those of the authors and do not represent views of the Institute or the U.S. Department of Education.

REFERENCES

Anderson, R. C. (1996). Research foundations to support wide reading. In V. Creany (Ed.), *Promoting reading in developing countries* (pp. 55–77). Newark, DE: International Reading Association.

Anderson, R. C., Wilson, P., & Fielding, L. (1988). Growth in reading and how children spend their time outside of school. *Reading Research Quarterly, 23,* 285–303.

Anglin, J. (1993). Vocabulary development: A morphological analysis. *Monographs of the Society for Research in Child Development, 58*(10, Serial No. 238).

Au, K. H. (1997). Ownership, literacy achievement, and students of diverse cultural backgrounds. In J. T. Guthrie & A. Wigfield (Eds.), *Reading engagement: Motivating readers through integrated instruction* (pp. 168–182). Newark, DE: International Reading Association.

Bannon, E., Fisher, P. J. L., Pozzi, L., & Wessel, D. (1990). Effective definitions for word learning. *Journal of reading, 34,* 301–302.

Baumann, J. F., Kame'enui, E. J., & Ash, G. E. (2003). Research on vocabulary instruction: Voltaire redux. In J. Flood, D. Lapp, J. R. Squire, & J. M. Jensen (Eds.), *Handbook of research on teaching the English language arts* (2nd ed., pp. 752–785). Mahwah, NJ: Erlbaum.

Beck, I. L., Perfetti, C. A., & McKeown, M. G. (1982). The effects of long-term vocabulary instruction on lexical access and reading comprehension. *Journal of Educational Psychology, 74,* 506–521.

Becker, W. C. (1977). Teaching reading and language to the disadvantaged—what we have learned from field research. *Harvard Educational Review, 47,* 518–543.

Blachowicz, C. L. Z. (1986). Making connections: Alternatives to the vocabulary notebook. *Journal of Reading, 29,* 643–649.

Blachowicz, C. L. Z., & Fisher, P. J. L. (2000). Vocabulary instruction. In M. L. Kamil, P. B. Rosenthal, P. D. Pearson, & R. Barr. (Eds.), *Handbook of reading research* (Vol. 3, pp. 503–523). New York: Longman.

Campbell, J. R., Voelkl, K., & Donahue, P. L. (1997). *NAEP 1996 trends in academic progress* (NCES Publication No. 97-985). Washington, DC: U.S. Department of Education.

Carlisle, J. (1995). Morphological awareness and early reading achievement. In L. Feldman (Ed.), *Morphological aspects of language processing* (pp. 189–209). Hillsdale, NJ: Erlbaum.

Carlo, M. S. (2009). Cross-language transfer of phonological, orthographic, and semantic knowledge. In L. M. Morrow, R. Rueda, & D. Lapp (Eds.), *Handbook of research on literacy and diversity* (pp. 277–291). New York: Guilford Press.

Casey, H. K. (2009). Engaging the disengaged: Using learning clubs to motivate struggling adolescent readers and writers. *Journal of Adolescent and Adult Literacy, 52,* 284–294.

Cunningham, A. E., & Stanovich, K. E. (1998). What reading does for the mind. *American Educator, 22,* 8–15.

Dickinson, D. K., & Smith, M. W. (1994). Long-term effects of preschool teachers' book readings on low-income children's vocabulary and story comprehension. *Reading Research Quarterly, 29,* 104–122.

Duffelmeyer, F. A. (1980). The influence of experience-based vocabulary instruction on learning word meanings. *Journal of Reading, 24,* 35–40.

Fischer, U. (1990). *How students learn words from a dictionary and in context.* Unpublished doctoral dissertation, Princeton University, Princeton, NJ.

Fisher, P. J. L., Blachowicz, C. L. Z., & Smith, J. C. (1991). Vocabulary learning in literature discussion groups. In J. Zutell & S. McCormick (Eds.), *Learner factors/teacher factors: Issues in literacy research and instruction* (pp. 201–209). Chicago: National Reading Conference.

Guthrie, J. T., Wigfield, A., Humenick, N. M., Perencevich, K. C., Taboada, A., & Barbosa, P. (2006). Influences of stimulating tasks on reading motivation and comprehension. *Journal of Educational Research, 99*, 232–245.

Gwynne, F. (1970). *The king who rained.* New York: Simon & Schuster.

Haggard, M. R. (1982). The vocabulary self-collection strategy: An active approach to word learning. *Journal of Reading, 26*, 203–207.

Hart, B., & Risley, T. R. (1995). *Meaningful differences in the everyday experience of young American children.* Baltimore: Brookes.

Jiminez, R. J. (1997). The strategic reading abilities and potential of five low-literacy Latina/o readers in middle school. *Reading Research Quarterly, 32*, 224–243.

Johnson, D. D., Toms-Bronowski, S., & Pittelman, S. D. (1982). *An investigation of the effectiveness of semantic mapping and semantic feature analysis with intermediate grade level students* (Program Rep. No. 83–3). Madison, WI: Wisconsin Center for Education Research, University of Wisconsin.

Lubliner, S., & Scott, J. A. (2008). *Nourishing vocabulary: Balancing words and learning.* Thousand Oaks, CA: Corwin Press.

Marzano, R. J., & Marzano, J. S. (1988). *A cluster approach to elementary vocabulary instruction.* Newark, DE: International Reading Association.

McKenna, M. (1978). Portmanteau words in reading instruction. *Language Arts, 55*, 315–317.

McKeown, M. G., Beck, I. L., & Worthy, M. J. (1993). Grappling with text ideas: Questioning the author. *The Reading Teacher, 46*, 560–566.

Nagy, W. E., Herman, P. A., & Anderson, R. C. (1985). Learning words from context. *Reading Research Quarterly, 20*, 233–253.

Nagy, W. E., & Scott, J. (2001). Vocabulary processes. In M. L. Kamil, P. B. Mosenthal, P. D. Pearson, & R. Barr (Eds.), *Handbook of reading research* (Vol. 3, pp. 269–283). New York: Longman.

Pressley, M., & Woloshyn, V. (1995). *Cognitive strategies: Instruction that really improves children's academic performance* (2nd ed.). Cambridge, MA: Brookline Books.

Readence, J. E., & Searfoss, L. W. (1980). Teaching strategies for vocabulary development. *English Journal, 69*, 43–46.

Roth, F., Speece, D., Cooper, D., & De la Paz, S. (1996). Unresolved mysteries: How do metalinguistic and narrative skills connect with early reading? *Journal of Special Education, 30*, 257–277.

Ruddell, M. R., & Shearer, B. A. (2002). "Extraordinary," "tremendous," "exhilarating," "magnificent": Middle school at-risk students become avid word learners with the vocabulary self-collection strategy (VSS). *Journal of Adolescent and Adult Literacy, 45*, 352–363.

Schwartz, R., & Raphael, T. (1985). Concept of definition: A key to improving students' vocabulary. *The Reading Teacher, 30*, 198–205.

Scott, J. (1991). *Using definitions to understand new words*. Unpublished doctoral dissertation, University of Illinois at Urbana–Champaign.

Snow, C. E. (1991). *Unfulfilled expectations: Home and school influences on literacy*. Cambridge, MA: Harvard University Press.

Stahl, S., & Vancil, S. (1986). Discussion is what makes semantic maps work in vocabulary instruction. *The Reading Teacher, 40*, 62–69.

Taeschner, T. (1983). *The sun is feminine: A study of language acquisition in bilingual children*. Berlin, Germany: Springer-Verlag.

Thaler, M. (1988). Reading, writing, and riddling. *Learning, 17*, 58–59.

Tunmer, W. E. (1990). The role of language prediction skills in beginning reading. *New Zealand Journal of Educational Studies, 25*, 95–114.

Tunmer, W. E., Herriman, M. L., & Nesdale, A. R. (1988). Metalinguistic abilities and beginning reading. *Reading Research Quarterly, 23*, 134–158.

Watts, S. M. (1995). Vocabulary instruction during reading lessons in six classrooms. *Journal of reading behavior, 27*, 399–424.

Chapter 11

Language Play

Essential for Literacy

Dale D. Johnson
Bonnie Johnson
Kathleen Schlichting

While recently riding a #2 New York City subway to Penn Station, we noticed two ads in the car: "Energy to scratch and claw your way out of the doghouse," sponsored by the National Peanut Board, and "Get Fat," sponsored by the New York State Lottery. On a rapid subway ride where visual stimuli compete for riders' attention, ad writers know that their work must be clever, memorable, understood by many riders, and say a lot in a few words. Regardless of geographic location, political persuasion, or demographics, figurative expressions are a part of modern Americans' vocabulary. In a recent issue of *Bon Appétit*, an article about a chef's abundance of serrano peppers carried the title "In a Pickle." A heading in the Business Day section of *The New York Times* asked, "Rotten Apple, or Sour Grapes?" Another *Times* Business Day section heading posed the question, "Which Grease for a Squeaky Wheel?" *The Wall Street Journal* chided, "Too Often, Chief Executives Sugarcoat the Truth." An Elkhart, Indiana, newspaper reported on a noodle-making factory under the headline "Using Their Noodles." As Johnson and Johnson (2011) pointed out, "We cannot be literate citizens unless we can understand figurative language" (p. 110). Figurative language, however, seems to be the elephant in the classroom. Linguist David Crystal (1998) noted:

> Given the high profile of language play within adult society, its prominence during the years when children are learning to speak, and its

210

relevance to literacy and verbal art, you would naturally expect that it would have a privileged place in those materials and settings where children are being taught to read and write, or to develop their abilities in the use of spoken language. . . . Well, if you do have these expectations, you will be severely disappointed. (p. 182)

Language play or *word play* refers to the adaptation or use of words to achieve an effect, and it is accomplished through the manipulation of meanings, arrangements, sounds, spellings, and various other dimensions of words, phrases, and sentences. Language play serves two critical roles in the home and classroom. First, a learner must be able to interpret and produce these linguistic manipulations to completely comprehend or generate oral or written language. A primary reason that American English is so colorful is because it is laced with word-play devices. The examples above show how widespread the use of idioms, proverbs, and ambiguity is in our everyday language. Second, children exhibit a natural interest in language from birth onward. They often explore and experiment with the sounds, the nuances, and the unpredictable qualities and complexities associated with language. Language can be a source of excitement and pleasure to children. As children observe and listen to others in their environment, they discover how to use language to communicate their wants, needs, and feelings. Children learn best when they have strong personal interest and are actively and interactively involved with learning. When children are having fun—when they see a purpose or direction to their learning—learning takes on a more authentic, more welcoming quality. As teachers, it is important that we incorporate language play activities in the classroom to stimulate, sustain, or recapture that natural interest. Some teachers recognize the value of engaging children in word-play activities. They observe the way children eagerly interact with this unique and playful aspect of language and how they revisit a familiar story, poem, or passage. Children return to a book such as *Tikki, Tikki, Tembo* (Mosel, 1968) to reread the story. They are heard during lunch and in hallways repeating its refrain.

Geller (1985), in the same vein as Crystal, stated that, based on her observations, language learning in classrooms is too often viewed as work rather than play:

> For me, as an educator, the anomaly in this situation has been the absence of word play from the classroom—especially classrooms of the primary and middle elementary years. Teachers of these ages are aware of youngsters' penchant for play; however, most see no educational reason to bring it into the classroom. The question generally posed is, What does word play have to do with language education? or, more to the point: What does word play have to do with the teaching of reading and writing? (pp. 2–3)

Word play has everything to do with language education and the teaching of reading and writing if we want students to be able to read an Internet site, a newspaper or magazine headline, understand a broadcast, read an ad on public transportation, or comprehend many narrative and expository texts. Below are seven categories of language play. In this chapter, we focus on two of the seven: figurative expressions and onomastics (the study of names) because of the categories' abundance in oral and written language.

THE SEVEN CATEGORIES OF LANGUAGE PLAY

1. Figurative language: idioms (*Hold your horses*), proverbs (*Too many cooks spoil the broth*), in-betweens (*greasy spoon*), catchphrases (*Don't call us, we'll call you*), slogans (*I Like Ike*), similes (*as due as the rent*), metaphors (*Steve is a walking dictionary*), hyperbole (*tons of money*), euphemisms (*between jobs*), oxymorons (*deliberate haste*).

2. Onomastics: proper names (*Bernadette*), nicknames (*Bernie*), pseudonyms (*Agatha Christie*), eponyms (*leotard*), toponyms (*paisley*), demonyms (*Long Islander*), place names (*Wilmington*), business names (*Movers not Shakers*, the name of a moving company in Brooklyn, New York).

3. Word associations: synonyms (*skinny–trim*), antonyms (*lively–dull*), homographs (*conduct*), homophones (*there–their*), collocations (*green grass*), coordinates (*pansy–daisy*), superordinates–subordinates (*flowers: tulips, daffodils*).

4. Word formations: affixes (*un-, -ous*), compounds (*homesick*), acronyms (*NATO*), initialisms (*FBI*), portmanteaus (*telecast*), neologisms (*twigloo*).

5. Word manipulations: anagrams (*teach–cheat*), palindromes (*star–rats*), rebuses (*2 4 T*).

6. Word games: alphabetic (*anagrams*), alliteration (*John Jones from Janestown*), rhyming (*swift gift*), riddles, tongue twisters (*sixty sticky thumbs*).

7. Ambiguities: ambiguous words, phrases, and sentences (*fish biting off the coast*).

RESEARCH REVIEW

Although word play has been described in books, specialized dictionaries, and periodicals, and despite its relevance to oral and written language development and maintenance, it has not received much recent research attention with school-age children. A few studies conducted in the 1980s and 1990s have examined acquisition and comprehension primarily of metaphors and idioms.

Ortony (1984) undertook a review of literature to answer the question of whether or not figurative language in written text was an important source of comprehension failure. He included such subcategories as similes, metaphors, irony, and other more obscure elements of figurative language. He defined figurative language as the use of language in which what is said is different from what is meant; the type of relationship between the two accounts for the different subcategories of figures of speech. Ortony concluded that "figurative (or at least metaphorical) uses of language do not require any special cognitive mechanism" (p. 466). He argued then that the greatest research needed was research related to instructional issues. Based on his review of research literature, he offered two suggestions for including this category of word play in classroom instruction:

> It would not be unreasonable at this juncture to wonder why one should bother to introduce figurative uses of language to young children. There are at least two answers to this. First, figurative language is a powerful way of relating old knowledge to new. Second, figurative language increases the expressive power of the available linguistic resources by permitting the expression of what might otherwise be difficult or impossible to express. How else can the opera singer's voice be described, if not by the metaphorical use of some word like *thin*? And, if ships don't plow the seas, what do they do literally? (p. 467)

Ortony argued for including appropriate use of figurative language from the earliest school years rather than waiting until middle grades, as is the current practice. Several authors who can skillfully help teach young children about the use of figurative language to create lasting images in the readers' minds are Patricia Polacco (2001), Chris Van Allsburg (1985), Barbara Park (1993), and David Shannon (1998).

Teresa Labov (1992) conducted a review of studies of adolescent slang. Based on her review and a questionnaire study of 89 slang terms used by high school and college students, she demonstrated differences in slang recognition. For example, more than 90% recognized *jocks* and *cool*, but only about 6% recognized *dexters* and *motorhead*. She found statistically significant differences for the recognition of specific slang terms by gender (e.g., *airhead* by girls), race (e.g., *homie* by African Americans), community type (e.g., *za* by suburbanites), school type (e.g., *dweebs* by private schoolers), coast (e.g., *wicked good* by East Coasters), and college year (e.g., *bag it* by college seniors).

Nippold, Uhden, and Schwarz (1997) demonstrated that language continues to develop through adolescence and into adulthood, especially in the interpretation of figurative language and expressions. Their study of low-familiarity proverbs with 353 subjects ranging in age from 13 to 79 showed this growth. Each proverb was used in a concluding sentence of a four-sentence story. The subjects read the paragraph silently and interpreted the proverb in writing. Nippold et al. noted that "performance on the task improved markedly during adolescence and into adulthood. It reached a plateau during the 20s" (p. 245).

Perhaps more studies of idiom comprehension have been reported than of any other category of language play. Studies have shown that older children comprehend more idioms than younger children and that the period between ages 7 and 11 is when idiom understanding is acquired most rapidly (Levorato & Cacciari, 1995). Other researchers have demonstrated that high-familiarity idioms such as *beat around the bush* are learned more easily than low-familiarity idioms such as *to take a powder* (Nippold & Taylor, 1995). Transparent idioms such as *to keep a straight face* are learned more easily than opaque idioms such as *talk through one's hat* (Gibbs, Nayak, & Cutting, 1989; Gibbs, 1991; Nippold & Taylor, 1995). Children of average intelligence are better at comprehending idioms than children with learning difficulties (Ezell & Goldstein, 1991).

Finally, children find it more difficult to produce idiomatic expressions than to comprehend them (Levorato & Cacciari, 1995). The implications of these studies on idioms are that school-age children can and do understand idiomatic expressions, their idiomatic facility develops through the school years, and some care must be taken by teachers in their own idiomatic usage with younger or academically less able students. Marvin Terban, an author of several books on idioms (*Punching the Clock*, 1990; *Mad as a Wet Hen!*, 1987; *Scholastic Dictionary of Idioms*, 1996), teaches children about the definitions and origins of idioms as he takes an everyday part of the English language and makes it engaging for students.

Holmes (1999) demonstrated that children use language play as a response to literature. The fourth graders in her study used conventional language play (e.g., metaphorical proverbs) and inventive language play (e.g., rhymes and colloquialisms) in both oral and written expression in response to stories.

FIGURATIVE LANGUAGE

Figurative language refers to the expressive use of language often in non-literal ways for special effects. It is more colorful than literal language and allows for greater range of interpretation. Figurative language is comprised of several subcategories; in this chapter we discuss *idioms, proverbs, in-betweens, catchphrases, slogans, similes, metaphors,* and *euphemisms.*

Idioms

An *idiom* is an expression in which the entire meaning is different from the usual meanings of the individual words. Idioms are often viewed as a single-vocabulary word in concept, even if they are made up of more than one word (e.g., *down in the mouth* means *sad*). As Crystal (1995) pointed out, no word in an idiomatic expression can be changed and retain the meaning of the idiom. For example, *a drop in the bucket* means a very small amount. The idiom cannot be changed to *a globule in the bucket* or *a drop in the pail*.

As we noted in an earlier work, "Understanding idiomatic expressions and other nonliteral figures of speech is particularly troublesome for learners who do not speak English fluently or for whom English is not the first language" (Johnson & Johnson, 2011, p. 114). There are approximately 5 million English learner (EL) students in U.S. schools who speak more than 400 different languages (Goldenberg, 2008). Classroom teachers find that many of their EL students need help with figurative language, in particular with idioms.

Perhaps the most surprising thing about idioms is that many are old. Three ancient idioms include *not out of the woods yet* (circa 200 B.C.E.), *to eat someone out of house and home* (40 C.E.), and *in one ear and out the other* (80 C.E.). Other comparatively old idioms include *in a pickle* (1585), *to walk on eggshells* (1621), and *to have bigger fish to fry* (1660).

Idioms that do not make literal sense to contemporary readers made perfectly good sense to speakers and the readers during the times in which they were coined. *To give someone the cold shoulder*, for example, can be traced to the 1800s. The idiom referred to the age-old problem of receiving unwelcome guests—usually right around mealtime. The guests were given a cheap shoulder cut of unheated meat to hasten their departure. *To have something up one's sleeve* is an even older idiom (1400s) that was used before pockets were invented; sleeves were used to keep items that we slip into pockets nowadays. We recommend the *Scholastic Dictionary of Idioms* (1996) by Marvin Terban for use with intermediate and middle grade students. The book contains the meanings and origins of more than 600 idioms. In the story *Junie B. Jones and a Little Monkey Business*, author Barbara Park (1993) offers students many examples of idioms.

A popular idiom exercise for younger students is to have them illustrate the literal meanings of the words within an idiom. For example, children learn that *in a pickle* means *in trouble* but would draw a picture of a person inside a gherkin (i.e., a fruit similar to a cucumber). In the second picture, students illustrate the figurative meaning of the idiom (i.e., to be in trouble).

Proverbs

A *proverb* is a short saying that offers guidance on how to live one's life. All cultures have proverbs because there never is a shortage of people, whether well-meaning or intrusive, who feel it necessary to provide advice to others. As with idioms, many proverbs are old and their originators have been lost with the passage of time. Examples include *Familiarity breeds contempt* (40s B.C.E.); *out of sight, out of mind* (1200s C.E.); *easy come, easy go* (1300s); and *Still waters run deep* (1400s). Some proverbs are contradictory. Examples include *The squeaky wheel gets the grease; Silence catches a mouse; Strike while the iron is hot; Haste makes waste; The more, the merrier; Two's company but three's a crowd.* Proverbs can serve a global purpose. Mieder (1986) wrote:

> In modern business and politics the understanding of proverbs plays a major role, often being the key to the success or breakdown of communications. It is a known fact that interpreters at the United Nations prepare themselves for their extremely sensitive job by learning proverbs of the foreign languages since politicians often argue or attempt to convince their opponents by the use of a native proverb. (pp. x–xi)

The study of proverbs fits into the study of any country or people. Proverbs used by particular cultures can provide insights into their guiding principles and show learners that there usually are common human threads and shared experiences regardless of geography or background. Here are a few: *Better a patch than a hole* (Welsh proverb); *No choice is also a choice* (Jewish proverb); *When the mouse laughs at the cat, there is a hole nearby* (Nigerian proverb); *Since the house is on fire, let's warm ourselves* (Italian proverb); *Never eat in a restaurant where the chef is thin* (Chinese proverb).

Although many familiar proverbs are old, some are fairly recent and have been created by Americans. Just three of many examples include *You can't unscramble eggs; An apple never falls far from the tree;* and *One who slings mud loses ground.* For those readers who want to investigate proverbs used in specific states in the country, a valuable resource is *A Dictionary of American Proverbs* (Mieder, Kingsbury, & Harder, 1992). Although the work is arranged according to key words (e.g., *clothes, meal, rule*), one can find proverbs used in certain states. From Louisiana comes *To know everything is to know nothing; When the outlook isn't good, try the uplook* was recorded in Illinois; and North Carolinians wisely say, *There's no beauty like the beauty of the soul.* Older students who grasp the meanings of these wise sayings will enjoy exploring books such as *Proverbs from Around the World* (Gleason, 1992) and the *International Dictionary of Proverbs* (de Ley, 1998).

In-Betweens

Slang, according to Lighter (1994), is "an informal, nonstandard, nontechnical vocabulary composed chiefly of novel-sounding synonyms for standard words and phrases" (p. xi). Slang expressions include *big bucks* (a lot of money), *burger joint* (a casual restaurant that features hamburgers on the menu), and *chicken feed* (a small amount of money). Slang has gotten a bum rap. Granted, some slang is fleeting and offensive; however, established slang adds variety and often amusement to our language. The importance of slang to our vocabularies has been supported by language scholars such as S. I. Hayakawa, H. L. Mencken, and Steven Pinker. Johnson and Johnson (2011) have coined the term *in-betweens* as a replacement for the word slang, because it has a more agreeable, less off-putting connotation.

Some words that we consider "legitimate" words started off as in-betweens and gradually worked their way into our everyday speech and writing. Examples include *number cruncher, cash cow, junk food, brown bag lunch, greasy spoon, puddle jumper, overkill, egghead, street smarts, tuckered out, wish list, sleazy, psyched up, nine-to-five, 24–7, to moonlight, low-life, high roller*, and tens of thousands more. There are in-between terms that are occupation-specific (e.g., a *bean counter*, a computer *hacker*), there are rhyming in-betweens (e.g., *fender bender, hodge-podge*), there are repeating in-betweens (e.g., a *no-no, so-so*), and there are in-betweens in which only a letter has been changed (e.g., *chit-chat, wishy-washy*). A useful resource for teachers is the *Random House Historical Dictionary of American Slang* (Lighter, 1994, 1997), which, when completed, will have three volumes. The etymologies of established slang are included. Some children's books that incorporate in-betweens include Alexandra Day's (1990, 1994) *Frank and Ernest* books, Diane Stanley's (1996) *Saving Sweetness*, and Jon Scieszka's (1989) *The True Story of the 3 Little Pigs*.

Catchphrases

Nigel Rees (1995) defined a *catchphrase* as "a phrase that has 'caught on' with the public and is, or has been, in frequent use" (p. vi). One might think that catchphrases are somewhat new expressions that have been helped along by the proliferation of contemporary media. Just as there are many old idioms, however, there also are many old catchphrases. *Avoid like the plague* was a catchphrase used during the fourth century; *Eat your heart out* was used in the 1500s. A catchphrase often wears itself out through overuse. A faux pas among those in the know is to date oneself by the use of an out-of-date catchphrase. As we examined catchphrases for this chapter, we noted that the older catchphrases (e.g., the journalistic *If in doubt, strike it out*, from 1894) seem fresher than the more recent ones

(*Are we having fun yet?* from 1984). Perhaps it is the nature of catchphrases to recycle themselves so that they appear clever to generations who don't remember them from their first time around.

Here is a list of just a few of the thousands of catchphrases in the English language. We have sequenced them according to the dates in which they became popular with large groups of people. These ten catchphrases are from Rees's (1995) *Dictionary of Catchphrases*:

- 1900: *It's all done with mirrors.*
- 1910: *Another day, another dollar.*
- 1920s: *Act your age.*
- 1930s: *Famous last words.*
- 1940s: *I don't mind if I do.*
- 1950s: *Be my guest.*
- 1960s: *Garbage in, garbage out.*
- 1970s: *Cry (or laugh) all the way to the bank.*
- 1980s: *Been there, done that.*
- 1990s: *Get a life.*
- 2000s: *It is what it is.*

Slogans

A *slogan* is a type of catchphrase that is used to promote a person, group, or product (Ammer, 1989). When we think of slogans, we often think of presidential campaigns and advertisements. Some memorable presidential campaign slogans include:

- *In Hoover we trusted, now we are busted* (Franklin Delano Roosevelt, 1932)
- *Dewey or don't we?* (1944, Thomas Dewey)
- *Phooey on Dewey* (1948, Harry S. Truman)
- *In your guts you know he's nuts* (1964, Lyndon B. Johnson, referring to Barry Goldwater)
- *What's wrong with being right?* (1964, Barry Goldwater); *Nixon is through in '72* (1972, George McGovern)
- *The nation needs fixin' with Nixon* (1972, Richard Nixon)
- *Yes we can* (2008, Barack Obama).

There is an onslaught of new political slogans every 4 years. As election time approaches in your community and state, have your students develop a collection of slogans used in ads by candidates or proponents of issues.

In addition to advertising slogans, of which there are many, slogans also can be found in public service announcements. The United States Post Office promises: *We deliver.* The Boys and Girls Club says, *Support the club that beats the streets. Only you can prevent forest fires* is Smokey the Bear's slogan. Johnson and Johnson (2011) state, "The sheer marketing objective of slogans is what differentiates them from catchphrases; they do not become popular accidentally as is the case with most catchphrases" (p. 194).

Similes and Metaphors

Similes and *metaphors* are literary devices that are used to make comparisons. *Similes* use the word *like* or *as.* Many familiar similes are relegated to the cliché pile, but to do so without studying their origins would be to miss out on stories that make our language captivating. We're not referring to *as thick as pea soup* or other obvious origins. Some, such as *neat as a pin*, are more difficult to figure out. For example, Johnson (1999) explained, "The simile 'neat as a pin' was recorded in the late 1700s as 'neat as a new pin.' Originally pins rusted quickly because they were made from iron wire. Only new pins were free of corrosion" (p. 171).

There are other intriguing origins for *know someone like a book, fit as a fiddle, as easy as pie, as happy as a clam*, and *as easy as falling off a log. Dictionary of Colorful Phrases* (Carothers & Lacey, 1994) is an easy-to-read resource for students and contains the stories behind some of our most commonly used similes. Children's literature is laced with similes that help students see language in different ways and discover the power of words to create lasting images. David Shannon (1998), Chris Van Allsburg (1985), and Denise Fleming (1996) are well-known authors who employ similes in their writing.

Metaphors are more abstract and implicit than similes in their comparisons. The words *like* and *as* are not used in metaphorical comparisons. For example, *New York City is as busy as an anthill* is a simile. *New York City is an anthill* is a metaphor. One type of metaphor is *personification* in which human qualities are given to nonhuman or inanimate entities. *The town slept* is an example of personification.

Euphemisms

Euphemisms are "feel good" words. A euphemism for *pain* is *discomfort*; a euphemism for *television commercial* is *message.* Many euphemisms are just good manners. *Passed* and *loss* are more sensitive word choices than *died.* It is especially important that students learn about the use of euphemisms because there is nothing playful about some of them. *Career change opportunity, repositioning,* and *streamlining* all mean that people will be fired. *Action entertainment* means violent entertainment. A *consideration* is a bribe. When someone is in a *reeducation camp,* they are behind bars. Large hog operators in Iowa refer to their hog-waste holding pits as *lagoons.* The real estate section of any newspaper contains euphemisms such as *cozy, mint condition,* and *handyperson's special* that can be translated into more accurate descriptions of the properties—and, in the process, improve children's critical reading skills.

For a class activity, divide your students into small groups. Each group can select or be assigned a type of figurative expression: idioms, proverbs, in-betweens, catchphrases, slogans, similes and metaphors, and euphemisms. The group is to compile a list of expressions in contemporary use through scanning Internet sites, newspapers, magazines, and by listening to conversations at school and at home. The groups can report their findings to the full class.

ONOMASTICS

Onomastics is the study of names. School lessons based on onomastics are scarce, perhaps because it is human nature to take for granted what is right in front of our noses. Names are everywhere—on street signs, inside shoes, on 18-wheelers, under our desk chairs. Although it is unusual to encounter the study of names in educational materials, the business world and some academicians take the study of names seriously. There are businesses that do nothing but create names for other businesses. Sam Birger, a psycholinguist who works for Whatchamacallit, a naming firm based in Boston and San Francisco, stated, "The whole point of the Rumpelstiltskin story is that when you have the right name for a thing, you have control over it" (Kaplan & Bernays, 1997, p. 110).

Research has shown that names do influence our feelings toward a person, place, or thing (Dickson, 1996). Brian Wansink (2006), director of the Cornell University Food and Brand Lab, found that when some foods were labeled with geographic (e.g., Minnesota wild rice), nostalgic (e.g., Grandma's sweet potato pie), or sensory terms (e.g., plump, succulent butter beans), the foods "were rated as more appealing and tastier than the identical foods with less attractive labels" (p. 126). Wansink also noted that, "The customers who ate the food with descriptive names had more favorable attitudes toward the cafeteria as a whole. Some commented that it was trendy and up-to-date. Others thought the chef was probably classically trained, perhaps in Europe" (p. 127).

Land developers, too, recognize the psychology at work behind a name. Bryson (1994) pointed out that a property name change can increase property values by as much as 15%. A name might also affect enrollment in some private prep schools. There is a school north of the city of Monroe, Louisiana that caters to fairly well-off families. The school is located on a street named *Finks Hideaway*. In every ad we have seen for the school of privilege, the street address is written as just *Hideaway*. The *Finks* has been dropped. Apparently the school leaders and parents decided that it wouldn't look or sound too impressive for their children to come from a school that is situated on a Hideaway of Finks—even though *fink* is outdated slang. To illustrate the playfulness of creating names, have your students create menu items using geographic, nostalgic, or sensory labels for the following foods: *broccoli, carrot cake, peanut butter, spinach, liver,* or other foods of their choosing.

Eponyms

An *eponym* is a word based on a person's name. Eponyms can be found in nearly every category of interest. In the category *plants*, there is the *Bartlett pear* (Encoh Barteltt, 1779–1860), the *Douglas fir* (David Douglas, 1798–1834), and the *Sequoia* (Sequoya, 1770?–1843). Under *clothing* there is the *cardigan* (seventh Earl of Cardigan, 1797–1868), the *leotard* (Jules Leotard, 1842–1870), and the *mackintosh* (Charles Mackintosh, 1766–1843). In the *measurement* category, we find the *Geiger counter* (Hans Geiger, 1882–1945), the *Richter scale* (Charles Richter, 1900–1985), *Fahrenheit* (Daniel Fahrenheit, 1686–1736), and *Celsius* (Anders Celsius, 1701–1744). From a *cookbook* we note chicken *tetrazzini* (Louisa Tetrazzini, 1872–1941), *peach melba* (Nellie Melba, 1861–1931), *Béchamel sauce* (Louis de Béchamel, died 1703), and *beef Wellington* (first Duke of Wellington, 1769–1852). There are tens of thousands of eponyms in the English language. The medical profession alone claims at least 15,000 eponyms (see *www.whonamedit.com*). *Alzheimer's disease* (Alois Alzheimer, 1864–1915), *Parkinson's disease* (James Parkinson, 1755–1824), and *Down's syndrome* (John Down, 1828–1896) are just three familiar medical eponyms.

Table 11.1 presents a short list of eponyms. Challenge your students to trace the story behind these and other eponyms. Some student-friendly sources that will tell the stories are Laura Lee's *The Name's Familiar: Mr. Leotard, Barbie, and Chef Boyardee* (1999), Eugene Ehrlich's *What's in a Name? How Proper Names Became Everyday Words* (1999), and *Webster's New World Dictionary of Eponyms: Common Words from Proper Nouns* (Douglas, 1990). Although *Webster's* is an older reference, it contains more than 800 eponyms.

TABLE 11.1. Eponyms

argyle	Dow Jones average	Oscar award
bibb lettuce	ferris wheel	reuben sandwich
Big Ben	frisbee	salmonella
blanket (noun)	Gallup poll	saxophone
blurb	graham crackers	schrapnel
boycott	guppy	stetson
boysenberry	macadamia nuts	Tony award
cobb salad	maverick	Venn diagram
doberman pinscher	ohm	watt

Toponyms

A *toponym* is a word named after a place. *Magenta* is a reddish-pink color, and it is a toponym. The rather upbeat color is named after a downbeat scene—the blood-soaked battlefield at the Battle of Magenta in Italy in 1859 (Freeman, 1997). Other toponyms include *duffel bag* (Duffel, Belgium), *sardines* (the island of Sardinia), and *paisley* (Paisley, Scotland). For fun, have your students look in local and large commercial cookbooks for toponyms.

Demonyms

A *demonym* is a word for people who live in a particular place. A *Baraboo-ian* is a person who resides in Baraboo, Wisconsin. Someone who lives in Fergus Falls, Minnesota is a *Fergusite*. A *Dane* lives in Denmark, and a *Florentine* hails from Florence, Italy. An indispensable book for the study of demonyms is Paul Dickson's *Labels for Locals: What to Call People from Abilene to Zimbabwe* (1997). There are some rather complex rules for creating demonyms, but Dickson stated that "people in a place tend to decide what they will call themselves, whether they be *Angelenos* (from Los Angeles) or *Haligonians* (from Halifax, Nova Scotia)" (p. x). Engage students in researching demonyms for schools, neighborhoods, communities, and states of interest. For example, one of us is a former *Tenth Warder*, an *Eau Clairian*, and a *Wisconsinite*.

Unusual Town and City Names

Each state in our country has colorful town and city names. There is a small town in Louisiana with a big name: *Transylvania*. It lies in the Mississippi delta region of the state, so the topography is flat. From miles away, travelers on the main highway can see the town's water tower with a gigantic drawing of a bat on it—just like in old Dracula movies and resembling Batman's logo. The Transylvania general store had a witty sign on its window until some town father or mother or skittish tourist convinced the proprietors to remove it. The sign said: "Welcome to Translyvania. We're always looking for new blood." Upon inquiring about the origin of the town name, the clerk in the general store told us that the name came from someone who had ancestors from Transylvania, which was a province in Romania.

Just as every word has a story behind it, every town has a story behind it. Some are amusing, some surprising. According to Gallant (1998), *Toast*, North Carolina, was a name submitted to the U.S. Post Office by a school administrator whose mind was on food. *Charm*, Ohio, was named for a charm that a local jeweler wore on his watch chain. *Only*, Tennessee, came from a store owner's preceding every price quote with "only" (e.g., "*only* ten cents, *only* a quarter"). *Snowflake*, Arizona, refers to Mr. Snow and Mr. Flake, the men who are credited with naming the town.

Table 11.2 gives a couple of examples of colorful town names in each state. ZIP codes are included in case you want your students to write to historical societies or town officials for the origins of the town names. As a follow-up activity, have students look in the index of an atlas or state highway maps for more unusual names. They are plentiful.

Odonyms

Odonyms are street names, and they can be quite colorful, too. Near Ruston, Louisiana, are a *Goodgoin Road* and a *Stone's Throw Road*. *Just Imagine Drive* is in Avon, Ohio; *None Such Place* is in New Castle, Delaware; and *Almosta Road* is in Darby, Montana (Wallechinsky & Wallace, 1993).

Dickson (1996) delineates three time periods in the naming of American streets. The first is from 1682 to 1945. William Penn is credited with numbering streets (e.g., First Street, Second Street) and using the names of trees for streets (e.g., Elm Street, Maple Street). Also during this time frame, streets were named after prominent people (e.g., Washington Street), business that was conducted on the street (e.g., Bank Street), and where the street led (e.g., Boston Street). The second era of street naming, according to Dickson, was from 1945 to 1960. Developers trying to cash in on the returning World War II veterans wishing to settle down and buy a home used enticing, relaxing type names with *Haven* or *Grove* or *Woods* in them. The third period, from 1960 to 1995, reflects streets named for a theme. If, for example, the developer wanted a medieval theme, he or she might call

TABLE 11.2. Colorful Town Names

Brilliant, Alabama (35548)	Flea Hop, Alabama (36078)
Eek, Alaska (99578)	Sourdough, Alaska (99586)
Carefree, Arizona (85377)	Surprise, Arizona (85374)
Cash, Arkansas (72421)	Greasy Corner, Arkansas (72346)
Cool, California (95614)	Jelly, California (96080)
Brush, Colorado (80723)	Tincup, Colorado (81210)
Headquarters, Connecticut (06759)	Puddle Town, Connecticut (06022)
Bakers Choice, Delaware (19946)	Shortly, Delaware (19947)
Picnic, Florida (33547)	Two Egg, Florida (32423)
Ideal, Georgia (31041)	Social Circle, Georgia (30279)
Happy Valley, Hawaii (96793)	Volcano, Hawaii (96785)
Bench, Idaho (83241)	Riddle, Idaho (83604)
Normal, Illinois (61761)	Roaches, Illinois (62898)
Fickle, Indiana (46041)	Santa Claus, Indiana (47579)
Gravity, Iowa (50848)	What Cheer, Iowa (50268)
Admire, Kansas (66830)	Neutral, Kansas (66725)
Quicksand, Kentucky (41363)	Rush, Kentucky (41168)
Plain Dealing, Louisiana (71064)	Sharp, Louisiana (71447)
Reach, Maine (04627)	Strong, Maine (04983)
Boring, Maryland (21020)	Cabin John, Maryland (20818)
Blissville, Massachusetts (01364)	Old Furnace, Massachusetts (01031)
Payment, Michigan (49783)	The Fingerboard Corner, Michigan (49705)
Staples, Minnesota (56479)	Young America, Minnesota (55494)
Hot Coffee, Mississippi (39428)	Rich, Mississippi (38617)
Cash, Missouri (63534)	Bland, Missouri (65014)
Circle, Montana (59215)	Truly, Montana (59485)
Superior, Nebraska (68978)	Worms, Nebraska (68872)
Jackpot, Nevada (89825)	Contact, Nevada (89825)
Beans, New Hampshire (03595)	Pickpocket Woods, New Hampshire (03833)
Deal, New Jersey (07723)	Yellow Frame, New Jersey (07860)
Dusty, New Mexico (87943)	House, New Mexico (88121)
Gang Mills, New York (14870)	Idle Hour, New York (11769)
Apex, North Carolina (27502)	Crisp, North Carolina (27852)
Cannon Ball, North Dakota (58528)	Zap, North Dakota (58580)
Dent, Ohio (45211)	Jumbo, Ohio (43326)
Boss, Oklahoma (74745)	Bunch, Oklahoma (74931)
Plush, Oregon (97637)	Remote, Oregon (97458)
Bonus, Pennsylvania (16049)	Eighty-Four, Pennsylvania (15330)
Harmony, Rhode Island (02829)	Hope, Rhode Island (02831)
Fair Play, South Carolina (29643)	Return, South Carolina (29678)
Parade, South Dakota (57647)	Promise, South Dakota (57601)
Difficult, Tennessee (37145)	Disco, Tennessee (37737)
Ding Dong, Texas (76542)	Wink, Texas (79789)
Bountiful, Utah (84010)	Bonanza, Utah (84008)
Mosquitoville, Vermont (05042)	Prosper, Vermont (05091)
File, Virginia (22427)	New Store, Virginia (23901)
Forks, Washington (98331)	Mold, Washington (99115)
Odd, West Virginia (25902)	Joker, West Virginia (26141)
Loyal, Wisconsin (54446)	Luck, Wisconsin (54853)
Ten Sleep, Wyoming (82442)	Halfway, Wyoming (83113)

the subdivision *Camelot* and name the streets *Castle Road, Knights' Lane*, and *Tournament Trail*. In one Green Bay, Wisconsin, subdivision named *Treasure Island*, there is a *Fortune Drive, Pirate Drive, Silver Drive, Jolly Roger Drive, Captain Kidd Drive, Spyglass Drive*, and *Stevenson Drive*. The appearances of the houses in the subdivision suggest that they were built during the third period of street naming. Using an online or other available map, have students note unusual street names in the community. They can investigate the origins of these names by checking with town clerks, city planners, or established realtors.

Anemonyms

Anemonyms are the names of storms. Among storms, only tropical storms and hurricanes have names. According to the National Hurricane Center (n.d.):

> Experience shows that the use of short, distinctive given names in written as well as spoken communication is quicker and less subject to error than the older more cumbersome latitude–longitude identification methods. These advantages are especially important in exchanging detailed storm information between hundreds of widely scattered stations, coastal bases, and ships at sea. (*www.nhc.noaa.gov/aboutnames.html*)

Male names were not given to hurricanes until 1979, whereas female names have been used since 1953. Since 1954, 73 names have been permanently retired by the National Hurricane Center. Among these are *Agnes, Andrew, Bob, Camille, Hugo, Katrina*, and *Rita*. The names of these particularly destructive hurricanes probably would cause needless anxiety if used again. Kaplan and Bernays (1997) noted that if the names were used again there could be confusion in insurance work and research studies. The names are selected by the World Meteorological Organization. There are different names for storms in the Atlantic (e.g., *Kate, Felix*), Central North Pacific (e.g., *Akoni, Peke*), Eastern North Pacific (e.g., *Sonia, Gil*), Western North Pacific (e.g., *Kai-Tak, Usagi*), Western Australian Region (e.g., *Emma, Daryl*), Eastern Australian Region (e.g., *Blanch, Ernie*), Northern Australia Region (e.g., *Kay, Sid*), the Fiji Region (e.g., *Atu, Drena*), the Papua New Guinea Region (e.g., *Tako, Upia*), and the Southwest Indian Ocean (e.g., *Bako, Ikala*). All the names can be found on the National Hurricane Center's website noted above. As a classroom activity, students can create names for particular storms of the type that are prevalent in their locales (e.g., blizzards in Nebraska, tornadoes in Texas, dust storms in Oklahoma, ice storms in Arkansas, gales in Maine) and give reasons for selecting the names.

CONCLUSION

Almost from birth children have a fascination with words and language, and before they ever enter a classroom, they exhibit natural talents for language manipulation. Teachers have the opportunity to build on children's instinctive capabilities as they stimulate and augment language acquisition through the school years. When children are actively and interactively engaged with language, they see learning as purposeful and enjoyable. Language play activities enhance this enjoyment. Through playing with words and expressions, children begin to discover and develop their own language abilities.

The English language abounds in language play. We recommend that teachers incorporate word play into their language and literacy programs. Such instruction will pay off in two ways: by generating and enhancing students' interest in language and by helping students experience the many facets of oral and written language as listeners, speakers, readers, and writers.

REFERENCES

Ammer, C. (1989). *Fighting words: From war, rebellion, and other combative capers.* Lincolnwood, IL: NTC.

Bryson, B. (1994). *Made in America: An informal history of the English language in the United States.* New York: Morrow.

Carothers, G., & Lacey, J. (1994). *Dictionary of colorful phrases.* New York: Sterling.

Crystal, D. (1995). *The Cambridge encyclopedia of the English language.* Cambridge, UK: Cambridge University Press.

Crystal, D. (1998). *Language play.* Chicago: University of Chicago Press.

Day, A. (1990). *Frank and Ernest play ball.* New York: Scholastic.

Day, A. (1994). *Frank and Ernest on the road.* New York: Scholastic.

de Ley, G. (1998). *International dictionary of proverbs.* New York: Hippocrene Books.

Dickson, P. (1996). *What's in a name?: Reflections of an irrepressible name collector.* Springfield, MA: Merriam-Webster.

Dickson, P. (1997). *Labels for locals: What to call people from Abilene to Zimbabwe.* Springfield, MA: Merriam-Webster.

Douglas, A. (1990). *Webster's new world dictionary of eponyms: Common words from proper nouns.* New York: Simon & Schuster.

Ehrlich, E. (1999). *What's in a name?: How proper names became everyday words.* New York: Holt.

Ezell, H. K., & Goldstein, H. (1991). Comparison of idiom comprehension of normal children and children with mental retardation. *Journal of Speech and Hearing Research, 34,* 812–819.

Fleming, D. (1996). *Where once there was a wood*. New York: Holt.

Freeman, M. S. (1997). *A new dictionary of eponyms*. New York: Oxford University Press.

Gallant, F. K. (1998). *A place called Peculiar: Stories about unusual place names*. Springfield, MA: Merriam-Webster.

Geller, L. G. (1985). *Wordplay and language learning for children*. Urbana, IL: National Council of Teachers of English.

Gibbs, R. W., Jr. (1991). Semantic analyzability in children's understanding of idioms. *Journal of Speech and Hearing Research, 34*, 613–620.

Gibbs, R. W., Nayak, N. P., & Cutting, C. (1989). How to kick the bucket and not decompose: Analyzability and idiom processing. *Journal of Memory and Language, 28*, 576–593.

Gleason, N. (1992). *Proverbs from around the world*. Secaucus, NJ: Citadel.

Goldenberg, C. (2008). Teaching English language learners: What the research does—and does not say. *American Educator, 32*(2), 10.

Holmes, L. A. (1999). Language play as response discourse. *Language Arts, 76*(3), 258–261.

Johnson, B. (1999). *Wordworks: Exploring language play*. Golden, CO: Fulcrum.

Johnson, D. D., & Johnson, B. (2011). *Words: The foundation of literacy*. Boulder, CO: Westview Press.

Kaplan, J., & Bernays, A. (1997). *The language of names: What we call ourselves and why it matters*. New York: Simon & Schuster.

Labov, T. (1992). Social and language boundaries among adolescents. *American Speech, 67*, 339–366.

Lee, L. (1999). *The name's familiar: Mr. Leotard, Barbie, and Chef Boyardee*. Greta, LA: Pelican.

Levorato, M. C., & Cacciari, C. (1995). The effects of different tasks on the comprehension and production of idioms in children. *Journal of Experimental Child Psychology, 60*, 261–283.

Lighter, J. E. (1994). *Random House historical dictionary of American slang: Volume I, A–G*. New York: Random House.

Lighter, J. E. (1997). *Random House historical dictionary of American slang: Volume II, H–O*. New York: Random House.

Mieder, W. S. (1986). *The Prentice-Hall encyclopedia of world proverbs*. New York: MJF Books.

Mieder, W. S., Kingsbury, S. A., & Harder, K. B. (Eds.). (1992). *A dictionary of American proverbs*. New York: Oxford University Press.

Mosel, A. (1968). *Tikki tikki tembo*. New York: Holt, Rinehart & Winston.

National Hurricane Center. (n.d.). *World-wide tropical cyclone names*. Retrieved from *www.nhc.noaa.gov/aboutnames.html*

Nippold, M. A., & Taylor, C. L. (1995). Idiom understanding in youth: Further examination of familiarity and transparency. *Journal of Speech and Hearing Research, 38*, 426–433.

Nippold, M. A., Uhden, L. D., & Schwarz, I. E. (1997). Proverb explanation through the lifespan: A developmental study of adolescents and adults. *Journal of Speech, Language, and Hearing Research, 40*, 245–253.

Ortony, A. (1984). Understanding figurative language. In P. D. Pearson, R. Barr, M. L. Kamil, & P. Mosenthal (Eds.), *Handbook of reading research* (pp. 453–470). New York: Longman.

Park, B. (1993). *Junie B. Jones and a little monkey business.* New York: Random House.

Polacco, P. (2001). *Betty doll.* New York: Penguin.

Rees, N. (1995). *Dictionary of catchphrases.* London, UK: Cassell.

Scieszka, J. (1989). *The true story of the 3 little pigs.* New York: Viking.

Shannon, D. (1998). *A bad case of stripes.* New York: Scholastic.

Stanley, D. (1996). *Saving sweetness.* New York: Putnam.

Terban, M. (1987). *Mad as a wet hen! And other funny idioms.* New York: Clarion.

Terban, M. (1990). *Punching the clock: Funny action idioms.* New York: Clarion.

Terban, M. (1996). *Scholastic dictionary of idioms.* New York: Scholastic.

Van Allsburg, C. (1985). *The polar express.* Boston: Houghton Mifflin.

Wallechinsky, D., & Wallace, A. (1993). *The book of lists: The '90s edition.* Boston: Little, Brown.

Wansink, B. (2006). *Mindless eating.* New York: Bantam Dell.

Part IV

Special Topics
of Vocabulary Instruction

Chapter 12

Vocabulary Assessment

Making Do with What We Have
While We Create the Tools We Need

P. David Pearson
Elfrieda H. Hiebert
Michael L. Kamil

After a long absence, vocabulary has returned to a prominent place in discussions of reading; it is alive and well in reading instruction and reading research. This is good news for teachers, teacher educators, and researchers. There is good reason to teach vocabulary more aggressively. After all, as many of the contributors in this volume illustrate, vocabulary is a strong predictor of comprehension, and the gap in the vocabularies of the "haves" and the "have-nots" is substantial on school entry. Without strategic and concerted efforts in schools, this initial gap may never be eliminated and, in fact, can easily be broadened. If effective instruction is to become commonplace, we must first address the vexing question of how we assess vocabulary knowledge and growth.

In this chapter, we argue that vocabulary assessment is grossly underdeveloped, both in its theoretical and practical aspects. On the theoretical side, it has been driven by tradition, convenience, psychometric standards, and a quest for economy of effort rather than a clear conceptualization of its nature and relation to other aspects of reading expertise, most notably, to comprehension. On the practical side, it has provided teachers with scores that tell them only how students perform in relation to other students (e.g., percentiles or grade norms); it has not given them data that indicate how well students have mastered particular domains of vocabulary, such as all of the key vocabulary associated with a fourth-grade reading level or with the central concepts of a topic such as habitats and ecosystems. We hope that this chapter serves as one small step in stimulating the development of strategic instruction and curriculum needs that students deserve.

We examine the literature—research, common practices, and theoretical analyses—on vocabulary assessment to answer three questions:

1. What do vocabulary assessments (both past and current) measure?
2. What could vocabulary assessments measure, as illustrated by conceptual frameworks, and what development and validation efforts are needed to make such assessments a reality?
3. What vocabulary assessments should teachers use, create, or modify while we wait for the research that is needed for wide-scale change?

VOCABULARY ASSESSMENTS: PAST AND PRESENT

A working definition of a domain is useful, prior to embarking on either the design or the review of the assessment of that domain. In the case of vocabulary, definitions that come from dictionaries are typically vague, such as "the words of a language" or "the stock of words used by or known to a particular people or group of persons" (Flexner, 2003). Because such definitions lack the specificity required for instruction or assessment, educators (e.g., National Institute of Child Health and Human Development, 2000) have typically turned to a two-by-two matrix where the use of vocabulary is on one axis (productive, receptive) and the mode of communication (written, oral) is on the other. This matrix implies four types of vocabulary: listening, speaking, writing, and reading.

The assessment of vocabulary, as it pertains to reading comprehension, has almost exclusively emphasized the receptive dimension of vocabulary. At least on large-scale reading tests, the mode involves reading, although within the most prominent norm-referenced vocabulary measure—the Peabody Picture Vocabulary Test (PPVT; Dunn & Dunn, 2007)—the mode is listening. Rarely is the productive aspect of vocabulary examined, especially as it relates to comprehension; for example, when students encounter (or are taught) new words in relation to new texts or topics in subject-matter classes, it would be useful to know whether these words spontaneously emerge in their speaking and writing. Small-scale analyses have documented students' spontaneous use of new, complex vocabulary in writing as a result of participating in intensive vocabulary instruction (Flinspach, Scott, & Vevea, 2010), but such projects are labor-intensive because students' writing must be collected and analyzed over extended periods of time.

More typically, the approach to assessment of vocabulary follows the patterns that can be traced back to the origins of standardized tests. In early tests of intelligence developed by Binet and Thurstone (see Pearson & Hamm, 2005), students were asked to define or explain words that they were likely encounter in schoolbooks (e.g., the function of a *fork*). With the movement toward mass testing prompted by the need to test recruits for World War I (Resnick & Resnick, 1977) came the need for easily administered and scorable assessments, which led to standardized, multiple-choice tests with items such as those illustrated in the first row of Table 12.1.

That sort of item dominated formal vocabulary assessment until the 1970s (Read, 2000), when changes in thinking about language and reading motivated more contextualized vocabulary assessments (see the second row of Table 12.1). The press for contextualization increased systematically, at least in the most ambitious context for vocabulary assessment, English as a second language (see Read, 2000; Nation, 2001), resulting in a progression of items as illustrated in the final three rows of Table 12.1.

Despite this history, many major assessments still use fairly isolated approaches. To illustrate the nature of current vocabulary assessments, we have analyzed items on four prominent vocabulary assessments that are among those that a national panel identified as fitting the criteria for use in Reading First (Kame'enui, 2002), a large-scale, federally funded national reading initiative: two individually administered assessments— the PPVT (Dunn & Dunn, 2007) and the Woodcock Reading Mastery Test (WRMT; Woodcock, McGrew, & Mather, 2007)—and two that are group administered—the Iowa Test of Basic Skills (ITBS; Hoover, Dunbar, & Frisbie, 2003) and the Stanford Achievement Test (SAT; Stanford Achievement Test, 2006). Items characteristic of those included in these assessments are presented in Table 12.2, except for the PPVT, which uses illustrations from which students select the word spoken by the test administrator (e.g., the stimulus for the word *surfing* might be a picture set of someone surfing, someone playing water polo, someone swimming, and someone driving a speedboat). In all of the items in Table 12.2 as well as in the PPVT example just described, there are rather simplistic word associations. None can be described as capturing the deep or multifaceted features of words that we know are important to vocabulary learning and, hence, to assessment.

TABLE 12.1. Sample Items of Different Eras

Time period	Sample item(s)
1915–1920: Decontextualized vocabulary assessment	Pick the word that fits in the blank. A _____ is used to eat with. —plow —fork —hammer —needle	Pick the best meaning for the underlined word. <u>Foolish</u> —clever —mild —silly —frank

1970s: Early efforts to contextualize vocabulary	Pick the best meaning for the underlined word. The farmer <u>discovered</u> a tunnel under the barn. —wanted —found —traveled —captured

1980s: Steps toward contextualization	In a (1) <u>democratic</u> society, individuals are presumed innocent until proven guilty. The (2) <u>establishment</u> of guilt is often a difficult task. One consideration is whether or not there remains a (3) <u>reasonable</u> doubt that the suspected persons committed the act in question. Another consideration is whether the acts were committed (4) <u>deliberately</u>.-

For each item, select the choice closest in meaning to the underlined word corresponding to the number.

(2)	(4)
1. attribution	1. both
2. business	2. noticeably
3. creation	3. intentionally
4. absolution	4. absolutely

Among a set of comprehension items, you might find the following:

In line 2, it says, "Two reasons are usually advanced to account for this <u>tardy</u> development; namely the mental difficulties . . . "

The word **tardy** in line 2 is closest in meaning to
1. historical
2. basic
3. unusual
4. late

Late 1990s: Computerized format	The Southwest has always been a dry country, where water is scarce, but the Hopi and Zuni were able to bring water from streams to their fields and gardens through irrigation ditches. Because it is so <u>rare</u>, yet so important, water played a major role in their religion.

Look at the word <u>rare</u> in the passage. Click on the word in the text that has the <u>same</u> meaning.

TABLE 12.2. Simulated Items of Vocabulary Tasks on Three Norm-Referenced Tests

Test	Prototypical item(s)
Iowa Test of Basic Skills	To <u>sink</u> in the water play rest wash go down
Stanford Achievement Test	Item type #1: To <u>cut</u> is to— slice bark run save Item type #2: Put the money in the <u>safe</u>. In which sentences does the word <u>safe</u> mean the same thing as in the sentence above? The puppy is <u>safe</u> from harm. I am <u>safe</u> at home. It is <u>safe</u> to go out now. Michael opened the <u>safe</u>. Item type #3: Ron only has one hat, but he has <u>several</u> coats. <u>Several</u> means— funny some hungry large
Woodcock Reading Mastery Tests	Subtest 1: Antonyms (Read this word out loud and then tell me a word that means the opposite.) near (far) dark (light) Subtest 2: Synonyms (Read this word out loud and then tell me another word that means the same thing.) cash (money) small (little) Subtest 3: Analogies (Listen carefully and finish what I say [text is visible but experimenter reads the text].) Dark–light night (day) Rain–shine wet (dry)

VOCABULARY ASSESSMENTS: DIRECTIONS FOR THE FUTURE

Words may seem like simple entities, but they are not. Their surface simplicity belies a deeper complexity. Scholars of vocabulary suggest a much richer view of vocabulary—and its assessment—than captured by current tools. Two of the most influential perspectives come from the work of Nagy and Scott (2000) and Read (2000).

Complexity of word knowledge is evident in Nagy and Scott's (2000) identification of five aspects of word knowledge used in reading. The first of these, *incrementality*, refers to the fact that knowledge about a word/idea becomes a little deeper and a little more precise with each encounter, leading to nuanced understanding and flexible use. As an example, consider the word *éclat*, in a phrase from a novel: "the éclat of love at twenty years of age" (Dumas, 1845). The use is ambiguous enough that a 21st-century reader may be a little unclear about its meaning. But, when encountered a second time, in another novel (Austen, 1790), it becomes clearer: "where we spent our little fortune with great éclat." On a third encounter—this time perhaps in an online review of an author's presentation at a local bookstore, where the audience's response to an author who has received otherwise modest acclaim is described this way, "They gave him more éclat than he really deserved," the reader is likely to feel fairly confident that the word means *enthusiasm* and might even be tempted to use it in a dinner-table conversation.

Multidimensionality, the second aspect, refers to qualitatively different types of word knowledge, including understanding nuances of meaning between words such as *glimpse* and *glance* or typical collocations of words (e.g., we can have a *storm front* but not a *storm back*).

The third aspect is one of the most critical and challenging for learning English—*polysemy*. Many words have multiple meanings, and the more common the word, the more meanings it is likely to have. The common word *set*, for example, has dozens and dozens of meanings, including ones that are part of unique phrases (e.g., *movie set*) and that take on different parts of speech (e.g., *set* the table, a *set* of drawers, a *set* direction). By contrast, an uncommon word such as *poinsettia* is likely to have a single meaning.

Interrelatedness involves learning or knowing a word, which often entails derivation (*commence–commencement*) or association with the meanings of related words, either in a linguistic context (*dogs bark* or *buffaloes roam*) or in one's semantic memory store (dogs are members of the canine category and related to cats because they share the attribute that they can be domesticated).

Heterogeneity refers to a word's meaning, which differs depending on its function and structure (e.g., frequency in written English, and syntactic roles). Contrast, for example, the sentences "I spilled the cocoa. Get a broom" with "I spilled the cocoa. Get a mop." Over time, by encountering a word such as *spill* in different contexts, we learn more about the range of its applications and the shades of meaning instantiated by different contexts and applications. In the case of the spillage of cocoa, comprehension depends on knowing that cocoa can be a bean, a powder, and a liquid and that brooms and mops, although both cleaning tools, have different properties.

Although these categories illustrate the complexity of vocabulary, few studies of vocabulary attend to these variables in any systematic fashion, especially when it comes to choosing the words for instructional interventions or assessments (Scott, Lubliner, & Hiebert, 2005). At the present time, these distinctions are unlikely to be highly productive as filters for reviewing assessments that are commonly used in large-scale assessment. These variables do, however, suggest important new directions for vocabulary research in both assessment and instruction.

A second framework comes from Read (2000), who has examined existing assessments and scholarship to understand how different test formats represent different kinds of vocabulary knowledge. Read's interest lies in the design of appropriate assessments for individuals learning English as a second language, but we believe that they are equally germane to the design of assessments for children learning to read English. Read has identified three continua for designing and evaluating vocabulary assessments: (1) discrete–embedded, (2) selective–comprehensive, and (3) contextualized–decontextualized.

The *discrete–embedded* continuum addresses whether vocabulary is represented by its own separate set of test items (discrete) or as part of the larger construct of text comprehension (embedded). In the vocabulary assessments summarized in Table 12.2, vocabulary is reported separately from comprehension (i.e., discrete). Most norm-referenced silent reading assessments and the National Assessment of Educational Progress (NAEP)—a Congressionally mandated assessment administered to a representative group of students in each state every few years—take an embedded stance, wherein contextualized vocabulary items contribute to an aggregate comprehension score. But the direction of the NAEP is changing. The 2009 NAEP framework (National Assessment Governing Board, 2005; Salinger, Kamil, Kapinus, & Afflerbach, 2005) mandated a discrete measure of vocabulary. This change could be reflected in the assessments that two state consortia—SMARTER Balanced Assessment Consortium (2010) and the Partnership for Assessment of Readiness for College and Careers (2010)—are developing in response to the Common Core State Standards (Common Core State Standards Initiative, 2010).

The *selective–comprehensive* distinction refers to the relationship between the sample of items in a test and the hypothetical population of vocabulary items that the sample represents. Thus, if one assesses students' grasp of the vocabulary in a story from an anthology or a chapter in a science text, the sample is inherently selective. Most vocabulary assessments, however, fall on the comprehensive side of the continuum, to the point where the domain sampled is a mystery. For example, consider the items in Table 12.2. Because the items on real tests are copyrighted and cannot be shared publicly, we had to create items that paralleled those of assessments. To create these items, we could find no guidelines, theories, or frameworks within test makers' technical reports or materials for users. We ended up choosing our parallel words by matching the word frequency and decodability of the target words in the actual items. Such a lack of clarity on the source of vocabulary is typical of current, large-scale assessments. Most of our current vocabulary assessments have no theoretically defined population of words at all or, if they do, are difficult (if not impossible) to infer from available documents.

We came away from the process concluding that psychometric criteria, not theoretical frameworks, drive the test-development process. Test developers obtain a group of words that is administered to a sample of students at known levels of reading development or expertise. The words are sorted by their difficulty, expressed often as the percentage of students in a particular population who answered the question correctly. Ultimately, scores for individuals on such a test derive their meaning from comparisons of particular students' performance on a particular test with the population of students—not from words, at large—which is why we call them norm-referenced tests. Under such circumstances, all we know is that a given student performed better, or worse, than the average student on the set of words that happened to be on the test. We know nothing about what the scores say about students' vocabulary knowledge of any identifiable domain or corpus of words.

In the next section, we illustrate a framework for a theoretically grounded selection of words for instruction and assessment. Theoretically grounded frameworks have yet to be used in designing assessments, but such frameworks exist and they suggest that it may be possible to move assessments toward the selective end of the continuum. Only when theoretically grounded frameworks drive assessments will it be possible to make claims that "The average student in a given school (or classroom) exhibits basic mastery over $X\%$ of the words in a given corpus (e.g., the words encountered in a given curriculum in a given grade level)."

Contextualized–decontextualized refers to the degree that textual context is required to determine the meaning of a word on an assessment. Table 12.3 includes several examples of the continuum. Item 1 falls firmly on the decontextualized side of the continuum. Even though context is provided for item 2, it is not needed if someone knows the meaning of

TABLE 12.3. Degrees of Contextual Reliance

1. <u>consumed</u>
   a) Ate or drank
   b) Prepared
   c) Bought
   d) Enjoyed
	2. The people <u>consumed</u> their dinner.
	   a) Ate or drank
	   b) Prepared
	   c) Bought
	   d) Enjoyed

3. The people <u>consumed</u> their dinner.
   a) Ate or drank
   b) Used up
   c) Spent wastefully
   d) Destroyed
	4. The citizens <u>consumed</u> their supply of
	   gravel through wanton development.
	   a) Ate or drank
	   b) Used up
	   c) Spent wastefully
	   d) Destroyed

consume as eating or drinking. In item 3, because all four meanings denote one or another meaning of *consume*, context is essential for zeroing in on the meaning as used in the sentence. Item 4 is even trickier than item 3. Unlike item 3, which requires the selection of the most common meaning of *consume*, item 4 requires a student to reject the default (most common) meaning in favor of a more arcane sense of *consume*. Note also that a very fine semantic distinction is required in item 4 to select *spent wastefully* over *used up*.

We know of no vocabulary initiative, be it a research study, a curriculum scheme, or an assessment development effort, with the aim of bringing together the criteria related to word knowledge (Nagy & Scott, 2000) and the criteria related to assessments formats (Read, 2000). There is a degree of overlap between the two schemes. For example, items that fall at the completely contextualized end of the continuum are almost without exception polysemous words because it is nearly impossible to assess vocabulary in context without distractor sets that reflect at least two of the meanings of each assessed word. On the other features, however, the two schemes represent important but unique aspects of the design of vocabulary assessments. However, if educators are to develop a true measure of their students' knowledge of vocabulary, just such an integration of word knowledge features and assessment features is needed.

In the framework that we unpack in the next section, we have not achieved such an integration of all variables in both schemes, but we begin a line of work that might lead to integration by addressing one issue in depth: the selection of words on assessments. This feature of assessments is at the core of understanding what students are learning and what needs to be taught and learned. It falls squarely into Read's selective–comprehensive issue and it also addresses, at least to some degree, some of the features of word knowledge. It is in the design of individual items, however, that issues raised by Nagy and Scott will be played out. Researchers are engaged in efforts that should provide insight into the manner in which features such as incrementality, multidimensionality, interrelatedness, polysemy, and heterogeneity can be best measured (Scott, Flinspach, Miller, Vevea, & Gage-Serio, 2009; Scott, Vevea, & Flinspach, 2010). With the validation of new item formats from projects such as these, educators can anticipate that richer views of the nature of students' vocabulary knowledge will be possible. For these rich views of students' vocabulary knowledge to ensure a closing of the vocabulary gap, it is imperative that the words on the assessments are *the right words*. By "the right words," we refer to information on the selection of words. It is that topic to which we turn our attention next.

An Illustration of a Theoretically Grounded Framework for Vocabulary Assessment

There are numerous ways of parsing the words of a vocabulary. Written words are, after all, multidimensional, as Nagy and Scott (2000) demonstrate in their analysis; they differ in orthographic forms, syntactic functions, and semantic roles, to name several important distinctions. In this section, we illustrate one way of organizing vocabulary that might increase our capacity to measure vocabulary acquisition in ways that will be more useful to educators across the disciplines of literature, science, social studies, and mathematics. The illustrative framework for vocabulary assessment is one on which one of us (Hiebert, 2011) has been working. We offer this categorization scheme not as the "be-all and end-all" of vocabulary schemes but to illustrate the manner in which assessments can be organized.

The three parts of the scheme, as depicted in Figure 12.1, are (1) *core vocabulary:* the 5,600 most common words (along with words that share the root word but have inflected endings) that constitute approximately 90% of running academic text; (2) *extended vocabulary:* the other 300,000–600,000 (Leech, Rayson, & Wilson, 2001; Oxford Dictionaries, 2010) words in English that, while occurring rarely, give detail to narratives and precision to informational texts; and (3) *word flexibility:* the capacity to negotiate the subtleties of word use (mainly due to polysemy and interrelatedness) in a variety of contexts. We illustrate the focus of each of the three components of the scheme, reminding readers that we provide this scheme primarily as an illustration of ways of specifying the words for vocabulary assessment.

Core Vocabulary

The vocabulary of English is distributed unevenly. A small group of words— approximately 5,600 (Carroll, Davies, & Richman, 1971; Zeno, Ivens,

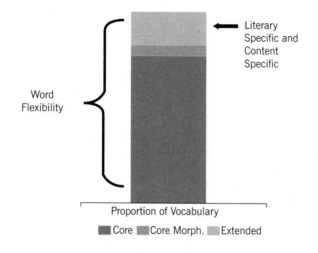

FIGURE 12.1. Framework for vocabulary. From Hiebert (2011). Reprinted with permission from the author.

Millard, & Duvvuri, 1995)—accounts for about 80% of all the words in all English texts, including those of college and the workplace. When inflected words (e.g., *looked* plus *look; happier* plus *happy*) are added, this group accounts for about 90% of the total words in English texts.

The other 10% of the total words that we encounter in printed English come from an enormous body of words—approximately 300,000–600,000, depending on how a word is defined—that occur with low frequency in texts. This 10% of the rarest English words is often the source for the items on vocabulary tests. To foreshadow our position, we will provide an alternative stance toward this 10%, what we will call *extended vocabulary*.

Ironically, it is the *core vocabulary* that has often been overlooked in vocabulary assessments. Typically, core vocabulary is viewed as the Dolch words—a small group of mostly abstract function words—which, in actuality, form only a small part of the approximately 5,600 words. But beyond the first 100 or so most frequent words, there are numerous core content words that carry the semantic load of sentences. Typically, these words represent general concepts (e.g., *mysteries, property, value,* and *interior*) and are versatile—hence, their frequency. By *versatile* we mean that these words often have multiple meanings, change their function as parts of speech (e.g., be a *force, force* an issue), share a root word with numerous other words (e.g., *spectacles, inspect, respect, spectrometer*), and often "travel" across disciplines (history, science, mathematics, and literature).

The 10% of the lexicon that occurs rarely provides much of the specificity in texts—words such as *anthill, commandant, rectory,* and *dirigible.*

But it is unlikely that a reader will be able to understand *dirigible* if he or she is not facile with the core vocabulary, at least in part, because core vocabulary provides the contextual and lexical fabric that allows us to infer the meanings of the rarer extended vocabulary. Consequently, an essential part of vocabulary assessment pertains to students' knowledge of the vocabulary that accounts for the majority of the texts that they read. If students can read these words, it is highly likely that they can figure out the "other 10%"—or at least make a sufficiently plausible inference about the meaning of these rarer words to make sense of the text as a whole. If students aren't facile with the core vocabulary, they will never be successful as readers—no matter how many engaging vocabulary lessons are taught that include challenging words from the 10%.

Despite the versatile nature of the core vocabulary, a basic issue has been viewed as an obstacle to textbook publishers, in designing instructional materials, and to test-makers in creating assessments. The issue is this: Just because two words happen to be in the same "band" of frequency, it does not follow that knowing one means that students are likely to know the other. Consider this set of words that share a predicted low frequency of 19 appearances per million: *mayor, measurement, mercury, microscope,* and *mysterious.* Words that have high imagery values or concreteness, such as *microscope, mercury,* and *mayor,* are fairly straightforward and likely tied to students' exposure to these words in everyday life or even through text. Words such as *measurement* and *mysterious* are more abstract and have nuanced meanings. If a student knows the meaning of *microscope,* it does not follow that he or she will know the meaning of *mysterious.*

Although membership in a particular band of frequency provides no indication of semantic relationship, it can be taken as an index of two important phenomena: (1) students' mastery of this important band of words and (2) the amount of exposure students have had to texts. The 5,600 words are predicted to occur at least 10 times or more per million words (with most occurring substantially more). Ten repetitions is the "rule of thumb" that has been associated with gaining working knowledge of a word (McKeown, Beck, Omanson, & Pople, 1985), although, as Landauer, Kireyev, and Panaccione (2011) have shown, concrete words representing specific objects or people (e.g., *microscope, mayor*) may require fewer repetitions. If, however, fourth graders have read approximately 500,000 words in school texts (a reasonable expectation, given what we know about curriculum and reading volume; Anderson, Wilson, & Fielding, 1988), they should have had exposure to a substantial portion of the core vocabulary. Thus, an assessment of words from particular bands of the core vocabulary could be taken as evidence that students have read critical benchmark amounts of text.

Extended Vocabulary

Now what about those 300,000–600,000 words in the extended vocabulary? They should be assessed somehow, for surely it is mastery of this vocabulary that sets apart the truly literate from the functionally literate individuals in our society. The extended vocabulary, as we discuss in the next section, differs as a function of text type. And the vocabulary assessments we use or design need to take those differences into account.

The percentage of extended vocabulary appearing in text is highly similar across narrative and informational categories through the elementary period, at which point the proportion of extended vocabulary in informational texts begins to creep ahead of the proportion in literary texts—roughly 15% of the total tokens in the text represent extended vocabulary.

What differs between narrative and informational text is the conceptual complexity and the relationships among the words in a text. Hiebert and Cervetti (Chapter 16, this volume) report that science words are longer, more conceptually complex, and more thematically related to one another and to the topic of the text than are narrative words. These differences suggest the need for unique instructional approaches and types of assessment. In science, for example, where unique words are conceptually complex but interrelated, assessing students' knowledge of relationships among key terms or their ability to use these words in talking or writing about the big ideas in the curriculum makes sense. Because the unique words of narrative texts represent familiar concepts with unfamiliar labels (e.g., *dejected/ sad, meticulous/careful*), assessments would emphasize either synonyms or perhaps the special nuance of meaning that is gained when a writer uses a rare word, such as *gargantuan*, rather than common synonyms such as *big* or *large*.

Nagy, Anderson, and Herman (1987) operationalized conceptual difficulty as the relationship of a new word's meaning to students' existing knowledge, with the key distinction made between words that are new labels for concepts already known to the learner (e.g., *apologize* for the known concept *saying you're sorry*) and words that require the acquisition of new factual information or a new system of concepts to learn (e.g., *divide* as the boundary between river systems). Nagy et al. (1987) found that conceptual difficulty was the factor that most strongly influenced whether students learned a given word from context while reading a text. Other word features that did not have a significant impact on learning from context in this study were word length, part of speech, morphological transparency, and proportion of students who reported knowing the word before reading. There was no evidence of incidental learning from context for words at the highest level of conceptual difficulty. In their analysis of text-level factors,

Nagy et al. found that the proportion of conceptually difficult words was also a significant negative predictor of word learning from context.

Semantic relatedness among word meanings is another critical part of conceptual difficulty: A word can be conceptually difficult because it is part of a system of related meanings that is new, not simply because its meaning is unknown. When the focus is on knowledge acquisition, these systems of related words become the unit of instruction, rather than individual words, particularly for content-area texts (e.g., all the words required to explain photosynthesis or the legislative process). The contrast is important: The unknown words in a narrative text are, for the most part, unlikely to be either related to one another or encountered again, whereas the new terms of one topic in a content area are (1) likely to be encountered many times in the chapter in which they initially occur, (2) likely to be related to one another, and (3) highly likely to be the conceptual foundation for the new ideas in the next chapter or topic.

Word Flexibility

This third issue of word flexibility involves the stance that learners can take as they encounter new words while reading. We have labeled it *word flexibility*, drawing liberally on Spiro and Jehng's (1990) notion of cognitive flexibility to define it. According to Spiro and Jehng, cognitive flexibility is the ability to adapt cognitive strategies to the particular situation we find ourselves in as learners. This adaptability is just as essential in navigating English vocabulary as it is in any other learning situation. When it is applied to vocabulary, however, it takes on a particular character that distinguishes it from other kinds of learning. To understand how word flexibility works, it is useful to revisit several of Nagy and Scott's (2000) dimensions introduced earlier, specifically, polysemy, interrelatedness, and multidimensionality.

To cope with polysemy, readers need to understand that the same written form of the word on the page can mean something different in different contexts; moreover, they must suppress alternate meanings in order to focus on the meaning at hand. The manner in which the word *conflict* is used, for example, in the sentence *The two groups have been in conflict with each other for years* is different from its use in the sentence *Armed conflict might be unavoidable*. These alternate meanings may seem slight, but they imply very different meanings about the world.

Word flexibility also involves an awareness of interrelatedness, particularly the expectation in complex texts that particular words often appear together. Using the word *conflict* again, the term *conflict of interest* illustrates a unique meaning for which a reader needs to have word flexibility. With respect to multidimensionality, readers need to anticipate that words take on different functions (i.e., parts of speech) and, in some cases, even different pronunciations. In the case of the word *conflict*, the stressed syllable changes when it moves from a noun (CON flict) to a verb (con FLICT). Another aspect of multidimensionality is the recognition of shared meanings across words. Many words, especially in the academic texts of the disciplines, come from the Romance language historical heritage of English. This means that adding prefixes and suffixes generates new forms of the word. The word *recommend* illustrates derivation of a word. *Recommend* is a member of a family that comes from the base word *commend*, and both *commendation* and *recommendation* represent additional derived forms. When readers possess the knowledge that English permits this sort of generative flexibility in forming derived forms, their capacity to understand and compose increasingly complex texts is greatly enhanced.

These three elements—core vocabulary, extended vocabulary, and word flexibility—are the concepts in our approach to vocabulary assessment—and instruction! We believe that they could be used to transform the way in which we assess vocabulary in schools as well as the decisions we make about what words to teach and how to teach them.

A Research Agenda for the Next Decade

We have raised this three-pronged framework of core vocabulary, extended vocabulary, and word flexibility as one means of identifying the parts of the lexicon for assessments. There is an enormous amount of work that needs to be done before such a framework—or others—can be used on a large-scale to assess students' vocabulary knowledge and growth that, in turn, guide practice and policy. In this section, we raise some of the research issues that need to be addressed before such assessments can be used on a large scale.

Criteria for Selection

We have offered one framework for making determinations along the selective–comprehensive continuum. The usefulness of assessments that capture bands within the core and extended vocabularies in guiding instructional practice is of the essence. Are such assessments any better than those that fall in the extremes of the comprehensive end of the continuum in supporting educators in closing the vocabulary gap?

Additional schemes require validation as well, such as Biemiller's (2009) designation of words worth teaching on the basis of data on students' familiarity with words. Beck, McKeown, and Kucan (2002) advocate focusing on words that are relatively rare synonyms of known concepts—just the sort of words that characterize literary texts. Determining bodies of words that belong to particular semantic clusters (e.g., ways that are used to communicate excitement) might be another way to narrow the sample of words within an assessment. These and other ways of configuring words need to be studied, as does the relationship of assessments with different bodies of vocabulary. In particular, performances on vocabulary assessments need to be considered in relation to different modes of use: receptive–productive and oral–written. How is vocabulary on a particular measure related to students' use of grade-appropriate vocabulary in writing? How well does a vocabulary assessment relate to students' ability to understand complex vocabulary in a listening or speaking mode? As much as we want to get the assessment of reading vocabulary right, we cannot do so at the cost of rich approaches to assessing it in other language modes.

Word Flexibility

For the large population of extended vocabulary, what we really need to know is how capable students are of determining the meanings of words that they have seldom, if ever, encountered. That presents a formidable challenge. What seems most promising to us is to conceptualize the process of determining word meaning as a problem-solving activity in which sentence contexts (both the one at hand and other "collocations" we could provide to students), morphological connections (it's a member of the *spec* family so it must have something to do with vision), and semantic connections (it's in the same conceptual family as other machines we use to measure eyesight) become the resources that students use to infer the meanings of unknown words they encounter in text. In short, we should move toward the assessment of students' word flexibility levels.

Vocabulary and Text Genre

It is clear that informational text typically carries a heavier vocabulary burden than does literary text. Currently, that difference is a hidden variable in many studies. Research is needed to untangle the relationship between text genre and vocabulary: (1) how words are chosen for instruction, (2) what's new for students—the ideas, the words, or both, and (3) how likely are words to be repeated in the texts in which they first occur. Regardless of the answers, they will have profound implications for vocabulary instruction and transfer. Because vocabulary is generally considered in a holistic fashion, one dividend might be to differentiate methods of vocabulary instruction by text genre.

Transfer of Vocabulary Knowledge

The preceding points all converge on the issue of transfer of vocabulary knowledge to other components of reading. The research alluded to here would almost certainly offer insights into the difficulties we have raised about issues of transfer and the specific effects of vocabulary instruction on comprehension; for example, which aspects of novelty (new ideas or new words) cause the most havoc with comprehension? More important is the explicit attention to the issues of transfer, both near and far, for the tasks under investigation. In addition, the strength and durability of transfer over time should be a part of this effort, particularly given the relatively short duration of many vocabulary instruction interventions in the literature. It is one thing to teach a word, but if it is forgotten in a few days, it hardly seems worth the effort.

Computerized Assessments of Vocabulary

Finally, we need to seriously address computerized assessments of vocabulary domains. In a better world, we would not be limited to conventional norm-referenced assessments of vocabulary acquisition, where our only benchmark for gauging vocabulary growth is the average performance of other students. We could opt instead for estimates of mastery over particular domains of interest (e.g., all of the words in a given curriculum or a given frequency band) or estimates of control over other characteristics that might prove to be effective indexes of vocabulary learning (e.g., all words with a common morpheme, such as *spec*, or all the words denoting some aspect of *power*). The work recently reported by Landauer et al. (2011) suggests that we may not be far off from providing what they describe as *personalized* assessments of students' vocabulary. For example, they are refining a word maturity algorithm to determine students' knowledge of words in a variety of contexts (i.e., heterogeneity). They can, over time, capture students' learning of a word (incrementality), and they can provide sufficient contexts for capturing at least some levels of interrelatedness. However, at this point, their digital assessment provides only one format that does not do justice to the dimensions of polysemy or multidimensionality. Nevertheless, efforts such as those of Landauer et al., indicate that we may not be far off from adaptive assessments that permit insight into the breadth and depth of students' knowledge of words.

VOCABULARY ASSESSMENT FOR THE PRESENT: WHAT TEACHERS CAN DO RIGHT NOW

So what's a teacher or a principal or a curriculum coordinator to do about vocabulary assessment in his or her situation while we wait for the revolution in research and development that we have just described as a set of goals for the future? Educators still have to make decisions about who possesses what levels of knowledge about what vocabulary. They still have to place students in programs, decide whether students have met standards, and determine whether their curriculum is doing the job they hoped it would do. So what can and should be done in the interim? Two general strategies, each supported by a set of specific tactics, seem appropriate to the situation educators face: (1) continue to use the norm-referenced tests currently in use but with explicit knowledge of their limitations clearly in mind, and (2) develop local assessments based on the advice offered in this chapter and tailored to a particular situation.

Making Judicious Use of the Current Crop of Commercially Available Assessments

In one sense, our critique of standardized comprehension assessments is culturally unfair. After all, these norm-referenced assessments have been used to make decisions about students' vocabulary knowledge for over a century. And what's wrong with knowing how a student "stands" in relation to other students around the country? Nothing . . . and everything. The problem with norm-referenced assessments is that they don't offer a clue about instruction. Just because you know that Tommy scores at the 32nd or 75th (or any other) percentile tells you nothing about what steps (or what specific words) you might teach to improve his vocabulary. A norm-referenced score thus provides a "screen" or an "early warning system" to let you know that something more ought to be done in this school or that you, as a teacher, need to learn about Tommy's vocabulary repertoire in order to zero in on an instructional plan (low norm-referenced scores = do something, quickly!), but they cannot and will not provide the plan. At best, they lead to prescriptions such as "Read more books, experience more of the world, and learn more words." In short, they tell you whether Tommy knows more or fewer words than the "average bear—nothing more, nothing less." As long as they are used with these limitations in mind, they can be helpful sources of information for evaluating the effectiveness of curriculum and instruction or determining who needs instructional attention. For greater instructional guidance, we will need tests that focus on students' relative mastery of particular collections of words.

Taking Our Advice Seriously

When it comes to vocabulary, what a teacher wants to know, in addition to how to teach it (a topic well addressed by the other chapters in this book), is how much of the corpus that Tommy *should* know does he *actually* know? And can the teacher learn that? It is, at once, the simplest and most complex of tasks. It is simple because it involves identifying the corpus (or population) of words of interest and then sampling words from that population to get good estimates of the proportion of words Tommy knows. It is complex because everything matters, as the following sections make clear.

Defining the Corpus

Twenty years ago, it would have been difficult to determine how many new words were introduced in a textbook, a unit, or a story. There were just too many, and it was too hard to keep track of them. Not so in the 21st century. Computers have changed all that. It is now possible, with most textbook curricula, to answer the question "How many new words are there?" for just about any unit of curriculum. One can usually get a computerized list, and with some help from your district technology experts, create a computerized portfolio of relevant lists of words. Users need to be aware of their options here: One can define the corpus very broadly (all the words in the K–12 curriculum) or very narrowly (all the new words introduced in this story or all the words that include the *spect-* morpheme).

Dividing the Corpus

Sometimes it is useful to divide the corpus in ways that provide answers to questions that matter about student performance. For example, we believe that it is useful to make separate judgments about students' mastery of words in different bands of frequency. Recall that a big dividing line for us is the core (the 5,600-plus inflected forms) and extended (the rest of the words in English) vocabularies. We would want to be able to answer questions like this: In this history text, what percentage of the new core words did my students know at the start of the semester (or year, depending), and what percentage have they learned through the semester (or year)? We would want to be able to answer the same question for extended vocabulary. Others might want to know the proportion of "academic" words known or learned that consist of a subset of words, mostly core, that are also on the Coxhead (2000) Academic Word List.

One can also imagine a plan in which at key points throughout a course, a unit, or a text, you and your colleagues assess mastery of vocabulary words that you have already taught versus those that are yet to be taught, to distinguish between intentional and incidental learning of vocabulary.

Keeping Track of Your Corpus

It's a good idea to create a spreadsheet to keep track of all of the relevant variables involved in classifying words. For each word, classify it by several categories (e.g., zone membership, letter–sound transparency, number of syllables, number of prefixes, number of suffixes, or inflection status). There are web resources to aid with this task (see Table 12.4 for a list of several, currently available sites).

Drawing Samples

Once a corpus has been defined, the task is to draw a representative sample of words from it, usually with an eye toward determining students' level of mastery over its contents. Drawing random samples of the words in the corpus is really the only defensible and appropriate strategy; the minute we begin to exercise judgment (let's pick this word rather than that word because it is more obscure or interesting) in selecting words, we compromise our ability to answer questions about level of mastery. Once you have committed to the logic of drawing random samples, you create a lot of options for yourself. The beauty of selecting random samples, provided that the corpus is sufficiently large, is that you can create an indefinitely large number of "forms" of the test—where a form equals a particular random sample of size N (# of items) from the corpus. And if your school has a large (and nimble) computer assessment capacity, a simple program could generate 30 different samples of words of a given size for the 30 students in your classroom. The advantage of this sort of system is that you can assess mastery of the corpus frequently (say, weekly or monthly) throughout the unit,

TABLE 12.4. Sources for Online Databases and Text Analyzers

Resource	Contents	Website
Web Vocabulary Profiler	This program tells you how many word types the text contains from the following four frequency levels: (1) the list of the most frequent 1,000 word families, (2) the list of the second 1,000 word families, (3) the Academic Word List, and (4) the words that do not appear in any of the preceding lists.	*www.er.uqam.ca/ nobel/r21270/textools/ web_vp.html*
Online Readability Index	On this University of Nebraska–Lincoln site you can input text to have it analyzed by Hiebert's word zones. You can also create custom zones using your own lists of content-specific words.	*cehs07.unl.edu/reading/ zone*

semester, or year without giving the students the "same" form of the test—a real benefit for monitoring progress. Experience with curriculum-based assessment (Deno, 1984) tells us that occasionally one will draw an "odd" sample, but over time, if assessments are given frequently, the "bumps" due to this sort of fluctuation will smooth out, giving us accurate and useful assessments of the domain of words at hand.

Determining Sample Size

Determining how large a sample of words to select for an assessment to be representative of a corpus of words is a complex task, and we have not made enough progress on this approach to assessment to offer unassailable advice. But there are a few rules of thumb, taken from the test development literature. For example, it is hard to achieve even a modicum of reliability for measuring a particular phenomenon (e.g., objective, standard, or domain) of interest with fewer than 10 items, and that number assumes that the items are developed with enough care to exhibit small errors of measurement. With lower-quality items, more items would be needed. For classroom assessment purposes, especially when teachers are gathering lots of evidence about mastery of a standard over several days, the 10-item rule of thumb can be relaxed a bit. And when there are fewer than 10 words in a particular domain, as there might be for a particular domain like "all of the new words in this selection," then the whole population of relevant words can be measured, and sampling is not an issue. Our advice is not to regard this issue lightly for the important reason that making an unreliable judgment about individual performance leads inevitably to poor pedagogical decisions for that student.

Item Format

The advice here is straightforward: Pick a format that matches your purpose for assessment. So, for example:

- If you want to know whether a student can "define" a word, then ask him or her to write or select a definition.
- If you want to know whether a student can determine the meanings of particular words in context, then ask him or her to write or select a definition after observing it in a sentence or paragraph context (even better, after seeing it used in three or four sentence contexts).
- If you want to know where a word "fits" into a knowledge base or a semantic network of related words, then assess student knowledge of words that are closely related to that word.

The Role of the Student

For years, teachers have been bringing students into the assessment process by asking them to rate their knowledge of particular words, either before or after a lesson or unit in which those words are used or taught. Scott et al. (2010) reported on a method of engaging students in estimating their personal knowledge of particular words. They asked students to make judgments about a word in four distinct and progressively discriminating test items:

1. Have you ever seen or heard this word before?
   a. Yes
   b. No
2. How confident are you about what you know about the word?
   a. I've heard it, but I'm not sure what it means.
   b. I think I know what this word means.

Items 3 and 4 for each word focus respectively on the word's semantic field and choosing a definition that also recognizes the part(s) of speech it exemplifies.

3. The word *flick* most likely has something to do with
   a. Dolphins
   b. Looking
   c. Fruit
   d. Movement
4. *Flick* means
   a. The seed of a jungle fruit.
   b. The way dolphins swim.
   c. Looking carefully.
   d. Moving something quickly.

The point is to involve students in the process of determining their own level of knowledge about words as early as they can begin to make those judgments. This can begin in grade 1, but it gets more important and more feasible in grades 3 and 4, and it can become a routine part of the introduction of new texts in middle and high school.

CODA: RECAPPING VOCABULARY ASSESSMENT

We wish we could offer our readers a more positive account of the state of vocabulary assessment, one in which we were able to either (1) express more confidence about the validity, appropriateness, and utility of the current crop of commercially available vocabulary assessments; or (2) provide a definitive set of guidelines that readers could use to do it on their own. We can't offer that sort of account because our reading of the evidence leaves much to be desired (and much to be done!). We can, however, be more confident about a future in which we adopt a different framework (core and extended vocabulary coupled with word flexibility) for thinking about vocabulary and look to different assessment tools and constructs (the ideas in our suggestions for future research section) to improve the way we assess knowledge of words and their linguistic environments. In the meantime, we can begin to improve the quality, relevance, and utility of the assessments we use in our classrooms, schools, and districts by keeping the limitations of current assessments clearly in mind as we use them, and by building a new generation of local vocabulary assessments that adhere to as many of the principles of a new generation of vocabulary assessments as we can manage. Finally, we hope that whoever writes this chapter a decade from now will have a happier tale to tell. Whether they do unwittingly depends upon what all of us who care about vocabulary learning and its assessment do over that decade.

ACKNOWLEDGMENT

Portions of this chapter, particularly the section titled "Vocabulary Assessments: Past and Present," are based on and adapted from Pearson, P. D., Hiebert, E. H., & Kamil, M. L. (2007). Vocabulary assessment: What we know and what we need to learn. *Reading Research Quarterly, 42*(2), 282–296. Copyright 2007 by the International Reading Association. Adapted by permission.

REFERENCES

Anderson, R. C., Wilson, P. T., & Fielding, L. G. (1988). Growth in reading and how children spend their time outside of school. *Reading Research Quarterly, 23*, 285–303.

Austen, J. (1790). *Love and freindship* [sic]. *www.gutenberg.org/files/1212/1212-h/1212-h.htm*

Beck, I., McKeown, M., & Kucan, L. (2002). *Bringing words to life: Robust vocabulary instruction*. New York: Guilford Press.

Biemiller, A. (2009). *Words worth teaching: Closing the vocabulary gap*. Columbus, OH: SRA.

Carroll, J., Davies, P., & Richman, B. (1971). *The American heritage word frequency book*. Boston: Houghton Mifflin.

Common Core State Standards Initiative. (2010). *Common core state standards for English language arts and literacy in history/social studies, science, and technical subjects.* Washington, DC: CCSSO & National Governors Association.

Coxhead, A. (2000). A new academic word list. *TESOL Quarterly, 34*(2) 213–238.

Deno, S. (1984). Curriculum-based measurement: The emerging alternative. *Exceptional Children, 52*(3), 219–232.

Dumas, A. (1845). *Twenty years after. www.gutenberg.org/files/1259/1259-h/1259-h.htm*

Dunn, L., & Dunn, P. (2007). *Peabody Picture Vocabulary Test* (4th ed.). San Antonio, TX: Pearson Assessments.

Flexner, S. B. (Ed.). (2003). *Random House Webster's unabridged dictionary* (2nd ed.). New York: Random House. Retrieved October 15, 2001, from *dictionary.infoplease.com/vocabulary*

Flinspach, S. L., Scott, J. A., & Vevea, J. L. (2010). Rare words in students' writing as a measure of vocabulary. In R. T. Jimenez, V. J. Risko, D. W. Rowe, & M. Hundley (Eds.), *59th annual yearbook of the National Reading Conference* (pp. 187–200). Oak Creek, WI: National Reading Conference.

Hiebert, E. H. (2011, June 7). The 90–10 rule of vocabulary in increasing students' capacity for complex text. Retrieved from *textproject.org/frankly-freddy/the-90-10-rule-of-vocabulary-in-increasing-students-capacity-for-complex-text*

Hoover, H. D., Dunbar, S. B., & Frisbie, D. A. (2003). *Iowa Tests of Basic Skills.* Rolling Meadows, IL: Riverside.

Kame'enui, E. J. (2002). *An analysis of reading assessment instruments for K–3.* Eugene, OR: Institute for the Development of Educational Achievement, University of Oregon.

Landauer, T. K., Kireyev, K., & Panaccione, C. (2011). Word maturity: A new metric for word knowledge. *Scientific Studies of Reading, 15*(1), 92–108.

Leech, G., Rayson, P., & Wilson, A. (2001). *Word frequencies in written and spoken English based on the British National Corpus.* London: Longman.

McKeown, M. G., Beck, I. L., Omanson, R. C., & Pople, M. T. (1985). Some effects of the nature and frequency of vocabulary instruction on the knowledge and use of words. *Reading Research Quarterly, 20,* 522–535.

Nagy, W. E., Anderson, R. C., & Herman, P. A. (1987). Learning word meanings from context during normal reading. *American Educational Research Journal, 24,* 237–270.

Nagy, W. E., & Scott, J. A. (2000). Vocabulary processes. In M. L. Kamil, P. Mosenthal, P. D. Pearson, & R. Barr (Eds.), *Handbook of reading research* (Vol. 3, pp. 269–284). Mahwah, NJ: Erlbaum.

Nation, I.S.P. (2001). *Learning vocabulary in another language.* Cambridge, UK: Cambridge University Press.

National Assessment Governing Board. (2005). *Reading framework for the 2009 National Assessment of Educational Progress.* Washington, DC: American Institutes for Research.

National Institute of Child Health and Human Development. (2000). *Report of the National Reading Panel: Teaching children to read: An evidence-based assessment of the scientific research literature on reading and its implications for reading instruction: Reports of the subgroups.* Washington, DC: Author.

Oxford Dictionaries. (2010). *Oxford dictionary of English* (3rd ed., rev.). New York: Oxford University Press.

Partnership for Assessment of Readiness for College and Careers. (2010). *The Partnership for Assessment of Readiness for College and Careers (PARCC) application for the Race to the Top Comprehensive Assessment Systems Competition.* Retrieved from *www.fldoe.org/parcc/pdf/apprtcasc.pdf*

Pearson, P. D., & Hamm, D. N. (2005). The history of reading comprehension assessment. In S. G. Paris & S. A. Stahl (Eds.), *Current issues in reading comprehension and assessment* (pp. 13–70). Mahwah NJ: Erlbaum.

Read, J. (2000). *Assessing vocabulary.* Cambridge, UK: Cambridge University Press.

Resnick, D. P., & Resnick, L. (1977). The nature of literacy: An historical exploration. *Harvard Educational Review, 47,* 370–385.

Salinger, T., Kamil, M. L., Kapinus, B., & Afflerbach, P. (2005). Development of a new framework for the NAEP reading assessment. In C. M. Fairbanks, J. Worthy, B. Maloch, J. V. Hoffman, & D. L. Schallert (Eds.), *55th yearbook of the National Reading Conference* (pp. 334–349). Oak Creek, WI: National Reading Conference

Scott, J. A., Flinspach, S., Miller, T., Vevea, J., & Gage-Serio, O. (2009, December). *Vocabulary growth over time: Results of a multiple level vocabulary assessment based on grade level materials.* Paper presented at the National Reading Conference, Albuquerque, NM.

Scott, J. A., Lubliner, S., & Hiebert, E. H. (2005). Constructs underlying word selection and assessment tasks in the archival research on vocabulary instruction. In J.V. Hoffman, D.L. Schallert, C.M. Fairbanks, J. Worthy, & B. Maloch (Eds.), *55th Yearbook of the National Reading Conference* (pp. 264–275). Oak Creek, WI: National Reading Conference.

Scott, J. A., Vevea, J. L., & Flinspach, S. L. (2010, December). *Vocabulary growth in fourth grade classrooms: A quantitative analysis of Year 3 in the VINE project.* Paper presented at the annual meeting of the Literacy Research Association, Fort Worth, TX.

SMARTER Balanced Assessment Consortium. (2010). *Race to the Top Assessment Program application for new grants: Comprehensive assessment systems CFDA Number: 84.395B.* Retrieved from *www.k12.wa.us/SMARTER/RTTTApplication.aspx*

Spiro, R. J., & Jehng, J. (1990). Cognitive flexibility and hypertext: Theory and technology for the nonlinear and multidimensional traversal of complex subject matter. In D. Nix & R. J. Spiro (Eds.), *Cognition, education, and multimedia: Exploring ideas in high technology* (pp. 163–205). Hillsdale, NJ: Erlbaum.

Stanford Achievement Test. (2006). *Stanford Achievement Test Series* (10th ed.). San Antonio, TX: Pearson Assessment.

Woodcock, R. W., McGrew, K. S., & Mather, N. (2007). *Woodcock–Johnson III.* Rolling Meadows, IL: Riverside.

Zeno, S. M., Ivens, S. H., Millard, R. T., & Duvvuri, R. (1995). *The educator's word frequency guide.* New York: Touchstone Applied Science Associates.

Chapter 13

Reading and Vocabulary Growth

Anne E. Cunningham
Colleen Ryan O'Donnell

Given the critical role that vocabulary knowledge plays in academic achievement and, most notably, in reading comprehension (Baumann, Kame'enui, & Ash, 2003), it is not surprising that teachers spend somewhere between 6 and 20% of their instructional time on activities geared toward vocabulary learning (Blachowicz, 1987; Blanton & Moorman, 1990; Scott, Jamieson-Noel, & Asselin, 2003) or that most comprehensive literacy curricula emphasize word analysis and the direct teaching of word meanings (National Institute of Child Health and Human Development, 2001). Indeed, direct vocabulary instruction and intentional word study are considered particularly important strategies for supporting children at risk for reading difficulties (Elleman, Lindo, Morphy, & Compton, 2009). However, although it is important for reading programs to include activities intended to develop oral language and vocabulary, theorists and researchers are also generally in agreement that language development and vocabulary learning transcend these structured lessons and are largely subconscious processes that occur in the context of functional language use (Chomsky, 1975; Halliday, 1975; Miller & Gildea, 1987; Nagy & Anderson, 1984; Neuman & Koskinen, 1992; Sternberg, 1985, 1987).

Consider the following: It has been estimated that an 18-month-old child learns an average of 5 new words a day in order to have an average vocabulary of approximately 8,000 words by the time the child is 6 years old (Sénéchal & Cornell, 1993). At the time of high school graduation, the average student is estimated to know approximately 40,000 words (Nagy,

Herman, & Anderson, 1985). In order to increase one's vocabulary from 8,000 to 40,000 in roughly 12 years time, a child needs to learn roughly 32,000 words between 1st grade and 12th grade (i.e., 7 words a day, every day of the year for 12 years). And although a vocabulary of 40,000 words may be average for a 12th-grade student, analyses of texts suggest that it would be insufficient to allow a reader unassisted comprehension of a newspaper and many high school-level novels (Nation, 2006)! Thus, students who excel academically are likely mastering an average of almost 100 words a week for 12 years. When we consider that the average program of direct vocabulary instruction covers only a few hundred words and word parts per year, it seems evident that the type of vocabulary development that is necessary for skilled reading is beyond the scope of even the most intensive programs of vocabulary instruction. Therefore, in addition to direct instruction, children's word knowledge must also be developed indirectly through authentic experiences with language.

The purpose of this chapter is to provide an overview of the critical nature of incidental word learning and specifically to establish the importance of exposure to print as yet another vehicle for supporting vocabulary growth. For the purposes of this chapter, *incidental word learning* or *incidental vocabulary development* is defined as the derivation and learning of new word meanings encountered through exposure to language (Swanborn & de Glopper, 1999). In addition, the term *print exposure*, which refers to the amount of text or print a child encounters as a result of experiences with books, is used synonymously with the terms *reading volume, shared reading*, and *independent reading*. In an effort to contextualize our discussion and establish the general importance of a robust vocabulary, we begin with a review of the research documenting the critical role that vocabulary plays in the reading process. We then turn to a targeted description of the unique value of print as a potent vocabulary builder across the developmental span and a discussion of the factors that appear to be related to variation in exposure to print. This discussion of the factors that are related to reading behavior is intended to provide educators with insights into the most effective ways to ensure that all children develop positive reading habits and reap the benefits that reading provides.

THE RELATIONSHIP BETWEEN VOCABULARY AND READING COMPREHENSION

Direct Associations between Vocabulary and Reading Comprehension

Research has consistently demonstrated that skills such as phonological processing (i.e., a child's ability to attend to and manipulate language at the sound level; Cunningham, 1990; Hagiliassis, Pratt, & Johnston, 2006; Share & Gur, 1999), orthographic skills (i.e., a child's knowledge of and ability to attend to the visual aspects of words and letter patterns; Castles & Holmes, 1996; Cunningham & Stanovich, 1990; Martin, Pratt, & Fraser, 2000), and rapid automatized naming (i.e., lexical access or a child's ability to efficiently access phonologically encoded information from long-term memory; Bowers & Newby-Clark, 2002; Bowers & Wolf, 1993) have a significant impact on the development of efficient word identification skills (i.e., the ability to accurately identify words in text) and that accurate and efficient word identification skills in turn support reading fluency and reading comprehension. However, recent research has also identified a category of struggling readers who, despite adequate word identification skills and fluency, have deficiencies in their ability to understand what they have read and gain meaning from text (i.e., they are "poor comprehenders"; Nation, 2005; Nation & Angel, 2006).

Consideration of theoretical models of the reading process, such as Hoover and Gough's (1990) "simple view of reading," provides a starting point for identifying the specific deficits of this group of poor comprehenders. According to the simple view of reading, reading skill is a simple reflection of an individual's skill with decoding (i.e., word identification) and his or her general ability to comprehend language. Thus, if the deficits of this group of struggling readers lie outside of their word identification skills, then it is logical to consider the possible impact of their general language development. Indeed, scientific investigations suggest that poor comprehenders have underlying weaknesses in the general verbal domain, as exemplified by poor listening comprehension, weak receptive and expressive vocabulary skills, and poor semantic processing skills (Cain, Oakhill, & Bryant, 2004; Catts, Adlof, & Ellis Weismer, 2006; Nation, Clark, Marshall, & Durand, 2004; Nation & Snowling, 1998; Ricketts, Nation, & Bishop, 2007; Stothard & Hulme, 1992; Yuill & Oakhill, 1991). Simply put, poor comprehenders struggle to understand what they have read in part as a result of weak vocabulary skills and limited word knowledge.

In many ways, the identified relationship between vocabulary and skilled reading requires no further explanation: Knowledge of words and their meanings is essential if one aims to understand and make sense of the words one has successfully identified. For example, if a reader does not know the meaning of the words *fabricating* and *whereabouts*, he or she is likely to struggle to understand the reason that the character in his or her book got a detention for "*fabricating* a story about the *whereabouts* of his homework." Consistent with this idea, in a study investigating the number of words required for unassisted comprehension of text (defined as 98% coverage of a text or the ability to read and understand 98% of the words in the text), Nation (2006) determined that in order to read a newspaper or a novel expected of upper-grade high school students (e.g., *The Great Gatsby* or *Lady Chatterley's Lover*), one must have a vocabulary of 8,000–9,000 *word families* (e.g., the word *abbreviate* is in a family of six words: *abbreviate, abbreviates, abbreviated, abbreviating, abbreviation, abbreviations;* other word families, such as *nation*, contain more than 20 words). Nation notes that even with this level of vocabulary knowledge (and 98% coverage of text), 1 out of 50 words is still unknown to the reader! His point is well taken (and perhaps understated) when one flips to the first page of F. Scott Fitzgerald's book *The Great Gatsby* (a text commonly read by high school students) and reads the following:

> Most of the confidences were unsought—frequently I have feigned sleep, preoccupation, or a hostile levity when I realized by some unmistakable sign that an intimate revelation was quivering on the horizon; for the intimate revelations of young men, or at least the terms in which they express them, are usually plagiaristic and marred by obvious suppressions. (1925, p. 7)

In this way, word knowledge has a direct and convincing impact on reading comprehension, and this example easily authenticates the research suggesting that a critical weakness of poor comprehenders (i.e., those with adequate word identification skills but poor reading comprehension) lie, in part, in the domain of general language development and vocabulary knowledge.

Indirect Associations between Vocabulary and Reading Comprehension

The connection between children's vocabulary and their reading comprehension is multifaceted and does not end with the direct relationship just described (i.e., knowledge of word meanings is essential to deriving meaning from text as a whole). Vocabulary also impacts reading comprehension indirectly through its less obvious association with word identification (Nation & Snowling, 1998; Ouellette, 2006; Ricketts et al., 2007). In a longitudinal study examining the relationship between general language skills and reading development, Nation and Snowling (2004) determined that, in addition to phonological skills, various aspects of oral language development, including vocabulary knowledge and listening comprehension, were unique concurrent predictors of both reading comprehension and word recognition in a sample of children approximately 8½ years old. Interestingly, they found that even after statistically controlling for the effects of initial reading skill and general intellectual abilities, vocabulary and listening comprehension contributed unique variance to individual differences in reading comprehension, word recognition, and exception word reading (i.e., identification of irregular/nondecodable words) 4½ years later (when the children were approximately 13 years of age). In addition, the investigators found that the extent to which children's word recognition skills departed from the level predicted by their decoding ability was significantly related to their oral language proficiencies. In other words, children who had adequate decoding skills but weak oral language skills struggled more with accurate word identification than their peers with commensurate word attack skills and well-developed vocabularies. These results help to refine our understanding of reading difficulties by suggesting a unique role for vocabulary in supporting the word identification process.

In subsequent research aimed at elucidating the relationship between vocabulary and word identification, Ricketts et al. (2007) determined that vocabulary has its greatest impact on the identification of exception words that can be identified only on the basis of contextual information (syntactical and morphological) in combination with the pool of words in one's oral lexicon that is consistent with the available (albeit somewhat unreliable) phonological information. For example, to successfully identify the irregular word *laughter* in the sentence *I could hear the gleeful sound of their laughter*, one must first know the meaning of the word *gleeful* in order to deduce that one needs to generate a "mental list" of words that represent joyful or happy sounds (e.g., *screeches* and *moans* are out of the running, whereas *giggles, laughter,* and *chuckles* may be considered). Once the reader has his or her mental list of words that is appropriate to the context, he or she will have to rely on the existing word-level information to narrow down a selection and successfully identify the word. Despite the fact that *laughter* is an irregular word, the reader must rely on the sounds that follow the "rules" (i.e., /l/, /a/, /t/, /r/) to narrow his or her mental list and arrive at an acceptable response (e.g., *giggles* and *chuckles* are out and only *laughter* remains). If the child's vocabulary is meager, then both the ability to benefit from context and the ability to successfully generate word options are diminished considerably, and, consequently, the likelihood of successfully identifying the exception words is dramatically reduced.

Thus, it appears that children with weaknesses in vocabulary are doubly disadvantaged when it comes to reading comprehension. Despite the presence of the phonological and orthographic skills required for successful decoding and word analysis, due to vocabulary weaknesses, these children struggle to identify critical words in text, which negatively impacts their ability to process and comprehend what they have read. Moreover, even when they prevail at word identification, they are unable to escape their vocabulary deficiencies and ultimately suffer as a result of their inability to make meaning from the words they have successfully identified.

VOCABULARY DEVELOPMENT: THE UNIQUE CONTRIBUTION OF PRINT

Given that children with large vocabularies are at a distinct advantage in reading and general academic development (Beck, McKeown, & Kucan, 2002, 2008), it is of critical importance that we understand the means by which vocabulary is developed. As reflected in other chapters in this volume, there is strong evidence of the value of providing children with direct and explicit vocabulary instruction as a means of building word knowledge. However, as argued earlier, there are also compelling reasons to believe that a sizable amount of vocabulary development occurs through authentic experiences with language. Although exposure to language of all kinds is of value in developing vocabulary (Heath, 1983/1996), there is sufficient evidence that, in comparison to oral language, written language (i.e., reading) provides a particularly rich source of language exposure.

The theoretical reasons for believing that reading is a more effective means of expanding a child's vocabulary are rooted in the differences in sophistication of the words found in print as compared to oral language. These differences between oral and written language are not merely a matter of speculation but rather have been borne out repeatedly in empirical investigations. For example, in a seminal paper, Hayes and Ahrens (1988) utilized standard word frequency counts (see Carroll, Davies, & Richman, 1971) to compare the median rank of words and the number of rare words[1] per 1,000 in three different categories of language. Specifically, they analyzed written language (sampled from genres as difficult as scientific articles and as simple as preschool books), words spoken on a variety of different television programs, and adult speech in two contexts of varying formality (i.e., expert testimony and casual conversation between college-educated friends/spouses). Their analyses unequivocally demonstrated that speech is "lexically impoverished" when compared to written language. For example, children's books had more rare words than any form of spoken language, including expert witness testimony. Children's books contained 50% more rare words than did adult prime-time television and the conversation of college graduates. Moreover, basic adult reading materials (e.g., books, popular magazines, newspapers) contained words that were two or three times rarer than those heard on popular prime-time television news programs. As one might imagine, these relative differences in word rarity

---

[1]A rare word is defined as one with a rank lower than 10,000—a word that is outside the vocabulary of a fourth to sixth grader.

have direct implications for vocabulary development. In order for a child to benefit from the word-learning opportunities that incidental exposure to language provides, he or she must regularly be exposed to words that are outside his or her existing oral lexicon. It is evident that the likelihood of this happening is far greater while reading than while watching television or even talking to well-educated adults.

The argument is sometimes made that the types of words that are found in text but not readily utilized in oral discourse are "unnecessary words—jargon, academic doublespeak, elitist terms of social advantage, or words used to maintain the status of the users but that serve no real functional purpose" (Cunningham & Stanovich, 1998, p. 3; Stanovich, 1993). Certainly, when one considers the types of words that have been identified as having "appreciable frequency" in written texts but rarely occur in oral language (e.g., *legitimate, infinite, invariably, luxury, maneuver, portray, provoke, relinquish, reluctantly*),[2] it is clear that these words are not essential to the basic ability to communicate one's thoughts, ideas, needs, or intentions. For example, it is possible to use the word *move* rather than *maneuver*, the word *cause* or *excite* rather than *provoke*, or the words *lots of* rather than *infinite*, and by doing so, one's basic point would be communicated adequately. However, to the extent that one of the primary benefits of a large vocabulary is its relationship to reading comprehension, it is also abundantly clear that being unfamiliar with these words could have a dramatic impact on readers' ability to understand what they have read (e.g., not knowing the word *invariably* when reading the sentence *It invariably snows in April in the Rocky Mountains* could have disastrous consequences for the prospective backpacker or hiker). Moreover, although perhaps not necessary for basic communication, these words convey subtleties of meaning, and the level of precision afforded by these terms undoubtedly puts one at an advantage in certain physical, social, and professional realms. As persuasively stated by Olson (1986),

> It is easy to show that sensitivity to the subtleties of language are crucial to some undertakings. A person who does not clearly see the difference between an expression of intention and a promise or between a mistake and an accident, or between a falsehood and a lie, should avoid a legal career or, for that matter, a theological one. (p. 341)

It is largely print that provides the exposure to these central but infrequent words, and it is for this reason that children's reading volume plays a fundamental role in their vocabulary development.

---

[2]See, for example, Berger (1977); Brown (1984); Carroll et al. (1971); and Francis and Kucera (1982).

The Contributions of Exposure to Print across the Developmental Continuum

Given the strong theoretical reasons to suspect a positive relationship between exposure to print and vocabulary development, it is not surprising to learn that this relationship is consistently demonstrated in empirical research. A number of scientific investigations have directly considered the impact that independent reading has on the development of language-based skills such as vocabulary (Cunningham & Stanovich, 1991, 1997; Martin-Chang & Gould, 2008; Stanovich & Cunningham, 1992, 1993). Time and again, these studies have demonstrated that individuals who read more have stronger oral language skills than those who read less frequently. Not surprisingly, when we look more broadly at research investigating the impact that literacy experiences have on cognitive and academic outcomes, we begin to understand that the powerful contributions of print to oral language development, and vocabulary development specifically, begin long before an individual is capable of independent reading. In fact, we argue that the relationship between print exposure and vocabulary is developmental in nature and begins before most children can even identify the letters of the alphabet. Specifically, print often gets its foothold in shaping vocabulary prior to school entry through shared book reading or read-aloud experiences.

Shared Book Reading

Reading aloud to children is a practice that has long been promoted in the field of education. In fact, many would argue that its importance cannot be overstated. In *Becoming a Nation of Readers: The Report of the Commission on Reading*, a canonical document in the field of reading research, Anderson, Hiebert, Scott, and Wilkinson (1985) argue, "The single most important activity for building the knowledge required for eventual success in reading is reading aloud to children" (p. 23). Given statements such as this, it is easy to conclude that shared book reading is tied to reading achievement in that it supports the development of the skills that lead directly to the ability to identify words (e.g., phonological awareness and orthographic knowledge). Many are surprised to learn that research has been quite *inconsistent* in verifying the direct impact that shared reading has on the development of these specific literacy skills (Bus, van IJzendoorn, & Pellegrini, 1995; Scarborough & Dobrich, 1994; Whitehurst et al., 1994). Although the nature of this relationship remains unclear, the value of shared book reading may be more distal in nature and occur through its role in developing oral language skills such as vocabulary. In other words, shared book reading *does*, as Anderson and colleagues argue, "[build] the knowledge required for eventual success in reading," but it does so by building a child's knowledge of words and their meanings rather than by developing the skills that directly support word identification.

Evidence for the role that shared book reading plays in developing vocabulary is perhaps best captured by a review of a recent meta-analytic project undertaken by the National Early Literacy Panel (NELP).[3] The purpose of the NELP (2008) study was to identify early literacy programs and interventions that lead to gains in the specific skills and abilities most linked to positive outcomes in reading, writing, and spelling. Using a meta-analytic approach, 7,313 publications were rigorously screened for inclusion in the analyses. This rigorous screening increased the likelihood that their results would represent causally interpretable effects and led to the categorization of 136 articles by intervention type. Shared reading was one of five categories of intervention investigated by the panel. Most of the studies in the shared reading category of interventions examined the impact of shared reading on oral language skills, while a few studies examined variables reflecting phonological awareness, general cognitive ability, alphabet knowledge, print knowledge, reading readiness, and writing.

The NELP's (2008) analysis revealed that shared reading interventions had the largest impact on oral language outcomes, with an average effect size of .68. This result means that, on average, children who received a shared reading intervention scored almost 0.7 of a standard deviation higher on measures of oral language than children who did not receive a shared reading intervention. This translates to a difference of roughly 11 points on most standardized assessments of language development. To put this in perspective, a Standard Score of 100 places a child in the 50th percentile, and a Standard Score of 89 places a child in the 23rd percentile. The panel found that these effects were consistent regardless of variations in the type of shared reading intervention and the child's age.

When we consider the types of books we typically read to children prior to school entry, it might be difficult to understand how the simplistic and juvenile nature of these texts could possibly create such dramatic differences in vocabulary development. However, a cursory review of popular children's storybooks such as Maurice Sendak's (1963) *Where the Wild Things Are* and Judi Barrett's (1978) *Cloudy with a Chance of Meatballs*, reveals words such as *marvelous, mischief,* and *gnashed*—words that, in speech, are likely to be eliminated altogether or replaced with simpler terms

---

[3] Meta-analyses are considered effective tools for summarizing the research in a specific area in that they provide a statistical analysis of the results of several individual studies and are specifically designed to integrate findings more rigorously than traditional narrative or descriptive review methods (Glass, 1976).

like *great* and *trouble*. Even simple board books for toddlers, such as the silly and poetic books by Sandra Boynton (e.g., *Moo, Baa, La, La, La* [Boynton, 1984]; *Birthday Monsters* [Boynton, 1993a]; *Oh My Oh My Dinosaurs!* [Boynton, 1993b]) include words such as *snort* and *crammed* and *confetti*. Although these terms might not be as urbane as those we typically associate with "vocabulary words," when we consider how relatively limited a young child's general exposure to language has been, it is easy to see how shared book reading could provide them with their first exposure to a wide variety of rich, academic, and descriptive words.

Several researchers have noted the dramatic differences in oral language development (i.e., vocabulary) that we see between children at school entry (Biemiller, 1999; Hart & Risely, 1995; Beck & McKeowen, 2001). As is evident from studies examining shared storybook reading, such as the NELP, these differences can, at least in part, be explained by the experiences that children have with books outside of school. As discussed, differences in vocabulary impact reading development through the role they play in supporting word identification and reading comprehension, and it is in this way that shared book reading contributes to reading development and reading achievement. Thus, the "achievement gap" that receives so much attention in both academic and political circles might actually be viewed as the "vocabulary gap" that begins with the wide disparity in children's early language and literacy exposure.

Independent Reading

To this point, we have reviewed the data highlighting the relationship between shared book reading and vocabulary development. As mentioned, the value of print in developing vocabulary spans the developmental spectrum, and research also consistently demonstrates that once children have learned to read, and are capable of reading independently, variability in exposure to print continues to play a role in creating disparities in exposure to words that are outside of a child's existing oral lexicon and, thus, vocabulary learning. For example, Cunningham and Stanovich (1991) investigated the relationship between print exposure (i.e., how much one reads, or reading volume) and several declarative knowledge bases (including vocabulary) in a sample of elementary school students. Specifically, in addition to obtaining information about independent reading behavior (i.e., reading volume or print exposure), the researchers gave measures of vocabulary, word knowledge, spelling ability, verbal fluency, and general knowledge. As predicted, they found that print exposure is significantly related to each of these declarative knowledge bases. A skeptic will easily point out that it is entirely possible (even likely) that the observed relationship between reading volume and these cognitive skills could be due to their shared relationship with a third and more salient variable such as IQ or reading ability (i.e., children who are smarter and/or better readers read more and children who are smarter or better readers also have more declarative knowledge). Thus, it is possible to argue that the identified relationship between reading volume and knowledge is not genuine but spurious. In order to account for this possibility, the researchers utilized multiple regression techniques to statistically control for the effects of both general intelligence (e.g., nonverbal reasoning) and basic reading skills (e.g., decoding ability/phonological processing). After statistically controlling variability associated with general intelligence and decoding abilities, print exposure accounted for *significant* and *independent* variation in spelling, vocabulary, verbal fluency, word knowledge, and general information, providing empirical evidence for the hypothesis that reading volume is a significant contributor to the development of cognitive capacities and, in particular, of vocabulary and word knowledge above and beyond general intelligence and reading ability.

These results were replicated in a subsequent study that utilized even more stringent tests of the contribution of reading volume to verbal skills by removing the contributions of general intelligence, decoding skill, *and* reading comprehension (Stanovich & Cunningham, 1992). This test was particularly rigorous because by removing the contributions of reading comprehension, a skill likely *developed* by print exposure, the researchers statistically removed some of the variance that rightfully belonged to reading volume. Despite the stringent nature of these analyses, print exposure still proved to be a powerful and unique contributor to the development of cognitive abilities, including vocabulary knowledge.

Further evidence of the power of reading volume as a unique mechanism for supporting vocabulary development across the lifespan is provided by a study involving students at the college level. Utilizing a sample of undergraduate students from the University of California, Berkeley (an institution known for high academic achievement), Stanovich and Cunningham (1993) demonstrated that the unique ability of print exposure to shape cognition persists long after students have become skillful, competent readers. In this study, the researchers collected data regarding general intellectual and academic abilities (i.e., high school grade-point average, nonverbal reasoning, reading comprehension, tests of math ability), print exposure, and general knowledge (e.g., practical and cultural information, vocabulary) from nearly 300 undergraduate students. After controlling for these general abilities, they found that reading volume was a robust predictor of variability in vocabulary as well as general practical and cultural knowledge. In other words, regardless of their baseline cognitive abilities, students who read more had more sophisticated vocabularies and knew more about the world. In sum, a wide variety of studies has successfully demonstrated what educators have long believed: At every stage of life and education, reading can (and does) shape the mind.

WHO READS?: VARIATION IN READING BEHAVIOR

Despite the preponderance of evidence suggesting that reading plays an important role in the development of critical cognitive skills and academic achievement, there is tremendous variation in the amount of reading in which individuals engage. Although some people choose to read abundantly, others rarely read outside of their work environments or the classroom. In their 2007 report, "To Read or Not to Read," the National Endowment for the Arts (2007) reported that only 22% of 17-year-olds read for enjoyment on a daily basis. Moreover, 65% of college freshman reported reading for pleasure less than 1 hour per week, and 39% reported not reading for pleasure. Obviously, this variation in exposure to print goes beyond the differences that exist between literate and nonliterate individuals. Within a literate population, and even among individuals with similar levels of reading ability and education, there are dramatic differences in the amount of reading in which people engage (e.g., see Anderson, Wilson, & Fielding, 1988). Some people fill every vacant moment of their day with text, never standing in line or sitting in a waiting room without something to read. By contrast, other people, despite adequate reading skill, rarely (or never) choose to read. Thus, the differences in print exposure between avid readers and infrequent readers are substantial. Anderson et al. (1988) used diary studies to estimate that a child who is an avid reader may read almost 2,000,000 words a year outside of school, whereas a child who reads infrequently reads only approximately 8,000 words a year—a difference of more than 200 times more words read in 1 year.

Matthew Effects: The Rich Get Richer

It does not require a sophisticated analysis to see a clear picture develop with respect to the trajectory of those children who are frequently engaged in literacy activities. As discussed, children enter school with varying levels of oral language skills and knowledge of words and their meanings. These initial differences provide children with a distinct advantage (or disadvantage) as they set out on the course of becoming skilled readers. Children with larger vocabularies are better at identifying words and better at comprehending what they have read. As a result, these children are able to read more, enjoy reading more, and are more inclined to read often. Because of their reading volume, their vocabularies are further developed, and they enjoy even greater benefit in the development of their reading skills. By contrast, children with weak vocabularies have more difficulty success-fully processing text, they enjoy reading less, and as a result, they read less—further exacerbating their deficits in vocabulary and reading achieve-ment. This scenario is often referred to as the "Matthew effects" in read-ing, describing the cycle through which the rich get richer and the poor get poorer, continually exacerbating the achievement gap that exists as early as school entry (Stanovich, 1986, 2000).

Identified Pathways toward Independent Reading: Practical Considerations

Given the importance of avid reading to vocabulary development, read-ing achievement, and academic success, it is useful to consider why some individuals choose to read abundantly, whereas others rarely engage in lit-eracy activities. Understanding the variables associated with the develop-ment of positive reading habits is a critical consideration in allowing us to determine the most effective ways to support all children in becoming avid readers. If we understand the conditions that appear to encourage positive reading habits, then we can work to level the playing field for our students by creating those conditions in our classrooms.

To date, we have approached the study of reading behavior by investi-gating cognitive, sociological, and ecological influences. Research in each of these areas has successfully illuminated different pathways toward avid reading and thus has contributed an additional layer to our understanding of this complex phenomenon. Specifically, we have documented the critical importance of reading ability, social support, and access to print as poten-tial pathways leading to the development of positive reading habits.

Reading Ability

A unique and particularly compelling study by Cunningham and Stanovich (1997) provided insight into one of the critical factors that determine read-ing behavior: reading ability. This study sought to examine the influence of speed of initial reading acquisition on later tendencies to engage in reading activities by examining the performance of a group of students that was assessed in first grade and then again 10 years later. The researchers found that first-grade decoding abilities, word recognition, and reading compre-hension (i.e., first grade reading abilities) all predicted 11th-grade reading volume. More importantly, the influence of first-grade reading ability on reading behavior later in life was observable after measures of 11th-grade reading comprehension had been controlled. In other words, regardless of the level of reading ability eventually attained, *early* success and skill in reading were important predictors of future reading behavior. Interestingly, in this study, first-grade assessments of general cognitive abilities did not provide a unique contribution to 11th-grade reading volume, suggesting that the relationship between initial reading acquisition and subsequent reading volume cannot be attributed simply to general cognitive ability. These findings are stunning because they debunk the hypothesis that only smart children read well and read more. Instead, they indicate that, regardless of initial intellectual abilities, students who get off to a fast start in reading (i.e., children who learn to break the alphabetic code early) are more likely to read more over the years, and as demonstrated, build vocabulary knowledge.

For teachers, this powerful finding can serve as a source of both reassurance and added pressure: We need not despair over our students who enter our classrooms with weak or limited cognitive skills. By helping them to become skilled readers, we can help to lay the foundation for our students to become avid readers and reap the cognitive benefits that reading affords. However, in order to do so, it is critical that we utilize instructional techniques that allow these students to experience success in the early years of learning to read. We have overwhelming evidence suggesting that providing direct, explicit, and systematic instruction is most effective in helping all students break "the code" (i.e., instruction in phonemic awareness and phonics instruction; NELP, 2008). Yet we also know that our approach to literacy instruction must be balanced, and that the best approach is one that not only addresses word recognition skills, but also includes methods to improve fluency and ways to enhance comprehension and engagement (NELP, 2008).

Social Support

In addition to reading ability, there is evidence suggesting that reading habits develop, in part, as a result of socialization. Children who have stronger reading support systems are more likely to develop an appreciation for reading and become active, successful readers (Baker, 2003; Foertsch, 1992; Klauda, 2009; Sénéchal & Young, 2008). Because of these support systems, these children are at an advantage when it comes to vocabulary learning, reading comprehension, and general academic success.

Although reading is an activity that requires only one participant, it is, in many ways, a social activity. Literacy is often viewed as a sociocultural process involving social and cultural interactions both at home and at school—children become literate as a result of experiences in their families, communities, and classrooms (Heath, 1983, 1996; Moll, 1992; Purcell-Gates, 2007; Schmidt, 1995). As such, environmental and social variables have a notable influence on reading volume, and children who come from homes in which parents and siblings read more have more opportunities to become interested and engaged in literacy activities.

Morrow (1983) investigated the differences between groups of kindergarten children rated as having either a high interest in reading or a low interest in reading. She found that the nature of children's home environments had a strong influence on their interest in and proclivity toward reading. In comparison to children who demonstrated low interest in literature and engaged infrequently in self-initiated literacy activities, children who demonstrated high interest in literature came from families that placed a high value on literacy. These children came from homes in which there were books in multiple rooms throughout the house, including the kitchen and the child's bedroom. Moreover, although the parents of both high- and low-interest readers spent relatively equal amounts of time reading the newspaper and technical materials related to work, the parents of high-interest readers were significantly more likely to read for pleasure as a leisure time activity. The relationship between parental reading habits and the reading behavior of children suggested by Morrow (1983) is well supported by the work of other researchers (Callaway, 1981; Chandler, 1999; Greaney, 1980, 1986; Greaney & Hegarty, 1987; Gauvain, Savage, & McCollum, 2000; Snow, Burns, & Griffin, 1998) and likely plays an important role in a child's proclivity toward reading. Thus, by modeling positive reading habits, and indirectly encouraging their children to read, parents play an important role in supporting the development of their child's oral language skills and reading engagement.

Given this knowledge, teachers (from preschool through high school) are encouraged to create "communities of readers" and to communicate the importance of leisure time reading to the family members of the children in their classrooms. Although it is a common practice for teachers to provide time for their students to read books at school, it is also important that children see the adults that they work with reading and enjoying books during their school day (e.g., leading book groups during free periods or lunch). Teachers who utilize weekly classroom newsletters might consider writing to parents about the importance of modeling positive reading habits and they might provide information about "story hours" and other similar events at local libraries. Schools that host "read-ins" or "readathons," where students, teachers, school staff, and parents get together in a fun, cozy, and festive environment to read as a community, create an excitement about reading that serves as a springboard for this valued activity. Children of all ages are enthusiastic about special classroom events such as "pajama parties" with popcorn and books or special guest readers such as the school principal, administrative assistant, or custodian.

Access to Print

One aspect of social support for reading that may serve to encourage the development of positive literacy habits is greater access to print or a general immersion in a literacy-rich environment. Researchers are virtually unanimous in concluding that students who have access to reading materials at home, in their communities, and in their classrooms read more often, report greater reading enjoyment, and experience superior reading achievement (Foertsch, 1992; Morrow, 1983; Neuman & Celano, 2001; Palmer, Codling, & Gambrell, 1994). "Opportunities for book borrowing and avenues for obtaining books for the home library are significant factors in reading motivation" (Palmer et al., 1994, p. 177). This is supported by the fact that children who have library cards (i.e., memberships in public libraries) are more likely to engage in leisure time reading (Baker, Simmons, & Kame'enui, 1995; Greany & Hegarty, 1987; Morrow, 1983).

Interestingly, a compelling body of research suggests that there are striking differences in access to print between children in low-income and middle-income communities. For example, in an extensive year-long study, Neuman and Celano (2001) compared the following variables in neighborhoods of differing incomes: availability of books for purchase; readable signage; public areas where children might observe literacy activities; and the quality and quantity of books in local child care centers, elementary schools, and libraries. The researchers concluded that whereas middle-income children have a wide variety of resources from which to choose in terms of access to print, low-income children rely on public institutions that provide unequal resources. Research also suggests that when low-income children are given increased access to print, their early literacy skills improve significantly (Neuman, 1996, 1999), as does their voluntary use of library centers during free-choice time in school (Morrow & Weinstein, 1986).

Neuman (1996) investigated the influence of an intervention strategy designed to increase access to books for economically disadvantaged children and their families and to provide increased opportunities for parent–child shared storybook reading. The results of the investigation indicated that increased access to literacy materials positively influenced parents' willingness to engage in literacy activities with their children and therefore increased children's exposure to print. Neuman (1999) also found positive effects of increased access to literacy materials in a study examining an intervention program designed to provide child care centers with high-quality children's books. The intervention resulted in greater physical access to books, greater verbal interaction around literacy, and more time spent reading. Due to the increased access to literacy materials, children's concepts of print, writing, letter-name knowledge, and narrative improved substantially and were maintained over a period of 6 months. Moreover, Neuman discovered that with increased access to high-quality literacy materials, children demonstrated an increased interest in books and began to self-select and initiate reading activities.

This information can be used by teachers to advocate to their school boards and district administrators regarding the importance of access to high-quality literacy materials for the overall academic success of students. Moreover, although the budgets for classroom supplies may be limited, it is of utmost importance that teachers understand the direct value of allocating a portion of funding to maintaining classroom libraries that include books ranging in difficulty and genre. If schools do not have libraries that allow children to borrow books, teachers might consider creating a "checkout" system in their class library or establishing a program whereby children share and/or trade personal books. For children who do not possess a library card, it would be time well spent to arrange a field trip to the library to allow them to investigate the process of obtaining a library card and learn about library procedures. We collaborate with teachers who are willing to serve as the liaison between the library and students with limited access to books, agreeing to borrow and return books on their students' behalf. In addition, summer reading programs have proven to be useful mechanisms for increasing print exposure over summer months and helping to bridge the academic regression that is common with extended school breaks (Kim & Guryan, 2010; White & Kim, 2008). Teachers and school administrators might consider ways to create "summer school" experiences that communicate the importance of reading for pleasure by allowing children to select, recommend, and discuss books they have read, perhaps in "book club" fashion, again, creating a community that values reading.

Personality

Factors such as ability and environment have a clear and established impact on reading behavior and reading volume; however there is also emerging evidence that a child's proclivity toward avid reading is, at least in part, determined by individual characteristics such as disposition or personality (O'Donnell, 2006). Recent scientific explorations provide preliminary support for what might be considered the "book worm hypothesis," suggesting that avid readers tend to be children who are more introverted and less socially active and, by contrast, children who are more gregarious, active, talkative, and energetic tend to engage in *less* reading for pleasure. Conceptually, this relationship makes sense. Reading is an activity that occurs in isolation of others. When reading, we must cease interactions with others, end social dialogue, and manage our activity level and energy in order to process the text and remain focused on the plot. In essence, the demand characteristics of reading almost require, at least temporarily, introverted qualities.

These data shed light on one possible reason that some children may avoid involvement in literacy activities—their overarching need for social interaction and external stimulation. Thus, it may be beneficial to consider ways to allow extroverted children to get their active, gregarious, and social needs met within the context of literacy activities. For example, more extroverted children might benefit from opportunities for shared storybook reading or interactive book reading. Perhaps these children would benefit from participation in book clubs or story hours—activities that simultaneously encourage literacy while meeting children's need to interact with others.

CONCLUSIONS

On an intuitive level, we have long recognized the value of a well-developed vocabulary. As a culture, we generally perceive people with rich vocabularies as bright, knowledgeable, well educated, and experienced. People with a deep knowledge of words and the nuances of language are able to communicate their thoughts more precisely, leading us to assume that they are able to think more deeply and critically. Verbally precocious individuals avoid the inconvenience of referencing the dictionary incessantly while reading Faulkner, they successfully complete the *New York Times* crossword puzzle, and they dwell in the limelight of being champions at the game of Scrabble. Indeed, it would be difficult to argue against the merits of a well-developed oral lexicon. But, as we have seen, a large vocabulary does not enjoy its finest moment with the thrill of a "triple word score." Instead, a large vocabulary serves as a launching pad for reading comprehension, reading achievement, and, ultimately, general academic success.

As a field, we have documented the importance of exposure to print as an effective and critical means of supporting word learning and vocabulary development. At the same time, we have identified remarkable differences in the amount of reading in which children engage. Thus, although some children continuously benefit from the "cognitive bootstrapping" that reading affords, others do not enjoy these same rewards, and as a result, some children are simply more equipped to learn to read and to read well.

Within the last 15 years, we have made significant progress in developing our understanding of reading behavior. Research efforts have successfully identified several variables that impact the likelihood of becoming an avid reader. Researchers have established that reading volume and reading behavior form a reciprocal relationship; in the same way that reading volume promotes reading skill, reading skill influences reading volume. In addition, research has successfully illustrated the ways in which environmental opportunities such as access to print and social support for reading influence reading behavior. Simply put, children who have more access to books and who receive more support for reading in their home and classroom environment are more likely to develop positive reading habits.

Armed with this knowledge, it is incumbent upon those of us who are involved in the education of children to find ways to support students in developing a love for reading. We must create learning environments that promote positive reading habits and positive attitudes toward literacy. This begins by involving children in high-quality shared reading experiences early in life, providing the types of curricular and instructional opportunities that have proven to support the development of solid basic reading skills, and establishing communities of readers within our classrooms.

REFERENCES

Anderson, R. C., Hiebert, E. H., Scott, J. A., & Wilkinson, A. (1985). *Becoming a nation of readers: The report of the Commission on Reading.* Washington, DC: National Institute of Education.

Anderson, R. C., Wilson, P. T., & Fielding, L. G. (1988). Growth in reading and how children spend their time outside of school. *Reading Research Quarterly, 23,* 285–303.

Baker, L. (2003). The role of parents in motivating struggling readers. *Reading and Writing Quarterly, 19,* 87–106.

Baker, S., Simmons, D., & Kame'enui, E. (1995). *Vocabulary instruction: Synthesis of the research* (Technical Report No. 13). Eugene, OR: National Center to Improve the Tools of Education.

Barrett, J. (1978). *Cloudy with a chance of meatballs.* New York: Atheneum.

Baumann, J. F., Kame'enui, E. J., & Ash, G. (2003). Research on vocabulary instruction: Voltaire redux. In J. Flood, D. Lapp, J. R. Squire, & J. Jensen (Eds.), *Handbook of research on teaching the English language arts* (2nd ed., pp. 752–785). Mahwah, NJ: Erlbaum.

Beck, I. L., & McKeown, M. G. (2001). Text Talk: Capturing the benefits of read-aloud experiences for young children. *Reading Teacher, 55,* 10–20.

Beck, I. L., McKeown, M. G., & Kucan, L. (2002). *Bringing words to life: Robust vocabulary instruction.* New York: Guilford Press.

Beck, I. L., McKeown, M. G., & Kucan, L. (2008). *Creating robust vocabulary: Frequently asked questions and extended examples.* New York: Guilford Press.

Berger, K. W. (1977). *The most common 100,000 words used in conversations.* Kent, OH: Herald.

Biemiller, A. (1999). *Language and reading success.* Cambridge, MA: Brookline.

Blachowicz, C. L. (1987). Vocabulary instruction: What goes on in the classroom? *Reading Teacher, 41*(2), 132–137.

Blanton, W. E., & Moorman, G. B. (1990). The presentation of reading lessons. *Reading Research and Instruction, 29,* 35–55.

Bowers, G. P., & Newby-Clark, E. (2002). The role of naming speed within a model of reading acquisition. *Reading and Writing: An Interdisciplinary Journal, 15,* 109–126.

Bowers, P., & Wolf, M. (1993). Theoretical links among naming speed, precise timing mechanisms and orthographic skills in dyslexia. *Reading and Writing: An Interdisciplinary Journal, 5,* 69–85.

Boynton, S. (1984). *Moo, baa, la la la.* New York: Simon & Schuster.

Boynton, S. (1993a). *Birthday monsters.* New York: Workman.

Boynton, S. (1993b). *Oh my oh my oh dinosaurs!* New York: Workman.

Brown, G. D. (1984). A frequency count of 190,000 words in the London–Lund Corpus of English Conversation. *Behavior Research Methods, Instruments, and Computers, 16,* 502–532.

Bus, A. G., van IJzendoorn, M. H., & Pellegrini, A. D. (1995). Joint book reading makes for success in learning to read: A meta-analysis on intergenerational transmission of literacy. *Review of Educational Research, 65,* 1–21.

Cain, K., Oakhill, J., & Bryant, P. E. (2004). Children's reading comprehension ability: Concurrent prediction by working memory, verbal ability, and component skills. *Journal of Educational Psychology, 96,* 31–42.

Callaway, B. (1981). What turns children on or off in reading? *Reading Improvement, 18,* 214–217.

Carroll, J. B., Davies, P., & Richman, B. (1971). *Word frequency book.* Boston: Houghton Mifflin.

Castles, A., & Holmes, V. M. (1996). Subtypes of developmental dyslexia and lexical acquisition. *Australian Journal of Psychology, 48,* 130–135.

Catts, H. W., Adolf, S. M., & Ellis Weismer, S. (2006). Language deficits in poor comprehenders: A case for the simple view of reading. *Journal of Speech, Language, and Hearing Research, 49,* 278–293.

Chandler, K. (1999). Reading relationships: Parents, adolescents, and popular fiction by Stephen King. *Journal of Adolescent and Adult Literacy, 43*(3), 228–239.

Chomsky, N. (1975). *Reflections on language.* New York: Pantheon.

Cunningham, A. E. (1990). Explicit versus implicit instruction in phonemic awareness. *Journal of Experimental Child Psychology, 50,* 429–444.

Cunningham, A. E., & Stanovich, K. E. (1990). Assessing print exposure and orthographic processing skill in children: A quick measure of reading experience. *Journal of Educational Psychology, 82,* 733–740.

Cunningham, A. E., & Stanovich, K. E. (1991). Tracking the unique effects of print exposure in children: Associations with vocabulary, general knowledge, and spelling. *Journal of Educational Psychology, 83,* 264–274.

Cunningham, A. E., & Stanovich, K. E. (1997). Early reading acquisition and its relation to reading experience and ability 10 years later. *Developmental Psychology, 33,* 934–945.

Cunningham, A. E., & Stanovich, K. E. (1998). What reading does for the mind. *American Educator, 22*, 9–15.

Elleman, A. M., Lindo, E .J., Morphy, P., & Compton, D. L. (2009). The impact of vocabulary instruction on passage-level comprehension of school-age children: A meta-analysis. *Journal of Research on Educational Effectiveness, 2*, 1–44.

Fitzgerald, F. S. (1925). *The great Gatsby.* New York: Scribner's.

Foertsch, M. A. (1992). *Reading in and out of school: Factors influencing the literacy achievement of American students in grades 4, 8, and 12, in 1988 and 1990.* Washington, DC: U.S. Department of Education, Office of Educational Research and Improvement.

Francis, W. N., & Kucera, H. (1982). *Frequency analysis of English usage: Lexicon and grammar.* Boston: Houghton Mifflin.

Gauvain, M., Savage, S., & McCollum, D. (2000). Reading at home and at school in the primary grades: Cultural and social influences. *Early Education and Development, 11*, 447–463.

Glass, G. V. (1976). Primary, secondary, and meta-analysis of research. *Educational Researcher, 5*(10), 3–8.

Greaney, V. (1980). Factors related to amount and type of leisure time reading. *Reading Research Quarterly, 3*, 337–356.

Greaney, V. (1986). Parental influences on reading. *The Reading Teacher, 39*, 813–818.

Greaney, V., & Hegarty, M. (1987). Correlates of leisure-time reading. *Journal of Research in Reading, 10*(1), 3–20.

Hagiliassis, N., Pratt, C., & Johnston, P. (2006). Orthographic and phonological processes in reading. *Reading and Writing, 19*, 235–263.

Halliday, M. A. K. (1975). *Learning how to mean: Explorations in the development of language.* New York: Elsevier.

Hart, B., & Risley, T. (1995). *Meaningful differences.* Baltimore: Brookes.

Hayes, D.P., & Ahrens, M. (1988). Vocabulary simplification for children: A special case of "motherese"? *Journal of Child Language, 15*, 395–410.

Heath, S. B. (1996). *Ways with words: Language, life and work in communities and classrooms.* Cambridge, UK: Cambridge University Press. (Original work published 1983)

Hoover, W. A., & Gough, P. B. (1990). The simple view of reading. *Reading and Writing: An Interdisciplinary Journal, 2*, 127–160.

Kim, J. S., & Guryan, J. (2010). The efficacy of a voluntary summer book reading intervention for low-income Latino children from language minority families. *Journal of Educational Psychology, 102*(1), 20–31.

Klauda, S. L. (2009). The role of parents in adolescents' reading motivation and activity. *Educational Psychology Review, 21*, 325–363.

Martin, F., Pratt, C., & Fraser, J. (2000). The use of orthographic and phonological strategies for the decoding of words in children with developmental dyslexia and average readers. *Dyslexia, 6*, 231–247.

Martin-Chang, S. L., & Gould, O. N. (2008). Revisiting print exposure: Exploring differential links to vocabulary, comprehension and reading rate. *Journal of Research in Reading, 31*, 273–284.

Miller, G. A., & Gildea, P. M. (1987). How children learn words. *Scientific American, 257*(3), 94–99.

Moll, L. C. (1992). *Vygotsky and education: Instructional implications and applications of sociohistorical psychology.* New York: Cambridge University Press.

Morrow, L. M. (1983). Home and school correlates of early interest in literature. *Journal of Educational Research, 76*(4), 221–230.

Morrow, L. M., & Weinstein, C. S. (1986). Encouraging voluntary reading: The impact of a literature program on children's use of library centers. *Reading Research Quarterly, 21,* 330–345.

Nagy, W. E., & Anderson, R. C. (1984). How many words are there in printed school English? *Reading Research Quarterly, 19,* 304–330.

Nagy, W. E., Herman, P. A., & Anderson, R. C. (1985). Learning words from context. *Reading Research Quarterly, 20,* 233–253.

Nation, I. S. P. (2006). How large a vocabulary is needed for reading and listening? *Canadian Modern Language Review, 63,* 59–81.

Nation, K. (2005). Picture naming and developmental reading disorders. *Journal of Research in Reading, 28,* 28–38.

Nation, K., & Angell, P. (2006). Learning to read and learning to comprehend. *London Review of Education, 4,* 77–87.

Nation, K., Clarke, P., Marshall, C. M., & Durand, M. (2004b). Hidden language impairments in children: Parallels between poor reading comprehension and specific language impairment. *Journal of Speech, Language, and Hearing Research, 47,* 199–211.

Nation, K., & Snowling, M. J. (1998). Semantic processing and the development of word recognition skills: Evidence from children with reading comprehension difficulties. *Journal of Memory and Language, 39,* 85–101.

Nation, K., & Snowling, M. J. (2004). Beyond phonological skills: Broader language skills contribute to the development of reading. *Journal of Research in Reading, 27,* 342–356.

National Early Literacy Panel. (2008). *Developing early literacy: Report of the National Early Literacy Panel.* Washington, DC: Author.

National Endowment for the Arts. (2007). *To read or not to read: A question of national consequence.* Washington, DC: Author.

National Institute of Child Health and Human Development. (2000). *Report of the National Reading Panel. Teaching children to read: An evidence-based assessment of the scientific research literature on reading and its implications for reading instruction* (NIH Publication No. 00-4769). Washington, DC: U.S. Government Printing Office.

Neuman, S. B. (1996). Children engaging in storybook reading: The influence of access to print resources, opportunity, and parental interaction. *Early Childhood Research Quarterly, 11,* 495–513.

Neuman, S. B. (1999). Books make a difference: A study of access to literacy. *Reading Research Quarterly, 34*(3), 286–311.

Neuman, S. B., & Celano, D. (2001). Access to print in low-income and middle-income communities: An ecological study of four neighborhoods. *Reading Research Quarterly, 36*(1), 8–26.

Neuman, S. B., & Koskinen, P. (1992). On forests and trees: A response to Kling-ner. *Reading Research Quarterly, 28*(4), 383–385.

O'Donnell, C. R. (2006). *Personality as a predictor of independent reading behav-ior.* Unpublished doctoral dissertation, University of California, Berkeley.

Olson, D. R. (1986). Intelligence and literacy: The relationships between intelli-gence and the technologies of representation and communication. In R. J. Sternberg & R. K. Wagner (Eds.), *Practical intelligence.* Cambridge, MA: Cambridge University Press.

Ouellette, G. (2006). What's meaning got to do with it?: The role of vocabulary in word reading and reading comprehension. *Journal of Educational Psychol-ogy, 98,* 554–566.

Palmer, B. M., Codling, R. M., & Gambrell, L. B. (1994). In their own words: What elementary students have to say about motivation to read. *The Reading Teacher, 48,* 176–178.

Purcell-Gates, V. (2007). *Cultural practices of literacy: Complicating the complex.* Mahwah, NJ: Erlbaum.

Ricketts, J., Nation, K., & Bishop, D. V. (2007). Vocabulary is important for some, but not all reading skills. *Scientific Studies of Reading, 11,* 235–257.

Scarborough, H. S., & Dobrich, W. (1994). On the efficacy of reading to preschool-ers. *Developmental Review, 14,* 245–302.

Schmidt, P. R. (1995). Working and playing with others: Cultural conflict in a kin-dergarten literacy program. *The Reading Teacher, 48*(5), 403–412.

Scott, J. A., Jamieson-Noel, D., & Asselin, M. (2003). Vocabulary instruction throughout the day in twenty-three Canadian upper-elementary classrooms. *Elementary School Journal, 103,* 269–286.

Sendak, M. (1963). *Where the wild things are.* New York: Harper & Row.

Sénéchal, M., & Cornell, E. H. (1993). Vocabulary acquisition through shared reading experiences. *Reading Research Quarterly, 28,* 360–374.

Sénéchal, M., & Young, L. (2008). The effect of family literacy interventions on children's acquisition of reading from kindergarten to grade 3: A meta-analytic review. *Review of Educational Research, 78,* 880–907.

Share, D., & Gur, T. (1999). How reading begins: A study of preschoolers' print identification strategies. *Cognition and Instruction, 17,* 177–213.

Snow, C. E., Burns, M. S., & Griffin, P. (1998). *Preventing reading difficulties in young children.* Committee on the Prevention of Reading Difficulties in Young Children. Washington, DC: National Academy Press.

Stanovich, K. E. (1986). Matthew effects in reading: Some consequences of indi-vidual differences in the acquisition of literacy. *Reading Research Quarterly, 21,* 360–407.

Stanovich, K. E. (1993). Does reading make you smarter?: Literacy and the devel-opment of verbal intelligence. In H. Reese (Ed.), *Advances in child develop-ment and behavior* (Vol. 24, pp. 133–180). New York: Guilford Press.

Stanovich, K. E. (2000). *Progress in understanding reading.* New York: Guilford Press.

Stanovich, K. E., & Cunningham, A. E. (1992). Studying the consequences of literacy within a literate society: The cognitive correlates of print exposure. *Memory and Cognition, 20,* 51–68.

Stanovich, K. E., & Cunningham, A. E. (1993). Where does knowledge come from?: Specific associations between print exposure and information acquisition. *Journal of Educational Psychology, 85*(2), 211–229.

Sternberg, R. J. (1985). *Beyond IQ: A triarchic theory of intelligence.* Cambridge, MA: Cambridge University Press.

Sternberg, R. J. (1987). Most vocabulary is learned from context. In M. G. McKeown & M. G. Curtis (Eds.), *The nature of vocabulary acquisition* (pp. 89–105). Hillsdale, NJ: Erlbaum.

Stothard, S. E., & Hulme, C. (1992). Reading comprehension difficulties in children: The role of language comprehension and working memory skills. *Reading and Writing, 4,* 245–256.

Swanborn, M. S. L., & de Glopper, K. (1999). Incidental word learning while reading: A meta-analysis. *Review of Educational Research, 69,* 261–286.

White, T. G., & Kim, J. S. (2008). Teacher and parent scaffolding of voluntary summer reading. *The Reading Teacher, 62*(2), 116–125.

Whitehurst, G. J., Arnold, D. S., Epstein, J. N., Angell, A. L., Smith, M., & Fischel, J. E. (1994). A picture book reading intervention in day care and home for children from low-income backgrounds. *Developmental Psychology, 30,* 679–689.

Yuill, N., & Oakhill, J. (1991). *Children's problems in text comprehension: An experimental investigation.* New York: Cambridge University Press.

Chapter 14

Powerful Vocabulary Instruction for English Learners

Patrick C. Manyak

Nearly 20 years ago, I sat around a table with my bilingual teaching colleagues at a Southern California elementary school. As a kindergarten teacher, I wanted to hear what knowledge or skills the upper-grade teachers wished their native Spanish-speaking students had when they entered the fourth and fifth grades. The teachers responded in unison, "Greater English vocabulary." A few years later I taught a combined fifth- and sixth-grade class of all native Spanish speakers and experienced firsthand the challenges that these students faced due to limited English vocabulary knowledge. Intelligent, hard-working students struggled to understand literary and social studies texts as a result of the high percentage of unfamiliar English words that these texts contained. Furthermore, due to their relative lack of vocabulary knowledge, my exceptional students performed only at an average level in English reading. Today, a growing body of research confirms what my teaching colleagues and I observed in our classrooms two decades ago: many English learners (ELs) face a large deficit in English vocabulary knowledge, and this deficit presents a major obstacle to achievement in critical areas such as reading comprehension (August, Carlo, Dressler, & Snow, 2005; Carlo et al., 2004; Garcia, 1991; August & Shanahan, 2006; Proctor, Carlo, August, & Snow, 2005; Saville-Troike, 1984; Snow & Kim, 2007).

In this chapter, I synthesize research studies addressing the English vocabulary development of ELs and instructional interventions aimed at enhancing this development. In addition, I offer insights gleaned from a project in which I am currently participating that is focused on developing and researching vocabulary instruction in fourth- and fifth-grade classrooms with a high percentage of ELs. In the following section, I stress the diversity that exists among ELs. In the subsequent sections, I summarize research focused on the vocabulary knowledge of ELs and vocabulary instruction targeting ELs. I conclude the chapter by offering key guidelines for planning and implementing powerful vocabulary instruction for ELs.

ENGLISH LEARNERS: A COMPLEX CATEGORY

The term *English learner*, like many categorical terms, can gloss over the diversity among students from families that speak languages other than English. Educators who have experience with ELs know that children in this category differ in many consequential ways. Without question, skillful teachers must account for these differences and carefully adapt instructional guidelines, materials, and activities according to the needs of their ELs. To prepare to make such adaptations, I find it helpful to consider six ways in which ELs may differ from one another.

1. ELs differ in age. Like their native English-speaking peers, a 5-year-old kindergarten EL and a 13-year-old eighth-grade EL differ greatly in their respective levels of cognitive development and world knowledge. Further, they participate in very different school settings with different linguistic, academic, and social expectations and tasks.

2. ELs differ by native language. Although ELs in the United States speak hundreds of different languages, nearly three-fourths of ELs come from Spanish-speaking homes (National Center for Education Statistics, 2004). Unlike spoken languages historically unrelated to English, Spanish shares many cognates with English—words that are spelled similarly and have similar meanings across languages. Thus, cognate knowledge represents a potentially important resource and instructional target for some ELs and a far more limited one for others (Nagy, Garcia, Durgunoglu, & Hancin-Bhatt, 1993). In addition, some ELs' native languages utilize alphabetic writing systems that are highly comparable to English whereas other ELs' native languages do not.

3. ELs differ in proficiency levels in their native language. Research has established that Spanish-speaking students' primary language (L1) vocabulary can impact their English reading comprehension (Proctor, August, Carlo, & Snow, 2006) and, more generally, that ELs' knowledge of literacy in their L1 may influence their English reading achievement (Dressler & Kamil, 2006). Thus, it is important to consider ELs' L1 oral knowledge and literacy skills.

4. ELs differ in their level of English language proficiency and level of exposure to English outside of school. One EL student may enter school with no knowledge of English whereas another may fall short of his or her native English-speaking (NES) peers only in some forms of academic English. Adding further complexity is the fact that ELs' levels of English proficiency and age often are not related in the ways that educators typically imagine. Although many ELs enter school in kindergarten with a limited knowledge of English and grow increasingly proficient as they progress through the grades, it is not unusual for a kindergartener who has been exposed to a great deal of English at home to enter school just slightly behind his or her NES peers, or, conversely, for a 13-year-old recent immigrant to enter eighth grade with no knowledge of English. Furthermore, outside of school, ELs experience a range of opportunities to hear and use English, and their level of access to support for English academic work varies widely.

5. ELs have different instructional histories, particularly with regard to language of instruction. ELs who immigrate to English-speaking countries after beginning school in their L1 may be highly proficient in that language. ELs who begin school in English-speaking countries such as the United States may experience English-only instruction throughout their school years or receive L1 instruction, to varying degrees of intensity and for varying lengths of time, in bilingual programs. Therefore, ELs differ with regard to exposure to English language instruction and to the language goals of their past and current school programs.

6. Finally, the language background of the student population of schools and classrooms that ELs attend differs greatly. ELs may find themselves in schools where an overwhelming number of students share the same L1, schools with a large number of ELs from diverse language backgrounds, or schools with a large percentage of NESs. Similarly, ELs may be placed in classrooms where all the students are ELs (who speak the same or various languages), in classrooms with a balanced number of ELs and NES peers, or in classrooms where they are a small minority. The composition of the school or classroom influences the language learning environment that ELs' experience and the teachers' instructional approaches for these students.

Recognition of these differences among ELs underscores the limitations of "one-size-fits-all" plans for vocabulary instruction for such students. Still, I believe that research supports a set of general guidelines for vocabulary instruction for most ELs. However, educators must knowledgeably translate these guidelines into instruction that best meets the specific needs of their particular students. Thus, whenever possible, I call attention to the ways that vocabulary research with ELs has addressed these elements of difference and suggest how teachers might take into account these differences in classroom instruction.

RESEARCH ON ENGLISH LEARNERS' VOCABULARY KNOWLEDGE

I began this chapter with a recollection of my own and my teaching colleagues' perceptions that our upper elementary ELs had limited English vocabulary knowledge and that this limitation presented a major obstacle to academic achievement. Today, an emerging body of research enables us to understand ELs' vocabulary development in greater depth and detail. In this section, I discuss findings related to the vocabulary knowledge of young and upper-grade ELs that I have distilled from numerous research studies. In each case, I state a broad finding and then offer a number of specific points that I believe are informative for teachers of ELs.

Starting Behind: Young English Learners' Vocabulary Knowledge

Common sense suggests that, on average, young ELs are likely to have more limited English vocabulary knowledge than their NES peers. Numerous studies support and further elaborate on this general assertion (Manis, Lindsey, & Bailey, 2004; Páez, Tabors, & López, 2007; Roessingh & Elgie, 2009; Umbel, Pearson, Fernández, & Oller, 1992; Verhoeven, 2000). Here, I discuss four points that extend our understanding of young ELs' vocabulary development.

Significant English Language Limitations

Many young ELs from low-income homes whose families use little English have very limited English language vocabulary. For example, Páez et al. (2007) provided evidence of the vocabulary size of developing Spanish–English bilingual children during their final year of preschool. The study included 319 children from low-income homes who were attending Head Start and public preschool programs. A large majority of the families (81%) reported using only or mostly Spanish at home. In a test of expressive vocabulary, the children averaged two standard deviations—a dramatic statistical difference—below the monolingual English norming population on two separate administrations of the assessment. Manis et al. (2004) reported similar findings from a group of 251 Spanish-dominant students in first and second grades. These students came from low-income families in a school district where the vast majority of the students were ELs who participated in a bilingual program in which they received Spanish language literacy instruction for a year and a half before transitioning to English language literacy instruction in the middle of first grade. The children scored at the 3rd percentile on a test of English expressive vocabulary at the end of first grade and at the 8th percentile at the end of second grade.

The Effect of Home Language Use

Home language use appears to significantly impact young ELs' English vocabulary knowledge. Umbel et al. (1992) assessed the vocabulary knowledge of first-grade upper-middle-class Latina/Latino children in Miami. They found that children from families that reported equal usage of English and Spanish performed significantly higher on an English vocabulary knowledge measure than children from the same socioeconomic level whose families reported speaking only in Spanish.

Qualitative Differences

Many young ELs with more advanced English proficiency demonstrate limited "lexical richness" (Roessingh & Elgie, 2009, p. 35) when compared to NES peers. Roessingh and Elgie (2009) offered evidence of this limitation in a study of 65 Canadian-born kindergarten ELs from a variety of language backgrounds. These children were asked to generate a narrative from a wordless picture book. Although there were no statistically significant differences in the average number of words in the narratives that the ELs produced when compared with a group of 25 NES peers, the ELs' narratives were filled with a significantly higher percentage of words from the 250 highest-frequency English words. The authors illustrated the difference between NES peers' and ELs' lexical richness with the following example: "In the frame where the boy is shaking his fist, ELL were limited to the word *mad, mad, mad* (or, *really, really, really MAD*). NS, on the other hand, used words such as *disappointed, angry, bothered*, or *mad*" (p. 40). The authors concluded that the ELs exhibited a "lack of low-frequency vocabulary, the key to longitudinal reading success" (p. 40).

L1–L2 Relationship

The relationship between L1 and L2 for young ELs is a complex one. In a study evaluating the relationship between the Spanish and English vocabulary knowledge of 1,300 kindergarten and first-grade ELs, Branum-Martin et al. (2009) revealed a number of variables that appeared to complicate the L1–L2 relationship. First, the students' performance on an expressive picture vocabulary measure (naming a picture) in the two languages was relatively unrelated, whereas their performance on an expressive narrative vocabulary measure (telling a story using a wordless picture book) was moderately positively correlated across languages. Thus, the team concluded, in keeping with their review of previous research, that the relationship between children's Spanish and English vocabulary knowledge is strongly affected by the nature and purpose of the assessment used. Second, children's vocabulary knowledge was highly influenced by the language of instruction at the classroom level, with more instructional time in a language producing higher vocabulary scores in that language. Thus, the research team concluded that a significant practical implication of the study was that "[language of] instruction matters" (p. 909), particularly with regard to children's acquisition of specific word knowledge.

This brief review of the research on young ELs' vocabulary knowledge provides a more nuanced understanding of the early English vocabulary development of young ELs and, perhaps most importantly, highlights the limited English vocabulary knowledge of many young ELs. Next, I turn to research on older ELs' vocabulary development.

The Continuing and Consequential Gap: English Learners' Vocabulary Knowledge in Upper Elementary Grades and Beyond

A number of studies indicates that many ELs in the upper elementary and middle school grades continue to lag far behind their NES peers in English vocabulary and that this lag has critical consequences for reading comprehension and other literacy tasks (Cameron, 2002; Garcia, 1991; Mancilla-Martinez & Lesaux, 2010; Geva, 2006; Proctor et al., 2005, 2006; Roessingh & Elgie, 2009; Snow & Kim, 2007). To elaborate on these general conclusions, I discuss five salient points.

The Continuing Deficit

At fourth and fifth grades, ELs, on average, score more than two grade levels behind their NES peers in English vocabulary knowledge. For instance, Proctor et al. (2005) found that a group of 132 fourth-grade Latina/Latino ELs scored at the late first-grade level in English vocabulary knowledge. Similarly, Mancilla-Martinez and Lesaux (2010) reported that 173 11-year-old, low-achieving, Spanish-speaking ELs scored at the 21st percentile in a standardized test of expressive English vocabulary, with their average raw score equivalent to that of an 8.5- to 9-year-old NES peer. Significantly, these students' percentile scores slowly increased from age 4.5 to age 8 and then decreased slightly from age 8 to age 11, suggesting that a vocabulary gap at the mid-elementary level may continue to widen as ELs progress through the grade levels.

The Effect of Language of Instruction

Children who participated in L1 instructional programs scored lower in English vocabulary than those who had received only English language instruction. Proctor et al. (2005) found that the fourth-grade students from a Spanish language program scored at a beginning first-grade level, whereas those who received English-only instruction scored at an end-of-second-grade level.

Variation in English Learners' Vocabulary Knowledge

Average group scores can mask the fact that ELs' vocabulary knowledge varies widely. For example, Proctor et al. (2005) noted that despite the low average vocabulary score of the ELs in their study, some of the students surpassed NES peer grade-level norms. In light of this finding, the authors declared, "low-socioeconomic status bilingual Latina/o students are capable of learning English to impressive levels" (p. 251). This conclusion is optimistic, suggesting that there is no inherent ceiling to ELs' English vocabulary development. However, it is also challenging, as it raises the possibility that many more ELs could acquire high levels of English vocabulary with the support of exceptional instruction.

English Learners' Vocabulary Knowledge and Reading Comprehension

English vocabulary knowledge plays a critical role in ELs' English reading comprehension (Mancilla-Martinez & Lesaux, 2010; Proctor et al., 2005). For example, the students in Mancilla-Martinez and Lesaux's (2010) study scored at the 22nd percentile in English vocabulary knowledge and at the 24th percentile on a comprehension test of English reading passages. Whereas this and other studies (Proctor et al., 2005) have focused on the relationship between the size of ELs' English vocabulary and their reading comprehension, Kieffer and Lesaux (2008) demonstrated that ELs' morphological awareness—the ability to derive a root word from a complex word in context (e.g., given the word *popularity*, students completed the sentence, "The girl wanted to be very _____") also significantly contributed to fifth-grade ELs' reading comprehension "independent of its association with breadth of vocabulary" (p. 799). This finding serves as an important reminder that in addition to breadth of vocabulary knowledge, the depth of such knowledge—in particular, an understanding of the morphological relationships among words—also appears critical for ELs' long-term academic success.

The Long-Term Vocabulary Gap

Many ELs in high school remain significantly behind their NES peers in English vocabulary knowledge. Cameron (2002) found that ELs averaging 14 years of age, despite having experienced approximately 10 years of English language schooling, continued to show gaps in knowledge of relatively frequent English words (i.e., those found within a list of the 3,000 most common words in printed English) and more significant problems in knowledge of less frequent words.

Clearly, as a group, ELs face an early deficit in English vocabulary that typically does not disappear as they progress through the grades. In fact, the research evidence suggests that at least some ELs may begin to lose ground in vocabulary knowledge vis-à-vis their NES peers after the age of 8 (Mancilla-Martinez & Lesaux, 2010) and continue to face a significant vocabulary deficit even after 10 years of English language instruction in typical schools (Cameron, 2002). Unfortunately, this deficit proves highly consequential in the critical academic skill of reading comprehension (Geva, 2006; Mancilla-Martinez & Lesaux, 2010; Proctor et al., 2005). For these reasons, the development of effective vocabulary instruction for ELs represents a pressing educational necessity. In the next section, I review research that focuses on instructional interventions aimed at enhancing the English vocabulary knowledge of ELs.

RESEARCH ON VOCABULARY INSTRUCTION FOR ENGLISH LEARNERS

The research that I discussed in the previous section maps out what Snow and Kim (2007) appropriately called the "large problem spaces" related to ELs' vocabulary knowledge. In this section, I examine the research designed to address these problem spaces through vocabulary instruction designed for and taught to ELs. In particular, I discuss recent studies that have reported on instruction at the primary grade, the upper elementary, and middle school levels.

Vocabulary Instruction in the Primary Grades

Most research on vocabulary instruction for primary grade NES peers has examined the read-aloud strategy for teaching individual words. Teacher read-alouds expose young children to sophisticated book vocabulary and provide a meaningful context for discussing unfamiliar vocabulary words. Thus, it is not surprising that recent research on vocabulary instruction with primary grade ELs has often focused on teaching words as a part of the read-aloud process. The results of this instruction have been positive: Introducing young ELs to new words through read-alouds and then providing further instruction on those words has consistently enabled ELs to acquire new word meanings (Beimiller & Boote, 2006; Silverman, 2007; Silverman & Hines, 2009). I now discuss four points that extend this general finding.

The Word Learning of English Learners and Native English Speakers

It appears that ELs can learn target words in the same settings and at the same rate as NES peers. Silverman (2007) investigated the word learning of children in five kindergarten classes composed of a mixture of ELs and NES peers. Instruction involved the introduction of words during read-alouds, explanation of target word meanings and questioning and prompting to help children process these meanings, provision of examples of the words in other contexts, children's acting out of word meanings, use of visual aids, calling attention to word pronunciations and spellings, comparison and contrast of word meanings, and review of the word meanings. Over the 14 weeks of the intervention, ELs learned the meanings of the target words at the same rate as their NES peers and showed a faster rate of general vocabulary growth than their NES peers.

Intensity and Quantity in Teaching Word Meanings

It appears that both the intensity of instruction and the number of words taught influence children's word learning. In a study of vocabulary instruction in kindergarten and first- and second-grade classes with approximately 50% ELs, Beimiller and Boote (2006) examined the impact of various instructional approaches and of the number of words taught. They found that children learned 12% of the target word meanings from repeated readings without further instruction, 22% of the word meanings when word explanations were added, and 41% of the word meanings when several review sessions of the word meanings were added and the number of words taught daily was increased from between four and six to between seven and nine words. Significantly, children who scored lower on a pretest of the target word meanings, learned as many or more words as children with higher pretest scores. Beimiller and Boote concluded that teaching a high number words and providing a basic review of word meanings that had been introduced and explained in the context of reading aloud constitutes an effective way of increasing the vocabulary knowledge of ELs and primary grade NES peers.

Multimedia-Enhanced Instruction

Multimedia-enhanced instruction appears to benefit young ELs' word learning. Silverman and Hines (2009) reported on the effects of an intervention in which teachers from prekindergarten through second grade taught word meanings to mixed NES–EL classes in the context of reading aloud thematically related science books. One hundred words were taught during a 12-week intervention, and in some classrooms approximately 5-minute video clips were shown and discussed for three days at the end of six book-reading days. The teachers in these classrooms reviewed the target words that would be illustrated in the videos, the students viewed the video clips without interruption, and then the teachers replayed the videos, stopping at key points to emphasize the target words. Results showed that although the video-enhanced instruction had no effect on NES word learning, ELs in the video condition demonstrated significant gains over ELs who reviewed the words in another manner and without the video-enhanced instruction. Further, Silverman and Hines reported that for the ELs who received the video-enhanced instruction, "the gap between non-ELL and ELL children in knowledge of words targeted during the intervention was closed and the gap in general vocabulary knowledge was narrowed" (p. 311). This conclusion highlights the potential of multimedia-enhanced vocabulary instruction for young ELs.

Long-Term Instruction

Intensive multiyear vocabulary instruction produces significant benefits for young L2 learners. Appel and Vermeer (1998) reported on the teaching of Dutch vocabulary to limited Dutch-speaking immigrants in The Netherlands. Although Dutch was the target language in this study, the context is highly comparable to that of ELs in English-speaking settings. The study involved an intensive 4-year vocabulary instruction intervention in six schools that aimed at closing the large vocabulary gap between Dutch L2 learners and native Dutch speakers during the early years of formal schooling. Specifically, the intervention taught 1,000 words a year, half from the regular Dutch learner curriculum and half from read-alouds, in each of the first 4 years of primary schooling. The researchers found that the schools implemented the program to about 80% of its full extent and that the children in the experimental classrooms learned significantly more target words than the control group, scored higher on general receptive and productive tests of Dutch vocabulary and a general Dutch reading test, and, as evidenced by results of a general vocabulary test given in seventh grade, continued to learn Dutch vocabulary at a higher rate than the control students during the 3 years after the intervention. Appel and Vermeer concluded:

> By the end of 4th grade [the students in the experimental condition] were one or two years ahead of their comparison group age peers in Dutch vocabulary, and were able to maintain their position three years after the experiment. They also performed better than the comparison children in the same experimental school. . . . However, they did not attain the level of their Dutch classmates, and were in fact still lagging one year behind. (p. 171)

This study is valuable because of the long-term nature of the vocabulary intervention. Although the intervention fell short of completely eliminating the vocabulary gap between Dutch learners and native Dutch students, it did have a large positive long-term effect on immigrant students' growth in Dutch vocabulary and reading. Further, as the researchers speculated, a complete implementation of this kind of vocabulary instruction program across 4 years or the extension of such a program for more years may actually enable language minority children to attain a similar vocabulary level as their native-speaking peers.

Taken together, these studies of vocabulary instruction for young ELs highlight the powerful potential of intensive, well-designed instruction that aims to teach a large number of word meanings. The long-term study of Appel and Vermeer (1998) calls attention to the benefits that such instruction may produce for ELs when extended across the primary grades. Now I examine vocabulary interventions targeting ELs in upper elementary and middle school grades.

Vocabulary Instruction in Upper Elementary and Middle School Grades

Recent research has documented a number of vocabulary interventions with ELs at the upper elementary and middle school grades (August, Branum-Martin, Cardenas-Hagan, & Francis, 2009; Carlo et al., 2004; Lesaux, Kieffer, Faller, & Kelley, 2010; Townsend, 2009; Townsend & Collins, 2009; Vaughn et al., 2009). These interventions have proven successful in teaching word meanings and other aspects of vocabulary knowledge. Here I discuss five important points that elaborate on the nature of these interventions and effective vocabulary instruction for older ELs.

Vocabulary Instruction in Mixed Classrooms

Vocabulary instruction provided in mixed NES–EL classrooms benefited both NES and ELs. Several vocabulary interventions for older students targeted classes with both ELs and NES (August et al., 2009; Carlo et al., 2004; Lesaux et al., 2010; Vaughn et al., 2009). August et al. (2009) underscore a critical issue regarding such instruction, stating that "the development of instructional methods to specifically benefit the ELL students in mixed classrooms cannot disadvantage those students in the same classrooms who are not identified as ELL students" (371). Thus, it is noteworthy that both at the upper elementary (Carlo et al., 2004) and middle school levels (August et al., 2009; Lesaux et al., 2010; Vaughn et al., 2009), vocabulary instruction designed for ELs resulted in comparable growth for NES and ELs in word meanings, aspects related to depth of word knowledge, and academic content knowledge.

Multifaceted Vocabulary Instruction

Vocabulary instruction for upper elementary and middle school ELs is often multifaceted, targeting both breadth and depth of word knowledge, as well as strategies for independently unlocking the meanings of unfamiliar words. For example, Carlo et al. (2004) examined the effects of teaching 254 fifth-grade NESs and ELs academic vocabulary and strategies for inferring word meanings. The instruction was organized around a social studies theme, lasted from 30 to 45 minutes a day, focused on 10–12 target words weekly, and involved repeated exposure to the words and consistent practice with word-learning strategies. The researchers believed that the development of the students' strategic knowledge was equally important as teaching individual words and thus provided "explicit instruction in using context to infer word meanings . . . , in depth of word meaning, in the possibility of polysemy [multiple meanings], in performing morphological analysis, in glossary use, and in cognate use" (p. 193). Results revealed that the intervention classes demonstrated greater growth compared to control classes in knowledge of the target words, in other aspects of word knowledge addressed by the instruction, and, to a small extent, in reading comprehension. Similarly, reflecting on their study of vocabulary instruction for 476 sixth-grade students, Lesaux et al. (2010) concluded: "Lessons that move beyond simple definitions to focus on building depth of word knowledge (multiple meanings, morphological analysis) over time show promise in bolstering vocabulary and comprehension skills of the middle schooler" (p. 220). Thus, although vocabulary instruction for ELs in the primary grades has focused on teaching individual word meanings, evidence suggests that by the upper elementary grades, such instruction should expand to include word meanings, deeper word knowledge about words, and word-learning strategies.

Diverse Pedagogical Strategies

The interventions not only targeted multiple goals, they also utilized a diverse set of pedagogical strategies to meet those goals. The vocabulary and content instruction in the interventions typically represented thought-ful packages of instructional strategies aimed at enhancing the comprehen-sibility of the vocabulary and content for ELs, developing deep vocabulary knowledge, and increasing student engagement and active participation (August et al., 2009; Lesaux et al., 2010; Townsend & Collins, 2009; Vaughn et al., 2009). For instance, Vaughn et al. (2009) developed an approach to vocabulary instruction within the discipline of social stud-ies that involved five key elements: (1) a daily overview of the big idea of the unit and an explicit introduction of four new vocabulary words; (2) the strategic use of brief video clips to build background knowledge and facilitate discussion; (3) teacher-led or paired student reading of the social studies text; (4) daily writing with graphic organizers to summarize lesson content; and (5) structured student-paired work for reading, writing, and discussion of vocabulary. These instructional strategies were aimed at scaf-folding ELs' background knowledge, providing multiple contexts for new vocabulary, and creating engaging social contexts for learning.

In a second example, Townsend and Collins (2009) developed Lan-guage Workshop, an instructional approach aimed at teaching academic vocabulary to middle school ELs in a voluntary after-school setting. Given the voluntary nature of the intervention, the authors focused on the need for fast-paced, engaging, and fun activities. Townsend (2009) described a num-ber of activities featured in Language Workshop as game-like, including the discussion of how puzzling pictures and popular music illustrated tar-get vocabulary and the adaption of vocabulary-oriented commercial games such as Taboo and Pictionary. Townsend found that students learned more word meanings during Language Workshop than they did when involved in other after-school activities for the same period of time and that they learned more target word meanings than comparable untaught word mean-ings.

Text-Based Content-Area Instruction

In general, vocabulary instruction in the upper-grade interventions involved reading short, engaging nonfiction texts or portions of content-area textbooks. The texts provided a context for the target vocabulary and facilitated discussion of the words and the academic content to which the words related. The interventions revolved around informational texts in social studies (Carlo et al., 2004; Vaughn et al., 2009), science (August et al., 2009; Townsend & Collins, 2009), or a variety of high-interest topics (Lesaux et al., 2010). Importantly, studies that measured students' growth in content knowledge in addition to vocabulary reported that ELs showed significant gains vis-à-vis control group students. With regard to the words taught, the majority of the interventions targeted high-utility academic words. In particular, word selection in several interventions was guided partially or fully by Coxhead's (2000) Academic Word List, a list of 570 of the most frequent general academic words found in texts across multiple disciplines (August et al., 2009; Lesaux et al., 2010; Townsend & Collins, 2009). Thus, it appears that effective interventions were text-based, often integrated with content-area instruction, and focused on carefully selected academic vocabulary.

Supporting High-Quality Instruction

It appears that the development of detailed instructional guides and materials and the provision of professional development facilitated implementation of the interventions, but teachers still faced challenges in providing instruction. Lesaux et al. (2010) researched teachers' perceptions of the ease of implementation of the intervention. Through interviews and surveys, they found that teachers grew to appreciate the high expectations the intervention set for the students, praised the use of high-interest texts to provide meaningful contexts for vocabulary words and rich discussion, and strongly endorsed the curricular materials, particularly the optional sample lessons (with scripted language for the teachers). Although Carlo et al. (2004) similarly reported a high level of teacher satisfaction with the provided materials and the general approach of their fifth-grade Vocabulary Improvement Program, they offered another revealing detail: The intervention had little impact on instruction outside of the specific lesson time, and importantly, teachers did not continue with it beyond the length of the formal study.

Like the research on vocabulary interventions targeting primary grade ELs, recent research on interventions for upper elementary and middle school ELs offers reason for optimism. The studies that I have discussed reveal that sophisticated, multifaceted instruction can produce significant benefits for ELs and their NES peers in breadth and depth of vocabulary knowledge, content-area knowledge, and reading comprehension. However, planning such instruction and preparing teachers to implement it clearly constitute major undertakings.

RESEARCH INTO PRACTICE: GUIDELINES FOR
POWERFUL VOCABULARY INSTRUCTION FOR ENGLISH LEARNERS

To conclude this chapter, I reflect on the research that I have reviewed with an eye toward classroom practice, articulating six key practical guidelines for planning and implementing instruction that I believe will have a powerfully positive effect on ELs' vocabulary development and long-term academic achievement.

1. Given the English vocabulary deficit with which many ELs begin school (Manis et al., 2004; Páez et al., 2007) and the sizeable vocabulary gap that older ELs continue to face (Cameron, 2002; Mancilla-Martinez & Lesaux, 2010; Proctor et al., 2005), schools that serve ELs, either through English immersion or bilingual instruction, must implement intensive vocabulary instruction across the grades. Such instruction should begin in kindergarten or, when possible, prekindergarten and continue through the secondary grades. In guidelines 2–5, I describe essential features of intensive vocabulary instruction for primary, upper elementary, and middle school grades. However, it is important to note that such instruction, although critical, will likely not eliminate, in and of itself, the vocabulary gap experienced by L2 learners (Appel & Vermeer, 1998). In light of this fact, schools should also make wide reading at all grade levels a priority. While I have focused on explicit vocabulary instruction for ELs in this chapter, it is clear that all students learn many word meanings incidentally through reading (Nagy, Anderson, & Herman, 1987; Swanborn & de Glopper, 1999). Although students successfully learn the meanings of only a small percentage of the unfamiliar words that they encounter while reading (Nagy et al., 1987), those who read a great deal over a number of years will acquire many more word meanings than students who read little. Therefore, I believe that a two-pronged approach involving intensive vocabulary instruction and the promotion of wide reading for ELs at all grade levels represents the optimal way that schools can facilitate ELs' English vocabulary development.

2. Implementing intensive vocabulary instruction while simultaneously meeting many other instructional goals requires efficient routines and integrated instruction. Together with James Baumann and Camille Blachowicz, I am currently involved in a research project focused on developing and examining the feasibility of a multifaceted, comprehensive vocabulary instruction program (MCVIP) for fourth- and fifth-grade NESs and ELs. In the early stages of the project, we recognized that MCVIP could take up a disproportionate amount of the school day. Consequently, we have worked with teachers to establish a viable balance between efficient instruction and richer activities that allow for deeper processing of target words and word-

learning strategies (Manyak, 2010). For example, the teaching of less familiar high-frequency words is a core activity in MCVIP classrooms. When
introducing and reinforcing the meanings of the target words, the teachers
utilize a 3-day instructional plan involving a variety of fast-paced activities.
While this plan, outlined in Table 14.1, provides students with a variety of
encounters with the target words, the teachers move quickly through the
lesson components and avoid lengthy discussions. However, several times
a week the teachers review previously taught words, often using strategies
that enable students to process the words deeply. For instance, I documented
one review session in which a fifth-grade teacher asked groups of students
to write and share sentences using two words from the word wall. As the
students shared, their peers evaluated the sentences, identifying when the
target words were used inappropriately and suggesting revisions for more
appropriate usage. This example illustrates the type of balance that the
MCVIP team has found necessary to make intensive vocabulary instruction both feasible and robust.

TABLE 14.1. Instructional Plan for High-Frequency Words

Day	Goal	Lesson components
1	Introduction of target words	1. Chorally reading phrases that contain the words. 2. Providing kid-friendly definitions ("*Aware* means noticing things going on around you."). 3. Providing examples of use ("We were aware that it was starting to rain. I was not aware that my shoe was untied until I tripped."). 4. Prompting students to create examples using the word or to evaluate whether sentences relate to the target word ("Say *aware* if this sentence is an example of someone being aware: 'The girl knew that her little brother was crying.' ").
2	Repeated reading and discussion of words in context	1. Repeated partner readings of a short passage that includes the target words. 2. Class discussion of questions about the passage that focus on the meanings or include usage of the target words ("What could have happened if the kids in the story did not become *aware* of the thunderstorm right away?").
3	Repeated reading and quiz to review and assess knowledge of word meanings	1. Repeated partner readings of a short passage that includes the target words. 2. Students take and then briefly discuss an 8- to 10-sentence quiz intended both as a review of the target words and as a formative assessment of their knowledge of the words ("I was _____ that it was much colder when I walked outside.").

Integration represents a second critical way to enhance the feasibility of intensive vocabulary instruction. The interventions described by August et al. (2009) and Vaughn et al. (2009) constitute exceptional models in which teachers covered required middle school content in effective ways while simultaneously providing explicit vocabulary instruction. However, teachers in these interventions utilized carefully developed instructional materials and received quality professional developmental. Realistically, we must be cautious about the ability of many teachers to develop and implement this kind of sophisticated instruction without such support. Nevertheless, all teachers can and should work toward the goal of integrating more effective vocabulary instruction into content area teaching.

3. Vocabulary instruction for ELs should target a number of word types. First, given the low average level of ELs' vocabulary knowledge throughout the elementary grades and the fact that 14-year-old ELs demonstrated a significant gap in knowledge of the 3,000 most frequent words in English (Cameron, 2002), I believe that ELs would benefit greatly from systematic instruction in relatively basic English vocabulary. In the MCVIP project, we have utilized materials based on Fry's (1999) list of the 3,000 most frequent words in English texts to address this level of vocabulary. Specifically, we designed instruction around the *Increasing Frequency with High Frequency Word Phrases* materials (e.g., see, Knoblach, 2007). These books include weekly lessons that present high-frequency words in phrases and short reading passages designed to improve reading fluency. To enhance students' knowledge of the meanings of these words, we selected four to six semantically rich, less familiar words for the type of lesson outlined in Table 14.1. Consequently, each week MCVIP students are exposed to approximately 20 relatively high-frequency English words through repeated readings of the passage and receive explicit instruction on the four to six least familiar words. I describe our use of the *Increasing Frequency with High Frequency Word Phrases* materials merely as example of what systematic instruction in this category of words might look like; I do not intend to recommend this specific set of materials and instructional activities to everyone. However, I strongly encourage schools that serve ELs to develop a similarly systematic way of providing explicit instruction in semantically rich, less familiar high-frequency English words.

In addition to more basic words, vocabulary instruction for ELs should also target a balance of high-frequency general academic words, academic vocabulary related to specific content areas, and useful lower-frequency words. Several interventions for older ELs utilized Coxhead's Academic Word List (2000) as a source of general academic vocabulary. Although this list was created using university-level texts and thus is better suited to the secondary grades, it does call attention to the category of general academic words (e.g., *analyze*). Furthermore, Coxhead's list is divided into 10 categories of approximately 60 words, with the first category representing the most frequent words. I suggest that upper elementary teachers of ELs become familiar with this category of the Academic Word List and use it to identify a smaller subset of words that would be appropriate for instruction. Finally, there is evidence that discipline-specific academic vocabulary and useful lower-frequency words also represent good targets for instruction (Carlo et al., 2004; Silverman, 2007; Silverman & Hines, 2009). Therefore, I recommend a balanced approach to selecting words for instruction that follows the general grade-level guidelines presented in Table 14.2.

4. At the primary grades, English vocabulary instruction for ELs should focus on teaching specific words in the read-aloud or text reading settings (Appel & Vermeer, 1998; Biemiller & Boote, 2006). This instruction should involve teaching a high number of words and include ongoing review (Biemiller & Boote, 2006). Specifically, Biemiller and Boote (2006) provided evidence that young ELs could learn 400 words a year if 1,000 words were taught and reviewed. This amounts to targeting approximately five or six words a day throughout the academic year. Boote and Biemiller confessed that teaching new words at this pace involves sacrificing extensive discussion of the words. In contrast, Silverman and Hines (2009) demonstrated the potential of multimedia-enhanced vocabulary instruction—specifically, the use of short video clips that illustrated the meanings of target words introduced during read-alouds—for young ELs.

TABLE 14.2. General Grade-Level Guidelines for Target Word Selection

	Primary	Upper elementary	Middle school
Less familiar words from the 3,000 highest-frequency words (e.g., *aware*)	30–50% of target words	20–35% of target words	
Discipline-specific academic words (e.g., *musket*)	25–30% of target words	20–35% of target words	30–40% of target words
General academic words (such as those in the first category of the Academic Word List) (e.g., *evidence*)		10% of target words	20–30% of target words
Useful lower-frequency words (e.g., *mesmerize*)	25–30% of target words	25–35% of target words	30–40% of target words

Thus, although I find the evidence for teaching a high number of new words to young ELs compelling, I suggest that teachers enhance such instruction and review with efficient use of visual aids, drama, and brief video clips whenever possible.

5. Beginning at third grade and increasingly through the middle school grades, vocabulary instruction should become multifaceted in nature, targeting a smaller number of specific words in order to invest some instructional time in other aspects of vocabulary knowledge, such as depth of word meaning, multiple meanings, morphological elements (prefixes, suffixes, and common word roots), use of context to infer word meanings, and cognate knowledge (Carlo et al., 2004; Lesaux et al., 2010). In addition, vocabulary instruction should be connected to the reading of anchor texts. Such texts provide a meaningful context for introducing new words and applying word-learning strategies; a focus for rich vocabulary-oriented and content-oriented discussion, and the opportunity to integrate vocabulary, reading comprehension, and content-knowledge instruction. Finally, effective upper-grade vocabulary should incorporate a variety of pedagogical strategies, including visual images and video clips to illustrate word meanings and build background knowledge, peer collaboration, graphic organizers, writing, and engaging game-oriented activities.

In MCVIP, we refer to many of these strategies as "minor modifications" that increase the comprehensibility of instruction and the active participation of ELs. For instance, MCVIP research teachers have taken the lead in providing visual images to illustrate word meanings and prompt discussion of them. Figure 14.1 presents a representative slide from one fourth-grade teacher's weekly introduction of target words. In addition, the MCVIP teachers have demonstrated the ability to scaffold attempts by students with more limited English proficiency to contribute to vocabulary-oriented discussion; this scaffolding often involves providing sentence frames

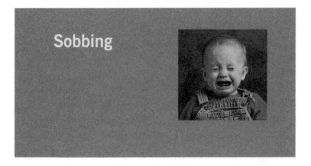

FIGURE 14.1. Visual images from a PowerPoint slide introducing new words to MCVIP fourth graders.

(e.g., "Try saying, 'I would like to go on an expedition to _____.'") or revising incomplete or awkward utterances into a model for the student to repeat. Such scaffolding, combined with deliberate strategies to ensure wide student participation, has led to highly inclusive discussions and a strong expectation that even ELs with limited vocabulary are responsible for learning and using the target words.

6. In order for schools to plan, and for teachers to implement, the kind of sophisticated instruction described in the previous guidelines, continuing professional development in vocabulary instruction for ELs must be a priority. Given the recent nature of the majority of the studies that I have discussed, it is not surprising that a large gap between research and practice appears to exist in the area of vocabulary instruction for ELs. I believe that it is critical that researchers, districts, and schools collaborate to close this gap by providing teachers with professional development experiences that will deepen their understanding of the vocabulary needs of ELs and equip them to provide effective vocabulary instruction to this student population.

Clearly, these guidelines do not constitute a simple, easy-to-follow recipe for powerful vocabulary instruction for ELs. Rather, they provide a mixture of general guidance and more specific suggestions for educators attempting to meet one of the most critical and difficult instructional challenges of our times: Closing the highly consequential English vocabulary gap that most ELs face.

Reading over the guidelines again, I am struck by the inspiring research evidence supporting them, the difficult challenge that they represent for schools and teachers that seek to translate them into exemplary everyday instruction, and the promise that they hold for lifting the long-term academic achievement of a large and long underserved population group. In the end, I hope that this chapter is not only informative but also energizing, that educators will be able to return to it to find not only practical guidance but also a dose of inspiration to bring about the kind of intensive, articulated, sophisticated vocabulary instruction that is critical to the academic success of ELs.

ACKNOWLEDGMENTS

The preparation of this chapter was supported in part by the Institute of Education Sciences, U.S. Department of Education, through Grant No. R305A090163 to the University of Missouri, the University of Wyoming, and National Louis University. The opinions expressed are those of the authors and do not represent views of the Institute or the U.S. Department of Education.

REFERENCES

Appel, R., & Vermeer, A. (1998). Speeding up second language vocabulary acquisition of minority children. *Language and Education, 12*, 159–173.

August, D., Branum-Martin, L., Cardenas-Hagan, E., & Francis, D. (2009). The impact of an instructional intervention on the science and language learning of middle grade English language learners. *Journal of Research on Educational Effectiveness, 2*, 345–376.

August, D., Carlo, M., Dressler, C., & Snow, C. (2005). The critical role of vocabulary development for English language learners. *Learning Disabilities: Research and Practice, 20*, 50–57.

August, D., & Shanahan, T. (2006). *Developing literacy in second-language learners: Report of the National Literacy Panel on language-minority children and youth.* Mahwah, NJ: Erlbaum.

Biemiller, A., & Boote, C. (2006). An effective method for building vocabulary in primary grades. *Journal of Educational Psychology, 98*, 44–62.

Branum-Martin, L., Mehta, P., Francis, D., Foorman, B., Cirino, P., Miller, J., et al. (2009). Pictures and words: Spanish and English vocabulary in classrooms. *Journal of Educational Psychology, 101*, 897–911.

Cameron, L. (2002). Measuring vocabulary size in English as an additional language. *Language Teaching Research, 6*, 145–173.

Carlo, M., August, D., McLaughlin, B., Snow, C., Dressler, C., Lippman, D., et al. (2004). Closing the gap: Addressing the vocabulary needs of English-language learners in bilingual and mainstream classrooms. *Reading Research Quarterly, 38*, 188–215.

Coxhead, A. (2000). A new academic word list. *TESOL Quarterly, 34*, 213–238.

Dressler, C., & Kamil, M. (2006). First- and second-language literacy. In D. August & T. Shanahan (Eds.), *Developing literacy in second-language learners: Report of the National Literacy Panel on language-minority children and youth* (pp. 197–238). Mahwah, NJ: Erlbaum.

Fry, E. (1999). *1,000 instant words by Dr. Fry.* Westminster, CA: Teacher Created Resources.

Garcia, G. (1991). Factors influencing the English reading test performance of Spanish-speaking Hispanic children. *Reading Research Quarterly, 26*, 371–392.

Geva, E. (2006). Second-language oral proficiency and second-language literacy. In D. August & T. Shanahan (Eds.), *Developing literacy in second-language learners: Report of the National Literacy Panel on language-minority children and youth* (pp. 123–139). Mahwah, NJ: Erlbaum.

Kieffer, M., & Lesaux, N. (2008). The role of derivational morphology in the reading comprehension of Spanish-speaking English language learners. *Reading and Writing, 22*, 993–1019.

Knoblach, K. (2007). *Increasing fluency with high frequency word phrases, grade 3.* Huntington Beach, CA: Shell Education.

Lesaux, N., Kieffer, M., Faller, S. E., & Kelley, J. (2010). The effectiveness and ease of implementation of an academic vocabulary intervention for linguistically diverse students in urban middle schools. *Reading Research Quarterly, 45,* 196–228.

Mancilla-Martinez, J., & Lesaux, N. (2010). Predictors of reading comprehension for struggling readers: The case of Spanish-speaking language minority learners. *Journal of Educational Psychology, 102,* 701–711.

Manis, F., Lindsey, K., & Bailey, C. (2004). Development of reading in grades K–2 in Spanish-speaking English-language learners. *Learning Disabilities Research and Practice, 19,* 214–224.

Manyak, P. C. (2010). Vocabulary instruction for English learners: Lessons from MCVIP. *The Reading Teacher, 64,* 142–146.

Nagy, W., Anderson, R., & Herman, P. (1987). Learning word meaning from content during normal reading. *American Educational Research Journal, 24,* 237–270.

Nagy, W., Garcia, G., Durgunoglu, A., & Hancin-Bhatt, B. (1993). Spanish–English bilingual students' use of cognates in English reading. *Journal of Reading Behavior, 25,* 241–259.

National Center for Education Statistics. (2004). *Language minorities and their educational and labor market indicators—recent trends.* Retrieved October 20, 2010, from *nces.ed.gov/pubs2004/2004009.pdf*

Páez, M., Tabors, P., & López, L. (2007). Dual language and literacy development of Spanish-speaking preschool children. *Journal of Applied Developmental Psychology, 28,* 85–102.

Proctor, C. P., August, D., Carlo, M., & Snow, C. (2006). The intriguing role of Spanish language vocabulary knowledge in predicting English reading comprehension, *Journal of Educational Psychology, 98*(1), 159–169.

Proctor, C. P., Carlo, M. August, D., & Snow, C. (2005). Native Spanish-speaking children reading in English: Toward a model of comprehension. *Journal of Educational Psychology, 97*(2), 246–256.

Roessingh, H., & Elgie, S. (2009). Early language and literacy development among young English language learners: Preliminary insights from a longitudinal study. *TESOL Canada Journal, 26,* 24–45.

Saville-Troike, M. (1984). What really matters in second language learning for academic achievement? *TESOL Quarterly, 18*(2), 199–219.

Silverman, R. (2007). Vocabulary development of English-language and English-only learners in kindergarten. *Elementary School Journal, 107*(4), 365–383.

Silverman, R., & Hines, S. (2009). The effects of multimedia-enhanced instruction on the vocabulary of English-language learners and non-English-language learners in pre-kindergarten through second grade. *Journal of Educational Psychology, 101,* 305–314.

Snow, C., & Kim, Y. (2007). Large problem spaces: The challenge of vocabulary for English language learners. In R. Wagner, A. Muse, & K. Tannenbaum (Eds.), *Vocabulary acquisition: Implications for reading comprehension* (pp. 123–136). New York: Guilford Press.

Swanborn, M., & de Glopper, K. (1999). Incidental word learning while reading: A meta-analysis. *Review of Educational Research, 69,* 261–285.

Townsend, D. (2009). Building academic vocabulary in after-school settings:

Games for growth with middle school English-language learners. *Journal of Adolescent and Adult Literacy, 53,* 242–251.

Townsend, D., & Collins, P. (2009). Academic vocabulary and middle school English learners: An intervention study. *Reading and Writing, 22,* 993–1019.

Umbel, V., Pearson, B., Fernández, M., & Oller, D. (1992). Measuring bilingual children's receptive vocabularies. *Child Development, 63,* 1012–1020.

Vaughn, S., Martinez, L., Linan-Thompson, S., Reutebuch, C., Carlson, C., & Francis, D. (2009). Enhancing social studies vocabulary and comprehension for seventh-grade English language learners: Findings from two experimental studies. *Journal of Research on Educational Effectiveness, 2,* 297–324.

Verhoeven, L. (2000). Components in early second language reading and spelling. *Scientific Studies of Reading, 4,* 313–330.

Chapter 15

Using Multimedia to Support Generative Vocabulary Learning

Jill Castek
Bridget Dalton
Dana L. Grisham

Digital media and Web 2.0 tools offer unique opportunities for students to explore vocabulary, create multimodal products, and collaborate in online communities. This chapter makes a case for the value of integrating multimodal expression into vocabulary instruction and offers several strategies and digital tools to promote students' active word learning. To illustrate this type of vocabulary learning in a classroom, consider the following vignette:

> "Greg, the Wimpy Kid" is a fourth grader who has learning difficulties. Although Greg usually receives instructional support in a Special Day class, he actively and enthusiastically participates in regular education when it comes time to create a digital response to literature.
>
> Today, Greg is recording on the computer, playing the part of Perez, the little brown mouse, a suitor of "Martina the Beautiful Cockroach" (Deedy, 2007). He speaks softly, but it is obvious he has given this task a great deal of thought. He begins enthusiastically, "Suddenly, quick as a mouse, he pours the coffee on her shoes and says he has a Cuban *abuela* also. So that means they will get married!"
>
> In listening to his recording, Greg's teacher is struck by his use of vocabulary from the story. Just yesterday, he was in the principal's office for a long list of poor behaviors, but today Greg

has created three images to go with his digital recording, scanned them, and saved them in PowerPoint.

Greg's multimodal response was combined with other students' recordings and drawings, which together formed a generative product. The PowerPoint "digital book" was featured on his classroom website and shared with parents, the principal of the school, and other students in classrooms around the country.

This scenario reminds us of the importance of motivation and authenticity in our students' education. Not only were Greg and his classmates engaged as they recorded digital responses to literature, they were also gaining experience with the technologies needed to read, write, and communicate in the 21st century. In the process, they were extending their vocabulary knowledge in powerful ways as they engaged in digital literacy events.

In this chapter, we suggest that that the use of digital media in vocabulary learning should not only be receptive (e.g., viewing vocabulary graphics), but also generative. We use the term *generative* to refer to instruction that actively engages students in using language and media to express themselves and to create products that represent their new knowledge. We argue that this type of vocabulary learning empowers students as agents of their own learning. The act of creation supports ownership, introduces authentic reasons for learning, and tangibly links reading, writing, and communication in ways that mirror learning outside of school. In the sections that follow, we consider learning in a digital world, provide a theoretical and research foundation for generative word learning, and offer examples of engaging interactive vocabulary learning experiences.

LEARNING IN A DIGITAL WORLD

The Internet has become the defining technology for literacy and learning in the 21st century (Coiro, Knobel, Lanshear, & Leu, 2008). In today's world, we participate in online communities where words are key; graphics and video are emerging as a dominant mode for communication and expression, especially among adolescents (Lenhart, Smith, Macgill, & Arafeh, 2008). Facebook, blogs, wikis, and texting (or instant messaging) are all examples of multimodal communities where words predominantly shoulder the communication burden. When students research topics of interest to them, they tend to search on the Web (Selwyn, 2006). Through the use of digital media, important connections can be forged between academic language, learning, and popular culture.

WHAT DO WE KNOW ABOUT WORD LEARNING?

Words represent concepts—the wider the conceptual knowledge, the deeper the new learning will be (Bravo & Cervetti, 2008; Marzano, 2004; Willingham, 2009). As new vocabulary is acquired, there is essentially no limit to the conceptual knowledge that individuals may develop—this is an unbounded variable (Paris, 2005).

The National Reading Panel (National Institute of Child Health and Human Development, 2000) identified guidelines for effective vocabulary learning that include (1) teaching vocabulary both directly and indirectly; (2) providing multiple exposures to new vocabulary; (3) situating vocabulary learning in rich contexts; (4) restructuring vocabulary tasks when needed to promote deeper learning; (5) designing learning tasks that maximize engagement; (6) using technology to help teach vocabulary; (7) extending incidental learning opportunities; (8) using assessment to guide vocabulary instruction; and (9) using multiple instructional methods to increase vocabulary learning. In addition, we know that vocabulary knowledge is a function of experience—whether real or virtual (e.g., as in reading). New words are learned incidentally through wide reading (Cunningham & Stanovich, 1998), and they are learned incrementally through repeated exposures (Beck, McKeown, & Kucan, 2002; Biemiller & Boote, 2006). Moreover, we recognize that students learn new vocabulary through interactions with others (Marzano, 2004), as part of home and outside cultures (Hart & Risley, 1995; Moll, Amanti, Neff, & Gonzalez, 1992), and as a result of socialization into various communities of practice (Scott, Nagy, & Flinspatch, 2008; Wenger, McDermott & Snyder, 2002). And finally, we know that an important distinction between spoken vocabulary and academic language should be made. Learning to use academic language is one of the greatest challenges of schooling because this register tends to be abstract and distant from spoken vocabulary (Kelley, LeSaux, Kieffer, & Faller, 2010; Zwiers, 2008). Learning to read, write, and communicate ideas in different academic registers is a highly valued skill, because it allows for a compact and precise expression of complex ideas (Scott et al., 2008). However, engaging in academic discourse requires extensive practice and multiple opportunities to interact with words in meaningful ways.

MULTIMODAL LEARNING AND VOCABULARY

The fact that we learn through multiple modes is evident on a personal level. Recall the last time you learned a new skill. Did it involve a combination of observation, action, listening, and reading? Clark and Paivio's (1991) dual coding theory and Mayer and colleagues' multimedia learning theory (Mayer, 2005) provide a basis for much of the research in this area. Dual coding research (Clark & Paivio, 1991) suggests that information held in both verbal and visual memory is retained more easily than information held in only one memory system. Additional research has shown that there is a threshold that limits the amount of information that an individual can absorb in a given time and context (Mayer & Moreno, 2003; Willingham, 2009). Because multimodal word learning provides complementary inputs that do not overload a child's working memory, vocabulary instruction that integrates multiple means of access, and also provides opportunity for expression, has the potential to spark powerful word learning.

In a recent review of the research, Fadel and Lemke (2009) found a positive effect of multimodal learning, with one of the strongest effects resulting from the combination of words and pictures. There is also support for direct manipulation of the learning materials, especially when the learning is complex. They caution, however, that the generally beneficial effect of multimodal learning is likely to be moderated by learners' motivation and efficacy, as well as the level of instructional scaffolding.

Focusing specifically on the role of technology and media in language and vocabulary acquisition, Zhao and Lai's (2008) review concluded that technology can be used to facilitate vocabulary acquisition by enhancing access efficiency through digital multimedia, enhancing authenticity using video and the Internet, enhancing comprehensibility through learner control and multimedia annotations, and providing meaningful and authentic communication opportunities.

Research on vocabulary learning suggests that students' active word learning should include opportunities to use the new words in their own oral and written communication (Lovelace & Stewart, 2009; Lubliner with Smetana, 2005; Lubliner & Scott, 2008; Silverman & Crandell, 2010). Several studies have explored students' multimodal vocabulary expression. Dalton and colleagues found that fifth-grade English-only and bilingual students developed vocabulary as they read scaffolded digital texts with multimedia vocabulary supports (Dalton, Proctor, Uccelli, Mo, & Snow, 2011; Proctor, Uccelli, Dalton, & Snow, 2009; Proctor et al., 2011). They developed knowledge of targeted vocabulary as they typed and audio-recorded personal connections, created captions for graphics illustrating the word, and completed interactive word maps. In a follow-up study, Proctor et al. (2011) found that students also significantly improved their vocabulary scores on a standardized achievement test.

It is clear that students are often motivated by creative and thoughtful integration of technology and media (in fact, this is usually the first outcome that teachers notice). Students often invest substantial effort in projects that make strategic use of digital media, producing work they publish to online audiences and view with pride. The Internet provides new social contexts within which to develop vocabulary knowledge and forges a tangible connection to students' out-of-school lives (Castek et al., 2008). By drawing in and making use of the technology experiences students bring to the classroom, we acknowledge students as valuable contributors to learning. This recognition has the potential to transform the learning environment in classrooms by encouraging students to collaborate, guide one another, and engage fully in vocabulary activities. As teachers, it is our charge to provide them with the means for such strategic engagement.

In summary, there is both indirect and direct research evidence for multimodal word learning. It makes sense to take what we know about vocabulary learning and instruction and extend it to digital environments, innovating and taking advantage of the affordances media offers. For example, digital media and the Internet offer multiple means of access to new words and concepts, including auditory, visual, and animated supports. Dalton and Grisham (2011) offer teachers 10 vocabulary-learning strategies for representing vocabulary in multiple modes—writing, audio, graphic, video, and animation—as well as engaging students in creating multimodal expressions and developing word curiosity and playfulness. In the sections that follow, we draw from best practices in vocabulary instruction and research on multimedia learning and vocabulary instruction, to offer several strategies for involving students in using and learning words through multimodal expression.

STRATEGIES FOR LEARNING WORDS THROUGH MULTIMODAL EXPRESSION

We learn words by using them. Vocabulary instruction generally relies on verbal language as the expressive medium of choice (because words are verbal, after all). Digital tools and media allow us to connect verbal language with other powerful modes of communication—visual, audio, and movement. Products from the vocabulary-learning strategies featured in this chapter, as well as additional ideas for multimodal expression, can be found on our blog at *www.literacybeat.wordpress.com*.

Vocabulary Videos

Today's students have grown up with YouTube, with many experiencing the ubiquitous family video camera and cell phone video as part of daily life. Student-created vocabulary videos (or "vocab vids") are 60-second videos that allow students to act out the word's meaning, situating it in a specific context (Dalton & Grisham, 2011; to view examples, go to Bridget

Dalton's blog post on *www.literacybeat.wordpress.com*). The strategic embedding of a word into a web of multimodal meaning helps make the word-learning experience memorable for both the vocab video producers and for their viewing audience.

To create a brief video that effectively communicates a target word requires some planning. First, show students one or two examples that illustrate how meaning can be communicated in 60 seconds or less, with few or no props, and only one to three students. For example, Dalton and Christian Ehret partnered to create a model that illustrates the power of video to illustrate word meanings (see Figure 15.1). Using a flip camera, they shot a video illustrating the word *overwhelmed*. The video opens with a shot of a desk piled high with books. Ehret is sitting on the floor, hidden by the desk. Suddenly, his hand appears, pulling a book off. More books disappear as he pops up repeatedly, looking increasingly distressed. At the end, Ehret appears with a sign displaying the word *overwhelm*, saying, "I'm *distressed*, drowning in a *deluge* of books. This is an *overwhelming* amount of books to read! Can you tell I'm feeling totally *overwhelmed*?!" Note that all of the italicized words were found on a thesaurus during a Web search the pair did to prepare for the video. They used different forms of the word (*overwhelm, overwhelmed, overwhelming*) and incorporated related words (*distress* and *deluge*) to aid in the development of word concepts.

Once students have participated in making one or two vocab vids with guidance, divide them into teams of three (one partner will need to film and often two others are needed to act out the scene). Let them know that they will have 5 minutes to plan, including searching in an online thesaurus designed for students, such as Merriam-Webster's Word Central

FIGURE 15.1. Christian Ehret's vocab vid illustrating *overwhelmed*. "I'm submerged in a deluge of books. Can you tell I'm feeling overwhelmed?"

(*www.wordcentral.com*), and a visual dictionary such as Visual Dictionary Online (*www.visualdictionaryonline.com*), for related words and potential contexts. As students plan, suggest that they make a sign with the targeted word to display at the end of the video. Let them know that they will have about 5 minutes to film, including review of the film and reshooting. Limiting the time keeps videos short, focused, and memorable.

As an alternative to shooting video, students can use free Web tools such as Xtranormal (*www.xtranormal.com*) and GoAnimate (*www.goanimate.com*) to create animations with avatars or cartoon figures. Students can also add audio recordings to a graphic (see student-created examples for *amble*, *headstrong*, and *fecund* at VocabAhead [*www.vocabahead.com*]).

Invite students to present their videos to engage the class in viewing and responding to the representation of the word. If time allows, encourage students to film an additional scene that illustrates a different meaning of the same word. Encourage students to link ideas across other vocab vids being filmed in class (e.g., "*Devastate* connects to *overwhelm*, because you can feel devastated when you have too much work to do!"). You can post students' videos to your class blog, or you may want to keep it offline, creating a PowerPoint word glossary with embedded videos.

Creating Vocabulary VoiceThreads

VoiceThread (*voicethread.com*) is an online tool for educators that allows students to create a multimedia slide show that encourages multimodal response in the form of text, recorded audio, or webcam-created video files. The value lies in the possibility of both representing and expressing word meanings multimodally in a social learning community. Figure 15.2 shows an example of a VoiceThread created for the famous Mad Tea Party incident in "Alice in Wonderland." The target word is *civil*, a word that has multiple meanings. In a social studies context, it relates to citizens or the state; in Alice's tea party setting, it means to be polite. The teacher's post introduces the task and reads aloud the text. The next three participants post written, audio, and visual responses to the concept of civil. To address multiple meanings and develop academic language, the teacher might post a second VoiceThread containing a photo of a civil rights protest. She would then ask students to respond to the word *civil* in the context of civil disobedience by composing responses with words, images, and/or songs.

Once they have participated in a few VoiceThreads, students can then collaborate to create their own vocabulary VoiceThreads for important words and phrases they are learning across disciplines. To ensure response, invite parents, teachers, and other students to participate in extending vocabulary learning by composing responses in multiple forms. VoiceThreads can be exported to an MP3 player for easy access.

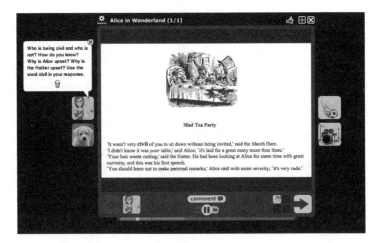

Student 1 (written response): I think the Hatter is rude because he told Alice to cut her hair. My sister would be very mad if you insulted her hair. Hatter is not **civil** to Alice.

Student 2 (audio-recorded response): I'm Alice, and this is what I'm thinking: I know I should be civil to them, it is their tea party and I'm only a guest. But aren't you supposed to be nice to your guests? I could say something very rude about the Mad Hatter's nose since it is strange looking, but I won't because my mother told me to be polite. Or should I say, **civil**!

Student 3 (video response): (*Child is wearing a baseball cap, and says*) "See this hat? If I wear it to a baseball game, I'm being civil. If I wear it at the dinner table, my mom says it's rude. (*Child takes off his hat.*) So, I take off my hat to show my mom that I can be civil when I want to be!

FIGURE 15.2. VoiceThread responses for *civil* (*ed.voicethread.com/share/1438491*). Reprinted with permission from VoiceThread.com.

Designing Multimedia Hypertext Versions of Poems, Quotes, or Short Text Excerpts

Students are often discouraged when asked to unpack the meaning of words and figurative language within a poem or passage. An alternative way to dive deep into word meaning is to engage students in creating hypertext versions of the text that include links to other media. The original text represents the first layer, and students' personal connections and interpretations represent the second, hyperlinked layer. This activity works well with partner groups because it encourages students to talk about and use the targeted words as they design their linked text.

PowerPoint, or other multimedia presentation software, can serve as the hypertext medium. To introduce this kind of vocabulary and figurative language exploration, create a three-slide PowerPoint template: Slide 1 explains the task and how to make a hyperlink within a slide show, slide 2 introduces an example, and slide 3 provides the actual text to be expanded with vocabulary hyperlinks. Instruct students to save the template with their own file name, delete the sample slides, and replace the template with their own slideshow. Figure 15.3 demonstrates how key words and phrases in the opening of Martin Luther King, Jr.'s "I Have a Dream" speech can be hyperlinked to students' elaborations and connections in different modes. In this example, WordSift's (*www.wordsift.com*) workspace was used to create the image collage on slide 4, a unique feature of this online resource.

Simulating Twitter to Get at the Heart of Word Meanings

The Twitter phenomenon tells us something important about language use and engagement. In 140 characters or less, information about "what's happening now" can be shared with an online community. Defining characteristics of a "tweet" are brevity, timeliness, and the ability to instantly respond to, and connect with, others. Without actually creating Twitter accounts, teachers can bring Twitter-like experiences into the classroom to expand vocabulary learning. To model a vocabulary-related Twitter, provide students with a target word or concept and challenge them to keep a related stream of tweets going as long as they can. Set the expectation that

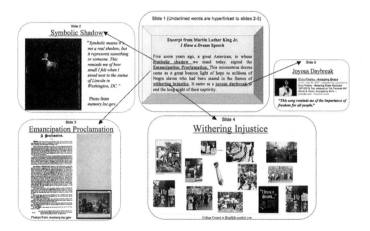

FIGURE 15.3. Hypertext "I Have a Dream" speech created in PowerPoint. The student hyperlinked underlined phrases to text, images, and a song to illustrate their meaning.

the target word and related words must be used in each tweet. Provide a context for using the new word, such as a breaking news event, a topic you're studying in class, or a book you are reading.

To simulate Twitter in a closed environment, try the free tool Wallwisher (*www.wallwisher.com*). Once you've set up the topic-themed wall, students can post together in a shared space without setting up individual accounts. Like tweets, comment space is limited (Wallwisher allows 160 characters). Alternatively, you may want to project a document and type in the posts as students say them aloud. If you have a wireless keyboard, students can pass it around to input their simulated tweet.

The following instructional setup may serve as a tangible example. Imagine that your students have been reading and watching online news reports about an oil rig explosion in the Gulf of Mexico. One way to extend the conversation and promote vocabulary building could be for students to create a Twitter-like stream to express reactions and pose questions, using the target words *pollution* and *disaster*. Before beginning, discuss the words' meanings and provide students a reference by writing the words and related forms on the board. Then introduce and talk through the following exchanges as a model.

Twitter-Like Stream

STUDENT 1: Bad news. An oil rig blew up in the Gulf of Mexico. Pollution is going to be a problem.

STUDENT 2: Oil will pollute the beaches. What a disaster!

STUDENT 3: You can't swim in polluted water.

STUDENT 4: The seagulls and pelicans will be hurt by the oil. It gets on their feathers.

This activity will also appeal to older students who might be researching the news event from the perspective of different stakeholders:

Twitter-Like Stream

SHRIMPER: Major disaster. Oil rig blew and oil gushing in Gulf of Mexico. Pollution might wipe us out.

OYSTERMAN: What about oyster beds? I have to fish. Polluted oyster beds mean no oysters. What a disaster for me and my customers.

BEACH LOVER: Gulf Shores beach has black oil washing up. Seagulls coated. Can't swim in polluted water.

CLEAN UP CREW: Dish detergent is the best thing to clean oil pollution from birds. Who knew?!!

OIL COMPANY: The faster we cap the oil rig, the faster the pollution stops.

Another approach would be to create a Twitter-like stream illustrating character traits or thematic elements. For example, students could take on the role of Alexander from Judith Viorst's (1972) funny story *Alexander's Terrible, Horrible, No Good, Very Bad Day* and create a series of tweets using multiple feeling words to express Alexander's journey of emotions over the course of the day. In this case, students would be developing a more nuanced understanding of different feeling words that express emotions.

Composing Multimodal Word Webs

Creating a multimodal word web is probably one of the simplest and most effective ways to use language and media to express word meanings and explore the relationship among words. Most schools have a graphic organizer program available, such as Visio for the PC (*visiotoolbox.com*) or Webspiration (*www.mywebspiration.com*). This expanded form of a traditional graphic organizer offers multimedia options for demonstrating an understanding of vocabulary and concepts. To begin, create a basic template that students can customize. At a minimum, the multimodal word web should include the target word or concept, an explanation, and examples of the word in a context. Further, at least two modes should be used, such as text, sound, graphics, and/or video. For example, when creating a word web for the target word *habitat*, students might include descriptive information that defines what a habitat is, as well as photographs of different habitats, video of wildlife in their habitat, and audio clips that offer a chance to hear sounds within a given habitat. In this sample word web (see Figure 15.4), readers can listen to whale sounds from the Arctic and watch a video clip showing how the polar bear learned how to survive in the Arctic, a habitat that offers few comforts.

Word webs can also be used to respond to literature. After reading the Newberry award-winning novel *The Tale of Despereaux*, by Kate DiCamillo (2003), invite students to illustrate the essential concept of *hero* with images of the comic book superhero Superman, and a photo of a "real-life" hero such as scientist Jane Goodall, a key quote from the novel that illustrates how Despereaux behaves like a hero, and a link to the song, "This Little Light of Mine." This song communicates the potential for heroism in all of us, great and small. As with all of these examples, sharing and publishing students' work is part of the learning process and provides an authentic audience.

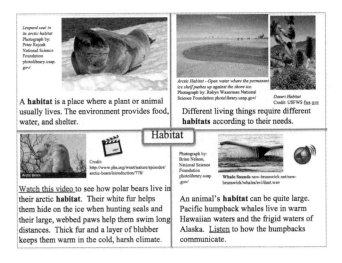

FIGURE 15.4. Multimodal word web illustrating *habitat*.

Creating Pictures Worth a Thousand Words

You know the saying, "A picture is worth a thousand words"? The same can be true of a word—what information, memories, images, and sounds are evoked when you hear the word *celebrate* or *grandmother*? While we share cultural understandings of some visual symbols, the ways that visual representations can be connected to words is limitless. Even for something as specific as a car, our image memories will vary. To develop both visual literacy skills and vocabulary, challenge students to connect words and images. In a recent project, Proctor, Dalton, and colleagues asked fifth graders to caption an image using a target word (Dalton et al., 2011; Proctor et al., 2011; Proctor, Dalton, & Grisham, 2007). When presented with an image of a person signaling a boat, some students wrote a description, whereas others experimented with dialogue and monologue and recorded responses with great expression ("Alright, when I give the signal! Bum-ba-ba-bum bum [*student hums dramatic music*] OW!").

It is also productive to reverse the direction of the connection, beginning with the key word and finding images that match it (see Figure 15.5). Once completed, ask students to add a title and explain why the images are a good representation of the word. This activity offers an excellent opportunity to teach students how to critically read images on the Web.

Show students how to search for images using photo repositories with public domain content (note that you will want to have an appropriate filter) and content designed specifically for educational purposes, such as NASA's

FIGURE 15.5. "A picture is worth a thousand words" illustrating *challenge*. Reprinted with permission from William Vann, EduPic Graphical Resource.

space photographs (*www.nasa.gov/multimedia/imagegallery/index.html*). To prepare for searching, have students brainstorm several different contexts for using the target word. For example, for the word *celebrate*, have students think through who might be celebrating, what they are celebrating, and where they might be celebrating. This would lead to searches for "cheering football fan"; "birthday party"; even "president wins election." As you might expect, the images are not always a good match for the target word, leading to productive discussions about why or why not to use a particular image. Once students have some experience finding images to illustrate vocabulary, ask for a more sophisticated selection and design process. For example, have students consider how their images include, or do not include, different kinds of people. Have them discuss who has power in their images and whether their images reinforce a negative stereotype. To extend the activity, ask students to communicate the target word with both an abstract image and a concrete image. Finally, ask them to find an image that contrasts with the target word and presents its antonym.

Having Fun with New Slang

The dynamic and inventive nature of language is dramatically evident in the torrent of new words we manage to create each year. While you may feel the need to chillax (calm down and relax) in the face of students' often unconventional vocabulary use, we recommend that you seize on the opportunity to build word curiosity and playfulness (Blachowicz & Fisher, Chapter 10, this volume; Johnson, Johnson, & Schlichting, Chapter 11, this volume; Scott et al., 2008). Three excellent Internet resources for learning about words and language are the Visual Thesaurus (*www.visu-althesaurus.com*), the *Cambridge Advanced Learners Dictionary* (*www. dictionary.cambridge.org*), and the *Oxford Dictionary of English* (*www. oed.com*). The latter two post a list each year of new words added to the dictionary (a cautionary note: Beware of the online slang dictionaries that often contain content not suitable for a K–12 audience). Wordspy (*www. wordspy.com*) also publishes neologisms (new word creations), many of which are slang and/or linguistic blends.

Multimedia and Internet resources can support the *fun* of word learning in numerous ways. Have students take turns creating a daily word podcast highlighting a new word, or a new use for an old word, that can be shared as part of the school's morning announcements, posted to a blog, or subscribed to via a smartphone. Offer one or more students the option of drafting a podcast script with or without sound effects. Then have them record and edit it using a free sound studio program such as GarageBand (*www.apple.com/ilife/garageband*) or Audacity (*www.audacity.source-forge.net*). Next, ask them to forward the audio file to to you for review and posting (Dalton & Grisham, 2011).

Games are fun, and word games are no exception. A popular vocabulary game played on the National Public Radio (NPR) radio show "Says You!" involves panelists who provide possible definitions for a given word. The trick is to guess which definition is correct—not so easy to do when some of the contenders are both hilarious and plausible. Your students can produce their own version of the game in a weekly podcast. They can also create a nonsense word with a realistic definition and create an online poll so that others can vote on whether it is a real word or not (and even rate how certain they are about their judgment).

Building a Cognate Catalogue

With more than 176 languages spoken nationwide, the United States is becoming increasingly multilingual. A growing body of literature details best practices for promoting vocabulary knowledge among English learners (ELs; August & Shanahan, 2006, 2010; Carlo et al., 2004). Although it is important to consider the needs of students from many language backgrounds, it is also clear that instructional strategies aimed at supporting the learning of Spanish speakers are especially relevant. Several studies suggest explicit instruction on identifying cognates—words that have similar spellings, meanings, and pronunciation in two languages (Lubliner & Grisham, in press). The cognate connection can be helpful for students who speak Latin-based languages, such as Spanish, French, Italian, Portuguese, or Romanian. Drawing attention to cognates promotes metalinguistic awareness (Scott et al., 2008).

Many words in English are a special kind of cognate in Spanish—the Spanish version of the word is a common word, and the English version is a more specialized word (e.g., *conserve/conservar* or *frigid/frío*). Since the origins of many words are Latin, cognates can help ELs identify shared roots or affixes that can be used to unlock the meaning of many words in English.

The instructional strategies highlighted in this chapter can each be adapted to include a cognate component. Vocab vids, VoiceThreads, student-created multimedia hypertexts, and multimodal word webs can easily include a component that identifies related cognates. An additional resource, Voki (*www.voki.com*), can be used to create personalized speaking avatars. With Voki, bilingual students can create a talking voice and record their own cognate catalogue that other students can access, helping the classroom community make connections between Spanish and English. These Vokis would serve as learning resources for other students, placing bilingual students in a role as a sought-after language expert. In addition, students can script their own avatars to promote curiosity about new words found in independent reading texts.

USING DIGITAL MEDIA TO TRANSFORM WORD LEARNING IN YOUR CLASSROOM

Whether you are a teacher with a laptop cart or have just a few computers, multimodal word learning can become a part of your classroom routine. For example, requiring students to plan out their multimodal vocabulary products before producing them digitally will automatically create a staggered completion rate. Taking time to conference with students increases their ability to set tangible goals for working with limited computer time and may increase the quality of student work. Schedule computer time on a routine basis and check in with students frequently to ensure that the time is used productively. Enlisting assistance from parents, the library media specialist, or computer lab supervisor may open up additional opportunities for computer time and assistance.

HOME–SCHOOL CONNECTIONS

Infusing generative vocabulary learning with digital resources can help students develop collaboration skills and forge positive home–school connections. For example, creating a digital archive of student-created resources can open up new avenues for learning within and beyond the school day. Creating a classroom wiki using a free service such as Wikispaces (*www.wikispaces.com*) is one option. You might also consider building the archive on your classroom or school website to provide easy access to resources both in and out of school. Encourage students to work with partners and parents to access, and add to, the resource bank both at home and at school.

ARCHIVING GENERATIVE WORD LEARNING

Archiving artifacts of word learning can be a powerful classroom resource, but having students save and access their work digitally may not be the most workable option. Printing out what students have created and making it available in paper form may be the most creative way to manage student-created resources. Binding resources into a series of class-constructed reference books, reserving a designated wall space, and creating a corner where digital content can be viewed on your computer might be more viable options to ensure that students have easy access to the content they created.

A WORD ABOUT COPYRIGHT

Today, educators have access to a vast, rich array of online materials, but care needs to be taken to help students learn to respect the rights of copyright holders (Hobbs, 2010). There are a growing number of websites that offer quality, copyright-friendly materials for educational projects. Pics4Learning (*www.pics.tech4learning.com*) and EduPic (*www.edupic. net*) offer copyright-free images for educational purposes, and Internet-4Classrooms (*www.internet4classrooms.com/graphics.htm*) contains a comprehensive listing for photos, clip art, sound clips, and video clips. The Library of Congress's American Memory collection (*memory.loc.gov*) offers an abundance of resources, including primary source materials, for use in student projects. Teaching students the limitations of copyrighted material and holding them to these guidelines in the educational products they create promotes a positive code of cyber ethics.

CONCLUSION

Technology and media can play an important role in developing students' vocabulary through generative, multimodal expression. Drawing on research investigating effective vocabulary instruction and multimedia learning, we have offered many instructional examples to illustrate how teachers can integrate media and technology in service of interactive and powerful vocabulary instruction in classrooms. We suggest that giving students experience with the digital technologies required in the 21st century will be motivationally as well as academically beneficial. As teachers try out these ideas (and invent new ones), we encourage them to embrace their students as collaborative learning partners. Together, we can generate many more innovative ways to use digital resources to support students' generative, expressive vocabulary.

REFERENCES

August, D., & Shanahan, T. (Eds.). (2006). *Developing literacy in second-language learners: Report of the National Literacy Panel on language-minority children and youth.* Mahwah, NJ: Erlbaum.

August, D., & Shanahan, T. (2010). Response to a review and update on developing literacy in second-language learners: Report of the National Literacy Panel on language-minority children and youth. *Journal of Literacy Research, 42*(3), 341–348.

Beck, I., McKeown, M. G., & Kucan, L. (2002). *Bringing words to life.* New York: Guilford Press.

Biemiller, A., & Boote, C. (2006). An effective method for building meaning vocabulary in primary grades. *Journal of Educational Psychology, 98,* 44–62.

Bravo, M., & Cervetti, G. N. (2008). Teaching vocabulary through text and experience in content areas. In A. Farstrup & J. Samuels (Eds.), *What research has to say about vocabulary instruction* (pp. 182–210). Newark, DE: International Reading Association.

Carlo, M. S., August, D., McLaughlin, B., Snow, C. E., Dressler, C., Lippman, D. N., et al. (2004). Closing the gap: Addressing the vocabulary needs of English-language learners in bilingual and mainstream classrooms. *Reading Research Quarterly, 39,* 188–215.

Castek, J., Leu, D. J., Jr., Coiro, J., Gort, M., Henry, L. A., & Lima, C. (2008). Developing new literacies among multilingual learners in the elementary grades. In L. Parker (Ed.), *Technology-mediated learning environments for young English learners: Connections in and out of school* (pp. 111–153). Mahwah, NJ: Erlbaum.

Clark, J. M., & Paivio, A. (1991). Dual coding theory and education. *Educational Psychology Review, 3,* 149–210.

Coiro, J., Knobel, M., Lankshear, M., & Leu, D. J. (2008). Central issues in new literacies and new literacies research. In J. Coiro, M. Knobel, C. Lankshear, & D. J. Leu (Eds.), *Handbook of research on new literacies* (pp. 1–21). Mahwah, NJ: Erlbaum.

Cunningham, A. E., & Stanovich, K. E. (1998). What reading does for the mind. *American Educator, 22*(1&2), 8–15.

Dalton, B. (2011, May 1). *Vocab vids: Making words come alive through digital role play.* Web log post on Literacy Beat, *www.literacybeat.wordpress.com*

Dalton, B., & Grisham, D. L. (2011). e-Voc strategies: 10 ways to improve vocabulary teaching using technology. *The Reading Teacher, 64*(5), 306–317.

Dalton, B., Proctor, C. P., Uccelli, P., Mo, E., & Snow, C. (2011). Designing for diversity: The role of reading comprehension strategies and interactive vocabulary in a digital reading environment for fifth-grade monolingual English and bilingual students. *Journal of Literacy Research, 43*(1), 68–100.

Deedy, C. A. (2007). *Martina the beautiful cockroach: A Cuban folktale.* Atlanta: Peachtree.

DiCamillo, K. (2003). *The tale of Despereaux.* Somerville, MA: Candlewick Press.

Fadel, C., & Lemke, C. (2008). *Multimodal learning through media: What the research says.* White paper. San Jose, CA: CISCO Systems. Retrieved October 20, 2010, from *www.cisco.com/web/strategy/docs/education/Multimodal-Learning-Through-Media.pdf*

Hart, B., & Risley, T. (1995). *Meaningful differences in the everyday experience of young American children.* Baltimore: Brookes.

Hobbs, R. (2010). *Copyright clarity: How fair use supports digital learning.* Thousand Oaks, CA: Corwin/Sage.

Kelley, J., Lesaux, N., Kieffer, M., & Faller, S. (2010). Effective academic vocabulary instruction in the urban middle school. *The Reading Teacher, 64*(1), 5–14.

Lenhart, A., Smith, A., Macgill, A. R., & Arafeh, S. (2008). *Writing, technology and teens.* Washington, DC: Pew Research Center. Retrieved September 16, 2009, from *pewresearch.org/pubs/808/writing-technology-and-teens*

Lovelace, S., & Stewart, S. R. (2009). Effects of robust vocabulary instruction and multicultural text on the development of work knowledge among African American children. *American Journal of Speech-Language Pathology, 18*(2), 168–179.

Lubliner, S. (with Smetana, L.) (2005). *Getting into words: Vocabulary instruction that strengthens comprehension.* Baltimore: Brookes.

Lubliner, S., & Grisham, D. L. (in press). Cognate Strategy instruction: Providing powerful literacy tools to Spanish-speaking children. In J. C. Fingon & S. H. Ulanoff (Eds.), *Learning from culturally and linguistically diverse classrooms: Using inquiry to improve practice.* New York: Teachers College Press.

Lubliner, S., & Scott, J. A. (2008). *Nourishing vocabulary: Balancing words and learning.* Thousand Oaks, CA: Corwin Press.

Marzano, R. J. (2004). *Building background knowledge for academic achievement: Research on what works in schools.* Alexandria, VA: Association for Supervision and Curriculum Development.

Mayer, R. E. (Ed.). (2005). *The Cambridge handbook of multimedia learning.* New York: Cambridge University Press.

Mayer, R. E., & Moreno, R. (2003). Nine ways to reduce cognitive load in multimedia learning. *Educational Psychologist, 38*(1), 43–52.

Moll, L. C., Amanti, C., Neff, D., & Gonzalez, N. (1992). Funds of knowledge for teaching: Using a qualitative approach to connect homes and classrooms. *Theory into Practice, 31*(2), 132–141.

National Institute of Child Health and Human Development. (2000). *Report of* the National Reading Panel. *Teaching children to read: An evidence-based assessment of the scientific research literature on reading and its implications for reading instruction* (NIH Publication No. 00-4769). Washington, DC: U.S. Government Printing Office.

Paris, S. G. (2005). Reinterpreting the development of reading skills. *Reading Research Quarterly, 40*(2), 184–202.

Proctor, C. P., Dalton, B., & Grisham, D. L. (2007). Scaffolding English language learners and struggling readers in a universal literacy environment with embedded strategy instruction and vocabulary support. *Journal of Literacy Research, 30,* 71–93.

Proctor, C. P., Dalton, B., Uccelli, P., Biancarosa, G., Mo, E., & Snow, C. E. (2011). Improving comprehension online: Effects of deep vocabulary instruction with bilingual and monolingual fifth graders. *Reading and Writing, 24,* 517–544.

Proctor, C. P., Uccelli, P., Dalton, B., & Snow, C. E. (2009). Understanding depth of vocabulary online with bilingual and monolingual children. *Reading and Writing Quarterly, 25*(4), 311–333.

Scott, J., Nagy, B., & Flinspatch, S. (2008). More than merely words: Redefining vocabulary learning in a culturally and linguistically diverse society. In A. Farstrup & J. Samuels (Eds.), *What research has to say about vocabulary instruction* (pp. 182–210). Newark, DE: International Reading Association.

Selwyn, N. (2006). Exploring the "digital disconnect" between Net-savvy students and their schools. *Learning, Media and Technology, 31*(1), 5–17.

Silverman, R., & Crandell, J. (2010). Vocabulary practices in prekindergarten and kindergarten classrooms. *Reading Research Quarterly, 45*(3), 318–340.

Viorst, J. (1972). *Alexander's terrible, horrible, no good, very bad day.* New York: Simon & Schuster Children's.

Wenger, E., McDermott, R., & Snyder, W. (2002). *Cultivating communities of practice: A guide to managing knowledge.* Cambridge, MA: Harvard Business School Press.

Willingham, D. T. (2009). *Why don't students like school?: A cognitive scientist answers questions about how the mind works and what it means to the classroom.* San Francisco: Jossey-Bass.

Zhao, Y., & Lai, C. (2008). Technology and second language learning: Promises and problems. In L. A. Parker (Ed.), *Technology-based learning environments for young English learners: In and out of school connections.* Mahwah, NJ: Erlbaum.

Zwiers, J. (2008). *Building academic language: Essential practices for content classrooms.* San Francisco: Wiley.

Chapter 16

What Differences in Narrative and Informational Texts Mean for the Learning and Instruction of Vocabulary

Elfrieda H. Hiebert
Gina N. Cervetti

We begin with four statements about influences on vocabulary instruction in schools. First, vocabulary is central to the comprehension of text (Davis, 1942; Thorndike, 1973). Second, the vocabularies of students when they enter school vary substantially (Hart & Risley, 1995). Third, the number of words in English is huge (Leech, Rayson, & Wilson, 2001). And, fourth, the amount of time in schools is limited (Fisher et al., 1980). All of these features combine to create a challenging situation for educators who aim to select vocabulary strategically in order to lessen the gap between the haves and the have-nots (Nagy & Hiebert, 2010).

Unfortunately, it appears that the choices made in schools regarding the teaching of vocabulary are often not strategic. In elementary schools, large blocks of time are devoted to reading/language arts instruction where, despite claims of increased access to informational texts, a narrative stance has continued to direct the selection of vocabulary and the form of vocabulary instruction (Norris, Phillips, Smith, Baker, & Weber, 2008). Whether the text is an informational or narrative one, teachers' guides of core reading programs recommend instruction of a handful of words. Typically, these words are treated in a similar manner—each is defined, discussed, and read in the context of a sentence from the text. Usually, the words are unrelated to one another but have been selected because of their perceived importance to the story content.

Such a perspective fails to recognize the differences in the vocabularies of narrative and informational texts. Typically, the registers of oral and written languages are recognized as unique, but these differences pale relative to differences in the features of narrative and informational genres. Through multidimensional analyses of spoken and written language samples, Biber (1988) concluded that particular types of speech and writing are more or less similar with respect to different dimensions. For example, a presentation or discussion at a meeting of a scientific society, although oral in nature, will vary considerably from a conversation between two friends over dinner. The vocabulary of a novel that includes substantial amounts of dialogue may have more in common with the dinner conversation than with a scientific report.

In this chapter, we examine the differences between the target vocabularies of an English/language arts (ELA) program that is dominated by narrative texts and a science program with informational texts. Our goal in this chapter is to accomplish three purposes: (1) Review what is known about the differences in the vocabularies of unique words in informational and narrative texts, (2) examine these differences in an analysis of the words from an ELA and science program, and (3) present suggestions as to what differences in the vocabulary of different text types mean for instruction.

WHAT IS KNOWN ABOUT THE DIFFERENCES IN THE VOCABULARIES OF NARRATIVE AND INFORMATIONAL TEXTS?

To understand differences in vocabularies of different subject areas requires a foundation in the features of words in written English. Differences in words have been identified on numerous dimensions, including, but not limited to their length, part of speech, and etymological origins. To describe the differences of the topic-specific words in different genres, we focus on four criteria: (1) frequency of the word and its morphological family, (2) familiarity, (3) conceptual complexity, and (4) relatedness within a thematic or semantic network of words.

Frequency of Words and Their Morphological Families

The approximately 750,000 words in the British National Corpus (Leech et al., 2001) can be sorted into three groups on the basis of frequency: (1) highly frequent, (2) moderately frequent, and (3) rare. The first group is made up of approximately 1,000 words that account typically for two-thirds of the total words in a text. The first row in Table 16.1 shows the high-frequency words within 50-word excerpts from two fourth-grade texts, one a narrative text (Gerson, 1994, as cited in Afflerbach et al., 2007) and the other an informational text (Cooney et al., 2006). Words such as *object, energy*, and *matter* in the first row of Table 16.1 show that all of the 1,000 most-frequent words are not simply glue words such as prepositions, pronouns, and question words. Some of the words in this group are there because they have multiple meanings. In science, words such as *energy* and *matter* take on quite precise meanings that differ from their common use. When only words from the 1,000 most-frequent group are available (as is the case in row 1 of Table 16.1), the context for the precise meanings of polysemous words is not available.

TABLE 16.1. Distributions of Words by Frequency in Exemplar Narrative and Informational Texts

	Narrative text	Informational text
High frequency	her and she the of that he showed her; the sand of the , the and of and in and the and in .	in an object move because they have energy. As an object becomes , its move . As the object , the move more slowly. energy is energy due to moving that make up matter. We feel the of energy as heat.
Moderate frequency	daughter loved husband, loved magic daylight beach, rows rows sunlight, feathered worn in harvest	Particles particles faster. particles flow
Rare	Iemanja's shimmering cocoa sugarcane baking sparkling jewels costumes festivals.	hotter, cools, Thermal thermal
Example texts	Iemanja's daughter loved her husband, and she loved the magic of daylight that he showed her; the shimmering sand of the beach, the rows and rows of cocoa and sugarcane baking in sunlight, and the sparkling jewels and feathered costumes worn in harvest festivals.	Particles in an object move because they have energy. As an object becomes hotter, its particles move faster. As the object cools, the particles move more slowly. Thermal energy is energy due to moving particles that make up matter. We feel the flow of thermal energy as heat.

A group of approximately 4,750 words appears with moderate frequency in written language—10–99 times per million words. Examples of words within this group are given in the second row of Table 16.1. Although some specific concepts are present (e.g., *Africa, France, Mexico*), the majority of words in this group represent common concepts (e.g., *lakes, villages, desert*). At times, words that represent common concepts (e.g., *flow*) can take on specific meanings, as is the case in the science text. With the addition of this group of moderately frequent words, readers can gain the gist of the text, such as the daughter's love of the light in the narrative example. Sufficient context is available to understand that a common word such as *flow* takes on a specific meaning in the science text.

The remaining words in written English—up to 745,000 words, according to the British National Corpus (Leech et al., 2001)—appear less frequently, if not rarely. As can be seen in the narrative excerpt in the third row of Table 16.1, some of these words are names of people. Others are representations of known concepts that authors use to give nuance to their writing—*shimmering, sparkling.* Still others are concepts unique to domains such as *thermal.* Approximately 15,000 of these words appear from 1 to 9 times per million words of running text. The remaining words of English—approximately 97% of the words in the language—can be expected to appear less than once per million words of text.

Many words in this group of approximately 725,000 rare words are archaic (e.g., *bap, snell*). The *Oxford Unabridged Dictionary* (Simpson & Weiner, 2009) identifies approximately 425,000 active words in English. When words are considered as morphological families, rather than as individual words, the volume of words is approximately five to six times smaller (Nagy & Anderson, 1984). Viewing the frequency of a word as a function of the size of its morphological family is justifiable in that nouns and their plurals as well as conjugations of verbs share a representation in the mental lexicon (Sereno & Jongman, 1997; Stanners, Neiser, Hernon, & Hall, 1979). While developing and struggling readers can be challenged by multisyllabic words (which most morphologically derived words are) (Nagy, Berninger, & Abbott, 2006), word meanings, even more so than features such as length and frequency, prove the greatest challenge to students' comprehension (Nagy, Anderson, & Herman, 1987). A word such as *energy*—used in a science text—has a specialized meaning that is different from the meaning communicated when a person moans in mid-afternoon, "I don't have any energy left to finish this work."

Conceptual Complexity

The essence of language is its meaningfulness, and it is the word that represents unique entities. Particular words may appear infrequently in written language, but they may be easy to understand for a number of reasons. For example, they may be highly concrete (e.g., *skateboard, mirror*) or can be easily understood from contextual use. A case of the latter is illustrated by the use of the word *madragada* in the following sentence from Gerson (1994, p. 32): "In Brazil the early morning is called the madragada."

Jenkins and Dixon (1983) identified four possible relationships between a learner and a new word: (1) unknown word but a known concept that can be expressed succinctly (*altercation/argument*); (2) unknown word with a simple synonym but student does not know the concept referred to by the synonym (*arcane/obscure*); (3) unknown word that does not have a simple synonym but can be described through experience (e.g., *odometer/* the item on the speedometer that tells how many miles you've gone); and (4) unknown word that does not have a simple synonym and for which students do not have extensive experiences to draw on (e.g., *legislature*). The density with which unknown words of the fourth type appear in texts is likely a strong influence on students' comprehension (Sternberg & Powell, 1983). Students may be able to establish the meaning of a conceptually complex word with an unknown meaning by using the meanings of known words in a sentence or paragraph, when the ratio of unknown to known words is low. Their comprehension may be compromised, however, when the ratio of unknown to known words reaches a particular threshold. They may also be unable to deepen their knowledge of new words when texts are dense with unknown words.

A study conducted by Nagy et al. (1987) confirms the hypothesis that the conceptual complexity of words influences students' ability to understand unknown words while reading. Third, fifth, and seventh graders were given texts that had unknown words that varied in conceptual complexity. Nagy et al. found that conceptual difficulty (using a scheme similar to that proposed by Jenkins and Dixon, 1983) was the only word feature from among several (including length, part of speech, and morphological complexity) that was significantly related to students' ability to understand the word meaning in context. The text properties that most influenced students' ability to learn word meanings from context were the proportion of unfamiliar words that were conceptually challenging and the average length of unfamiliar words (an indicator of morphological complexity).

Semantic Relatedness

Words enter the lexicon as humans make distinctions about features of the world around them, both internal and external. Consider, for example, two words that have been officially recognized by lexicographers over the last year (Oxford Dictionaries, 2010): *neuroprotective* and *spyware*. Words such as these are not the product of random word generators but of human beings making unique distinctions of entities or experiences in their environments. Words are parts of a richly interconnected network (Entwisle, 1966; Levelt, Roelofs, & Meyer, 1999). Common relationships among words include semantic classes (e.g., *eggs/food*), collocation of words that commonly occur together (e.g., *a dozen eggs*), superordination (e.g., *sedimentary/rock*), and synonyms (*glittering/sparkling*). Within the mental lexicon, words are related in other ways as well, such as part–whole (*branch/tree*), instrumentality (*broom/floor*), and theme (*hospital/nurse*) (Moss, Ostrin, Tyler, & Marslen-Wilson, 1995).

In a curriculum area such as science (Marzano, 2004), words are clustered within thematic groups. Marzano's analysis of standards documents produced by five national organizations (e.g., National Science Teachers Association) through 2000 showed that science vocabulary was associated with particular topics, such as weather in the K–2 grade span (e.g., *weather conditions, weather patterns, seasonal change, precipitation*). The vocabulary within the nine standards documents (e.g., National Council of Teachers) produced through 2000 for ELA had clusters related to a common topic (e.g., *vowels, consonants*). These topics, however, were ones used in instructional conversations and lessons given by teachers to describe features of language and texts. The vocabulary in the ELA standards were not words that typically appear in texts read by students. For example, although *vowels* and *consonants* might appear in an ELA workbook, it would be an unusual story that would contain these words.

Words that appear in the moderately frequent and rare categories of the narrative text in Table 16.1 (e.g., *feathered, loved*) did not appear in the standards documents in the Marzano (2004) review as recommended concepts. The typical response to this observation is that the variety in the words used in stories is great, making systematic selection of vocabulary in ELA standards documents impossible. However, if literary words such as *costumes, shimmering, festivals*, and *feathered* are seen as members of larger semantic clusterings of ideas, a systematic and cohort approach to the selection of words may be possible, if not the identification of specific sets of words.

A proposal based on research of semantic connections suggests a way in which vocabulary might be taught. This proposal came from Marzano and Marzano (1988), who organized 7,300 words from word lists for elementary students into 61 superclusters of words (e.g., types of motion) that were further broken into 430 clusters where words had closer semantic ties (e.g., *taking/bringing* and *tossing* within the motion supercluster). The clusters were made up of 1,500 miniclusters such as the eight within the *taking/bringing* minicluster (*take, return, get, send, remove, put, deliver, import*). Such a system has support in the research literature where teaching groups of words that are semantically related, such as *law/police, leaf/ tree*, and *learn/school*, has proven to positively impact learning (Tinkham,

1997). Nagy and Hiebert (2010) have suggested that similar words might be taught gradually with a known member of a semantic set serving as an anchor, because teaching words that are too similar in meaning can interfere with student learning (Tinkham, 1993; Waring, 1997). In other words, all of the words in one of the Marzano and Marzano (1988) miniclusters would not be taught simultaneously, but words in texts that share semantic clusters and miniclusters would be taught in relation to known words within the clusters and miniclusters. For example, *shimmering* and *sparkling* might be taught in relation to the likely known word *shining*. Nagy and Hiebert emphasize that the goal of a curriculum is to teach concepts, not just individual words. When *shimmering, sparkling,* and *shining* are viewed as part of a network of words having to do with light, their meanings can be related to additional words such as *luminous* and *radiant*.

Distinctions in the Vocabularies of Narrative and Informational Texts

The words from the exemplars in Table 16.1 provide a strong indication that the unique words of moderate and rare frequency within narrative and informational texts are different from one another in the concepts that they represent. These differences were observed in an essay by Armbruster and Nagy (1992), wherein they identified three important differences in the unknown words of narrative and informational texts: (1) knowing these words is likely more crucial to getting the gist of informational than of narrative texts; (2) these words are likely more conceptually challenging in informational than in narrative texts; and (3) the words in informational texts are likely more interrelated thematically than those in narratives. However, empirical verification of these differences has been limited.

Although the nature of the language used has been identified as one of the distinguishing features of genres (Biber, 1988), descriptions of the features of vocabulary in narrative and informational texts used in elementary schools have been limited. We have found a single study that has analyzed differences in the words in narrative and content-area texts. This study—by Gardner (2004)—focused on the number of infrequent words that were shared or unique to narrative or informational texts drawn from the same three themes (mummies, mystery, and westward movement). After Gardner had eliminated the words on the General Service List (GSL; West, 1953) and the University Word List (Coxhead, 2000), there were 23,857 unique words (from a total sample of approximately 1.4 million words. Of these 23,857 words, 42%, appeared only in narrative texts, and 30% appeared only in informational text. The remaining 6,566 unique words that were found in both narrative and informational texts were analyzed to determine how many appeared 10 times or more within both genres, a level that Gardner identified as a sufficient number of repetitions for meaningful acquisition. This group of shared unique words with 10 or more repetitions comprised 233 words. What is clear from this analysis is that the vocabularies that appear in these different genres have limited overlap, even when the texts have been chosen to represent the same topics. Gardner (2004) did not conduct additional analyses to determine what distinguished the three groups of unique words. Without greater understanding of the characteristics of the many words that are unique to one or the other genre, publishers and educators are left uncertain as to how words should be chosen differentially and what these features mean for instruction. To ameliorate this gap, we conducted an analysis of the features of words identified for instruction in ELA and science programs.

WHAT DIFFERENCES WERE APPARENT IN AN ANALYSIS OF THE VOCABULARIES OF NARRATIVE AND INFORMATIONAL TEXTS?

Although scholars have concluded that the vocabularies of narrative and informational texts have unique characteristics (e.g., Armbruster & Nagy, 1992), descriptions of these differences are limited. Consequently, we conducted an analysis of the features of the vocabularies of these two types of texts for this chapter. We analyzed the features of all of the words that have been identified for instruction and assessment within an ELA and science program. We also analyzed the words from exemplar texts from each program.

An Analysis of the Word Features

Our analysis of the word features of narrative and informational texts focused on all of the words that were designated for instruction (and subsequently assessment) from the fourth-grade ELA (Afflerbach et al., 2007) and science (Cooney et al., 2006) programs of the same publisher (Scott Foresman) for the entire school year. The ELA program had 209 words, and the science program had 207 designated for instruction and assessment.

A prefatory comment is needed about the attribution of *narrative* to the vocabulary and texts of the ELA program. As has been documented recently (Norris et al., 2008), the genres evident in current core reading programs include informational text focusing on science and also social studies. Although potential exists for developing the vocabulary of content areas with these texts, Norris et al. reported that most of the recommended instruction and assessment is appropriate primarily for literary texts. Our perusal of the vocabulary in the ELA program confirmed the findings of

Norris et al. For example, in a text on the tracking of hurricanes, vocabulary that mirrored the vocabulary in narratives (e.g., *expected, shatter, destruction*) was highlighted rather than the scientific vocabulary in the selection (e.g., *anemometer, meteorologists, tornadoes, satellite, storm surge*). Although a significant portion of the texts in the ELA program came from content-area sources, criteria for selecting vocabulary from these texts appeared to be the same ones as those used for narrative texts.

Although the number of lexical items identified for instruction was similar across the ELA and science programs (209 for the former; 207 for the latter), there was a notable difference in the size of the vocabulary "item": 22% of the science vocabulary consisted of complex phrases, whereas none of the ELA took this form. These complex phrases in science were primarily two-word phrases (e.g., *chemical change*), but some were three or more words (e.g., *wheel and axle*). Exclusion of these items would have limited an understanding of the science vocabulary. At the same time, including words such as *change* in the phrase *chemical change* or *and* in *wheel and axle* might underestimate the difficulty of the vocabulary learning task in science. Consequently, the decision was made to analyze the rarer of the words in a phrase (e.g., *chemical* rather than *change* in *chemical change* and *wheel, axle* and not *and* in *wheel and axle*).

Seven features of the words (209 from the ELA program and 207 from the science program) were established, five of which have been used in numerous studies of vocabulary: (1) length of words (in letters); (2) predicted frequency per million words of text (Zeno, Ivens, Millard, & Duvvuri, 1995); (3) morphological frequency: predicted frequency per million words of text of the words transparently related to the focus word (e.g., *revolve, revolving* for *revolution* but not *revolt*; Zeno et al., 1995); (4) familiarity based on the Living Word Vocabulary (LWV; Dale & O'Rourke, 1976) and its extension by Biemiller (2008); and (5) dispersion, which indicates how widely a word appears in different subject areas (Zeno et al., 1995). We use the remaining space available in this chapter to describe the two features of focus—conceptual complexity and relatedness. Readers interested in more extensive descriptions of the other five variables are encouraged to examine the literature review provided by Scott, Lubliner, and Hiebert (2005).

With respect to conceptual complexity, Nagy et al. (1987) reported that a dichotomous grouping of their categories (i.e., categories 1–3 vs. category 4 [highly complex]) accounted for differences in readers' knowledge of vocabulary, not all four categories. After numerous iterations of a coding system, we developed a 3-point system that made use of digital technology. Words that were defined by one or two words that were among the 2,000 most frequent words on the GSL (West, 1953) were rated as "1" (the least complex). For example, *anticipation* was coded as "1" because it was defined as *hope*, which appears on the GSL. Words with single-word definitions that were not among the 2,000 most frequent words on the GSL were designated as category 2 (e.g., *quarantine* was defined as *isolation*). Where definitions consisted of phrases where all words were within the GSL, the word was also coded as "2" for conceptual complexity (e.g., "tool that measures wind speed" for *anemometer*). Definitions with phrases or clauses where at least one key word was not within the GSL were designated as the highest level of complexity. For example, *rotation* was defined as "the spinning of a planet, moon, or star around its axis." Because both *planet* and *axis* are not in the GSL, *rotation* was rated as having the highest level of complexity—coded 3.

The *relatedness* measure drew on Marzano and Marzano's (1988) categorization of 7,300 words into 61 superclusters. After eliminating grammatical categories and consolidating several superclusters (e.g., facial expressions with communication), Hiebert (2010) identified 13 megaclusters that pertain to "big" ideas about story elements (e.g., Communication, Emotions/Attitudes) and the content of informational text (e.g., Social Systems, Human Body). Whereas the original superclusters (Marzano & Marzano, 1988) were presented in order of size, Hiebert has suggested that the vocabulary megaclusters be considered in three large groups: (1) words that would be expected to be distinctive of narrative vocabulary (e.g., Emotions and Character Traits), (2) words shared by both types of texts (e.g., Comparatives and Causes), and (3) words that are most prominent in informational texts (e.g., Natural Environment).

Results

Means and standard deviations for the measures, except for relatedness, are presented in Table 16.2, as are results of statistical comparisons of features across the two sets of vocabularies. Differences were statistically significant for all of the measures except for the frequency of morphological families of words and the dispersion index (i.e., whether a word appears in a single or multiple-content areas). The narrative vocabulary is more likely to be familiar to students, but the words are predicted to appear less frequently than those in the science corpus. Although less familiar but more frequent, the science words are significantly longer and have more conceptually complex definitions than the narrative set of words.

Semantic relatedness was considered by examining the number of megaclusters represented within the target words for a unit of text (i.e., a story in the ELA program and a chapter in the science program). A ratio was developed for the average number of target words per instructional unit (7 in the ELA program; 11 in the science program) and the number of megaclusters represented in that group for an individual instructional unit. The ratio for ELA vocabulary was 7:5 and for the science vocabulary,

TABLE 16.2. Means (and Standard Deviations) for Features of Words in Narrative and Informational Texts

	Narrative	Informational	F (significance level)
Familiarity (LWV grade)	6 (2.5)	7.5 (3.4)	42.752 (.000)
Frequency (U function)	13.7 (52.4)	39.1 (118.1)	28.039 (.000)
Frequency of morphological family	26. 7 (116.4)	31 (78.4)	.275 (.600)
Dispersion index	.60 (1.9)	.61 (1.9)	3.289 (.070)
Length	7.3 (1.9)	7.8 (2.6)	28.677 (.000)
Conceptual complexity	1.4 (.6)	2.3 (.5)	275.941 (.000)

11:4. A *t*-test indicated that the difference in the ratios was statistically significant ($t = 8.2$, $p = .000$). Most target words in an ELA unit did not come from closely related semantic clusters, whereas the vocabulary for an instructional science unit had at least several words with close semantic connections.

We were also interested in whether particular megaclusters were associated with particular text types. The percentages of the two vocabularies falling into the megaclusters are presented in Table 16.3. As has been predicted (Hiebert, 2010), particular megaclusters such as Emotions/Attitudes and Character Traits were heavily represented in the ELA vocabulary but not in the science vocabulary. Both vocabularies had a substantial number of words within the Natural Environment, but this megacluster accounted for almost half of the words in the science vocabulary and only about 20% of the words in the ELA vocabulary.

An Analysis of the Features of Exemplar Texts

Characteristics of words identified within published programs for instruction and, subsequently, assessment are important. An understanding of how these words represent all of the words in a text is also critical to understanding the demands of vocabulary in different types of texts. To capture the nature of vocabulary in entire texts of the two text types, an exemplar was chosen from each program. The exemplars were the texts from which the two excerpts in Table 16.1 were taken. Both ELA and science texts came from the same place in their respective programs—the third text of the third unit. For the ELA program, the text was *How Night Came from the Sea: A Story from Brazil* (Gerson, 1994, as cited in Afflerbach et al., 2007) and for the science text, the selection was "Why Does Matter Have Energy?" (Cooney et al., 2006). The former consisted of 1,250 words and the latter, 1,350 words.

TABLE 16.3. Distribution of Megaclusters in Vocabularies of Two Types of Texts

Dominant/shared text types	Megacluster	Narrative text	Informational text
Narrative dominant	Emotions and Attitudes	.09	0
	Character Traits	.09	0
	Social Relationships	.02	.01
Narrative/content shared	Action and Motion	.12	.06
	Communication	.10	.09
	Characters	.10	.07
	Places and Events	.06	.01
	Social Systems	.06	.01
	Physical Attributes (objects, events, time)	.05	.08
	Comparatives and Causes	.03	.05
Content dominant	Natural Environment	.19	.48
	Machines	.08	.07
	Human Body	.03	.07

Three features of the vocabulary in these two texts were of interest: (1) the ratio of different or unique words to total words, (2) the distribution of the unique and total words across different frequency groups, and (3) the number of repetitions of the targeted or assessed vocabulary within the texts. For the second feature, words were clustered into three groups based on the predictions of Zeno et al. (1995) for appearances of words per million words of text: (1) highly frequent words (appearances of 100 or more per million words), (2) moderately frequent words (appearances of 10–99 per million words), and (3) rare words (appearances of 9 or less per million words).

Results

The ELA text had a higher ratio of unique words than the science text: .33 for the ELA text (410 unique words: 1,250 total words) relative to .24 for the science text (328 unique words: 1,350 total words). The information in Table 16.4 shows that twice as many of the unique words in the ELA text fell into the rare category than was the case with the science vocabulary. To be proficient at reading, the ELA text requires that readers have a considerably greater capacity in recognizing unique words and in either already knowing the meaning of these words or being able to extract their meaning from the context of the text.

TABLE 16.4. Distribution of Word Zones: Narrative and Informational Exemplars

Word Zones	Narrative Text			Informational Text		
	Total words ($n = 1{,}250$)	Unique words ($n = 410$)	Average no. of appearances	Total words ($n = 1{,}350$)	Unique words ($n = 328$)	Average no. of appearances
Rare (WZ 5, 6)	.06	.15	1.2	.04	.03	5.4
Moderate (WZ 3,4)	.14	.24	1.8	.27	.16	6.6
High (WZ 0–2)	.79	.61	4.0	.69	.81	3.5

The number of appearances of words according to word zones is evident in Table 16.4. The patterns for words appearing with rare and moderate frequency differ substantially in the narrative and informational texts. Few of the rare words appeared more than once in the narrative text, whereas rare words in the informational texts appeared an average of five times. The pattern was the same for the words of moderate frequency, with substantially more appearances of these words in the informational than in the narrative texts. In the informational text, students have the opportunity to become facile with the same word as it appears repeatedly in the text. The narrative text, on the other hand, requires that students have facility in understanding many unique words that happen a single time in the text and that they are unlikely to have encountered in previous texts.

WHAT MIGHT THESE DIFFERENCES IN THE VOCABULARIES OF NARRATIVE AND INFORMATIONAL TEXTS MEAN FOR INSTRUCTION?

The patterns from our study showed both quantitative and qualitative differences in the words identified for instruction with ELA and science texts. First, the exemplar ELA text had *more* unique words and more of these unique words were *rare* than the words in the science text. The words called out for instruction accounted for 1% of the unique words in the ELA text. Of these unique words, 15% fell into the rare category of words that are unlikely to be encountered frequently in written language. By contrast, 3% of the words in the science text fell into this category. With few exceptions, these words were the focus of instruction. Even within a text-based vocabulary effort that the ELA program represents, instruction focuses on only a very small percentage of the words that are likely challenging for many students, especially the two-thirds of an American fourth-grade cohort that fails to be reading at a proficient level (Daane, Campbell, Grigg, Goodman, & Oranje, 2005). Especially in schools where the majority of students fall into this latter group, teachers will need to do a substantial amount of scaffolding for students to recognize vocabulary and to gain sufficient facility with a critical portion of the vocabulary to comprehend narrative texts with any depth.

A second way in which the two exemplar texts differed was in the repetition of the targeted vocabulary. As well as scaffolding students' recognition of the many words that fall outside the instructional focus, teachers will need to do considerable scaffolding of the words chosen for instruction in the ELA text, because almost all of the instructional words appeared a single time. Research is limited on the number of encounters that are required for a word to be known with any level of facility and precision (Swanborn & De Glopper, 1999). A single encounter with a word may be sufficient for learning to pronounce a word (Share, 1995). It is unlikely that a single encounter in a text will result in substantial learning. The general range of encounters appears to be, at least for unknown words, around 8–10 encounters (McKeown, Beck, Omanson, & Pople, 1985). Teachers will need to create the meaningful and repeated experiences with the words called out for instruction in the ELA texts. This analysis did not address the quality of the recommended experiences in the teachers' guide for this vocabulary and the likelihood that students would retain more than a passing recognition with the words. Opportunities for a rich textual context to support students' understanding of the words are limited in these texts.

A third difference in the vocabularies of the two programs offers a potential solution for what appears to be an insurmountable instructional challenge for teachers in ELA programs: The vast majority of the words called out for instruction in the ELA program (58%) were of the simplest conceptual complexity. Only 3% of the ELA vocabulary was of the highest level of conceptual complexity, and these words came from the limited number of informational texts that were part of the program. All but a handful of the words in the ELA program can be explained easily relative to students' existing concepts.

When combined with a fourth difference between the two vocabularies, a direction for instruction of the vocabularies in ELA texts that are primarily narrative in character becomes even clearer. The unique vocabularies in the two text types come from different vocabulary megaclusters. Half of the words for the ELA texts came from five clusters that have to do with Characters—their names, Traits, ways of Communicating, Actions and Motions, and Emotions/Attitudes. Although the relatedness of words in an individual ELA story was limited, the connectedness *across* stories was substantial. This connectedness reflects the nature of narratives, not any concerted effort on the part of the publisher. The publisher does not give a rationale for the selection of particular words for particular stories, but we suspect that particular megaclusters would have been even more heavily populated, had all of the unique, rare words for the stories in the ELA program, rather than the target vocabulary, been analyzed.

As Biber (1988) and other linguists have pointed out, authors of narrative and informational texts have different goals and, as a result, use words in very different ways. To underscore a theme in a story, Gerson (1994), in *How Night Came from the Sea*, does not repeat any single word describing brightness, but she does repeat the concept of brightness with numerous different words (e.g., *shimmering, gleamed, brightness, brilliant, glittering*). By contrast, the authors of the science text (Cooney et al., 20006) repeat words such as *heat* and *radiation* numerous times. Cooney et al. are intent on developing a precise meaning of radiation and heat, whereas Gerson wants the reader to get a sense of the dilemma of the goddess's daughter who longs for respite from the relentless Sun. The characteristics of characters and contexts are repeated in the same narrative but with different words. Even more critically, the same underlying concepts of traits, communication, features of contexts, and the nature of problems can be expected to appear *across* narratives.

The situation is quite a different one in a science text. A text on the life cycle of amphibians will contain very different words and descriptions than a text on the ways in which thermal energy is created. Authors of these texts will use different words as well as different text structures to communicate these constructs. But, within a particular topic such as thermal energy, the same words are likely to appear again and again.

These different purposes and their resulting different vocabularies indicate a need for significantly different programs for instructional concepts and vocabulary in ELA versus science. Although it would take a book-length manuscript to flesh out all of the details and uniquenesses of the vocabulary programs called for with different subject areas, we outline the main elements of these two types of vocabulary instruction.

Implications for the Instruction of Vocabulary in Science Texts

We begin with two caveats about the vocabulary in science texts. First, while we explore what the differences in word features mean for instruction related to the texts that students read, we want to emphasize that we are not viewing the words of science texts as simply learned through vocabulary lessons. To understand radiant heat or convection requires numerous activities in addition to reading. In the Seeds of Science/Roots of Reading project where we have worked to integrate literacy and science content and instruction (Cervetti, Jaynes, & Hiebert, 2009), a four-part mantra guides the lessons: Do it, read it, write it, talk it. Words such as *convection, conduction*, and *insulators* are used dozens of times in discussions, demonstrations, and writing activities. At least preliminary evidence suggests that such multimodal experiences appear to support the learning of conceptually complex words in science (Cervetti, Barber, Dorph, Pearson, & Goldschmidt, 2009).

A second caveat is that, because our analysis considered science texts only, conclusions cannot be generalized to other content areas such as social studies. A perusal of Marzano's (2004) summary of the vocabulary found in national and state standards suggests that two features that were associated with science vocabulary may be even more pronounced in social studies than they were in the present analysis: complex phrases and polysemous words. Some of the observations that follow about these two features are likely also applicable to social studies vocabulary, but we caution that this is an hypothesis only.

With respect to the complex phrase in science, 22% of the words in the sample were accompanied by one or more words (*solar cell, solar energy, solar system*). Even when words function as a single idea, it is rare that these words are presented as compound words or even hyphenated to alert the reader to their concatenation. The complex phrase has a unique meaning that cannot necessarily be determined by understanding common meanings of each word individually. The presence of numerous complex phrases adds a challenge to students in reading science that needs to be addressed through instruction. This instruction is unlikely to occur if vocabulary is primarily emphasized in narrative. Only one of the words in the ELA vocabulary sample was a phrase (*boarding school*).

A second feature of the science vocabulary that has consequences for instruction was the higher average frequency rating of these words than for those in the ELA sample. The unique words in informational texts are often more frequent because they have multiple meanings—meanings that can be challenging to teach and to learn. Many of the fundamental ideas within the science vocabulary—*work, speed, energy, force*—have common meanings. The word *work* has 53 common meanings, according to *dictionary. com*. In the science program, one meaning only—and in this case, a very precise one—is developed which is work as "using force in order to move an object a certain distance" (Cooney et al., 2006, p. EM9). For both students and teachers, the ordinary, everyday meanings of such a word may mean that knowledge of the word is assumed. It is also the case that the everyday meanings of words that have popular meanings in nonscience contexts can interfere with students' understanding of the scientific meaning (Cervetti, Hiebert, & Pearson, 2010).

Critical distinctions in the meanings of scientific vocabulary will be made only through multiple forms of inquiry and discussion. Further, because the majority of science words represented conceptually complex ideas—even with ordinary labels such as *work, force, energy, speed, tissue, matter*—meanings need to be taught in relation to one another. A thematic map with the interrelationships among vocabulary words is provided in Figure 16.1 to illustrate the connections among the complex ideas in the exemplar science text. The meaning of one conceptually complex word typically relies on an accurate (and precise) meaning of another conceptually complex word. These understandings are built through demonstrations, illustrations, DVDs, discussions, experiments, and writing. Everything in science cannot be experienced firsthand, but there are numerous ways in which background knowledge can be built through second-hand observation and inquiry.

The network of complex concepts also depends on experiences over time. The concepts in this unit (matter and thermal energy) were part of units in the primary grades. These concepts will be revisited in subsequent grades in even greater depth. If science is given short shrift in the primary grades, students will not have the foundation for the elaborations of existing concepts and new concepts that are added to the thematic networks in higher grades. They will not have the capacity to read the increasingly more complex texts that is the goal of the Common Core State Standards (CCSS; Common Core State Standards Initiative, 2010).

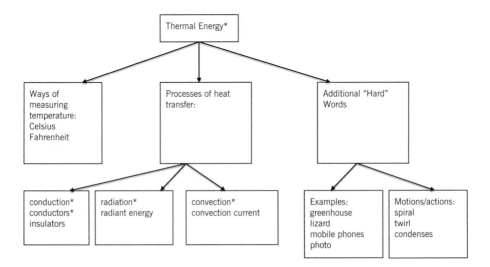

FIGURE 16.1. Thematic clustering of unique, rare words within a science prototypical text. *Words highlighted in instructional materials accompanying the exemplar text.

Implications for the Instruction of Vocabulary in Narrative Texts

Whereas the vocabulary of science is conceptually complex and requires intensive experiences over time, the vocabulary of the ELA program is dense with rare words. These rare words are typically not members of heavily populated morphological networks, as is the case with the rare words in science (e.g., *shimmering* in the former; *nonrenewable* in the latter). They do not have the thematic connections within or across stories that characterizes the words of the science curriculum. In the core ELA program of *Houghton Mifflin's Reading* (Cooper et al., 2004), vocabulary instruction for fourth graders, for example, focuses on *homage, commotion, hosted, severed*, and *fluffed* for a week, whereas students in states or districts that have selected Scott Foresman's *Reading Street* (Afflerbach et al., 2007) are learning *chorus, coward, gleamed, shimmering*, and *brilliant*. From one program to another, there is little overlap (except in the few cases where the same story appears, and even then, target words vary considerably). There is no rhyme or reason to the vocabulary instruction in the ELA programs where the lion's share of class time is spent in American classrooms.

Nagy and Hiebert (2010) have identified criteria for the selection of vocabulary in ELA programs. They underscore that, to close the vocabulary gap, instruction with narrative texts should focus on the unfamiliarity of words. This may sound like a strange criterion, but research over an extended period of time suggests that students already know many of the words identified for instruction in basal reading programs. Roughly 50 years ago, Gates (1962) demonstrated that the majority of words chosen for instruction in basal reading programs were already known sufficiently for students to comprehend the texts. Over twenty years ago, Stallman and colleagues (1990) confirmed the same pattern. Although we did not test students' understanding of the core vocabulary from a current core reading program (Afflerbach et al., 2007), 37% of the target vocabulary was rated as familiar for fourth graders (Biemiller, 2008; Dale & O'Rourke, 1976) and 60% of the words could be defined with a single word from the 2,000 most-frequent words in written English (West, 1953).

A second criterion suggested by Nagy and Hiebert (2010) is that instruction of literary vocabulary should emphasize a metalinguistic perspective wherein groups of words and underlying linguistic features are the focus, rather than a word-by-word perspective. The exemplar text, *How Night Came from the Sea* (Gerson, 1994), is typical of narrative texts in that it has numerous words that belong to rich semantic clusters. Nuanced words are used to convey how characters communicate, how they feel, and how they resolve their dilemmas and problems. Most fourth graders, even those who struggle as readers, have an understanding of basic concepts such as cowardice, yearning, fascination, and destruction. They may not use these words or the thousands of other nuanced words that describe the ways in which human communication and experience occur. All of these words cannot be taught, but readers can be taught to be aware that writers use multiple ways to label basic concepts about communications, feelings, traits, and settings. To expand vocabularies, students require the fundamental ideas of what stories are about and how writers of stories use rich vocabulary to communicate the human experience. Instructional scaffolds such as story structure and the cluster approach, which have fallen by the wayside over the past two decades, we propose, are resources for both teachers and learners in developing richer vocabularies and more efficacious vocabulary instruction. In Figure 16.2, we have mapped out the numerous unique words in the exemplar text. Most words appeared a single time in the text and communicate nuances that readers require to grasp the style and gist of the text. When the words are viewed in relation to

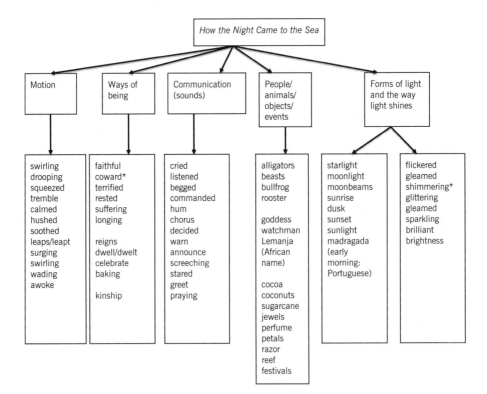

FIGURE 16.2. Semantic clustering of unique, rare words within an ELA prototypical text, *How the Night Came to the Sea*, by M. Gerson (1994). *Words highlighted in instructional materials accompanying the exemplar text.

underlying concepts that cut across stories, however, numerous words can be addressed. Such an approach offers a way to expand students' vocabularies substantially more than the identification of seven or eight of the many unique words in the texts, most of which come from discrete vocabulary clusters.

In this chapter, we have illustrated the substantially different kinds of vocabularies offered in ELA and science programs. These differences in vocabularies lend themselves to significantly unique instructional approaches. In science, most words are conceptually complex and represent new concepts for many students. These concepts are not learned by rote but evolve from extensive discussions, demonstrations, and experiments. The words that are unique to narrative texts are often many in number but represent concepts with which most students are familiar. Students may never have encountered the particular words that an author uses to convey a particular trait or motive of a character. It is likely, however, that even younger elementary students have underlying knowledge about the traits, motives, ways of moving, and emotions of characters. To become adept with narrative texts requires that students understand the ways in which authors vary their language to ensure that readers grasp the critical features of the story. If the vocabulary gap is to be narrowed for the students whose academic learning experiences occur primarily in schools, educators will need to develop unique selection criteria and instructional strategies for the vocabularies of *both* narrative and informational texts.

REFERENCES

Afflerbach, P., Blachowicz, C. L. Z., Boyd, C. D., Cheyney, W., Juel, C., Kame'enui, E. J., et al. (2007). *Reading street.* Glenview, IL: Scott Foresman.

Armbruster, B. B., & Nagy, W. E. (1992). Vocabulary in content area lessons. *The Reading Teacher, 45*(7), 550–551.

Biber, D. (1988). *Variation across speech and writing.* Cambridge, UK: Cambridge University Press.

Biemiller, A. (2008). *Words worth teaching.* Columbus, OH: SRA/McGraw-Hill.

Cervetti, G. N., Barber, J., Dorph, R., Pearson, P. D., & Goldschmidt, P. G. (2009, April). *Integrating science and literacy: A value proposition?* Symposium paper presented at the annual meeting of the American Educational Research Association, San Diego, CA.

Cervetti, G. N., Hiebert, E. H., & Pearson, P. D. (2010). *Factors that influence the difficulty of science words.* Santa Cruz, CA: TextProject.

Cervetti, G. N., Jaynes, C. A., & Hiebert, E. H. (2009). Increasing opportunities to acquire knowledge through reading. In E. H. Hiebert (Ed.), *Reading more, reading better* (pp. 3–29). New York: Guilford Press.

Common Core State Standards Initiative. (2010). *Common core state standards for English language arts and literacy in history/social studies, science, and technical subjects.* Washington, DC: CCSSO and National Governors Association.

Cooney, T., Cummins, J., Flood, J., Foots, B. K., Goldston, M. J., Key, S. G., et al. (2006). *Scott Foresman science.* Glenview, IL: Pearson.

Cooper, J. D., Pikulski, J. J., Ackerman, P. A., Au, K. H., Chard, D. J., Garcia, G. G., et al. (2004). *Houghton Mifflin reading.* Boston: Houghton Mifflin.

Coxhead, A. (2000). A new academic word list. *TESOL Quarterly, 34*(2) 213–238.

Daane, M. C., Campbell, J. R., Grigg, W. S., Goodman, M. J., & Oranje, A. (2005). *Fourth-grade students reading aloud: NAEP 2002 special study of oral reading* (NCES 2006-469). Washington, DC: Government Printing Office.

Dale, D., & O'Rourke, J. (1976). *The living word vocabulary.* Elgin, IL: Field Enterprises Educational.

Davis, F. B. (1942). Two new measures of reading ability. *Journal of Educational Psychology, 33*, 365–372.

Entwisle, D. R. (1966). *Word associations of young children.* Baltimore: Johns Hopkins University Press.

Fisher, C., Berliner, D., Filby, N., Marliave, R., Cahen, L., & Dishaw, M. (1980). Teaching behaviors, academic learning time and student achievement: An overview. In C. Denham & A. Lieberman (Eds.), *Time to learn* (pp. 7–32). Washington, DC: National Institute of Education.

Gardner, D. (2004). Vocabulary input through extensive reading: A comparison of words found in children's narrative and informational reading materials. *Applied Linguistics, 25*(1), 1–37.

Gates, A. I. (1962). The word recognition ability and the reading vocabulary of second and third grade children. *The Reading Teacher, 15*(6), 443–448.

Gerson, M. (1994). *How night came from the sea: A story from Brazil.* New York: Little, Brown.

Hart, B., & Risley, T. (1995). *Meaningful differences in everyday parenting and intellectual development in young American children.* Baltimore: Brookes.

Hiebert, E. H. (2010, November). *Growing capacity with the vocabulary of English language arts programs: Vocabulary megaclusters* (Reading Research Report #2). Santa Cruz, CA: TextProject.

Jenkins, J. R., & Dixon, R. (1983). Vocabulary learning. *Contemporary Educational Psychology, 8*(3), 237–260.

Leech, G., Rayson, P., & Wilson, A. (2001). *Word frequencies in written and spoken English based on the British National Corpus.* London: Longman.

Levelt, W. J. M., Roelofs, A., & Meyer, A. S. (1999). A theory of lexical access in speech production. *Behavioral and Brain Sciences, 22*, 1–38.

Marzano, R. J. (2004). *Building background knowledge for academic achievement.* Alexandria, VA: Association for Supervision and Curriculum Development.

Marzano, R. J., & Marzano, J. S. (1988). *A cluster approach to elementary vocabulary instruction.* Newark, DE: International Reading Association.

McKeown, M., Beck, I. L., Omanson, R. C., & Pople, M. T. (1985). Some effects of the nature and frequency of vocabulary instruction on the knowledge and use of words. *Reading Research Quarterly, 20*(5), 522–535.

Moss, H. E., Ostrin, R. K., Tyler, L. K., & Marslen-Wilson, W. D. (1995). Accessing different types of lexical semantic information: Evidence from priming. *Journal of Experimental Psychology: Learning, Memory, and Cognition, 21*(4), 863–883.

Nagy, W. E., & Anderson, R. C. (1984). How many words are there in printed school English? *Reading Research Quarterly, 19*(3), 304–330.

Nagy, W. E., Anderson, R. C., & Herman, P. A. (1987). Learning word meanings from context during normal reading. *American Educational Research Journal, 24*, 237–270.

Nagy, W., Berninger, V. W., & Abbott, R. (2006). Contributions of morphology beyond phonology to literacy outcomes of upper elementary and middle-school students. *Journal of Educational Psychology, 98*(1), 134–147.

Nagy, W. E., & Hiebert, E. H. (2010). Toward a theory of word selection. In M. L. Kamil, P. D. Pearson, E. B., Moje, & Afflerbach, P. P. (Eds.), *Handbook of reading research* (Vol. 4, pp. 388–404). New York: Longman.

Norris, S. P., Phillips, L. M., Smith, M. L., Baker, J. J., & Weber, A. C. (2008). Learning to read scientific text: Do elementary school commercial reading programs help? *Science Education, 92*(5), 765–798.

Oxford Dictionaries. (2010). *Oxford dictionary of English* (3rd rev. ed.). New York: Oxford University Press.

Scott, J. A., Lubliner, S., & Hiebert, E. H. (2005). Constructs underlying word selection and assessment tasks in the archival research on vocabulary instruction. In J. V. Hoffman, D. L. Schallert, C. M. Fairbanks, J. Worthy, & B. Maloch (Eds.), *55th yearbook of the National Reading Conference* (pp. 264–275). Oak Creek, WI: National Reading Conference.

Sereno, J., & Jongman, A. (1997). Processing of English inflectional morphology. *Memory and Cognition, 25*, 425–437.

Share, D. L. (1995). Phonological recoding and self-teaching: *Sine qua non* of reading acquisition. *Cognition, 55*(92), 151–218.

Simpson, J., & Weiner, E. (2009). *Oxford English dictionary.* New York: Oxford University Press.

Stallman, A. C., Commeyras, M., Kerr, B., Meyer Reimer, K., Jiménez, R., Hartman, D. K., et al. (1990). Are "new" words really new? *Reading Research and Instruction, 29*(2), 12–29.

Stanners, R. F., Neiser, J. J., Hernon, W. P., & Hall, R. (1979). Memory representations for morphologically related words. *Journal of Verbal Learning and Verbal Behavior, 18*, 399–412.

Sternberg, R., & Powell, J. S. (1983). Comprehending verbal comprehension. *American Psychologist, 38*, 878–893.

Swanborn, M. S. L., & De Glopper, K. (1999). Incidental word learning while reading: A meta-analysis. *Review of Educational Research, 69*(3), 261–285.

Thorndike, R. L. (1973). *Reading comprehension education in fifteen countries.* Stockholm, Sweden: Almquist & Wiksell.

Tinkham, T. (1993). The effect of semantic clustering on the learning of second language vocabulary. *System: An International Journal of Educational Technology and Applied Linguistics, 21,* 371–380.

Tinkham, T. (1997). The effects of semantic and thematic clustering on the learning of second language vocabulary. *Second Language Research, 13*(2) 138–163.

Waring, R. (1997). The negative effects of learning words in semantic sets: A replication. *System, 25*(2), 261–274.

West, M. (1953). *A general service list of English words.* London: Longman.

Zeno, S. M., Ivens, S. H., Millard, R. T., & Duvvuri, R. (1995). *The educator's word frequency guide.* New York: Touchstone Applied Science Associates.

Index

f following a page number indicates a figure; *t* following a page number indicates a table.